The Russian Challenge
and the Year 2000

The Russian Challenge and the Year 2000

Alexander Yanov

Translated by Iden J. Rosenthal

Basil Blackwell

Copyright © Alexander Yanov 1987

First published 1987

Basil Blackwell Ltd
108 Cowley Road, Oxford, OX4 1JF, UK

Basil Blackwell Inc.
432 Park Avenue South, Suite 1503
New York, NY 10016, USA

British Library Cataloguing in Publication Data

Yanov, Alexander
  The Russian challenge : the USSR and the
  year 2000.
  1. Soviet Union — Politics and
  government — 1953—
  I. Title
  320.947   JN6531

  ISBN 0-631-15334-9

Library of Congress Cataloging in Publication Data

Yanov, Alexander, 1930—
  The Russian challenge and the year 2000.

  Bibliography: p.
  Includes index.
  1.   Soviet Union — Politics and government — 1953—
2.   Dissenters — Soviet Union.   3.   Solzhenitsyn,
Aleksandr Isaevich, 1918—   I.   Title.
DK288.Y36   1987   947.085   86-32082
ISBN 0-631-15334-9

Typeset in 10 on 12 pt. Astro
by Pioneer Associates, Perthshire
Printed in Great Britain by
TJ Press Ltd, Padstow

To Robert and Margaret Reilly

'The West has supped more than its fill of every kind of freedom, including intellectual freedom. And has this saved it? We see it today crawling on hands and knees, its will paralyzed, in the dark about the future, spiritually racked and dejected.'

... Alexander Solzhenitsyn

'The messianic significance of Russia in relation to the West is beyond doubt. Slavophilism alone can still save the West from parliamentarism, unbelief, and dynamite.'

... Aleksei Kireev

'If we presume the coming transformation of the Communist Party into the Russian Orthodox Party of the Soviet Union, we would obtain truly the ideal state, one which would fulfill the historical destiny of the Russian people. It is a question of the Orthodoxization of the entire world.'

... Gennadii Shimanov

'Without the Communist Party, by the year 2000 the Zionists will physically exterminate the Russian people together with all our problems.'

... An anonymous Russian 'patriot'

Contents

Foreword

In May 1981, at a conference in Washington devoted to Russian nationalism, I was left dumbfounded by the presentation of Jerry Hough, one of the most well-known and radical revisionists in American sovietology. The gist of his speech was that all Russians are nationalists. Andrei Sakharov, for example, is just as much a nationalist as Alexander Solzhenitsyn or Leonid Brezhnev. Of course, Hough continued, we must differentiate between the good Russian nationalists and the bad ones, but in principle the problem is clear: when dealing with Russians, no matter who they may be, we are dealing with nationalists.

Richard Pipes, one of the most well-known and radical traditionalists in American sovietology, arrived late at the conference and so missed the presentation of his antipode. The reader may imagine the audience's astonishment when in his speech Pipes, virtually word for word, reiterated Hough's tirade.

On one and the same day to hear one and the same speech from the mouths of two experts who over the course of years have invariably contradicted one another on everything that concerns Russia was, it seems, the most surprising experience of my life in America — all the more so since I too was no novice in the single topic on which these two irreconcilable opponents had, before my eyes, come to terms. Three years earlier, in April 1978, I had even published my first book on this subject, *The Russian New Right*. The documents I presented there in great number fully excluded everything that this ideological duet composed of the leading figures of both opposing sovietological schools had pronounced in Washington.

To appreciate fully the degree of shock I experienced in listening to Hough and Pipes, the reader must imagine how, say, the author of a book about Catholicism in the sixteenth century would have felt, having heard from respected academics that all Europeans were

Catholics at that time and that the only difference between Martin Luther, the leader of the Reformation, and Ignatius Loyola, leader of the Counter-reformation, was that one was a bad Catholic and the other a good one. In other words, Protestantism was not an independent ideology in its own right that gave rise to a precisely outlined political doctrine in opposition to Catholicism, but only bad Catholicism.

In May 1981, during that conference, I began to regret having published my *Russian New Right* as early as 1978 — outside the context of the Western intellectual debate on Russia. Only recently arrived from Moscow, having been nurtured in a completely different school of thought and fresh from embittered skirmishes with Russian nationalists back at home, I had naively assumed that I was speaking in one and the same conceptual language as my new American readers. I believed that the phenomenon of Russian nationalism meant for them the same as it did for me and my fellow-thinkers and opponents in Russia: an age-old, powerful and attractive *ideology*, the main antagonist to traditional Russian liberalism (Westernism). I assumed that my readers would know its history and its political doctrine, that they would know how graphically this doctrine repudiates the central postulate of Western political thought — the separation of executive, legislative and judicial powers — offering instead a mediaeval postulate about *the separation of functions between secular and spiritual authorities*. I assumed that I would not need to explain to my readers that this doctrine conceives of its political ideal not as popular representation, but as a nation-family not requiring political guarantees; that separation of church from state is alien to it; that, in other words, the ideology of Russian nationalism is antagonistic to all the main principles on which modern democracy is based.

Hough and Pipes's duet convinced me that there is a chasm between how the term Russian nationalism is used in Washington and how it is used in Moscow. This rift seemed all the deeper to me when I learned that, in certain run-of-the-mill courses on the subject at American universities, the Westernism of the last century is calmly interpreted as a component part of Russian nationalism, thus confusing the Sakharovs of Russia's past with her Solzhenitsyns, just as American sovietologists had done in Washington, before my eyes, with respect to modern times. Then, after another conference in Washington in October 1985, I became almost despairing when the American politicians and experts present concluded almost unanimously (I was the sole exception) — and entered into the conference record!

— that Russian nationalism is 'the operative ideology' of the present-day Soviet government. The conceptual language of my readers clearly had nothing in common with the language in which my book was written.

As a rule, this conceptual language does not view Russian nationalism as a particular ideology, or even as a political doctrine. It sees it more as a feeling or sentiment which is merely *expressed* by ideological symbols. These symbols can either be positive (and then this nationalist sentiment is called patriotism) or negative (in which case it is called chauvinism). For what lies between these two emotional poles — nationalism as such, the ideology of nationalism — *there is no symbol*. It is a kind of no one's land, a blank spot on the ideological map, lacking political substance of its own and therefore accepting any content the observer brings to it.

There is no doubt that the Soviet leadership, as long ago as the 1930s, incorporated symbols of patriotism into its own ideology in order to exploit people's patriotic emotions. However, though this may have confused Western observers, it did not fool Russian nationalists. The ideological explosion of the 1960s described in *The Russian New Right* was the most convincing evidence of the gaping chasm between the 'emotional' exploitation of ideological symbols in Soviet propaganda and the genuine ideology of Russian nationalism. If nationalism really were serving as the 'operative ideology' of the Soviet government, the revolt of Russian nationalists that erupted in the 1960s almost simultaneously in both the dissident samizdat and the officially censored Soviet press, would defy explanation. Russian nationalists graphically and unambiguously refused to recognize the official Soviet ideology as their own, regardless of how many patriotic symbols it expropriated. The Soviet government, for its part, likewise refused to recognize the Russian nationalists as their own. On the contrary, it unleashed its KGB on them, hustling some off to prison and forcing others to fall silent. Why?

Neither Jerry Hough nor Richard Pipes can provide an answer to this decisive question. They confuse patriotic emotions (or, in the other interpretation, chauvinist excesses) with the ideology of Russian nationalism, and that has made it impossible for them to understand the nature of the phenomenon.

This, apparently, would explain the unexpectedly different reactions of readers to *The Russian New Right*. Some saw it as an attack on Russian patriotism and were duly offended. Other interpreted it as an assault on Russian chauvinism and duly rejoiced. In reality, however, the book was neither one nor the other. Generally, it was not intended to have any relation to emotions whatsoever. It described the — at first glance — inexplicable resurrection of the ideology of Russian nationalism in the modern-day Soviet Union (where, according to all sovietological cliches, such a thing could not happen). It dealt with Russian nationalism's revolutionary origins in the mid-1960s, its split into a dissident faction and an establishment faction toward the end of that decade, and the transformation of the latter into the USSR's unofficial shadow ideology. It went on to describe how these two factions grew ideologically closer and how they were repressed by the police in the mid-1970s. The book also offered an hypothesis about the potential political consequences for Russia and the world in the event of a new, and this time victorious, resurrection of the ideology of Russian nationalism at the end of the second Christian millennium.

I tried to show the reader how Russian nationalism's main traits were formed: its militant anti-Westernism, rendering it similar to the ideology of the Ayatollah Khomeini; its dogmatism and intolerance, bringing it closer to contemporary Soviet Marxism; its extremism and explosive potential, resembling Bolshevism abroad at the beginning of the century. However, even those reviewers most well disposed toward the book did not take all this seriously. For the majority of them it was a book about a bizarre chauvinist wing (the 'lunatic fringe') of Soviet dissidence, a kind of Russian Ku Klux Klan; interesting and even entertaining, with a mass of exotic details, but lacking any immediate political significance.

Suppose, right at the start of the twentieth century, immediately after the emergence of Bolshevism, someone had written a book about the sudden birth in Russia of a potentially powerful ideological alternative to the then ruling, and seemingly unshakable, tsarist regime. Suppose the author of this book had warned that, in the event of Bolshevism's triumph, it could totally transform Russia's role in the world and restructure the entire political arena of the twentieth century. Suppose, furthermore, that well-wishing critics had interpreted the phenomenon of Bolshevism described in this book as a marginal wing of contemporary Russian dissidence — unpleasant, perhaps ominous, but not of any immediate political interest. There would, of course, have been other critics too, Bolshevism's 'fellow-travellers', who might have accused the author of painting Bolshevism black and reducing it to a lowest common denominator, when in fact, they may have argued, there are good Bolsheviks and bad ones. The good ones should be supported, they might have said, because they are selfless fighters against accursed tsarism, (which suppresses human rights and organizes Jewish pogroms) and are thus our natural allies.

This was very similar to the position I found myself in after the publication of my *Russian New Right* in 1978. The only difference was that I had written not about Bolsheviks, whose role has become somewhat clearer over the past seven decades, but about Russian nationalists, whose role as yet remains just as dark as that of the Bolsheviks in 1903. In just the same way, those critics who wished me well and were full of revulsion for Russian chauvinism failed to take this new ideological phenomenon seriously as a real political alternative to the existing regime. At the same time, the nationalist Western 'fellow-travellers' attacked me for slandering Russian patriotism, because there are good nationalists too — selfless fighters against accursed Communism (which suppresses human rights and hinders Jewish emigration out of the Soviet Union) and are thus our natural allies.

It is for these reasons that I have written another book about Russian nationalism, in which all the i's will be dotted, and all the t's crossed, and which, hopefully, will not be so open to misinterpretation. In the final analysis, Russian nationalism did not come into the world yesterday or in the 1960s. It has a long history, rich in events. It arose at approximately the same time as Marxism, a century and a half ago. It underwent its own complex and dramatic evolution, it had its ups and downs and its metamorphoses, which contemporary nationalists are now repeating just as unsuspectingly as their contemporary Western readers. Its political doctrine was worked out long before the 1917 revolution. Its response to that revolution was fascism. Its political potential has been clearly and unambiguously demonstrated. Its resurrection in the Soviet Union in the 1960s was predictable, in the same way as its emergence in the 1830s. It answered deep needs within the Russian political system in the first half of the nineteenth century, just as it answers them today in the second half of the twentieth.

The entire historical drama of the ideology of Russian nationalism, or the Russian Idea, as Nikolai Berdiaev so aphoristically named it in the twentieth century, was omitted in *The Russian New Right*. That book was devoted exclusively to one short episode in the history of the Russian Idea — the ideological explosion of the 1960s. To that extent, it is my fault that the resurrection of the Russian Idea was received as an isolated and exotic episode in the history of Soviet dissent. Only in the broad historical perspective can it be understood that this explosion, though put down by police repression in the mid-1970s, was not, and could not have been, crushed completely. In just the same way, the Bolsheviks were put down but were never completely crushed by the repressions accompanying the dramatic explosion of 1905—07. The year 1917 was still in store for them, just as the year 2000 may still be in store for the champions of the Russian Idea. At least they hope so, as the reader of this book will discover.

The present book is constructed in an entirely different way from *The Russian New Right*, though it does include several chapters updated and revised from the earlier work. Here, I describe events that took place at the end of the 1970s and beginning of the 1980s after the publication of *The Russian New Right*. But more importantly, I also try to capture the historical drama of the Russian Idea, from the point of its very conception up to its crushing defeat in the period 1917—21. In presenting the subject thus, I want to make it clear that in the Russian Idea we have a phenomenon of first-order political significance which could enjoy a new and triumphant resurrection at the end of this century, if Gorbachev's 1980s reforms come to naught (in just the same way as Bolshevism enjoyed a resurrection after the collapse of Stolypin's reforms at the beginning of this century).

Above all, this book is intended to help Western readers gain an understanding of the fanciful intricacies of the Russian Idea, of the complexities of its political doctrine, and peripeteia of its historical drama. It should then be less easy to confuse it with the patriotic emotions or ideological symbols that Soviet propaganda seeks to exploit. I therefore hope that reviewers will not mistake the book for either an assault on Russian chauvinism or an attack on Russian patriotism. I, no less than they, deplore chauvinism in any form and respect each and every patriotism. But that is not my object here. My book is about the future of Russia — and quite possibly the world — should the Russian Idea be fated someday to triumph. This is the Russian challenge I am concerned with. We may not have seen the worst of it yet.

In conclusion I want to thank all my friends and readers who supported me throughout the fierce campaign waged against me by almost the entire emigre press after the publication of *The Russian New Right*, and which, alas, the Russian Idea's Western fellow-travellers joined. I also want to thank the magazines *Sintaksis* and *22* for not having joined this campaign. Finally, I am deeply indebted to the Harry Frank Guggenheim Foundation for making it possible for me to research the misadventures of the Russian Idea at the beginning of the twentieth century.

1

Introduction: Russia vs. Russia

My book *The Russian New Right* made its appearance during one of the most dramatic periods in modern history, when the era of detente between the superpowers was already over, but humanity did not yet know what kind of new era it was entering. Would there be a revival of the Cold War, or perhaps an open confrontation between the superpowers, or even another world war? Eugene Rostow summed up the mood of those years exactly when he said, 'We are living in a pre- not a post-war world.'[1] The very air was saturated with apocalyptic premonitions. Everything, it seemed, heralded a new world crisis. The deployment of SS-20 rockets on the European territory of the USSR was interpreted as preparation for the 'Finlandization' of Western Europe. Soviet exploits in Africa seemed to be aimed at a total breach of communications between the US and its allies. The invasion of Afghanistan looked like the first step toward an assault on the oil-fields of the Middle East.

In short, it would be difficult to imagine a less appropriate time for the appearance of a book on the revival of Russian imperial nationalism.[2] What serious person could be expected to take an interest in the sudden rebirth of a distant alternative to Soviet Marxism in Moscow when fear of an impending confrontation between Communism and anti-Communism was reaching its apogee? It is true that the resurrection of imperial nationalism precipitated a split within the Soviet dissident movement and potentially threatened to cause one in the Soviet establishment as well. Still, who cared about mere potentials when it seemed the very fate of humankind was at stake? *The Russian New Right* required of its readers a theoretical effort to overcome the stereotypes that have been hardening over decades. But in the urgency of the current crisis, what was important was practice, not theory. The book's very tone seemed irritatingly out of place against the backdrop of Shakespearian political passions then being played out across the world stage.

That is how the world looked at the end of the 1970s and early 1980s through the eyes of the American press — both popular and intellectual. Who would have been interested in a book about the emergence of Bolshevism in Russia, say, in 1911, at the time of the Balkan crisis that eventually led to World War I? Ironically, it was the Shakespearian passions boiling in the American press that were irrelevant; no Shakespearian tragedy was taking place in the world and none was foreseen. What was happening bore as much resemblance to the Balkan crisis as a gentle autumnal shower does to a typhoon. In fact, nothing was threatening humankind in those years. But if one wants to speak of threats, then the revival of Russian imperial nationalism was a hundred times more dangerous than Soviet adventures in Africa. But, in order to understand this, one had to have a much deeper and more sensitive conception of how the Russian political system functions than the familiar 'totalitarian' stereotypes and cliches of American politicians and academics would allow. Despite the hundreds of books and thousands of articles written about Soviet politics in the postwar decades, they proved unprepared for a new turn in relations between the superpowers. Why?

The answer to this question is far beyond the purview of a book about the resurrection of imperial nationalism in Russia. Yet the subject presents us with a chance to examine this question in greater detail and at least to try to offer a hypothetical answer.

The Battle of Metaphors

Let's first take an overview of the intellectual confrontation at the time. The prognosis of Senator Daniel Patrick Moynihan was, in effect, that once having placed Europe on its knees ('Finlandized' it) and isolated the United States, Russia intended to undertake a fateful assault on the Persian Gulf: 'The short run looks good [for the USSR], the long run bad. Therefore move. It was the calculation the Austro-Hungarian Empire made in 1914.'[3] Moynihan's Austro-Hungarian metaphor was opposed by another, suggested by Norman Podhoretz, the editor of *Commentary*: 'The Soviet Union is similar in character to Nazi Germany: a revolutionary totalitarian power bent on establishing a new world order in which it would enjoy hegemony.'[4] Out of this naturally followed an unambiguous prognosis: world war is inevitable and therefore negotiations senseless; 'appeasement' is criminal; the policy of detente is tantamount to the Munich agreement. For those who accepted the German analogy, it was hard to escape its logical conclusion. Thus Frank R. Burnett asserted that, 'The U.S. today is about where Britain was in 1938 with the shadow of Hitler's Germany darkening all over Europe.'[5]

Practically the whole intellectual debate in America at that time was reducible to the conflict between these two positions. As James Fallows explained later, 'The fundamental intellectual difference between the sides is the historical prism through which their perceptions are bent. When the liberals look at the 1980s, some of them see 1914. When the conservatives look at the 1980s, nearly all of them see 1938.'[6]

I will return once again to this debate in my conclusion. Suffice it to say, here, that in principle the outcome of this struggle did not change the apocalyptic mood of those years: both the 1914 and the 1938 comparisons signified the terrible imminence of a final world conflict — between Russia and the West, between Communism and anti-Communism. The fatal 'window of vulnerability' was supposed to open up sometime in the mid-1980s. As always, this apocalyptic mood was expressed at its most extreme by the Russian emigre press. 'Each minute we live,' wrote Alexander Solzhenitsyn, 'no fewer than one country (sometimes two or three at once) is gnawed away by the teeth of totalitarianism. This process never ceases and has already been going on for almost forty years. . . . Each minute we live, somewhere on earth one, two, or three countries are being freshly ground up by the teeth of totalitarianism. . . . The Communists are already on the march everywhere — in Western Europe, and in America. And all today's distant viewers will soon be able to see it all without a television set, and then they will feel it personally — but only after they've already been swallowed.'[7]

If we estimate the number of minutes in forty years as roughly twenty million and the number of countries as 150, then, arithmetically speaking, each country in the world has already been 'gnawed away' and even 'freshly ground up' by the Communists at least 133,333 times. But few care about emigre arithmetic when speeches such as the following are made on the floor of the US Senate. 'I guess Ronald Reagan is a warmonger just like Winston Churchill. . . . And we can find lots of examples of Neville Chamberlains, the appeasers of this world who never seem to learn the lessons of history' (Jake Garn of Utah); or: 'Don't tell me there is no lesson to be learned there' (John Tower, Texas).[8]

Russia's Historical Choice

Just one detail was omitted from this impassioned debate in which the lessons of German (or Austro-Hungarian) history were discussed: the lessons of Russian history. For this reason alone the examples cited were academic to the questions that really mattered. Had the senators followed their own advice and turned to the only history whose lessons are essential for a proper understanding of Soviet behaviour in world politics at the end of the 1970s, the picture perceived by them would probably have been different. In *The Russian New Right* I tried to sketch out this picture, tracing the long-term patterns of Russian political change over the last half-millenium, since the time when Russia became a nation-state.

According to this perception, the degree of Russia's aggressiveness and expansionism in world politics generally depends not so much on the character of the dominant ideology (as the stereotype holds) as on the character of a particular regime. The tsarist ideologies of 'Russia as the Third Rome' or 'Orthodoxy, Autocracy and Nationality' did not prevent Russia from being transformed into a gigantic empire occupying one-sixth of the earth's land surface, any more than the Communist ideology hindered Nikita Khrushchev from curtailing territorial expansion.[9] The Soviet government of the 1970s, which overturned Khrushchev's regime of reform but was not prepared to pass the whole way into becoming a regime of counter-reform, represented, according to this picture, merely a temporary and transitional regime of political stagnation. In this sense, and only in this sense, was it reminiscent (if we must draw analogies with other countries) of the Weimar Republic. It could have led Russia into a new counter-reform or into a new reform, but it was incapable of leading it into an all-out confrontation with the West. Historically, the only thing such a regime has been able to accomplish is to steer the nation into a profound political, cultural and economic decay at home and grab whatever is lying in temptation's way abroad.

This is why, according to the metaphor of transitional or 'Weimar' Russia, the world could not have been approaching a global crisis in the late 1970s. Instead, it was Russia which was once again approaching the same fateful historical crossroads where, as always after a regime of stagnation, she is faced with a choice — between radical reform and no less radical counter-reform.

Russia is the only European country which, time and again, over the course of her entire tragic history, has been forced to make this choice. It began as long ago as the 1550s when her first grandiose effort to join world civilization, 'to seek and find herself in mankind' as Petr Chaadaev was later to say, suffered a crushing defeat and ended instead in the grandiose counter-reform and fierce garrison-state dictatorship of Ivan the Terrible.[10] Since that time, over the course of centuries both Russia's reformist efforts as well as her counter-reforms have taken on the greatest variety of ideological integuments. Her reforms have always been attempts to join civilization while her counter-reforms have always been efforts to perpetuate her split with civilization. Now, at the end of the twentieth century, the choice before Russia is still the same — despite all her ICBMs, computers, and other outward attributes of modernity. 'Russia has never come out of the Middle Ages', Nikolai Berdiaev insightfully remarked as long ago as 1923.[11] Therefore she may now once again try to 'open up' to the world, as China has been doing over these last years, or, alternatively, issue another challenge to civilization, escaping from her present historical decline at the cost of once more transforming herself into a garrison-state empire.

Perhaps the most widespread illusion of the past seven decades has been that the Communist metamorphosis of 1917 somehow broke the long-term patterns of Russian political change and thus struck from the agenda of world history the issues raised by Russia as 'the sick man of Europe' and the progressive degeneration of the world's last empire. The 1980s should have brought with them the insight that Communism, just like Ivan the Terrible's 'Orthodox tsardom' or Peter the Great's garrison-state empire, was in fact only a postponement, a temporary remission for 'the sick man of Europe', a mere detour by which Russia — at the price of unheard-of sacrifices and trials — has returned to the same 'accursed questions' which 1917 had promised to rid her of for ever. Once again she is in decline and once more she faces her old traditional choice.

The world could ignore this recurrent Russian choice as long as Russia was just an obscure province procrastinating on the margins of civilization. It can no longer afford to do so in the nuclear age, now that intercontinental ballistic missiles have made this choice central to the survival of civilization. Such is the logical conclusion of the Weimar Russia metaphor.

Comparing Metaphors

The problem presented by *The Russian New Right* was that it did not comply with either of the contending metaphors, but instead proposed its own. Thus it landed beyond the limits of the main current of America's Soviet debate, for, from the standpoint of the metaphor it offered, nothing at all dramatic was going on in the world of the late seventies. It gave no grounds for apocalyptic prognoses nor did it promise any 'window of vulnerability' in the mid-eighties. The Soviet expansion of that time merely marked the agony of a regime of political stagnation. For the actions which the West was expecting of Brezhnev's Russia, an altogether different kind of political regime was necessary. This was something which just did not exist in the Moscow of the late seventies. Therefore, the deployment of SS-20s was not a portent of Europe's 'Finlandization'; Soviet operations in Africa did not promise to cut NATO's vital communications; and the Soviet army in Afghanistan was destined to be bogged down in that country for a long time to come. Neither 1914 nor 1938 were on their way back at the end of the 1970s. Munich and Neville Chamberlain had nothing remotely to do with the situation, nor did the calculations of the Austro-Hungarian Empire on the eve of World War I. In spite of Solzhenitsyn's jeremiads, Communism was not 'on the march — in Western Europe and in America', nor did US television viewers face the prospect of having to verify this prophecy only after they had 'already been swallowed'.

Now, in the mid-1980s, you may judge for yourself which of the metaphors offered at the end of the last decade has withstood the test of history. Who recalls the example of 1914 today? Who any longer speaks of 1938? What has become of the 'window of vulnerability', that was supposed to be opening? Where is the prophecy about Europe's Finlandization? Do we still hear so much about Soviet plans to take over the oil-fields of the Persian Gulf?[12] The hysteria is over, the drama gone. They have given way to what is almost a euphoria. American politicians have been speaking a completely different language by the mid-1980s.

'The Soviets', said Secretary of State Shultz, 'face profound structural economic difficulties, a continuing succession problem and restless allies; its diplomacy and its clients are on the defensive in many parts of the world. We can be sure that the 'correlation of forces' is shifting back in our favor.'[13] Richard Allen, former presidential

National Security Advisor, fully agreed with this analysis. If anything, the picture of Russia's decline he was drawing was even more sombre: 'The Soviet leadership is in the throes of a profound systemic crisis, one aggravated by political instability. . . . Combined with deeply rooted, some would say ineradicable, economic problems and widespread unease among the many nationalities of the Soviet Union, not to mention the mounting anti-Sovietism in Eastern Europe, the Soviet Union desperately needs breathing space.'[14]

What exactly are they talking about? The all-out confrontation which both the American metaphors were predicting at the end of the 1970s? The general state of decline envisaged by the metaphor of Weimar Russia? Which of these approaches toward explaining Russia's behaviour in world politics has come off better — the one based on coincidental and superficial analogies with the behaviour of some other power in another set of circumstances, or the one which appealed to the long-term patterns of Russian political change?[15]

An Alternative Approach

We have examined here only one case in which both of the major approaches in America's Soviet debate (the ideological one, which seeks to explain the 1980s in terms of 1938, and the geopolitical one, which does the same in terms of 1914) have proved incapable of understanding the present behaviour of Russia or predicting its future course. (We will encounter other similar cases later.) The Russian political system has always turned out to be more complex than such explanations allow. It has been developing cyclically; it has been pulsating; time and again it has entered into zones of decline, like the Austro-Hungarian Empire, but has never even come close to disintegrating. Instead, it has emerged from each agony renewed, ever a greater threat, more powerful and menacing. In fact, it has been like this throughout history (see Fig. 1. in the Appendix).

The Muscovite tsardom was quietly flickering out in the late seventeenth century on the periphery of Europe. Yet, in another quarter-century it had swiftly moved out of the zone of decline and, so far from remaining a provincial backwater kingdom, emerged before the world as the mighty Petersburg empire which for the first time tried to assert Russian control over Eastern and Central Europe. The establishment of Petersburg Russia, with its officers arrayed in uniforms with shining epaulettes and speaking French better than they did Russian, was just as unrecognizably different from the bearded boyars of earlier Muscovite Rus' as the elites of Soviet Russia are from their tsarist forbears. Peter's revolution changed the country no less than Lenin's, and it promised Russia a flight to the pinnacle of world power. As early as the second half of the eighteenth century Catherine's chancellor Bezborodko boasted that, 'not a single cannon in Europe would dare fire a shot without our permission'. By the middle of the next century, Petersburg Russia had reached its apex, having become a superpower and the gendarme of Europe, the chief anti-communist force in the world, which Karl Marx (just like President Reagan later) saw as an 'evil empire', and 'the bastion of world reaction'. This was the time when the Russian historian Mikhail Pogodin exclaimed, 'I ask, can anyone compete with us, and whom do we not compel to obedience? Doesn't the political destiny of the world rest in our hands, if only we should care to decide it . . . ? The Russian sovereign is closer than Charles V and Napoleon were to their dream of universal empire!'[16]

What happened then? Only a few decades later we see Petersburg Russia in the same desperate straits it had once led Muscovy out of, having lost the proud status of superpower, once more provincial and agonizing. Vladimir Il'ych Lenin was destined to do for Russia at the beginning of the twentieth century what Peter had accomplished at the start of the eighteenth — dismantle her political system's outdated format in order to rescue its medieval, quasi-Byzantine imperial essence. Once more — this time with its communism, its International, and its single party system — it differed so much from its predecessor as to seem another country. Again it rose to the heights of military might and became a superpower. By mid-century it had achieved what Peter could not, and had swallowed Eastern and part of Central Europe, with a population of 111 million, without so much as missing a stride. And then what? A few decades later we find Soviet Russia in the same situation of historical eclipse it had once led the Petersburg Empire out of, again agonizing with the long litany of seemingly incurable diseases recited by Shultz and Allen. Truly, one has to ignore completely Russia's past if one is to believe that this is the final chapter in the history I have just been trying to sketch. In fact, the farther Russia progresses on the path of historical decline, and the closer she comes to the moment of national crisis, when once again — for the third time in as many centuries — it will be decided which path she will take to halt her current decline, the more perilous the world situation becomes. Euphoria is no more appropriate now than panic was of the late 1970s. If ever in the last half-millenium the West had vital need of a precise, well thought-out, and potent strategy capable of influencing Russia's historical choice, then it is right now, in the nuclear age, in the face of a national crisis unfolding in Russia before our very eyes.

Therefore, this book's primary goal is to show the reader that Russia's impending crisis at the end of the twentieth century is no less real than were those she underwent at the close of the seventeenth and nineteenth centuries. If Russia again fails to direct the national energy that has been bottled up by the political stagnation of the last decades into the channel of peaceful reform, as she has failed to do in the past, this crisis may result in the emergence on the world stage of a monstrous garrison-state nuclear empire far more dangerous and aggressive than today's skidding USSR.

Mikhail Gorbachev has his predecessors. Both at the end of the seventeenth century and the beginning of the twentieth, relatively young and dynamic leaders advanced to Russia's helm. Vasilii Golitsyn in the first case and Petr Stolypin in the second tried to avert the danger of a garrison-state counter-reform by instituting bold reformist plans. They were both inventive and energetic individuals who achieved a great deal. But they lost in the end. Their opponents, the leaders of the garrison-state counter-reforms, won out, Peter in the first instance and Lenin in the second.

Thus the second aim of this book is to show the reader that the possibility of a counter-reform in Russia at the end of this century or the beginning of the next is just as real as it was at the close of the seventeenth or the start of the twentieth centuries. Moreover, the ideology for a modern counter-reform is being intensively developed and has been since the mid-1960s, both inside Russia and within the emigre community, by groups of intellectuals whom collectively I refer to as the Russian New Right.

The third and last, but by no means least, goal of this book is to show the reader that the key to understanding this peril — and consequently to avoiding it — lies in comprehending the nature of the ideology of counter-reform as it attacked in the 1970s a decayed regime of political stagnation from the right.

This task is perhaps more difficult than the others, if only because in a conflict between a cynical police state and a handful of fearless opponents (as the struggle of the Russian New Right is most often presented to the world) our sympathies are naturally on the side of the persecuted. If, in addition, one takes into account that at least the dissident (and emigre) faction of the Russian New Right loudly proclaims its anti-Communism to one and all, then the sympathies of all the world's anti-Communists must also be with them. The fact that they oppose a mediaeval system from a mediaeval position, that is, struggle not to dismantle, but rather revitalize it in a still more organic and aggressive form, might seem under the circumstances insignificant — particularly to those who espouse an ideological approach toward Russia. For, if Communism is the ultimate evil, then what could be worse? Unfortunately, neither the experience of Stalinism nor that of Nazism has taught these people anything. It is just such short-sightedness that makes it so difficult to understand the real function of the Russian New Right in the Soviet political system.

Try to explain, say, to American neo-conservatives that their support for a Russian anti-Communist inspired by mediaeval ideas is more dangerous than Neville Chamberlain's appeasement at Munich. They will never understand you, nor could they be expected to. To comprehend what is at issue, one must first grasp Russian history as a perpetual struggle that has been going on for centuries between reforms striving to destroy the Russian autocracy and counter-reforms seeking to perpetuate it. The ideological approach does not give one the opportunity even to glimpse the complexity of the issue — just as the liberals' geopolitical approach deprives them of the opportunity to see that the behaviour of Russia in world politics depends not so much on her imperial dynamics as on the character of the particular regime in power.

In other words, the role of the Russian Idea in the country's contemporary history simply cannot be understood by American intellectuals and politicians within the framework of their conventional approaches to Russia. The limits to their vision are rigidly set by these approaches, which invariably lack any historical dimension. Therefore, a book about Russian nationalism will not be properly received by them unless and until an alternative — that is, an historical — approach has acquired its legitimate place in America's Soviet debate. This is what I did not comprehend seven years ago when I was writing *The Russian New Right*.

An Explanation to the Reader

It is true that the book received commentaries and reviews in many languages and, consequently, was discussed in many countries of the world. Indeed, the list of responses it elicited, even leaving aside the storm of fury it provoked in the Russian emigre press, looks impressive.[17] However, the function for which the book was intended, remained unfulfilled. This was partly my fault. I naively assumed that the facts would speak for themselves, that documents work more effectively than intellectual stratagems, that examples are more persuasive than philosophical concepts, and that the capacity of a free mind to accept new ideas is unlimited. I was very much mistaken.

As one who left a country dominated by state censorship, I believed that the problem ended there — that censorship was the only thing limiting our view of the world. I now understand that there exist other, no less rigid limitations, which no one imposes on us from the outside. We impose them on ourselves by our intellectual approach to problems and by the logic of our struggle with opponents, which may have absolutely no relation to the problem at hand. That is why, in order to introduce into the public discourse a new set of ideas which contradict the conventional approaches, one has to have something more than facts. In the first place, the futility and shortsightedness of these approaches must be pointed out. Secondly, one must have an intellectual alternative to offer.

I am saying all this to 'my' reader since I assume that 'other people's' readers will already have long since slammed this book shut, never to open it again. I am saying this to my reader in order to explain why I have begun the introduction to a book about the contemporary Russian reactionary opposition with an analysis of the obvious inadequacy of America's Soviet debate. This simply reflects all that I have learned since 1978. It is also a promise not to repeat the same mistake. The Russian Idea will be examined here not only in the context of Russian intellectual and political history, but also in that of the American debate. I shall also address the question of what the West can do in order, in this nuclear age, to assist Russian reform rather than counter-reform.

The Lesson

There is still another reason why this book may succeed in achieving what *The Russian New Right* did not. The dissident segment of the Russian New Right (I call it this to distinguish it from its establishment counterpart in Moscow) has given the Western public a series of instructive lessons in the intervening years. The most recent of these I shall now recount briefly.

On 20 January 1981, the Governing Board of the Russian National Union in West Germany addressed a congratulatory letter to the new president of the United States. The letter was a long one, but its essence was contained in its last paragraph: 'Communism in all its ideological and practical applications is the major and mortal enemy of humankind. The path of seeking conciliation with it leads to inevitable catastrophe. To avert catastrophe there remains one path still open — that of finding an alliance, an understanding, and an honest friendship with the Russian people' who, it is said in another part of the letter, have nothing in common with the powers that be in the USSR, but on the contrary, represent 'the first and most suffering victim of Communist dictatorship'.[18]

The call was heard. A year later the new American administration restructured the staff of Radio Liberty and the Voice of America in order to adapt American radio broadcasting into the USSR to the ideas of the Russian New Right. This is what resulted.

At the end of January 1985 the New York *Daily News* asked its readers: 'Did you know your tax dollars were being used to transmit Antisemitic broadcasts into Russia? . . . And instead of spreading the message of freedom and democracy that President Reagan declared to be our contribution to the modern world, Radio Liberty is often pro-tsarist as well?'[19] According to the *Los Angeles Times*, anti-semitism and tsarist ideas were disseminated, specifically, in the broadcast of 'a passage of Alexander Solzhenitsyn's book *August 1914*, dealing with the 1911 assassination of a tsarist prime minister by a Jewish anarchist. The broadcast picked up several phrases that have been traditionally used by Russian anti-semites and even quoted a passage from the *Protocols of the Elders of Zion*.'[20]

According to an editorial in *The New Republic*, all this began in 1982, when the Reagan administration appointed George Bailey, a close associate of Solzhenitsyn's, as Radio Liberty director. Bailey, in turn, the editorial continues, 'installed a group of Russian emigre broadcasters who share Solzhenitsyn's particular Russian nationalist views. To be sure, this ideology is anti-Communist. But it also glorifies Czarist Russia and regards both Bolshevism and parliamentary democracy as equally decadent "Western" ideologies with no place in Russian society, and it has historically contained a strong element of anti-semitism.'[21] *The Christian Science Monitor* was more concrete:

> During the two and a half year tenure of RL director George Bailey, the US-funded and directed station claimed on the air that:
> Western democracy is corrupt and unsuitable for the Soviet Union.
> US pressure on right-wing authoritarian regimes to observe human rights is counterproductive and immoral.
> Liberal opponents of the tsarist autocracy were in error and contributed to the Bolshevik takeover.

Jewish revolutionaries bear direct responsibility for the destruction of the old regime.

Jewish pogroms in the Ukraine during the Civil War — however unfortunate — should be understood in the context of Jewish support for the Reds.

The SS division Galitchina, whose Ukrainian volunteers fought for Hitler in France, among other places, represented the commendable aspirations of freedom-loving Ukrainians.[22]

Moreover, the same newspaper reported that, 'one of the editors of Radio Liberty (an old associate of Bailey's) asked rhetorically in an interview in his presence: "And who has established that anti-semitism is wrong?"'[23]

There is an old African proverb that says: 'If a crocodile wants to eat your enemy, that does not mean he is your friend.' Hitler, who in his time aspired to devour both Communist Russia and parliamentary Europe indiscriminately, showed how true this is. But have we learned very much from it?

Russia vs. Russia

What is the point of the lesson offered by the Russian New Right to the American administration, which was just trying to make use of its anti-Communist potential? How, one wonders, was this administration to know that the Russian New Right stands not for the Russia of Pushkin and Tolstoy, but for the Russia of Purishkevich and the Union of the Russian People, which has been hostile to the other Russia since time immemorial? It was that Russia which, in the very first months of Alexander III's regime of counter-reform, began the first era of mass Jewish pogroms in modern history, and which, in the struggle against reform, launched the first mass-based proto-fascist party on to the world. It was that same one which, in its further struggle against reform, fabricated the vile and vicious anti-semitic document *The Protocols of the Elders of Zion*. Clearly the American administration was unaware of all this, since these events took place long before the Communist Revolution, in the days of the tsarist and thoroughly anti-Communist Russia which the Russian New Right seeks to restore.

Could the ideological approach to the USSR, which, one must assume, inspired the bulk of the Reagan administration, have warned it of the dangers of an alliance with the party of Russian counter-reform? It could not. The people who believe in this approach don't even suspect the existence of the struggle Russia vs. Russia, reform vs. counter-reform that constitutes the essence of Russian history. Could the administration's opponents have warned it of its mistake, given that their geopolitical approach ignores this struggle just as much as its ideologically oriented counterpart does? Clearly, they could not.

In truth, without an alternative, historical approach toward Russia, the West is simply not in a position to evaluate the intellectual and political complexity of the problem that confronts it in the second half of the twentieth century. Furthermore, the complexity of the problem cannot be fully grasped without coming to grips with the nature of the Russian New Right and its role in Russian history. It is for these reasons that the mid-1980s call for a new book about Russian nationalism. With each year that passes, Russia's new historical decline is becoming more obvious. The path that she chooses to escape this decline as the year 2000 approaches, will affect the fate of the world.

Notes

1   Quoted in Robert Scheer, *With Enough Shovels*, Random House, 1982, p. 5.
2   Imperial nationalism significantly differs from what is commonly understood as 'nationalism' in the social sciences. It expresses the interests not of small oppressed nations struggling for liberation from the imperial yoke (such as contemporary Poland), but of the dominant 'imperial' nation — in other words, not the object, but the subject of oppression. The late Andrei Amal'rik described this difference in the following words: 'The nationalism of small peoples is understandable as a means of self-defence for the people and their culture, though even in these cases it sometimes takes on unattractive forms. But the nationalism of a great people is a means not of defence, but of pressure applied both inwardly and outwardly.' (*Zapiski dissidenta*).
3   *Newsweek*, 19 Nov. 1979, p. 147.
4   *U.S. News and World Report*, 6 Sept. 1982, p. 35.
5   Quoted in Robert Scheer, *With Enough Shovels*, p. 28.
6   *Atlantic Monthly*, July 1983, p. 34.
7   Quoted from *Veche* No. 5, 1982, pp. 10, 12.
8   *Atlantic Monthly*, op. cit., p. 34.
9   Over the course of a decade of reform (1953—64) the Soviet Union abandoned its military bases in Finland, Austria and China, relinquished its territorial claims on Turkey, significantly reduced the size of its armed forces, refused to take part in the strategic arms race, normalized diplomatic relations with Israel, Yugoslavia and Japan, and so forth. Not

a square inch of new territory under direct Moscow control has been added to the empire during the entire Khrushchev decade.

10 See Alexander Yanov, *The Origins of Autocracy*, Univ. of California Press, 1981.

11 Nikolai Berdiaev, *Novoe Srednevekov'e* [*The New Middle Ages*],Berlin: Obelisk, 1924.

12 In January of 1980, at the height of the panic and anticipation of disaster, one of my colleagues at Berkeley asked me whether the Afghan resistance to the Soviet invasion forces would last two or four weeks. I bet him a bottle of cognac that a year later, in January 1981, the resistance would still be continuing, and in January of 1982 as well; that, in other words, the Soviet army would not only be bogged down in Afghanistan for some time to come, but also, without a radical change of regimes in Moscow, would be unable to make any move toward the Persian Gulf oil-fields. Needless to say, I won my cognac.

13 *U.S. News and World Report*, 18 February, 1985, p. 44.

14 Ibid., p. 47.

15 The methodology of this approach is complex and I certainly don't want to burden the reader with its theoretical intricacies. There is a table in the Appendix which lists all Russia's major reform attempts as well as all counter-reforms, and another which illustrates the structure of her historical cycles, i.e., periods separating one counter-reform from the other. Let me say only that this approach distinguishes between Russia's political *system* (which I call autocracy and which is centuries old), its *subsystems* (the Muscovite subsystem lasting from 1564 to 1700; the Petersburg one — from 1700 to February 1917; and the Soviet — from October 1917 until whenever), and its *political regimes*. The number of regimes in each cycle varies. In the most developed cycles, as can be seen from Figure 2 this number reaches six. But the three main types of regimes — reform, counter-reform, and stagnation — are more or less clearly visible in each cycle. Each of these regimes has a different function and these functions, in turn, are quite independent of the intentions of their leaders. The function of a counter-reformist regime is to perpetuate the system, that of a reformist one is to disintegrate it, while a regime of stagnation aims to restore the system's equilibrium after it has been shaken by both extremes in turn. Thus, functionally speaking, each regime is antagonistic to its predecessor, i.e., bent on the destruction of its political legacy. This is clearly reflected in the priorities of each regime. While a regime, like Stalin's (counter-reform), distinctly prefers guns to butter, and a regime, like Khrushchev's (reform), just as distinctly prefers butter to guns, a regime, like Brezhnev's (political stagnation) tries to combine both. The de-Stalinization following Stalin, the de-Khrushchevization after Khrushchev, and the de-Brezhnevization after Brezhnev support this argument. If one looks further back into Russian political history, however, one would find a comparable 'de-Petrinization' or 'de-Katherinization' in the Petersburg subsystem as well as a 'de-Ivanization' in the Muscovite one. In other words, the major patterns of political change hold their own despite all the tremendous ideological and social upheavals of Russian history both before and after 1917.

16   M. Pogodin, *Sochineniia*, v. 4, pp. 7, 10.
17   Here are some of the pieces (those I know) in which *The Russian New Right* was discussed: 'The Left Right', Stephen Cohen, *New York Times Magazine*, 7/1/79; 'The Roots of Reaction', Leonard Schapiro, *Times Literary Supplement*, 10/11/78; 'The Russian New Right', Abraham Brumberg, *The New Republic*, 5/5/79; 'Russia's New Fascists', Peter Dreyer, *Spectator*, 9/9/78; 'The Russian New Right', John Campbell, *Foreign Affairs*, Fall 1978; 'L'Audience de Solzhenitsyn en Occident et en USSR', Olga Carlisle, *Le Monde Diplomatique*, 2/9/78; 'La Nuova Destra', Luciano Tas, *Occidente*, No. 6, 1978; 'The End of Marxism-Leninism: Anti-Semitism Institutionalized', Reuben Ainzstein, *New Statesman*, 15/12/78; 'La Renaissance du Nationalisme Russe', Abraham Brumberg, *Le Matin*, 14/2/79; 'Khomeini ante portas?' Helen von Sachno, *Süddeutsche Zeitung*, 3/3/79; 'The Russian New Right', S. Enders Wimbush, *The Russian Review*, January 1980; 'Los Ultras Estan Conquistando El Poder En La USSR', Ignacio Carrion, *ABC* (Madrid), 21/3/80; L'orso russi guardera a destra', Lia Wainstain, *La Stampa*, 17/7/81; 'The Russian New Right', Victor Zaslavsky, *Theory and Society*, v. 6, 1978; 'La cultura dell' isolazionismo in USSR', Juliano Torlontano, *La Voce Republicana*, 4/9/81; 'Bulldoggarna slass under mattani Kremlin', Disa Hastad, *Dagen Nyheter*, 9/6/82; 'Quando la Santa Russia inspira i dissidente', Rita di Leo, *La Republica*, 12/1/79; 'The Coalition of Fear', Peter Dreyer, *San Francisco Review of Books*, vol. 4, No. 3, September 1978; 'Anti-Semitism, the New Soviet Religion', Reuben Ainzstein, *Jerusalem Post*, 28/12/78; 'The Russian New Right', Jonathan Harris, *American Political Science Review*, vol. 73, 1979; 'The Linchpin is Anti-Semitism', Irving Louis Horowitz, *Present Tense*, Fall 1979; 'Russian New Right May Play Role', Ernest Conine, *Herald Tribune*, 1/9/82.
18   Quoted from *Veche*, No. 1, 1981, pp. 197, 196.
19   Lars-Erik Nelson, 'Radio Liberty: Tax-Paid Anti-Semitism', *Daily News*, January 1985.
20   'International Bloopers', *Los Angeles Times*, 28 January 1985.
21   'Taking Radio Liberties', *The New Republic*, 4 February 1985.
22   Dimitri Simes, 'The Destruction of Liberty', *Christian Science Monitor* 13 February 1985.
23   Ibid.

I

The Historical Drama of the Russian Idea and America's Soviet debate

2
The Russian Idea: Between Two Hatreds

The Russian Idea, as I refer to the theoretical nucleus of the Russian New Right's ideology, emerged at approximately the same time as Marxism, the theoretical nucleus of Bolshevik ideology, in the years 1830—50. But it had no equivalent of Karl Marx. It was founded by a group of Moscow intellectuals, K. Aksakov, A. Khomiakov, I. Kireevskii, Yu. Samarin, A. Koshelev, P. Kireevskii and others, whose opponents dubbed them Slavophiles (which, incidentally, they did not object to being called). The philosophical, historiographical and religious aspects of Slavophilism were rather well studied in pre-revolutionary Russia and in the West. Unfortunately, the same cannot be said for its political doctrine (partly because the Slavophiles despised politics, relegating it to a minor place in their writings). Still less well studied are the complex metamorphoses which this doctrine underwent in the years 1860—80, and very little is known about its further transformation in the years 1890—1910. Nothing at all has been written on the connection of Slavophile political doctrine with the unexpected, unforeseen and wholly unexplained reappearance of the Russian Idea in Communist Russia during the 1960s.

Unlike Marxism, which has whole libraries devoted to it, the Russian Idea's political doctrine remains a relatively unilluminated subject even as far as its initial, Slavophile catechism is concerned. Its historical development from the 1830s to the 1980s has never been traced by anyone before. Perhaps this is why the addresses of its most famous contemporary spokesman, Alexander Solzhenitsyn, so shook America and Western Europe between 1975 and 1978. They seemed like a fresh wind from the East, something completely unheard of, the anguished cry of the Russian soul oppressed by Communism.

Hardly anyone suspected that Solzhenitsyn was merely repeating, often word for word, the 150-year-old postulates and formulas of the

Russian Idea. Significantly, Solzhenitsyn himself did not make any particular effort to direct the attention of his listeners and readers to the source of his inspiration. For some reason he did not wish to disclose his political genealogy to the world. Nor have any of his numerous biographers done this for him. The origins of his views therefore remain mysterious, at least for the general reader, and probably not for him or her alone.

Genesis

The Russian Idea emerged in the early nineteenth century, out of the noble aspiration to liberate Russia from 'soul-destroying despotism' and a 'police state,'[1] and Europe from 'parliamentarism, anarchism, unbelief and dynamite'.[2]

Out of the very dual character of this messianic task emerged the primordial duality of the Russian Idea's philosophical doctrine. If it's true that the problem of the devil (or, if you like, the antagonist) is a kind of theodicy for any ideological construct, the justification of its god,[3] then the Russian Idea's duality, its own peculiar trap, was that it had two devils. It was condemned to toss and turn between two hatreds, since the evil from which Russia was to be saved was completely unlike the one from which it intended to save Europe. Russia was to be saved from too little freedom and Europe from too much of thereof.

First let's turn to the second of these devils. 'Look at the West', wrote Ivan Aksakov, 'The peoples [there] have become carried away by vain motives, [they have] put their faith in the possibility of governmental perfection, made republics, built constitutions — and impoverished their souls, they are ready to collapse at any moment.'[4] Similarly, 'The messianic significance of Russia with respect to the West is beyond doubt . . . Slavophilism alone can yet save the West from parliamentarism, anarchism, unbelief and dynamite.'[5] Today [1974] Western democracy is in a state of political crisis and spiritual confusion . . . crawling on its hands and knees, its will paralyzed, in the dark about the future, spiritually racked and dejected . . . powerless before a pack of snotty terrorists.'[6] This is happening because the West 'hasn't realized that freedom is rooted in religious depth . . . in religion, and not in political institutions'.[7] 'In our country', Aksakov complained, 'they often clamour for guarantees and see these precisely in the western European legal order. But if the latter serves as the foundation of the guarantee, then what is it that guarantees the legal order itself, in other words: what guarantees the guarantee?'[8] Europe naively believes in the capacity of good constitutions to protect it from catastrophe, believes in political variety, in pluralism.

> Demagoguery about pluralism grows from a political understanding of freedom. We in Russia evaluate freedom above all as a deeply spiritual phenomenon. A person must be free internally in order to become free politically. And this again comes out of the teachings of the gospels: 'Know the truth and the truth shall set you free.' Thus, if we find freedom in our own souls, I assure you, society will be free politically as well. If we begin with political freedom, we shall unfailingly arrive at spiritual slavery. And that is what is taking place in the West at every step.[9]

Four generations of adherents of the Russian Idea have passed before us from 1850 to the 1970s. All of them have identified the evil that is leading the West to catastrophe in the same way: as the supplanting of the religious by the political, the fatal confusion of 'external' (political) freedom with 'internal' (spiritual) liberty and the resulting faith in parliaments, constitutions and republics. This is the devil from which the Russian Idea intended — and still intends — to save the West. In short, parliamentarism was the Russian Idea's 'European' hatred.

The devil which confronted it at home, its principal 'Russian' hatred, looked completely different. 'Where does the internal depravity, corruption, robbery and falsehood that overflows Russia emanate from?'[10] asked Konstantin Aksakov, the most remarkable spokesman of nineteenth-century Slavophilism. Why does 'Russia's contemporary condition present a picture of internal depravity, concealed by shameless falsehood . . . why does everyone lie to each other, see it, and continue to lie, and who knows what it will lead to?'[11] Why, on top of this 'internal discord', has a 'shameless toadyism grown up, which seeks to assure everyone we are living in universal prosperity'?[12] Because, Aksakov answers with courage worthy of Solzhenitsyn, 'the government has interfered in the moral life of the people . . . [it has] thereby passed over into soul-destroying despotism, oppressing the spiritual world and human dignity of the people and, finally, signifying the breakdown of moral fibre in Russia — and public corruption.'[13] That is why, he says, 'the government, despite all the lack of limitations on its power, cannot achieve truth and honesty . . . the universal corruption and weakening of the moral foundations of our society has reached enormous proportions . . . it has already turned from a private sin into a public one and has come to represent the entire social structure's immorality.'[14]

Thus 'soul-destroying despotism' (or totalitarianism, judging from how Aksakov describes it) threatens Russia with catastrophe. 'The longer the Petrine governmental system goes on,' Aksakov warns, 'making out of the subject a slave, the longer principles alien to Russia will continue to enter into her . . . the more threatening will be the menace of revolutionary attempts finally shattering Russia, when she ceases to be Russia.'[15]

This letter of Aksakov's to the tsar differs, of course, from Solzhenitsyn's letter to the leaders of the Soviet Union. Naturally, Solzhenitsyn did not describe Russian despotism as 'the Petrine governmental system' nor did he refer to 'soul-destroying despotism', but rather a 'black whirlwind from the West' and 'ideology'. The chronology does not correspond either. Aksakov says, for example, that 'the people wish . . . the state not to interfere in the independent life of their spirit, in which [the state] has interfered and which the government has oppressed for 150 years,'[16] while Solzhenitsyn says 'sixty-seven years'. Given that Aksakov wrote his letter 120 years before Solzhenitsyn and that in his opinion soul-destroying despotism existed in Russia at least 150 years before that, he could not have described despotism as having been carried in by that same 'black whirlwind' from the West. Aksakov, however, would not have objected to Solzhenitsyn's 'black whirlwind' in principle. Like Solzhenitsyn, he too was sincerely convinced of the Western origins of Russian evil and was also a prophet of the Russian Idea. The only difference is that, according to his calculations, the whirlwind struck Russia somewhere around 1700.

However, all that is detail. What is important is that in both letters despotism (tsarist in one case, Communist in the other) is leading Russia to disaster, and that in both instances the Russian Idea, as expressed by its leading proponents, promises to save the country from this awful fate.

Could it be that Solzhenitsyn is silent today about his spiritual forebears because the Russian Idea failed to fulfil the solemn promise it gave its people and the world a century and a half ago?

The test of history

Horace White once observed that the Constitution of the United States 'is based upon the philosophy of Hobbes and the religion of Calvin. It assumes that the natural state of mankind is a state of war, and that the carnal mind is at enmity with God.'[17] Whether that is good or bad is beside the point. It cannot be denied, however, that on the basis of this religious-philosophical attitude was founded a quite practical political doctrine (parliamentarism) which managed to survive all the great crises of the twentieth century — political, military and economic — and consequently escaped the calamity foretold for it by the Slavophiles one and a half centuries ago. 'The men who drew up the Constitution in Philadelphia during the summer of 1787 . . . did not believe in man,' Richard Hofstadter notes, 'but they did believe in the power of a good political constitution to control him.'[18] They didn't expect from us a spiritual rebirth or moral revolution — in a word, a miraculous transformation into paragons of virtue. 'It was too much to expect that vice could be checked by virtue; the Fathers [of the Constitution] relied instead upon checking vice with vice.'[19]

The American Constitution would not have come into existence if they had for a moment assumed that spiritual freedom must precede a political one. Even discussion of this topic, which has already absorbed advocates of the Russian Idea for centuries, would have seemed to them a pointless waste of time. Not a single democracy would exist in the world today — and consequently the present-day proponents of the Russian Idea would have nowhere to take refuge from the despotism of their native land — if Western leaders had once upon a time followed the advice of Slavophile spiritual forebears and considered parliamentarism a global evil.

I would not presume to set myself up as a judge in the dispute between the philosophies of Calvin and Hobbes on the one hand and of the fathers of the Russian Orthodox church on the other. Perhaps the latter were incomparably more pious and 'spiritual' than the former. However, the followers of Calvin and Hobbes kept their promise to provide their countries with freedom while the followers of the fathers of the Russian Orthodox church failed to keep theirs. The idea of neutralizing vice with vice has turned out to be the more practical politically, whereas the idea of a renaissance of virtue neutralizing vice has turned out to be a fruitless dream capable only of perpetuating despotism.

With all due respect for the spiritual quest of the Russian Idea's founding fathers, it must be pointed out that their primordial contempt for politics and hatred of parliamentarism punished them with political bankruptcy. It is precisely parliamentarism, the thing from which they intended to save Europe, that in reality did save Europe. It has proved to be the single method known to man for preventing despotism. The Russian Idea, as history has shown, was not an alternative to parliamentarism: it was merely an impractical and, as we shall see later, dangerous utopia.

For the moment, let us imagine two neighbours, each of whom has managed his business according to a different principle: the one, parliamentarism, the other, the Russian Idea. The first, for better or worse, has survived the crises that have shaken his enterprise and moved forward, while the other has gone broke. What right, one might ask, do the bankrupt's heirs have to denounce their neighbour's business as 'decaying', 'ready to collapse at any minute' and 'spiritual slavery'?

Of course, they may object — as they often do — that today Russia would be the focal point of world civilization if it hadn't been conquered by Western communism in 1917, if Orthodoxy had been given the chance to travel the course God had charted for it, and if the proponents of the Russian Idea had not had their hands tied. In fact, their political forebears had from the 1830s to the turn of the century and beyond, when Russia was the leader of world anti-communism, Orthodoxy was its state religion and when, consequently, their hands were not tied, to try out their historical experiment and indeed attempted to do so. How did it end? In such a way that today their heirs are forced to mimic the same unworkable formulas, bankrupt rallying cries and failed prognoses.

We shall return to these issues later. First, let us summarize the fundamentals of Slavophilism's initial catechism, developed by the founding fathers of the Russian Idea and today repeated by their heirs.

Russia's mission

The Russian Idea proceeded, as we already know, from the belief that the contemporary world was suffering from a global spiritual crisis 'carrying humankind headlong toward catastrophe'[20] (in the words of a present-day prophet). It pointed to the inability of the secularized, materialistic and cosmopolitan West to come to grips with this crisis, whose historical source lay in the secular Enlightenment: in the West's rejection of religion as the spiritual basis of politics and in its inability to realize that not the individual but the nation is the foundation of the world order conceived by God; that 'humankind is quantified by nations'.[21]

The Russian Idea pointed to the providential role of Orthodoxy, as uniquely capable of pulling back the world from the brink of the abyss, and to Russia as the instrument of this great mission. While the Russian Idea rejected the 'government's interference in the moral life of the people' (the police state), it also denounced the 'people's interference in state power' (democracy). To both of these it opposed the 'principle of AUTHORITARIAN power'.[22] The state, it taught, must be unlimited because 'only under unlimited monarchical power can the people separate the government from themselves and free themselves to concentrate on moral-social life [*nravstvenno-obshchest-vennaia zhizn*], on the drive for spiritual freedom.'[23]

The Russian Idea did not acknowledge the central postulate of Western political thought concerning the separation of powers (as the institutional embodiment of the neutralization of vice by vice). Instead, it advocated the principle of *separation of functions* between temporal and spiritual powers: the state guards the country against external foes and the Orthodox church settles the nation's internal conflicts. In place of Hobbes's misanthropic philosophy it offered a naive, but pure, faith in relations of love and goodness throughout the whole hierarchy of human collectives which make up society — the family, the peasant commune (*obshchina*), the monastery, the church and the nation. It cherished the ideal of the nation cum family, requiring neither parliaments, political parties, nor separation of powers. Like the family, the nation would have no need of legal guarantees or institutional limitations on state's power and its focus should not be the rights, but rather the obligations of its members. The nation's conflicts, according to the Russian Idea, must be reconciled by spiritual, rather than constitutional, authority.

The ideal of the nation as family presupposed the need for salvation from the sinful influences of the 'street' (the West) and, consequently, for a spiritual rebirth and a moral revolution. In the course of this Russia would return 'home' to its pure rural roots, to the tsarist *Rus'* (pre-Petersburg in the old version; pre-Communist in the new), *Rus'*, a land supposedly free from despotism, police terror, and official state lies.

Slavophilism

Such was the basis of the Russian Idea, which took many by surprise when it was resurrected, completely unaltered, in Communist Russia, more than a century after its birth. Whatever one may think of it, the nobility of its scheme and the purity of its intentions cannot be denied. Essentially, Slavophilism was an opposition movement.

Although its first advocates were themselves nationalists, they hated official nationalism, the ideology of Nicholas I's dictatorship. They passionately opposed human oppression in all its forms, whether serfdom, censorship or official lies. They called upon people not to live by lies. Moreover, although they claimed Russia's spiritual, cultural and potential political superiority over the West, this superiority was not to be used to harm the West. The Slavophiles wished merely to open the West's eyes to the ultimate truth, and in a spirit of generosity to extend a helping hand.

It is true that Slavophilism was a 'retrospective utopia', as Petr Chaadaev called it. It was also both reactionary and reactive: that is, it was at one and the same time a Romantic reaction to the bankruptcy of eighteenth-century European Rationalism and a political reaction to the new decline of the Russian empire begun in 1830—50. In the event, it was incapable of fulfilling any of its solemn promises, either to save Russia from the calamity that was indeed approaching (which, it must not be forgotten, Slavophilism was the first to sense and reflect in its impassioned writings), or — fortunately — to save Europe from parliamentarism. But, in all fairness, it should not be forgotten that the starting point of the Slavophiles' political quest was freedom, even if only spiritual and not political.

However, its catechism was alarmingly simple: despotism and parliamentarism at the negative pole, the 'principle of authoritarian power' — unlimited power which somehow provides spiritual freedom — at the positive one; rationalism at the negative pole, faith at the positive; individualism negative, collectivism positive; and, finally, cosmopolitanism negative, nationalism positive. When, at the start of the nineteenth century, the formula Freedom = Rationalism + Individualism + Cosmopolitanism appeared bankrupt, proponents of the Russian Idea reshuffled it to obtain a new one: Freedom = Religious faith + Collectivism + Nationalism.

The liberal opposition

The contemporaries of the early Slavophiles, whether liberal western-izers such as Alexander Herzen or populists (*narodniki*) like Nikolai Chernyshevskii, well understood the reactionary nature of Slavophil-ism, but none the less valued the drive for freedom that powered it (much as Western academic fellow-travellers of today's anti-communist Russian Idea understand and value Solzhenitsyn and his comrades-in-arms). Herzen wrote: 'We saw in their teachings a new oil for anointing tsarism, a new chain laid on thought, a new subordination of the conscience to the servile Byzantine church.'[24] At the same time he admitted, 'Yes, we were their opponents, but very strange ones: we shared one love with them, but not an identical one . . . like Janus or the two-headed eagle, we were looking in different directions while our hearts were beating as one.'[25] Chernyshevskii, albeit more prosaically, confirmed this view: 'It's too little to say in justification of Slavophilism that its effect is [only] either relative or negative. There are unquestionably some good sides to it as well . . . As far as its aspirations are concerned, one has to do full justice to them.'[26]

By contrast there is nothing sympathetic in the attitude of contemporary liberal Moscow thinkers toward the present-day anti-communist Russian Idea. Andrei Sakharov,[27] Leonid Pinskii,[28] Grigorii Pomerants,[29] Andrei Siniavsky,[30] Valerii Chalidze,[31] Boris Shragin[32] and Andreii Amal'rik, have all regarded the regenerated Russian Idea with suspicion, if not outright hostility. None of them would say, as Herzen did, that he and the Russophiles (as the new proponents of the Russian Idea are known) together shared 'one love' or that their hearts 'beat as one' with them. Yet they would immediately denounce the Russophiles' ideas as 'a new chain laid on thought' and protest against 'a new subordination of the conscience to the servile Byzantine church'. Why? What has brought about such a change in attitude?

None of those named have the slightest sympathy for Communism. On the contrary, they are all opponents of the regime and many of them made their names in the dissident struggle. It would be tempting to explain their hostility to the regenerated Russian Idea by arguing that the Soviet liberal-intelligentsia is more intolerant than its pre-revolutionary counterpart. However, if we compare what some of the best Russian liberal thinkers of the 1880s and 1890s had to say, such as S. Trubetskoi, M. Stasiulevich, A. Gradovskii, P. Miliukov or V. Solov'ev, surprisingly we would have to conclude that Russia's present-day liberals are far more tolerant toward the Russophiles than their pre-revolutionary forebears were.

So what was it that critics of the Russian Idea discovered in the 1880s and again in the 1980s which people of Chernyshevskii's and Herzen's generation could not know and which its Western fellow-travellers do not understand to this day? Why were they willing to raise their swords against it so quickly and without hesitation? What happened to the noble retrospective utopia after Konstantin Aksakov? We will never manage to grasp this unless we return to the Russian Idea's genesis and the process of its ideological development.

Notes

1   Ivan Aksakov in *Teoria gosudarstva u slavianofilov* [*The Theory of the State in Slavophilism*], St. Petersburg: 1898, pp. 32, 180.
2   Quoted from *Vestnik Evropy*, 1894, No. 8, p. 510.
3   See Alexander Yanov, 'Rabochaia tema', *Novyi mir*, 1971, No. 3, p. 247.
4   *Teoria* . . . , p. 31.
5   *Vestnik Evropy*, 1894, No. 8, p. 510.
6   *Iz-pod glyb*, Paris: YMCA Press, 1974. [English translation: *From Under the Rubble*, Boston: Little Brown, 1975], pp. 21, 25.
7   B. Paramonov, 'Paradoksy i kompleksy Aleksandra Yanova', *Kontinent*, No. 20, 1980, p. 241.
8   Ivan S. Aksakov, *Polnoe sobranie sochinenii*, Moscow, 1886, v. II, pp. 510—11.
9   V. Maksimov, 'Svoboda dukhovnaia dolzhna predshestvovat' svobode politicheskoi' [Spiritual Freedom Must Precede Political Freedom], *Novoe russkoe slovo*, 18 June 1978.
10 *Teoria* . . . , p. 49.
11 Ibid., pp. 38—9.
12 Ibid.
13 Ibid., pp. 32—3.
14 Ibid., p. 39.
15 Ibid., pp. 37—8.
16 Ibid., p. 41.
17 Richard Hofstadter, *The American Political Tradition*, Vintage Books, 1948, p. 3.
18 Ibid.
19 Ibid., p. 7.
20 *Iz-pod glyb*, p. 78.
21 Ibid., p. 19.
22 Ibid., p. 23. Emphasis in capital letters is in original.
23 *Teoria* . . . , p. 57.
24 Alexander Herzen, *Byloe i dumy* [*My Past and Thoughts*], Leningrad, 1947, p. 284.
25 Ibid., p. 304.
26 N. G. Chernyshevskii, *Pol'noe sobranie sochinenii*, v. III, Moscow, 1947, pp. 85—6. Other opponents of the Slavophiles in this generation spoke of them in a similar vein (see, for example, Nikolai Ogarev, *Izbrannye sotsial'no-politicheskie i filosofskie proizvedenia*, Moscow, 1952, v. 1, p. 409; Vissarion Belinskii, *Polnoe sobranie sochinenii*, Moscow: 1953, v. X, pp. 17—18).
27 See, for example, A. D. Sakharov, *O pis'me Solzhenitsyna vozhdiam SSSR* [*On Solzhenitsyn's Letter to the Leaders of the USSR*], New York: 1974.
28 See N. Lepin, 'Parafrazy i pamyatovaniia', *Sintaksis*, No. 7, 1980.
29 See, for example, Grigorii Pomerants, 'Son o spravedlivom vozmezdii', *Sintaksis*, No. 6, 1980.

30 See, for example, 'Solzhenitsyn and Russian Nationalism', *New York Review of Books*, 22 Nov. 1979.
31 See, for example, 'Khomeynizm ili natsional-kommunizm?' [Khomeiniism or National Communism?'], *Novoe russkoe slovo*, 27 Oct. 1979.
32 See *The Challenge of the Spirit*, New York: Alfred Knopf, 1978.

3

The Russian Idea: Genesis and Degeneration

The Russian Idea arose at the height of Nicholas I's dictatorship (a regime of counter-reform in my terminology). Of course, political terror was, as always, one of the means this regime used to assert itself. Another, no less important means — perhaps even more important — was its ideology. It was the very ideology of counter-reform that not only disarmed but even, for a time, attracted to its side almost the whole of Russia's intellectual elite. The Slavophiles were by no means behaving like radical heretics when they called Nicholas' dictatorship despotism. The dictator himself took pride in this. 'Yes,' he said with disarming frankness, 'despotism still exists in Russia, for it comprises the essence of my rule, but it is in agreement with the nation's genius.'[1]

It was this notion of despotism 'agreeing with the nation's genius' that was at the heart of the ideology of 'official nationality' which ruled Russia for a quarter of a century. It was, in essence, a kind of powerful secular religion thrust upon a society that had been frozen up after the desperate attempt at reform in 1825 had come to grief. It amounted to a deification of the state to the point of political idolatry. The very best Russian minds of that time — Pushkin, Tiutchev, Belinskii, Gogol', Viazemskii, Zhukovskii and Nadezhdin — proved unable to resist its temptation. This was the time when Pushkin's 'To Russia's Slanderers' and 'Stanzas' were published and Gogol's intensely nationalistic 'Selected Passages from Correspondences with Friends'. This was when Belinskii wrote, 'in the tsar is our *freedom* because from him comes our new civilization, our enlightenment, just as from him comes our life . . . unconditional obedience to tsarist authority is not just useful and necessary, but also the supreme poetry of our life, it is our *national trait [narodnost']*'[2] and Nadezhdin — most declamatory of all — expressed the general mood: 'In our country there is one eternal unchanging force of nature: the tsar! One source for all national life: sacred love of the tsar! Our history has up to now been like a great poem in which there is *one* hero, *one* character. That's the distinctive original characteristic of our past. It shows us our great *future* predestination as well.'[3] Very obviously, an ideology of political idolatry (a cult of personality, in modern terms) was a real, and for some time crucial, fact of Russian cultural life.[4]

The first commandment of this religion ran: the state is the intellect of the nation, its spiritual pastor, its consciousness. The state is all-knowing, all-seeing, all-loving and all-powerful. A Russian's principal civic virtue was his or her faith in the infallibility of the state. This pagan-like deification of authority was unprecedentedly dangerous for Russian culture because it threatened to bring with it intellectual degradation.

The mechanism of official nationalism was craftily constructed. The trio of Orthodoxy, Autocracy and Nationality artfully interwove despotism with religion, reaction with patriotism, and serfdom with sense of nationality. In rising up against despotism, one risked striking a blow against patriotism, and in rising up against reaction, one risked challenging religion. It was a resourceful construct, an ideological trap of enormous potency. Only by basing one's argument on its particular groundwork was it possible to tear 'the nation's genius' away from despotism, patriotism away from serfdom, and Orthodoxy from political idolatry.

Slavophilism fulfilled just this function in Russian political history. On the basis of defending Russian Orthodoxy, it attacked the official religion as heresy. From the position of defending unlimited power, it attacked the deification of the state as blasphemy. From the position of an offended sense of patriotism it attacked 'official nationality' as a perversion. In short, it fought for the secularization of power. It fearlessly declared that 'a yoke of state has arisen over the Russian land and it has become as though conquered, and the state as though conqueror. The Russian monarch has obtained the status of a despot and his freely subject people that of imprisoned slaves.'[5] If Marx was correct in asserting that 'criticism of religion is the prerequisite for all other criticism',[6] then this was the way in which Slavophilism fulfilled its historical mission. Its service to Russian culture must not be forgotten.

Paradoxically, however, it is from just this point that the drama of the Russian Idea begins. As long as it was fighting against the pagan-like deification of the state, it remained relevant and useful. When political-idol worship collapsed along with the regime of counter-reform in 1855, the progressive historical function of the Russian Idea was exhausted. From what it had once been only the idea of a retrospective utopia remained.

The proponents of the Russian Idea did not know that one of the fundamental patterns of political change in Russia is that no Russian despot has ever been able to make a regime of counter-reform outlive him. After Nicholas I another despot was impossible (just as after Stalin). After each of these despots an era of reform and political crisis had to ensue. This constitutes the second of the patterns of Russian political change, of which the proponents of the Russian Idea were also unaware, which was eventually to prove fatal to them.

A choice of evils

Slavophilism, having superbly mastered the tactics of ideological combat in the era of dictatorship, proved to be completely unready for the reality of political combat in the epoch of reform. Like all utopians, the Slavophiles knew quite precisely what they sought to do away with but only very vaguely what they wished to set up in its place. Their hatred was utterly concrete, while their love was woolly and abstract. Was it possible to have such a thing as a 'State of the Land' (*zemskoe gosudarstvo*), that is, an unlimited power that didn't interfere in the affairs of the 'land' [society], which, according to their scheme, was supposed to take the place of despotism? Post-dictatorial Russia, a Russia of reform, had no interest in this question. Instead, it split into two major irreconcilable camps: liberals and conservatives. The liberals aimed at following up the social reforms of the 1860s with a constitution — in other words the parliamentarism that the Slavophiles despised. The conservatives on the other hand, fought for the preservation of autocracy, increasingly striving for the restoration of the Slavophiles' no-less hated 'soul-destroying despotism'. As for the utopian 'principle of authoritarianism', which comprised the nucleus of the Russian Idea's political doctrine, its only proponents were the Slavophiles themselves.

The political crisis that ensued demanded from this magnanimous, naive, and anti-political ideological movement a tough choice: whom to support and whom to oppose. The reality of the crisis did not permit them to toss and turn between two hatreds. Slavophilism made its decision: 'Now the situation is such that there is no middle ground — either side with the nihilists and the liberals or with the conservatives. As sad as it is, we have to go with the latter.'[7] Such was the choice of Ivan Aksakov, the younger brother of Konstantin, who headed Slavophilism after its founding fathers (K. Aksakov, I. Kireevskii, and A. Khomiakov) had passed on. To a survivor of old Slavophilism and preserver of its early dogmas, taking sides with despotism was still a sad thing. Only with difficulty did Aksakov tear the ideal of a 'State of the Land' from his heart, but he was still laying tactical plans: first, to beat off parliamentarism, working alongside those who wished to restore despotism, and then. . . . But there wasn't to be any then. If the regime didn't want a 'State of the Land' when it was weak, then even discussion of such a thing would be out of the question when it became stronger. After making a temporary concession to devil number one in its alliance with despotism, while retaining a 'State of the Land' as its distant dream, Slavophilism emerged from this union with completely new ideas about the world.

Twin nationalisms

The Russian Idea's degeneration, which began with this fatal choice, is strikingly reminiscent of an analogous process that was taking place at the same time in another ideological movement. It too was a Romantic reaction against the bankruptcy of eighteenth-century Rationalist doctrines and might, analogous to Slavophilism, be called Teutonophilism. At its source, animated by the purest of visions of national regeneration, were Johann Gottlieb Fichte, with his fiery 'Speeches to the German nation', and the resurrector of German folklore, Jakob Grimm. They were the respective counterparts of Russia's Konstantin Aksakov and P. Kireevskii. Schleiermacher, with his 'Speeches about religion', and Novalis, with his 'Fragments about Christianity', were comparable to I. Kireevskii and A. Khomiakov. In the same way as the Slavophiles viewed Oleg's campaigns against Constantinople, their German colleagues revered Arminius's battles with the Romans and the triumphs of the medieval Teutonic orders. In deifying their nation, in what Vladimir Solov'ev later called 'idolatry of the folk', the two movements resembled each other like twin brothers. Moreover, as with Slavophiles, the insidious embraces of pan-Germanism lay in store for the Teutonophiles. Ultimately, it was to be a similarly tragic metamorphosis, later expressed in the form of fascist messianism, that awaited them too.

In the 1880s the proponents of degenerated Teutonophilism exported anti-semitism to Russia. As one German historian noted, 'the idea of anti-semitism has revealed the full measure of its venomousness only in Russia . . . Berlin's anti-semitic leaders provided the Russian hooligans with the [ideological] ammunition they needed. Stoecker and Ahlwardt became the true fathers of Russia's pogroms.' Meanwhile, the Teutonphiles congratulated themselves that, 'with a weapon from our ideological arsenal the Russian folk can now free itself from its mortal enemy'.

In the 1920s the proponents of degenerated Slavophilism were to repay this debt with interest to their German counterparts by exporting to Germany the *Protocols of the Elders of Zion* and the idea of Bolshevism's identity with World Jewry.

In the 1830s the classical authors of Slavophilism were engrossed in reading Hegel and Schelling. In the 1880s their degenerate intellectual progeny were to do the same with Theodore Fritsch and Hermann Goedsche, the great grandparents of German anti-semitism. If, during the first half of the nineteenth century, Slavophilism and Teutonophilism resembled one another but travelled separate paths, then one might say that during the second half their degenerate intellectual offsprings were reunited. Fifty years further on, this collaboration had managed to bring the world to the brink of the very catastrophe from which the founding fathers of Slavophilism had originally intended to save it.

Metamorphosis

To the defenders of the restoration of despotism, into whose camp Slavophilism crossed over in the 1870s, neither its 'freedom formula' nor its call to save Europe from parliamentarism were of any interest. In the immediate political crisis at hand, something completely different was demanded of Slavophilism's second generation: a rationale for unlimited power — irrespective of whether that power interfered in the 'moral life of the people' — and a justification for imperial expansion. The Slavophiles of the second generation willingly responded to the autocracy's political needs and tailored their doctrine to fit the required conditions.

Their main ideologue was Nikolai Danilevskii who, in the words of his younger contemporary Konstantin Leont'ev, 'explained the essence of the Slavophiles' teachings better and more clearly than the fathers of these teachings themselves'.[8] This essence, according to Danilevskii, consisted in the view that Russia could only fulfil her historical mission after transforming herself into a giant superpower. Moreover, the sense and content of all of Russian history, in his view, had been leading Russia to nothing less than repossession of Constantinople. 'The goal of the Russian people's strivings since the very dawn of their statehood, the ideal of enlightenment, glory, luxuriance and grandeur for our ancestors, the centre of Orthodoxy — what a historic meaning Constaninople would have for us, torn from the hands of the Turks in spite of all Europe!'[9] Fedor Tiutchev expressed this second generation Slavophile ideal in splendid verse:[10]

> When Byzantium is restored to us
> The ancient vaults of Saint Sophia
> Will shelter the altar of Christ anew.
> Kneel then before it, O Tsar of Russia —
> You will arise all Slavdom's Tsar!

Indeed, having taken Constantinople, Russia 'would be the restorer of the Eastern Roman Empire.'[11]

Thus, the main requirement for Russia was not reform, let alone a constitution, but rather military power and, above all, to be stronger than Europe. Moreover, this was not something so difficult to achieve given that parliamentary Europe, or 'the dual-foundation Romano-Germanic historical type' as Danilevskii put it, was — through its parliamentarism — 'decaying'. This was a view the second generation Slavophiles clung to from the Russian Idea's original catechism, and its significance for Russian autocracy's imperial strategy proved priceless. Conviction in the 'spiritual decay' of the West lent a moral justification to such designs. In order to become stronger than 'rotting Europe', Russia also needed, according to Danilevskii, something else — monolithic internal order, that is, tsar and people united around state power for the sake of Russia's grand historical mission. The old 'freedom formula' was totally redundant to this purpose since 'for any Slav, after God and the holy Church, Slavdom must be the highest idea, higher than freedom, higher than education, higher than any earthly blessing.'[12] It was only one short step from this to the fundamental conclusion Konstantin Leont'ev reached a decade later: 'The Russian nation has expressly not been created for freedom.'[13]

This pronouncement was made in the 1880s, at a time when a new counter-reform was trying to return the country to the dark days of Nikolaevian dictatorship. Undoubtedly, the ideas of the second generation of Slavophiles assisted the gradual slippage of the 1860s reform regime into one of political stagnation in the 1870s. Ivan Aksakov was still alive at the time and distant recollections of the ancient 'freedom formula' still held sway among the heirs of the initial catechism. Danilevskii himself, as we shall see later, was a 'liberal imperialist': that is, he was ready to give his blessing to a liberalization of the domestic order as soon as Russia was isolated from pernicious Western influences and a great Slavic Federation had slammed the 'window on Europe' tightly shut. Danilevskii was essentially the first representative of that strange amalgam of isolationism and expansionism which was to become the principal characteristic of the Russian Idea after his time.

The arrival of Alexander III's new counter-reform in 1881 — after some timid reformist attempts at the start of the decade had been crushed — revealed how far the revision of the Russian Idea's initial catechism had progressed in the second Slavophile generation. Ivan Aksakov himself was suspected of seditious liberalism, while Konstantin Leont'ev declared of himself that he was a Slavophile 'strictly in the cultural sense', which, incidentally, was closer to true Slavophilism 'than semi-liberal Slavophiles of the immobile Aksakov cast'.[14] It was at this time that Slavophiles pronounced that it was not with sadness that they had made their peace with despotism as the old patriarch Aksakov had said, but because they saw in it the superior strength and wisdom of the nation. The liberal positions of the initial catechism were subsequently discarded as subversive and a hindrance to the autocracy from leading Russia toward its grand goal. Rather like a sad memorial to the Nikolaevian ideology of 'official nationalism', the augmentation of state power was again proclaimed the nation's goal.

Now, however, this was not going to be advocated by state officials or muddle-headed intellectuals whose dishonesty and official lies had been uncovered by founding fathers of the Russian Idea. This time, it would be preached by its own new prophets with new rallying calls.

Down with everything that undermines the state's power! Down with the intelligentsia (the 'smatterers', as Solzhenitsyn was to call them a century later). 'The rotten West', — wrote Leont'ev, '— yes, rotten, it spatters and stinks from every quarter wherever our intelligentsia has been involved.'[15]

Down with mass education! 'Compulsory literacy will only bring good fruits when the landowners, officials, and teachers are made into still much greater Slavophiles than they have become under the influence of nihilism, the Polish mutiny, and European spite.'[16]

Down with Europe! 'The destruction of Western culture will instantly alleviate our cultural task [the resurrection of Byzantium] in Constantinople.'[17]

Long live the state which 'is obliged to be menacing, at times cruel and merciless, and must be severe sometimes to the point of savagery.'[18] Long live socialism, for 'socialism is the feudalism of the future . . . what is now extreme revolution will become conservation [*okhranenie*], a tool of strict coercion and discipline, partly even slavery.'[19] 'What in the West signifies destruction, for the Slavs will be creative endeavour.'[20]

Never before in Russia had slavery been preached by such august voices, so boldly and with such remarkable power of foresight. The syllogism was complete and the trap snapped shut. The tsar and people merged in an apotheosis of the 'Slavic cultural-historical type'. The Russian Idea, which only a generation ago had so passionately repudiated politics, had finally acquired politics of its own — those of despotism and imperial expansion.

A new crusade

However, the historical cycle of its ideological evolution did not conclude there. Alas, a still more gloomy end lay in store for it. Danilevskii, himself history's revenge on Slavophilism for its romantic-ist utopianism, was to suffer retribution of his own. Had he relied more on political reality and less on Slavophile dogma, he would have seen it coming. Contrary to this dogma, Europe was not in the least decaying. Furthermore, it had no use for the Russian Idea or Danilevskii's theory about the superiority of the 'Slavic cultural-historical type' over the 'Romano-Germanic' one. It had managed to arrive at its own racist conceptions without Slavophile help. According to the conclusions reached by the Teutonophiles from their own anthropological inquiries, the Slavs were by no means God's chosen people (that is to say, the most advanced cultural-historical type) — quite the reverse. The Slavs, the Teutonophiles believed, suffered from a manifest lack of Aryan credentials. Thus, in the area of theory, Slavophilism had run into a brick wall.

In practice, would Europe really have surrendered Constantinople without a fight? Moreover, there was every reason to suppose that the prerequisite for capturing Constantinople would have been the all-out conquest of Europe. On the evidence of the historical experience of Teutonophilism, we see that *Anschluss,* (the reunification of all Germans by means of seizing all the territories which they inhabited) proved possible in practice only within the framework of the Nazis' 'new order' in Europe. In other words, Europe truly did have to be conquered first to enable it to succeed.

The Slavic *Anschluss* preached by Danilevskii offered much the same prospect. But such a perspective was hardly realistic for Russia in a period of her historical decline — even if all the wishes of the degenerate Russian Idea were fulfilled to the letter: even if the whole population was as one in its suport for the tsar and the objective of *Anschluss*, and the heretical intelligentsia were eliminated. Even at a higher point of new historical ascendancy, in the era of Stalin's 1940s counter-reform regime, Russia was unable to realize fully Danilevskii's pan-slavic utopia: Yugoslavia defected from the empire while Constantinople, the utopia's central focus, proved unattainable. In the 1880s such plans were all the more naive. Thus, the third generation of Slavophiles proved incapable of fulfilling Danilevskii's dream, and the Russian Idea's new pan-Slavic catechism found intself in need of revision.

In particular, the traditional dogma about 'rotting' Europe proved completely unrealisitic and it vanished from Slavophilism's third catechism. Whereas for Danilevskii 'both France and Germany are, in essence, [Russia's] ill-wishers and enemies',[21] for third-generation Slavophiles there existed only a beautiful France and a sinister Germany, maliciously baring its wolf's fangs.

In order to comprehend the full implications of this revision, one must remember that precisely France, according to Leont'ev, was the 'worst of Europes', and Paris had to be destroyed along with Russia's annexation of Constantinople. To the second generation of Slavophiles, Paris was the world centre of 'liberal-egalitarian putrefaction'. Leont'ev had said: 'our luck is that we are *im Werden*, rather than at the peak, like the Germans, and, moreover, we haven't started to decline, like the French.'[22] Danilevskii had asserted: 'Russia is the head of the world that is advancing, France represents the world that is falling back.'[23] Nothing of this remained in the Russian Idea's new, third, catechism. Though the first 'white general', Skobelev, with a general's directness, called for instilling France with 'an awareness of the connection that exists today between the legitimate resurrection of Slavdom [read: the seizure of Constantinople] and the return to France of Metz and Strasbourg and perhaps the whole course of the Rhine',[24] the ideological leader of the new generation, the editor of the journal *Russkoe Delo (Russian Affairs)*, Sergei Sharapov, revised Danilevskii's catechism more profoundly and interestingly.

According to him, it is simply the case that, 'The French have already outlived their Latino-Germanic civilization.' For them it is in the past. Moreover, insofar as 'a ray is shining from the East, the heart is warmed, and this heart opens up trustingly', so that, 'in

France we will encounter no ill will towards us.' But, 'Germany is another matter. A later child of the Latino-Germanic world, possessing no ideals except those it has borrowed from Jewry, [Germany] cannot but hate the new culture and new light of the world.'[25] The Russian Idea, the noble romantic utopia which dreamed of a 'freedom formula' and of smashing despotism, proved to be flexible enough to adapt to the pragmatic calculations of imperial expansionism as well. A theoretical basis had been formed. The rest remained only a matter for practitioners, who generally considered 'civilian theories out of place here', since 'it's time to finish once and for all with all sentimentality [read: Slavophile utopianism] and remember only our own interests.'[26] Coming from Skobelev, such a tirade could mean only war: War with a capital 'W'; War as a crusade; War with Germany. 'The path to Constantinople', stated the catechism of Slavophilism's third generation, 'must be chosen not only through Vienna, but also through Berlin. . . . There is one war which I consider holy. It is necessary that the devourers of the Slavs be in turn themselves devoured.'[27]

Anti-semitism

Strange as it may seem today, the Russian Idea began the twentieth century looking into the future with confidence. Though its advocates still called themselves Slavophiles, not so much as a trace remained of the original catechism's first — and main — hatred, that of Russia's native despotism. Whereas Ivan Aksakov had felt some regret in allying with despotism in order to defend 'Russian originality' (*samobytnost*) and 'original culture' from the encroachments of the Westernizers, the third generation already poked fun at this timid defensive tactic:

> Not very long ago Aksakov had to fight for originality. What originality is there [to fight for] when the whole West has succeeded in under-standing that the Russian genius shall not be defending itself from Western attacks but will itself turn around and subordinate everything, introduce a new culture and new ideals into the world and breathe new spirit into the decrepit body of the West.[28]

The third generation, militarist and pragmatic, has already forgotten even to think about retrospective utopias. They were totally absorbed by their grandiose dreams of a future in which they saw Russia stretching out over half of Europe and dominating the remainder, which at that time found itself 'in complete subordination to the Jews'.

In this degenerate Russian Idea, nothing remained even of the second of the Slavophiles' original hatreds, parliamentarism. Its devil became 'The Protocols of the Elders of Zion'. Its rallying cry became smashing the worldwide Jewish conspiracy. To the new Slavophiles the principal confrontation of the contemporary world, seen by Danilevskii in the second generation as 'Russia versus the West', seemed hopelessly outdated. 'Not in the past', wrote Volzhskii, 'in what is finished and done, but in what's to come, in what the future holds, is Russia, according to common Slavophile thought, called upon to reveal the Christian truth about the earth.'[29] This truth consisted in the view that the fundamental confrontation of the contemporary world was 'Russia versus Jewry'.

Sharapov's vision

There is an astounding document at our disposal which leaves absolutely no doubts as to how Slavophile ideologues of the last pre-revolutionary generation saw the 'Christian truth about the earth.' The most vivid and prolific among them was Sergei Sharapov, who expressed his vision through a novel entitled *Cherez polveka* (*Fifty years on*), which was published in 1901.

'I wanted,' the author explains, 'to give to the reader in imaginary form a practical collection of Slavophile dreams and ideals, to show what could be if Slavophile views became the guiding ones in society.'[30] Here's how Sharapov saw Moscow in the year 1951. A Muscovite of the 1950s meets a person from the past and answers his amazed questions.

'Is Constantinople really ours?'
    'Yes, it's our fourth capital.'
    'I beg your pardon, and the first three are?'
    'The government is in Kiev. The second capital is Moscow, and the third is Petersburg.'[31]
    'What are the borders of this new Russia?'
    'Persia is our province, just as Khiva, Bukhara, and Afghanistan. The western border is by Danzig. [It includes] all of East Prussia, further [along] Austria, Bohemia and Moravia, [it runs] past Salzburg and Bavaria and then goes down to the Adriatic Sea, surrounding and including Trieste. This Russian Empire contains the Polish Kingdom with Warsaw, the Western Ukraine and Galicia with L'vov, Bohemia

with Vienna, Hungary with Budapest, Serbo-Croatia, Rumania with Bucharest, Bulgaria with Sofia and Adrianople, and Greece with Athens.'[32]

Doesn't one get the feeling from this astounding prophesy that — paradoxically — the true heir to the degenerate Russian Idea proved to be the Communist emperor Josef Stalin? We will return to this later. For now, let's just say that in some details Sharapov was, of course, in error. Austria and Greece were off the mark, as were Serbo-Croatia and Trieste. Iran was never part of the Soviet Slavophile empire, and as for Afghanistan, measures were undertaken only later. However, the general vision of an empire dominating Eastern and Central Europe as well as central Asia, proved exact. But how does this compare with Danilevskii's idea of a Slavic Federation?

'We dreamed', says the Russophile from the past, 'that a Slavic Union would form and the Russian empire would be dissolved in it.'

'Listen, that's laughable. Look how immense Russia's greatness is and how tiny an appendage western Slavdom is to it. Would it really be fair to us, to the victors and folk first in Slavdom, and now the world, to have to squat for the sake of some kind of equality with the other Slavs?'[33]

It proved to be so easy for 'the folk first in the world' to discard not only the Slavophile but also the Pan-Slavic mask. And behind that mask turned out to be the naked drive for world hegemony. It is hardly surprising that 'autocracy not only was maintained, but was extraordinarily strengthened and finally acquired the appearance of the most freedom-loving and most desirable form of rule.' Of the ancient Slavophile devotion to the one-time 'freedom formula' a single vague recollection was all that remained: 'Our historical road is the harmonious combination of autocracy and self-government.'[34]

But by way of compensation, a large part of the novel is devoted to the battle that would be raging in Moscow in 1951 around the most urgent problem of the modern world. 'The topic was the inordinate growth in Moscow of the Jewish and foreign element which was turning the old Russian capital into a completely international Jewish city.'[35] It had become so bad that 'at all institutions of higher and middle education the percentage quota for the number of Jews permitted to study there was abolished.'[36] Even set in an imaginary future such liberal depravity horrified the author. As we now know, however, there was no need for him to be appalled. In accordance with the first commandment of the degenerate Russian Idea, the percentage quota was in fact piously restored in Moscow. Even more importantly, if we recall the campaign against 'rootless cosmopolitanism' and the Jewish 'doctor-poisoners' that truly did shake Russia in 1951, then the main part of Sharapov's prophecy really did come true. The Communist emperor did indeed transform the Jewish question into the most urgent issue in Moscow a half-century later. As we now know, only death prevented him from implementing its 'final solution' in Russia.

The key point, however, is that for Sharapov as well as Stalin the solution to the Jewish question in Russia was only the obverse of the global struggle against world evil. To both, Russia's Europeanization, which her 'smatterers' had been carrying on over for an entire century, meant in fact its Judaization. The fundamental postulate of the Russian Idea has emerged again: as before, Russia stood in opposition to the rotten West. Only, in the new reformulated doctrine of world evil, the West's rottenness was rooted not in its parliamentarism, as the naive first generation of Slavophiles had imagined, nor even in capitalism, as the naive Bolsheviks had believed, but in Jewry, which had been responsible for forcing parliamentarism and capitalism upon the world.

According to Sharapov, the final solution of the Jewish question was to be achieved rather simply: by a gigantic nation-wide boycott of all of Jewry on the part of 'native Russian people, who finally had come to feel themselves masters in their own land'.[37] Jews were simply not to be hired for any kind of work except under the table. The degeneration of the pre-revolutionary Russian Idea was at last complete. It had merged with the Black Hundreds.

Hitler's mentors

How did such people react to their resounding defeat in 1917? Earlier, they had been full of euphoric anticipation of the empire's imminent and final victory over what they considered to be the last barrier to world supremacy — Jewry. Not surprisingly, they felt their defeat to be a disaster of apocalyptic proportions that portended the end of the world. But, above all, they saw what had happened as a triumph of the world Jewish conspiracy. They simply were incapable of interpreting it otherwise without having to reject their own doctrine, from which it logically followed that Russia had been conquered by Jewry. The following extract by one of the emigre carriers of the Russian Idea is not untypical.

Now Russia in the full and literal sense of the word, is Judea, where the ruling and dominant people are the Jews and where the Russians are allotted the pitiable and humiliating role of a conquered nation that has lost its national independence . . . To summarize everything that has been argued up to this point, one can plainly say that the Jewish yoke over the Russian people is an established fact which can be denied or unnoticed only either by perfect cretins or scoundrels who are completely indifferent to the Russian nation, its past, and the fate of the Russian people . . . Vengeance, cruelty, human sacrifice, and streams of blood is how one could characterize the methods the Jews use to rule over the Russian people. There can be no hopes for humaneness, compassion or human mercy for the victims of Jewish despotism, for these sentiments are beyond the Jewish people, who for centuries have nourished an insatiable hatred toward other nations, a folk whose whole essence thirsts for blood and destruction.[38]

The belief that the Russian Revolution was the 'action of the Antichrist in the form of Israel is as beyond doubt', wrote another champion of the defeated Russian Idea, 'as will be the brutal awakening after the crowning of the Antichrist, in the person of a Universal Despot from the House of David, foretold to us by the Apocalypse and now manifestly being prepared to enter the scene by the Jew-Freemasons with the worldwide support and complicity of "Christian" govern-ments, three-quarters composed of representatives of the "chosen people" and their Christian hirelings, the proteges of the anti-Christian Freemason-Kike secret alliance!'[39]

As we see, after almost a century of change in the Russian Idea catechism that spanned three generations, its supporters remained politically chaste. Even into the 1920s, they still did not comprehend that the solution of the land question was incomparably more important in peasant Russia than the Jewish question — however 'final' its solution — and that, after three years of carnage, what the country thirsted for most of all was peace, not the realization of imperial ambitions. The great adversary of the Russian Idea, Russian Marxism, did understand this. A young, dynamic, and flexible utopia of left-wing extremism, unencumbered by prejudices or a reactionary political constituency, it promised Russia what the old, moribund utopianism of right-wing extremism and imperial fantasies could not. The Russian Idea could not offer land to the peasants (it supported the landlords), nor peace to the people (that would contradict its sense of patriotism and the dream of Constantinople), nor self-determination to the national minorities (because of its dogma of the 'unified and indivisible' empire), nor, finally, even one-party dictator-ship (because of its traditional hatred of political parties and attachment to absolute monarchy). Therefore it was doomed from the moment the leaders of Russian Marxism offered, and were able to deliver, to Russia all these things (not for long, it's true, except for the dictatorship).

But even such an elementary political analysis did not occur to the supporters of the emigre Russian Idea. The shock of their defeat, which seemed final at the time, disposed them rather toward an eschatological and metaphysical explanation of their calamity. For them, the Bolsheviks' victory

> testifies with irrefutability that a force is operating in the world . . . that is steadfastly striving to realize its dream — the affirmation of the worldwide supremacy of the 'chosen people', and which now already heads Russia officially and covertly runs all other states. For there is literally not a single state in the world where behind the representatives of official power aren't standing kikes, the true power-brokers of international politics and inspirers of internationalist socialist forces [which include the] representatives of all socialist parties, without exception, and of the working class — blind executors of the will of the 'Internationals' — tool of the Freemason-Kike potentates.[40]

In his book *Russia and Germany*, in a chapter 'Hitler's Mentors', Walter Laqueur provides documentary evidence to show that the very 'idea of anti-Bolshevism as a central plank in Nazi ideology and propaganda and [the equation of] Bolshevism with World Jewry'[41] was adopted by Hitler from Russian emigres living in hopes that, 'Russia too would one day be able to boast of a Hitler movement.'[42] Entire fortunes taken out of Russia were disposed of by the inhabitants of 'Russian Koblenz' to support right-wing extremism in Germany.[43] All that, in Laqueur's opinion, gives us grounds to speak about the 'Russian sources of National Socialism'.[44] Advocates of the Russian Idea, having suffered an epoch-making defeat in their own country, scattered throughout the world and doomed, it seemed, to political extinction, nevertheless managed to find themselves a surrogate homeland in Germany as it marched toward fascism — that same Germany which not too long ago they had characterized as 'possessing no ideals except those it has borrowed from Jewry'. N. E. Markov, a deputy of the Russian Duma famous for his pogrom speeches and one of the apostles of the degenerate Russian Idea, ended his days as a consultant for the Gestapo on Russian affairs.

There is, of course, a cruel irony in this, all the more so because, in a certain sense, the emigre proponents of the Russian Idea were right to mourn over Russia. Nothing good could be expected for her under the left-extremist utopian regime for which, as for any utopia, degradation was in store. It too was to degenerate and its ideology be transformed into one of political idolatry. It is no coincidence that Moscow in 1951 — at the height of a regime of counter-reform — was more reminiscent of Sharapov's vision than Lenin's. Yet, none the less, unlike the Russian Idea, the left-wing ideology found in itself the strength for fierce self-criticism, for the destruction of its own cult of political idolatry and for a desperate new attempt at reform in the 1960s. But that's already a different story, one with other heroes and one which is the subject of another of my books.[45]

For now, let's just say that for anyone who agrees with the historical approach toward Russia that forms the basis of my analysis of the evolution of the Russian Idea, the mistake of its emigre proponents is obvious: eschatology had nothing to do with what began in Russia in 1917. As for the Antichrist, I can only paraphrase the answer of Laplace to Napoleon: an historical explanation of the Russian tragedy does not require this hypothesis. In fact, in none of Russia's historical cycles, beginning with the middle of the sixteenth century, has her reformist potential been capable of more than two efforts at reform. Furthermore, after both of these had ended in defeat, a brutal counter-reform invariably took their place, transforming Russia into a dictatorship, and at times a fortress state. (The difference between Russia's counter-reformist regimes is important and we will come back to it in the conclusion.) By October 1917, after the failure of both reformist attempts (one in 1905—07 and the second in 1917 from February to September), a counter-reform was, in essence, predetermined. The only thing that wasn't clear, and was only decided in the course of a bloody civil war, was which of the two extremist utopias, left- or right-wing, Communist or fascist, would win the titanic struggle over who should determine the ideology of Russia's new counter-reform (and thereby to decide her fate in the twentieth century). The left won, the Communist utopia. However, metaphysics were not to blame for this, nor were the machinations of an approaching 'Universal Despot from the House of David'.

We know now that the victory of V. Lenin and L. Trotsky's Communist government was indeed a great misfortune for Russia. What we don't know is whether the victory of a N. Markov and V. Purishkevich fascist government would have been a greater or lesser misfortune. Wouldn't such a government have restored Russia to a garrison-state empire under the banner of the world-wide struggle against the Freemason—Kike conspiracy? We can obtain some kind of idea of the possible program of such a government just from the following prophecy of Yu. M. Odinzgoev, which should not be forgotten.

> The same path is in store for Europe . . . The day of reckoning for mindless complaisance toward the scum of the earth approaches, and the peoples of Europe, who have been deceived by their own leaders, shall not be long in realizing from their own experience the nightmarish future that's been prepared for them, the Socialist-Bolshevik Eden, under the power of the Jewish *Sovnarkom*, which will, without a doubt, not delay in revealing its true essence — that of an inhuman, misanthropic and anti-Christian super-government striving to reduce everyone to a common denominator, to turn them into slaves of the 'chosen people' and its tsar-despot of Zionist blood. The catastrophe is near, it is at the doors. . . .[46]

However, inasmuch as the Russian Idea was not fated to lead the salvation of Europe from the 'despot of zionist blood' that threatened it in the 1920s and '30s, the only practical function it could serve was to help Nazism achieve victory in Germany and unleash it on the 'New Judea' (Russia) and the rest of Europe (ruled, as you recall, by the 'Freemason—Kike' secret alliance). Thus the noble retrospective utopia of Russian nationalism, which arose out of a dream of saving Russia and Europe from historical catastrophe, completed its first century by being transformed into an instrument of that catastrophe.

Notes

1   M. Lemke, *Nikolaevskie zhandarmy i literatura 1826—1885 gg.*, St. Petersburg, 1909, p. 142.
2   Quoted from *Voprosy literatury*, 1969, No. 5, p. 115.
3   M. Lemke, op. cit., p. 598.
4   'Calling his Majesty an earthly god, although it has not become a title, is, however, tolerated as an exegesis of the tsar's authority,' wrote Konstantin Aksakov indignantly. 'His Majesty is [referred to as] some kind of mysterious force that may not be talked or thought about and which, in addition, supplants all moral forces. Deprived of moral forces, a person becomes feckless and, with an instinctive guile, is able to plunder, rob, and swindle . . .' Things reached such a point, Aksakov fumed, that even 'in the form of written regulations . . . has been added something strange for Christian society. Namely, that "For his subjects, his Majesty is their supreme conscience," as though [their] personal consciences were idle.' (*Teoria* . . . , pp. 40, 49).

5   *Teoria . . .* , p. 36.
6   Karl Marx and Friedrich Engels, *Polnoe sobranie sochinenii*, Moscow, v. 1, p. 414.
7   *Moskovskii sbornik*, Moscow, 1887, p. 81.
8   K. N. Leont'ev, *Vostok, Rossia i slavianstvo*, Moscow, 1886, v. 2, p. 156.
9   N. Danilevskii, *Rossia i Evropa*, St. Petersburg, 1871, pp. 407—8.
10 Ibid., p. 338. [The stanza is from a poem entitled 'A Prophecy'. The English translation is from Jesse Zeldin, *Poems and Political Letters of F. I. Tiutchev*, University of Tennesee Press, Knoxville, 1973, p. 132].
11 Ibid., p. 406.
12 Quoted from A. Volzhskii, *Sviataia Rus' i russkoe prizvanie*, Moscow, 1915, p. 36.
13 *Russkoe obozrenie*, 1895, No. 1, p. 264.
14 K. N. Leont'ev, *Sobranie sochinenii*, Moscow, 1912—14, v. 6, p. 118.
15 K. N. Leont'ev, *Vostok, Rossia i slavianstvo*, v. 2, p. 13.
16 Ibid., p. 24.
17 Quoted from *Vestnik Evropy*, 1885, No. 12, p. 909.
18 *Pamiati K. N. Leont'eva*, St. Petersburg, 1911, p. 157.
19 *Russkoe obozrenie*, 1897, No. 5, p. 400.
20 Leont'ev, *Sobranie sochinenii*, v. , p. 500.
21 Nikolai Danilevskii, *Sbornik politicheskikh i ekologichesckikh statei* [*Collection of Political and Ecological Articles*], St. Petersburg, 1890, p. 23.
22 K. N. Leont'ev, *Sobranie sochinenii*, v. 7, p. 203.
23 Ibid., v. 6, p. 76.
24 V. Apushkin, *Skobelev o nemtsakh* [*Skobelev on the Germans*], Petrograd, 1914, p. 92.
25 *Moskovskii sbornik*, p. xxvi.
26 A. Volzhskii, op. cit., p. 86.
27 Ibid.
28 *Moskovskii sbornik*, p. xxv.
29 A. Volzhskii, op. cit., p. 23.
30 S. F. Sharapov, *Cherez polveka* [*Fifty Years on*], Moscow, 1901, p. 3.
31 Ibid., p. 23.
32 Ibid., p. 45.
33 Ibid., p. 59.
34 Ibid., p. 60.
35 Ibid., p. 24.
36 Ibid.
37 Ibid., p. 36. In fairness I must add that other representatives of the degenerate Russian Idea differed from Sharapov in the methods they proposed for the 'final solution'. Whereas Yu. M. Odinzgoev supported the idea of a total boycott against the Jews — 'Boycott by Christians of all press organs with a kike slant, boycott in industry and trade, boycott of the kike element in all the decisive spheres of human activity, coupled with the cleansing of it first and foremost from the organs of authority' (*V dni tsarstva Antikhrista: Sumerki khristianstva* [*In the Days of the Reign of the Antichrist: the Twilight of Christianity*], p. 225) — V. M. Purishkevich proposed resettling all the Jews to the Kolyma region of Siberia north of the Arctic Circle (an idea which was subsequently

picked up and modified by Stalin). The most radical, however, was N. E. Markov who once declared in the Duma that all Jews, 'to the last one', would be exterminated in pogroms. (See Alexander B. Tager, *The Decay of Czarism*, Philadelphia, 1935, p. 44). This idea was subsequently picked up on by Hitler, also with certain modifications. The variations in these different approaches however, as one can see, were strictly tactical.

38   Vasilii Mikhailov, *Novaia Iudeia ili razoriaemaya Rossia* [*The New Judea or Russia Being Ravaged*], Trudovaia Rossiia, New York, 1921, pp. 6, 15, 9.

39   Yu. M. Odinzgoev, op. cit., pp. 204, 225. Unfortunately, this book does not contain either a year, place of publication, name of a publishing house, or even the author's real name (Odinzgoev is clearly a name made up from the Russian for 'one of the goys' — *odin iz goev*). It can be deduced from the text, however, that the book was published after the defeat of Wrangel and before the Genoa Conference, i.e., apparently in 1921. Incidentally, the same ideas expressed in the very same words can be found in a small two-volume work by N. E. Markov *Voiny temnykh sil* [*The Wars of Dark Forces*] (Paris, 1928) and in the book by G. Bostunich *Masonstvo v svoei sushchnosti i proiavleniakh* [*Masonry in its Essence and Manifestations*] (Published by M. G. Kovalev, Belgrade, 1928). About Bostunich, Walter Laqueur had this to say: 'He became a confidant of Himmler and a friend of men like Heydrich, Ohlendorf and Karl Wolff, and a fairly high ranking member of the SS.' 'The Bostunich case . . . shows . . . the kinship between the Black Hundred ideology and Nazi thought' (*Russia and Germany, A Century of Conflict*, Weidenfeld and Nicholson, 1965, pp. 122, 125).

40   Yu. M. Odinzgoev, op. cit., pp. 204, 205.

41   Walter Laquer, op. cit., p. 57.

42   Ibid., p. 75.

43   Ibid., p. 62. There is a solidly rooted cliche according to which 'Russian Koblenz' consisted entirely of homeless writers and former colonels who all drove taxis. The evidence, however, shows otherwise. For example, the wife of one of the pretenders to the Russian throne (Prince Kyrill of Coburg), Viktoria Fedorovna, set at the disposal of General Ludendorf an 'enormous sum' between 1922 and 1924 for distribution among German right-wing extremist organizations. Others too donated to the struggle against the worldwide Jewish conspiracy — Gukasov, Nobel, Lenisov, to mention only a few. Baron Koeppen spent his entire fortune in contributions to these causes.

44   Ibid., p. 51.

45   *The Drama of the Soviet 1960s: A Lost Reform*, Institute of International Studies, Berkeley: 1984.

46   Odinzgoev, op. cit., pp. 207, 213.

4
The Russian Idea and its Critics

This short chapter deals with the evolution of the Russian Idea from 1830 to 1930 and is intended to answer the questions which ended the second chapter. Why don't contemporary Russian liberal thinkers in Moscow and the emigre community share the same feelings towards the present-day Russian New Right as the generation of Herzen and Chernyshevskii did towards the early Slavophiles? Why did the most prominent liberal thinkers of the 1880s and 1890s feel so differently towards proponents of the Russian Idea of their day — even to the extent that a respectable person in Moscow at the time would have refused a Russophile his hand? The shortest answer to all these questions is that Slavophilism as an ally in the struggle against 'soul-destroying despotism' no longer existed by the 1880s.

No one has explained this better than Vladimir Solov'ev, himself a former Slavophile and leading religious thinker:

> I have been reproached of late for supposedly crossing over from the Slavophile camp into that of the Westernizers, entering into an alliance with liberals and the like. These personal reproofs only give me occasion to pose now the following question, one of a completely non-personal character: where is that Slavophile camp in which I could have and was supposed to remain today located? Who are its representatives? What and where do they preach? Which scholarly, literary and political periodicals are expressing and developing 'the great and fertile Slavophile idea'? It's enough to pose this question to see immediately that Slavophilism is at present a non-existent phenomenon . . . and that the Slavophile idea is not being represented nor developed by anyone, if we don't count as its development those views and tendencies which we find in today's 'patriotic' press. Even with all the distinctions made between their various tendencies, from pro-serfdom to populism and from tooth-gnashing obscurantism to reckless mockery, the organs of this press adhere to one common principle — an elemental nationalism, lacking in moral substance, which they take for and pass off as true

Russian patriotism; they all join together too in the most graphic application of this pseudo-nationalist principle — anti-semitism.[1]

The most striking of Solov'ev's articles dedicated to the nationalities issue in Russia is even called 'Slavophilism and its Degeneration'. The term 'degeneration' applied to Slavophilism became standard usage in the Russian liberal press in the 1880s. This is testimony that Russian thinkers at the time superbly understood the essence of this process and wrote about it with a lack of inhibition that far exceeds anything present-day critics of the Russian Idea permit themselves. They used expressions like 'tooth-gnashing obscurantism' (V. Solov'ev) and 'mysticism with a crude predatory lining' (M. Stasiulevich).[2] We can find nothing similar among today's opponents of the Russian Idea.

The critics of that time naturally wished to understand the sources of this degeneration and thus carefully examined the Russian Idea's initial catechism, trying, as Solov'ev said, to find 'in old Slavophilism the imprint of today's jingoism.'[3] They unanimously discovered this 'imprint' in the *duality* of the Slavophile catechism. As S. Trubetskoi said, for example, in his article 'A Disillusioned Slavophile', in Slavophilism 'there were both progressive, highly humanistic and universalist tendencies as well as conservative retrograde nationalism . . . The Slavophiles' ideal was a Panslavic Orthodox culture of the future that would renew the world and, at the same time, pre-Petrine Russia . . . in her alienation from Europe.'[4] In 'Slavophilism and its Degeneration' Solov'ev says essentially the same thing, only in religious terms: 'The contradiction is between the universal ideal of Christianity and the pagan tendency toward aloofness.'[5] He denies the Slavophiles even the genuineness of their Orthodox faith, accusing them of being a 'tribe of Russian Orthodox heathens'. He puts Slavophile Orthodoxy in quotation marks because, he says, 'according to its psychological motif, [it] was more a faith in the people than a people's faith.'[6]

S. Trubetskoi dedicated another article, 'Protivorechiia nashei kul'tury'[7] ['The Contradictions of Our Culture'], to this same duality in Slavophilism's initial catechism, as did Pavel Miliukov in his famous lecture 'The Disintegration of Slavophilism'.[8]

The duality problem

The hypnotic power of the classical critique of the Russian Idea, based on its 'duality formula', was strong. When in 1969 I began a debate about Slavophilism in a Moscow academic journal, this formula still seemed to me not only adequate, but the only possible approach to the problem. It formed the basis of my first article, 'Zagadka slavianofil'skoi kritiki' ['The Enigma of the Slavophile Critique'], which opposed both orthodox Marxists and proponents of born-again Slavophilism inspired by the Russian Idea.[9] However, already in the course of the debate I understood — and this was reflected in my concluding article, 'Reply to My Opponents' — that such a meta-ideological critique of the Russian Idea, lumping together sociology with historiography, and politics with religion, is unsatisfactory. It proved to be too easy for my Marxist opponents to stretch the argument of Slavophile political doctrine into the realm of sociology ('they were all landlord serf-owners'), and for the Russophiles to argue on grounds of cultural philosophy and religion ('Slavophilism was not a political but a religious and cultural doctrine'). Switching back and forth like this, the debate soon lost its focus, which the duality formula did not help, but rather hindered it from finding.[10] Obviously, something very important — perhaps even decisive — was lacking, but at that time I did not know quite what it was. I was therefore not in a position to formulate precisely my objection to the classical critique.

Only in the course of working on my three-volume *A History of Political Opposition in Russia*, which saw the light of day — if one could call it that — only in Soviet samizdat,[11] did I manage to define what seemed to be lacking in the classical duality formula: it was devoid of a political dimension.

Of course, the classical authors were right. The duality of initial Slavophilism (as of today's Russian New Right that follows in its footsteps) is beyond doubt. Trubetskoi proved its philosophical duality and Solov'ev its religious duality. It also contained a duality, as Miliukov had shown, in its ideological goals as well. *Yet in its political doctrine this duality was missing*.

From the very beginning (and completely unambiguously), it opposed to both native despotism and Western parliamentarism its 'principle of authoritarianism', which repudiated the doctrine of the separation of powers, that is, the only mechanism known to human-kind for limiting the state's arbitrariness. Thus from the very start it was reduced to having to rely on the Russian Orthodox church as the sole guarantor of this constraint. It thereby supplanted, in essence, politics with religion, and the separation of powers with the principle of separation of functions between spiritual and temporal authorities. This, in turn, rendered it incapable of developing a political mechanism to prevent either the occurrence of periodic catastrophes in Russian history or its own degradation. From the very beginning it considered political parties, constitutions, republics — everything that was focused for it in the hated term 'parliamentarism' — as unconditional evils. Thus from its inception it built a political trap into its own world view. Its arguments served it superbly in the ideological struggle, but proved useless in the political arena. In fact, what was such a doctrine supposed to do when in a crisis situation it was faced with a purely political choice and was firmly restricted to only two possibilities — either for or against parliamentarism? In such an event wouldn't it naturally prefer despotism as the lesser evil?

Thus, despite the formula of the classical critique, it was precisely *the absence of duality* in Slavophilism's political doctrine, precisely its singularity (as opposed to duality), that proved to be the decisive factor that lay behind its degeneration. If this is so, then the drama of the Russian Idea was first and foremost a *political* drama. In a land where the combat between despotism and liberalism had dominated the political tradition for centuries, it sought to be the ideology of the authoritarian 'middle'. Sooner or later there had to come a time when it would become clear that, at the height of a national crisis in Russia, in Aksakov's famous expression, 'there is no middle.' For early Slavophilism, this moment of truth occurred in the 1870s. Thus the real enigma of the Russian Idea is that its own political doctrine invariably paralyses it just when it is faced with the kind of political choice that proves imperative at a moment of crisis. Here lies the seed of its degeneration. And, once degenerated, it is transformed into its own opposite — an ideology of 'soul-destroying despotism' and counter-reform.

Contemporary critics of Russian nationalism cannot know when such a moment of truth will come for its present heirs, the Russian New Right. They only know, on the basis of historical precedent and analysis of its political doctrine, that this moment will one day come. They have no reason to suppose that today's New Right will behave any differently when it does than Slavophiles have done in the past.

Critics and fellow-travellers

It should now be clear to the reader why contemporary critics of the Russian Idea are much closer in attitude to Solov'ev and Trubetskoi than to Herzen or Chernyshevskii (or Western fellow-travellers). Moreover, they know something about the Russian Idea that Solov'ev and Trubetskoi could not have. They know about its transformation into Black Hundreds-ism and Fascism. They know that even with its last breath it blessed Hitler's crusade against Russia and Europe. It is for these reasons that they do not allow the liberating anti-Communist rhetoric of the Russian New Right to push the 'tooth-gnashing obscurantism' of its political doctrine into the background. Understandably, they do not trust this rhetoric in the mouths of those who, like the first prophets of the Russian Idea, toss and turn between the same two hatreds.

When Western academic fellow-travellers applaud Solzhenitsyn's passionate declamations of freedom, as Herzen and Chernyshevskii in their time applauded those of Aksakov, and when they gently chide him for anti-parliamentarism, contemporary Russian critics see in the duality of his catechism the disastrous potential that Solov'ev and Trubetskoi saw in the duality of Slavophilism. They know that Konstantin Aksakov was replaced by Danilevskii and Leont'ev, and they fear that when today's Danilevskii and Leont'ev declare themselves the true spokesmen of the Russian Idea they will be replaced by a latter-day Sharapov and Skobelev. Moreover, as the reader of this book will soon see, in the compressed times we live in all these personages are already there, at the very heart of the Russian New Right. Its fateful evolution has already begun. The degeneration is gathering speed.

Denial of history

Of course, nothing on this earth is inevitable. Perhaps the coming degeneration of the Russian Idea can be prevented if an effort is made to do so. The attitude of Russian critics toward it might change if the New Right would admit its grave ideological heritage and acknowledge that its political doctrine is prone to degeneration no less than Marxism or Teutonophilism; if its spokesmen were prepared, frankly and dispassionately, to discuss the vulnerable points of their ideology, in order to try to ameliorate its weaknesses and offer new solutions to old problems; or, finally, if they would approach their own views with at least as great a degree of self-criticism as Russian neo-Marxists in Moscow and the emigre community do. They don't attempt to hide the fact that their initial catechism has become scandalized the world over. They seek dialogue and argument, in an effort to explain the reasons for its degeneration, to figure out its ideological and political mechanism and to offer new solutions. They would never try to follow Marx or Lenin mechanically, in the way Solzhenitsyn repeats Aksakov and Shimanov repeats Leont'ev. Neo-Marxist doctrine has not become any more convincing because of this, but at least its critics are persuaded that they are dealing with sincere people who are prepared to defend their convictions in argument against criticism from outsiders or each other. Critics of neo-Marxism aren't presented with outmoded dogmas that are held up as the ultimate truth, nor are they declared to be cretins or scoundrels when they express doubts about Marxism.

By contrast, no one has ever heard a single word of self-criticism from any ideologue of the Russian New Right. They are absolutely certain of the infallibility of their own moribund catechism. To get an idea of the style of their polemics, let us return to the jeremiad of V. Mikhailov quoted earlier:

> To summarize everything that has been argued up to this point, one can plainly say that the Jewish yoke over the Russian people is an accomplished fact which can be denied or unnoticed only either by complete cretins or scoundrels who are completely indifferent to the Russian nation, its past, and the fate of the Russian people.

If you replace the word Jewish with the word Communist you will have the standard response of Russian New Right ideologists to their opponents.[12]

While they fiercely attack the degeneration of Marxism, they never speak about the degeneration of Slavophilism. They fulminate against Lenin but have nothing to say about Leont'ev. History, in their opinion, is good for exposing the past failures of Marxism but ceases to exist as soon as the discussion turns to their own ideological roots. One of these preachers, V. Maksimov, explained that the Soviet system isn't of 'materialistic, but rather metaphysical, origins and we must approach it as such. If we do not, Western civilization is doomed to extinction.'[13] But didn't we hear this very same argument and the identical prophecy from Yu. M. Odinzgoev in 1921?

To find the perfect example of someone to whom Santayana's remark 'he who forgets history risks repeating it' would apply, one need look no further than the contemporary evangelists of the Russian Idea. They categorically deny their own past. But it is not, I suspect, out of forgetfulness or ignorance that they refuse to touch upon it themselves or let anyone else do so, but rather out of fear.

Russian extremism

If the critics of the Russian New Right cannot hope to receive a reply to their questions from the movement's ideologists, then perhaps their academic fellow-travellers will answer for them — even if they answer only the most essential of the questions. One of these is the following: if the old Russian Idea didn't save Russia from historical catastrophe, as it solemnly promised to do and which was, in essence, its very raison d'etre, why should we suppose that the new one will do any better? Why should we expect that it, like its spiritual mother, will not degenerate into Black Hundreds-ism and Fascism?

Indeed, the fellow-travellers try to respond in various ways. One proposes as a guarantee against this metamorphosis the Orthodoxy of the Russian people;[14] another emphasizes its presumed attachment to monarchy.[15] What are we to make of these arguments, however, when we note that all the proponents of the old Russian Idea were to a man Russian Orthodox and all were attached to monarchy to the bitter end? By the same token, all pre-revolutionary Russian tyrants were just as Orthodox and, one must assume, just as attached to monarchy. But did this circumstance prevent the Russian political system from periodically falling into horrors of 'soul-destroying despotism', or prevent the metamorphosis of the old Russian Idea into Black Hundreds-ism? Did Orthodoxy and monarchy succeed in protecting Russia from historical catastrophe in 1917? Of course, the answer to all these questions is 'no'.

Alas, to an equal degree they failed to protect her between 1560 and 1580, when a cruel dictator, over the course of a quarter-century-long reign of terror, forced autocracy and serfdom upon her. They didn't protect her from catastrophe in the 1700s either, when another dictator forced total militarization upon her, transformed serfdom into legal slavery and placed a guards colonel in charge of Russian Orthodoxy. They didn't protect her from Paul I's disastrous counter-reform in 1796, Nicholas I's in 1825, or Alexander III's in 1881 (any more than the Communist Party, I might add, which, under Soviet conditions, fulfils the traditional role of the Orthodox church, was able to protect Russia from the catastrophe of Stalinism in 1929).

Perhaps the problem is therefore not with Orthodoxy and monarchy, but in the theoretical foundation of *all* Russian extremist utopias, whether Russian Marxism or the Russian Idea, both of which repudiate the doctrine of separation of powers. Maybe the 'spiritual power' embodied in the institution of the Orthodox church or the Communist Party is simply incapable of fulfilling the function of curbing an autocratic state. Perhaps that is the reason why the replacement of the Orthodox church by the Communist Party has led to no fundamental change in the prevailing patterns of Russian history. If so, then how can we reasonably expect things to be very different from the reverse operation, if the Communist Party is exchanged for the Orthodox church?

It is an elementary rule of arithmetic that the sum of an addition is not changed by rearranging the order of its components. But isn't this rearrangement of components the crux of the entire political program of today's Russian nationalists?

It has not occurred to any of the fellow-travellers to ask whether the Russian problem might simply be incapable of a resolution by mechanically rearranging institutions and ideologies that preach an identically extremist political doctrine. Could it be that the problem has nothing at all to do with ideology, but everything to do with the fundamental postulate concerning the separation of functions between temporal and spiritual powers which determines the political platforms of both the Russian Idea and Russian Marxism?

Unfortunately, Russian nationalism's fellow-travellers (like Russian Marxism's fellow-travellers before them) are quite unaware of such considerations. For even to notice the similarity between the two extremist ideologies is impossible if one ignores Russian history — something which the fellow-travellers do just as scrupulously as their patrons. Consequently, they are forced to reason in the same black and white categories (Communist vs. anti-Communist) as the fellow-travellers of Russian Marxism before them. Only the attitude to the Russian problem has changed: what to some was a good, to others has become an evil. The methodology, however, has remained the same.

Russian nationalism's fellow-travellers argue that there are many faces[16] to the movement, that it is divided into hawks and doves or Orthodox and heathen or liberal 'Mensheviks' and 'national Bolsheviks' — in short, good nationalists and bad nationalists, patriots and chauvinists. In other words, they revive the classic duality formula, though not in an ideological, but in a, so to speak, personalized context. We shall examine this argument in detail in the next chapter. Suffice it to say, here, that the fellow-travellers are repeating the mistake of Trubetskoi and Solov'ev in ignoring the decisive fact that in Russian nationalism's *political* doctrine there is no duality, that both its hawks and its supposed doves despise Western parliamentarism and — most importantly — reject the doctrine of separation of powers. Thus, as far as political doctrine is concerned, they are indistinguishable, not only from one another but also from Russia's Communists (not to mention her Fascists).

It is no accident that among Russian Communists, there is no shortage of keen advocates of the Russian Idea. Irreconcilable enemies on the surface, the hawks and the doves of Russian nationalism, and Communists and anti-Communists, would all seem to stem from the same root — Russian extremism. They are not simply enemies, they are fraternal enemies. That is where the danger in the present-day political situation in Moscow lies. Once again, as on the eve of the Civil War, these fraternal enemies stand against one another: the Russian Idea and Russian Marxism. Sadly, like in the Civil War, any future open confrontation between them will not benefit Russia or the world, whichever of them wins. Of course, it may not come to open confrontation, but the fellow-travellers hope it will.

Notes

1   Vl. Solov'ev, *Sobranie sochinenii*, St Petersburg, 2nd edition, v. 5, p. 356.
2   *Vestnik Evropy*, 1894, No. 10.
3   Vl. Solov'ev, op. cit., p. 356.
4   *Vestnik Evropy*, 1892, No. 10, p. 777.
5   Vl. Solov'ev, op. cit., p. 173.
6   Ibid., p. 169.
7   *Vestnik Evropy*, 1894, No. 10.
8   Pavel N. Miliukov joined the liberal attack on the degenerated Russian Idea later than others (in the 1890s). Initially 'The Disintegration of Slavophilism' was a lecture read on 22 January, 1893 in the auditorium of the History Museum in Moscow. Afterwards it was published in issue number 2 of the journal *Voprosy filosofii i psikhologii* [*Problems of Philosophy and Psychology*] of the same year and reprinted in a collection of articles entitled *Iz istorii russkoi intelligentsii* [*From the History of the Russian Intellegentsia*] (St Petersburg: 1903).
9   This article was reprinted in English in the *International Journal of Sociology* (Summer—Fall 1976). Another of my articles relating to this discussion, *Slavianofily i Konstantin Leont'ev*, was published in the journal *Voprosy filosofii* (1969, No. 8) and reprinted in English while I still lived in Moscow in the journal *Soviet Studies in Philosophy* (Fall 1970) and in Polish in *Człowiek i Swiatopogład* (1973, No. 10). The debate was continued in issues 5, 7, 10 and 12 of *Voprosy literatury* (1969). In the last issue of that year my concluding article entitled *Otvet opponentam* [*Reply to My Opponents*] was published.
10 When this debate from the 1960s was unexpectedly continued in the West (after the publication of *The Russian New Right* in 1978), the emigre epigones of V. Kozhinov and A. Ivanov, who represented the Russian Idea in the Moscow debate, again tried to escape discussion of their political heritage by the same old method, that is, by scrambling together different aspects of Slavophile catechism. B. Paramonov wrote, for example, 'Slavophile nationalism was not politics, but cultural philosophy — a lesson about the organic roots of culture.' Already in the

next paragraph Slavophilism proves to be a lesson about 'the supra-cultural and supra-historical sense of human existence' (*Kontinent*, No. 20, 1980, p. 247), and in a few more lines it is asserted that 'the religious *problematique* of classical Slavophilism was *substituted* by cultural philosophy' (*Ibid.*, p. 248, my emphasis). Apparently, this author was not troubled even by the fact that this whole confusion in terminology ('cultural philosophy', 'lesson about the supra-cultural' and so on) completely contradicts the absolutely clear postulates of the founding fathers of Slavophilism themselves. Like Konstantin Leont'ev, he seems to know better than they did just what it is they wanted to say: 'The astounding terminological helplessness (if not incapacity) of the Slavophiles (who failed to even think up their own name) did them a disservice this time as well. Where he needed to say 'culture', Aksakov said 'state'; where he needed to say 'sky', he said 'earth'. What was, essentially, an eschatological doctrine, was expressed instead in political terms.' (*Ibid.*, pp. 247–8). I do not know whether it would please today's evangelists of the Russian Idea if tomorrow some other B. Paramonov tried to explain, say, Solzhenitsyn's hatred for the state structure of present-day Russia by attributing it to his 'terminological incapacity' (he said 'Communism' when he should have said 'hell', and 'authoritarianism' where he meant to say 'sky', thus expressing an 'essentially eschatological doctrine . . . in political terms'.) This all seems to me an intentional — and tactless with respect to the forefathers of the Russian Idea — attempt to distract the reader from the concrete problems that exist with Slavophile politics.

11   My book *The Origins of Autocracy: Ivan the Terrible in Russian History,* published only in English (University of California Press, 1981) and Italian (Edizioni di Communita, 1984) contains sections from this samizdat manuscript.

12   See, for example, A. Solzhenitsyn, 'Nashi Pluralisty' ['Our Pluralists'], *Vestnik russkogo khristianskogo dvizheniia,* No. 139, 1983.

13   *Novoe russkoe slovo,* 18 June 1978.

14   M. Agurskii in *Novyi zhurnal* (No. 118, 1975).

15   John B. Dunlop, *The Faces of Contemporary Russian Nationalism,* Princeton University Press, 1984.

16   John B. Dunlop, 'The Many Faces of Contemporary Russian Nationalism', *Survey,* Summer 1979, v. 24, No. 3, p. 108.

5

A Witness for the Defence?

John Dunlop, one of the most devoted fellow-travellers of the Russian New Right, wrote a book entitled *The Faces of Contemporary Russian Nationalism*. It is permeated with sympathy for the Russian Idea and sets itself the goal of defending its aspirations before the American administration (the book contains recommendations to the government) and public. Of course, it follows the fellow-travellers standard methodology in dividing contemporary Russian nationalists into 'Mensheviks' and 'Bolsheviks'. For the former, however, Dunlop has coined a new term *vozrozhdentsy* (from *vozrozhdenie*: renaissance), while the latter he just refers to as 'National Bolsheviks'. He freely admits that

> the similarities between National Bolshevism and fascism are striking: a strong impulse toward deification of the nation; the desire for a strong totalitarian state; a powerful leadership impulse . . . ; a belief in the necessity of the existence of an elite; a cult of discipline, particularly discipline of the youth; heroic vitalism; an advocacy of industrial and military might . . . ; a celebration of the glories of the past; and a militant, expansionist dynamic.[1]

Based on this, Dunlop concludes, very logically, that, 'in National Bolshevism we have an essentially fascist phenomenon, a radical right movement in a state still adhering nominally to a radical left ideology.'[2]

Although the whole point of his book is to prove that the *vozrozhdentsy* critically differ from the fascist National Bolsheviks, Dunlop none the less admits that there exists no 'Great Wall of China' between them: 'the two tendencies are often able to recognize a communality of interest, as in Solzhenitsyn's generally approving comments, contained in his literary memoirs, on Viktor Chalmaev and the *Molodaia gvardia* [Young guard] orientation of the late sixties.'[3] In general, from a political standpoint, the difference between the *vozrozhdentsy* and the National Bolsheviks consists, in Dunlop's opinion, in the fact that the former possess a mass base of support (having in mind 'their close ties to the fifty-million-member Russian Orthodox Church'), whereas 'the National Bolsheviks would seem to be better positioned actually to assume power.'[4] Dunlop thinks that, 'An implementation of their ideas would probably lead to what French sovietologist Alain Besançon has called a "pan-Russian police and military empire". A military dictatorship directed by a junta or a party dictatorship (with the CPSU becoming a fascist-style "Russian Party").'[5]

Such a turn of events I call Russian counter-reform: one of those periodic catastrophes in Russian history mentioned earlier, to which Russia is particularly susceptible in an era of historical decline. The extremist tendencies of both degenerate utopias, that of Russian Marxism and of the Russian Idea, would combine into a single fascist monster, capable of restoring not only mass terror in Russia, but also the threatening pre-war atmosphere of the 1930s, full of hysteria and uncertainty. In a nuclear age, such global hysteria could, in the light of the perpetual nuclear arms race, last indefinitely, destroying the whole foundation of international relations and, in essence, of civilization as well. It is this potential for just such a calamity before the year 2000 to which all my books are addressed. If I could persuade at least one American scholar to perceive this threat as I do, I should be well pleased with my efforts. So far, however, that pleasure has been denied me.

Though Dunlop describes the contours of this threat very realistically, he fails to perceive the threat itself. In fact, he argues that such a turn of events would be highly desirable: 'if the National Bolsheviks were to come to power, they would be much more vulnerable to the arguments of the intellectually more sophisticated *vozrozhdentsy*, with whom they have numerous ideational and emotional links . . . A possible scenario, therefore, would be a brief National Bolshevik interregnum followed by a *vozrozhdenets* period of rule.'[6]

Thus, Dunlop's cheerful scenario promises us a happy ending. A revolution occurs in Moscow — with, one must assume, all the attendant bloodshed and strife of civil war that accompanies revolution. Somehow, as a result, a fascist Russian Party takes power. Yet, having proven strong enough to crush everything in their path to power, the hawks suddenly defer to the arguments of the 'intellectually more sophisticated' doves and voluntarily hand over to them the power they have won. From this moment a golden age begins. This scenario has one obvious drawback: we have only Mr. Dunlop's word for it. I shall not at this point dwell on the fact that the *vozrozhdentsy* have plenty of their own hawks, as we will see later, or that both factions of the Russian New Right are permeated by a spirit of fascism. Indeed, Dunlop himself admits that the *vozrozhdentsy* 'have numerous ideational and emotional links' with the fascists and, if for only that reason, it is difficult to accept that they are as politically virtuous as he assumes. But leaving that aside, what chance would they really have of wresting control from a 'National Bolshevik' Russian Party that had just seized power?

Did the Russian Mensheviks have any chance of wresting power from the Bolsheviks after October 1917? Were not the Mensheviks also 'intellectually more sophisticated' and did they not have 'numerous ideational and emotional links' with the Bolsheviks? Did this then make the Bolsheviks 'vulnerable to their arguments'? Hardly. Didn't the Mensheviks — precisely because of their ideological closeness — end up among the first victims of the Bolshevik dictatorship? It could not have been any other way. In all revolutions, without exception, the extremists, after having seized power, have always decimated and terrorized first and foremost their closest rivals — those most closely related to them politically. So the Jacobins did with the Girondists, the Bolsheviks with the Mensheviks, the Stalinists with the Bolsheviks, and Khomeini extremists with Khomeini moderates. There has never been an instance — in revolutions in Asia or in Europe — where extremists, having established their dictatorship, suddenly turned around and voluntarily handed power over to moderates.

There is a wealth of documentary evidence which testifies to the genuine hatred of Dunlop's National Bolsheviks for the *vozrozhdentsy*. Some of these documents will be presented later. For the time being, it is worth citing two cases. Nikolai Yakovlev, whom Dunlop counts as a leading National Bolshevik,[7] both wrote a book entitled 'The CIA vs. the USSR' (in the opinion of Michael Scammel, Solzhenitsyn's biographer, 'a textbook of the cold war which strives to show that . . . all unofficial literature and art [in the USSR] is the product of CIA infiltration and manipulation'[8]), and spoke out as the most frenzied of Solzhenitsyn's 'academic' persecutors. Sergei Mikhalkov, also according to Dunlop a National Bolshevik, was among the initiators of a smear campaign against Solzhenitsyn in the Soviet press. Nothing these people have written gives us the slightest cause to suppose that once they had taken power they would be 'vulnerable to the arguments' of the Orthodox doves.

Thus, the logical conclusion to be drawn from Dunlop's book is irreconcilable with his declared intention to defend the noble anti-Communist aspirations of the Russian New Right. His painstaking documentation is evidence of just the opposite — the unprecedented threat posed by the New Right. For, if having seized power in Moscow, the National Bolsheviks whom Dunlop himself describes as open fascists remain in power, the West will be confronted for the first time in history with a fascist nuclear superpower.

Even though Dunlop's thesis doesn't stand up to close scrutiny, the scenario for a Russian counter-reform he describes — albeit unsuspectingly — is truly alarming. For the first time an American scholar, a product of Western training, has presented his readers with a possible scenario for Russia's future (in accordance with all the standards of modern political science) of a kind which before Dunlop no one, aside from myself, had tried to introduce into the currency of Western political thought — a scenario for counter-reform, something which neither the conservatives nor the liberals in the Western sovietological debate wanted to hear about.

As for John Dunlop, a man who sincerely believed he was speaking as a witness for the defence of the Russian Idea in the court of history, I hope the reader is now satisfied that in reality he is taking the stand in the opposite capacity, as a witness for the prosecution.

Notes

1 Dunlop, op. cit., pp. 256—7.
2 Ibid., p. 257.
3 Ibid., p. 264.
4 Ibid., p. 265.
5 Ibid., p. 262.
6 Ibid., p. 265. The reader may encounter some difficulties in connection with Dunlop's classifications (inasmuch as the single dividing line between *vozrozhdentsy* and National Bolsheviks in his scheme of things is profession of the Russian Orthodox faith). How would we categorize, say, the 'Union of Christian Socialists', first mentioned by Maxim Gorky ('Novaia zhizn'' ['New Life'], 20 May 1918)? On the one hand, this organization touted the physical and moral supremacy of the Aryan race and its slogan was 'Antisemites of the world, unite!' From this standpoint, it would have to be counted among the ranks of the National Bolsheviks. On the other hand, all the members of this union were Russian Orthodox, which obliges anyone adhering to Dunlop's system of classification to group them with the *vozrozhdentsy*. The participation of such obvious *vozrozhdentsy* as Antonii, Bishop Volynskii, Germogen, Bishop Saratovskii, Ilidor (Sergei Trufanov) and I. I. Vostorgov in the Black Hundreds in no way helps us resolve this problem. Nor, moreover, does the fact that the

Black Hundreds' 'emblems and banners are kept in churches, so it's clear to everybody that the Holy Orthodox Church fully approves of and blesses the lofty patriotic sacred cause of the Union of the Russian People and takes its activity under its own protection'. I am quoting this from Walter Laqueur's *Russia and Germany* (p. 85), which Dunlop, judging by his book, has also read. Nevertheless, this did not prevent him from including all Russian Orthodox adherents of the Russian Idea in the camp of the *vozrozhdentsy*, whose future 'rule' he portrays as a victory of good over evil.

7   Ibid., pp. 261—2.
8   Michael Scammel, *Solzhenitsyn: A Biography*, W. W. Norton, 1984.

6
The Western Debate and the Russian New Right

The time has come to turn to the Western debate on Russia and see what our study of the degeneration of the Russian Idea has to add. Does the historical approach toward Russia that lies at the foundation of this study strengthen or undermine the main arguments, of, for instance, liberal sovietology in the debate? Does the historical drama of the Russian Idea interrelate with the main arguments of conservatively oriented sovietology? At first glance, the answer is 'no'. However, first impressions can be deceiving.

First, let us look at the argument that links the scale and intensity of Russian expansionism with Communist ideology. It's true that only a Communist dictatorship managed to realize (at least in part) the expansionist program of the degenerate Russian Idea. It's also true that it succeeded — by means of very brutal counter-reform — in restoring serfdom to Russia and even for a time in making slave labour the foundation of Soviet production relations. Furthermore, in 1951 it made a 'final solution' of the Jewish question the most urgent problem in Russia. But what does all this prove? Is it not evidence that degenerate left-wing Russian extremism turned out to be a tool for implementing the program of degenerate right-wing extremism; that the debilitated form of Russian Marxist ideology proved to be the reverse side of the debilitated Russian Idea?

If this is correct — that any Russian extremist ideology has a tendency to degenerate and, once degenerate, proves to be an ideology of imperial expansionism — then, one might ask, why draw a connection between expansionism and Communist ideology? Where is the sense in supporting one form of Russian extremism against another (which is the de facto policy of the Reagan administration)? We may recall that the program of the pre-revolutionary Russian Idea required the domination of 'Judaized' Europe, in essence a 'New European

Order'. The full realization of this program proved beyond the means of even a Communist dictatorship at the height of counter-reform. We cannot know whether it would also prove to be beyond the capacity of a fascist dictatorship in a similar situation, should, God forbid, Dunlop's scenario come to pass. In any event, no policy could be more absurd than one which helped to bring about a new historical catastrophe in Russia by supporting Fascism against Communism — if only because, as the Russian proverb says, horseradish is no sweeter than radishes (six to one and half a dozen to the other).

The ideological approach toward Russia (extremist anti-Communism) taken by the conservatives in the Western debate deprives us of the opportunity to view the present political situation in its historical context, to adopt a perspective that relates the past to the future. It lives only in one dimension — the present. But to neglect the past means not to think about the future. As we shall see, the liberal geopolitical approach toward Russia suffers from the same shortcoming.

In order to show this, I shall examine here two main arguments of each of the two schools which dominate America's Soviet debate. In addition, I shall try to show that only an historical approach teaches us not to place our trust in any Russian extremist utopias, however much goodness and prosperity they may promise Russia and the world. Most important, however, is that only an historical approach can uncover the fundamental patterns in Russian political behaviour — and so help Western leaders not to stumble about in the dark, or, at the very least, save them from such errors as occurred in the Radio Liberty scandal.

An historical approach opposes in principle the conventional wisdom shared by all sides in America's Soviet debate, which holds that 'the secretive nature of Soviet society makes it something of a "black box" to us,'[1] and because of this the 'Soviet Union will remain both an enigma and an inescapable fact.'[2] Although such a defeatist and self-deprecating position indeed logically follows from both of the conventional approaches, in fact we have no need to blame the Russian political system or 'the secretive nature of Soviet society' for this. We ourselves have restricted our vision of Russia to only the two or three generations since 1917. We ourselves have refused the broader perspective that is opened up by analysis of the political behaviour of at least twenty generations of Russians (we shall discuss this in greater detail later). From the standpoint of an historical approach, we are the ones who have transformed Russia into a 'black box'.

The conservatives' flawed argument

The first, and main, argument of conservative sovietology I would formulate thus: successful resistance to Communist totalitarianism can be achieved only by a policy of actively undermining Communist regimes, and ultimately by overthrowing Russia's Communist regime. In the pre-nuclear age such a policy, if consistently conducted by an American administration, would have led to a new world war. Had the West won such a war, it could then have occupied the Soviet Union, broken apart its empire and forced upon occupied Russia a more or less liberal constitution. That would be the 'Japanese model' for forcibly transforming military autocracy. To put it another way, in the pre-nuclear age such a policy would have made some sense, if, of course, the West were willing to take the risk and pay the price of a new world war in order to break the centuries-long patterns of the Russian political system's behaviour. But what sense does such a policy make in the nuclear era? Now that a new world war and occupation of Russia are unthinkable, the possibility of breaking these patterns by imposing a new regime does not exist, and, even if Communist power were overthrown internally, Russia would continue to function according to the same old pattern.

Have the conservative ideologues ever pondered this perspective? How do they picture Russia's future in the event of the policy they propose being successful? We simply do not know, because they have never provided any answers. The most cursory glance at Russian history, however, should be enough to convince us that Russia responds to a situation of supreme danger created by a hostile international environment by turning itself into a garrison-state dictatorship. In other words, the only conceivable result of the policy proposed by the conservatives, if it were successful, would be Dunlop's scenario, a terroristic counter-reform leading to Russia's transformation into a Fascist nuclear superpower. Is this the result the conservatives are aiming for?

In this, more than anything else, they paradoxically resemble early twentieth-century Russian left-wing extremists and in particular the Bolsheviks. They too were blinded by their hatred for tsarism, seeing it as the ultimate evil, and thought that the liberation of Russia from tsarism would bring prosperity to their country and to the world. If we recall the ominous imperial fantasies of the Russian Idea, at the height of its expansionist ambitions and those of the Black Hundreds, there was probably more substance in this extremist anti-tsarism than today we are ready to admit. Its great mistake, however, was the same as that of contemporary conservatives: it planned to quench the inferno with more fire, to replace one form of extremism with another. We know what came of this.

Two extremes

The degeneration of extremist ideologies and the fact that, once degenerate, they are transformed into their opposites, represents one of the fundamental patterns of political change in Russia. For the reader who was not convinced of this by my outline of the degeneration of the Russian Idea, I shall try to show briefly how the same thing happened to its antithesis, Russian Marxism.

Consider the enormous gulf that separated Sergei Sharapov's Russophile utopia from Vladimir Lenin's original vision when he first took charge of the Russian empire. Sharapov's utopia foresaw an empire that had trampled dozens of nations underfoot who were obliged to Russia for having saved them from the threat of 'Jewish slavery' and 'a Universal Despot from the House of David'. Lenin's catechism, on the other hand, proclaimed the end of empire:

1. The equality and sovereignty of the peoples of Russia.
2. The right of the peoples of Russia to national self-determination up to and including secession and the formation of independent states.
3. The abolition of all privileges and restrictions based on nationality and national-religious affiliation.[3]

Sharapov's utopia, anticipating Hitler, saw the world's liberation in the final solution of the Jewish question. Lenin's catechism opposed to this the liberation of the proletariat from alienated forced labour. For Lenin, the resolution of the nationalities' question was merely part and parcel of eliminating man's exploitation of man. In this sense, the Jewish question as such did not exist for him. In any event, it was not supposed to exist any more by 1951. By that time all nations were supposed to have joined together into one noble humane family. Such was the promise of Communism. Also by 1951, according to Lenin, Communism (with a capital C) was supposed to have triumphed in Russia as the final and perfect phase of human history. 'The generation whose members are now around fifty', said Lenin in October 1921, 'cannot count on seeing a Communist society. This generation will die off before that time. But the generation which is now fifteen years' old, it shall see a Communist society'.[4]

The generation to whom Lenin promised that they would see the completion of history, the generation born about 1905, was in power in Russia in 1951. Brezhnev, Kosygin, Suslov and Kirilenko were all born around 1905. And what was it they saw? They saw the re-establishment of the Russian empire, once again, as before the revolution, tightly buttoned into military and paramilitary uniforms with shining epaulettes, medals and marshals' stars. They saw a patriarchate of the Orthodox church, reinstated along with serfdom, something not even the last tsars had managed to do. They saw the Jewish question on the eve of a 'final solution', and a soldier-emperor leading his nation to world hegemony.

The Leninist utopia, so decisively and (it seemed) for all time having done away with Sharapov's vision, yielded to it totally just three decades later. The generation that was fifteen years' old at the time of Lenin's solemn promise saw, not a miraculous and unprecedented historical leap 'from the kingdom of necessity to the kingdom of freedom', but the apotheosis of imperial slavery foretold by the prophets of the Russian Idea. The original catechism of Russian Marxism truly did degenerate and become transformed into its very opposite. In this sense, its fate was very much the same as that of the Russian Idea's original catechism.

An historical hypothesis

This brings us to yet another conservative argument, used mainly by the Russian New Right and on occasion by their Western academic 'fellow travellers'. It runs as follows: Russia would have avoided all those misfortunes and not been transformed into an 'evil empire' (would not have suffered a counter-reform, in my terminology) if that 'black whirlwind' of Western ideology had not caught her unawares in 1917; if this malevolent whirlwind, at first in the form of the pack of irresponsible liberals who toppled the tsar, and then as a gang of Bolshevik conspirators funded by German money and leaning for support on Latvian bayonets, had not treacherously seized power in Russia.

However, the centuries-old patterns of political change in Russia testify to the contrary. The terroristic counter-reform was brought about by the collapse of reform and not by the intrigues of any 'whirlwind', black or otherwise. It would have occurred even if there had been no German money, Latvian bayonets or Bolshevik conspirators, even if the contemporary prophet of the Russian Idea, Purishkevich, had ended up in power instead of Lenin. His government would have still needed terror in order to halt the disintegration of the empire, curb the spontaneous seizures of landlord estates by peasants and factories by workers and deal with the anarchy and demoralization that gripped the country after three long years of slaughter. They would still have needed an ideology to justify this terror and the restoration of the empire, and to justify making war on the peasantry, the working class, and any national minorities who tried to secede from the empire. They had no other ideology suited to this role at their disposal, apart from the 'tooth-gnashing obscurantism' of the degenerate Russian Idea. No other means besides terroristic counter-reform would have saved the empire. It suffices to recall the most famous prediction of Konstantin Leont'ev:

> My feelings tell me that someday a Slavic Orthodox tsar shall take the socialist movement in hand and, with the blessing of the Church, set up a socialist form of life in place of the bourgeois-liberal one. And this Socialism will be a new and severe threefold form of *slavery*: to the communes, to the Church and to the Tsar.[5]

Vasilii Rozanov insightfully remarked on this point, 'One who knows and senses Leont'ev, has to agree that, given free reign and the power (with which Nietzsche wouldn't have done anything), he would plunge Europe by fire and bloodshed into a monstrous political turn of events.'[6] So much for the fellow-travellers' assurances that the Russian Idea could not give birth to a Stalin.

The laissez-faire argument

At first glance, the liberal arguments look much more rational and, if I may say, secular. The liberals do not keep talking about crusades and they don't bring the religious and ideological dimensions of superpower confrontation to centre stage. Their geopolitical metaphors cast Russia as a new superpower which, like imperial Germany on the eve of World War I, is challenging the old world order (or, like a new Austria—Hungary, is trying to save itself from disintegration by means of imperial expansion). This form of the Western debate lacks the flavour of the medieval dispute of the conservatives' argument. Indeed, liberal sovietology recognizes the problem of political change as 'absolutely fundamental for our conception of the Soviet Union.'[7] Moreover, it believes that 'it is precisely here where our stereotypes are the most strikingly outmoded.'[8]

All this notwithstanding, if one listens closely to their discussion, it is difficult not to feel that such arguments belong more appropriately in the mouths of Enlightenment philosophers or the fathers of the American constitution. Certainly, after the heated medieval atmosphere of conservative disputes, it's pleasant to find oneself in the cool climate of detached rational doctrines of, say, the Encyclopedists of the eighteenth century, with their unshakeable faith in the panaceas of enlightenment and progress. However, it is hard to imagine such doctrines leading to a concrete set of policies appropriate to the nuclear age.

Their basic argument can probably be summed up thus: if we do not embark upon an active crusade, as advocated by the conservatives, but instead leave the Soviet Union in peace, limiting ourselves to the containment of its expansionist tendencies and of the arms race, then Russia will somehow, all by herself, not only overcome her historical decline, but also gradually liberalize her regime, thereby resolving for us the fatally dangerous problem of confrontation with a totalitarian superpower. In contrast to the feverish anti-Communist activism of conservatives, this postulate requires from the West simply caution, exactness and tact (plus, of course, the wish to stop the insane nuclear arms race by means of control agreements). Progress and enlightenment will take care of the rest, either with the help of generational change within the Soviet leadership or because the imperative of modernizing the economy will sooner or later force the leadership to move toward political liberalization.

Timothy Colton epitomizes this abstract belief in progress with the following statement: 'The ultimate Western resource for influencing the Soviet society is . . . the slow-acting magnet of Western culture.'[9] He understands that 'altered attitudes and values take generations.'[10] Yet we simply can do nothing more to move Russia 'in the direction congenial to Western interests.'[11]

Such is the thrust of all liberal arguments. Let us examine them one by one, beginning with 'the slow-acting magnet of Western culture.'

Didn't this magnet exist throughout all the five centuries of Russia's imperial history? It did. Why then did it fail, over the course of twenty generations, to move Russia in the direction congenial to Western interests? What grounds do we have to expect it to accomplish in future generations what it failed to do in all the preceding ones? Even more to the point, does humanity have at its disposal these future generations in the nuclear age? Let us turn to Colton's own prediction that in the event a new reform in the 1980s fails, Russia would face an unprecedented crisis as early as the next decade: 'If conservatives or reactionaries gain the upper hand in the 1980s, or if bungled reforms come to naught . . . the likelihood would then be high that the 1990s would bring a crisis of legitimacy and far more searching dilemmas for the regime, with its core structures and values open to question and under attack as never before'?[12]

It appears that the 'slow-working magnet' would be too slow to prevent such lamentable developments. So what does liberal sovietology recommend in this case, besides a remedy which surely wouldn't be ready in time, if ever? What would happen to Russia, and to the world, if its leadership finds itself 'under attack as never before'? There are no answers to these crucial questions in Colton's book. It is here where the quick generational change comes to the rescue of the 'slow-working magnet.'

> The engine of change is the emergence of new generations, with new expectations and experiences, . . . The younger elites are well educated and competent. Not liberals in a Western sense, their thinking is nevertheless far more sophisticated than that of high-level party members, which has been characterized by parochial fundamentalism. They are free of the formative influences of the Revolution and the Stalinist terror and are relatively knowledgeable about the outside world and prepared to learn from it.[13]

This implies that, as a result of the gradual transition of the Soviet elite, and consequently the government, from socialist fundamentalism to, let us say, socialist enlightenment, political change in Russia will progress in a positive, liberal direction.

The problem with this argument is that, unfortunately, it does not adequately describe political change even in the Soviet period of Russian history (insignificant though this may be on the chronological scale). The present-day Soviet government is indeed younger and more educated than its immediate predecessor. It is *not*, however, younger or more educated than the first Soviet government, its predecessor's predecessor. Lenin did not live to reach the same age at which the 'youngster' Gorbachev became general secretary, and Lenin was significantly older than his colleagues. In reality, the first Soviet government probably was the youngest and most educated one in Russian history. This circumstance in no way prevented it, however, from *presiding over a regime of counter-reform*.

Subsequent Soviet governments were increasingly older and less educated, until, at last, they lapsed into the aforementioned parochial fundamentalism, which nevertheless did not prevent some of them from presiding over a relatively liberal regime in the 1920s and others over a regime of terroristic counter-reform in the 1930s and '40s. Once again, irrespective of age and level of education, the post-Stalinist governments presided over a regime first of reform in the 1950s and early '60s and then of political stagnation in the 1970s. Nikita Khrushchev was significantly older than Leonid Brezhnev, something which did not hinder him from being a bold and colourful reformer, whereas Brezhnev and his generation, the very same one to whom Lenin had promised the Communist dream fulfilled, landed the country in a quagmire of stagnation.

In other words, facts show that the rhythm of political change in Russia has *never* corresponded to generational changes or changes in the age and level of education of the political elite — even in the Soviet period. All the more so, the theory of generational change proves a completely unreliable guide to the labyrinths of the Russian political system once we reject the postulate of Soviet Russia as a 'black box' and move beyond the boundaries of the Soviet sub-system of Russian autocracy. Here it turns out that our study of the degeneration of the Russian Idea (as well as Russian Marxism) has a very direct relation to America's Soviet debate. History, in essence, strips us of the optimistic hope that everything in Russia will take care of itself with the mechanical change of generations, that biology will serve as a substitute for sound policy, which is what the liberal thesis ultimately comes down to. One generation of Russian political ideologists after another has passed before us and each was less and less liberal and more and more bellicose and expansionist than the one before. If Konstantin Aksakov were to be called a fundamentalist of the Russian Idea, who would argue that Danilevskii was more liberal than him, not to speak of Leont'ev or Sharapov?

There is no doubt that the generation which replaced the one to whose lot it fell to live under the quarter-century terroristic dictatorship of Ivan the Terrible came to power with 'new expectations and experiences' and was 'more educated and competent' than its predecessors. It too truly did make an effort to reform the Russian political system, just as Khrushchev's generation tried to. Yet it was defeated, and the generation which succeeded it, still more educated and competent one must assume, none the less landed the country in a political quagmire, as did Brezhnev's generation. The same scenario was almost totally re-enacted after the generation that lived under the dictatorship of Peter the Great,[14] and after Paul I and Nicholas I. This pattern has continued to operate right up until the end of Stalin's dictatorship — and beyond.

Hence, we would seem to be dealing with a model of political change in Russia that includes two further patterns. According to one of them, generational change does not influence the archetype of this change. According to the second, the political history of Russia over the last eighteen to twenty generations has in effect been a story of *failed and reversed reforms*. Each of these either gave way to political stagnation or provoked a terroristic counter-reform. Even if everything else did in fact radically alter in Russia with the change of generations, the *patterns of political change* did not — either before or after the Revolution. That is the answer to the first argument of liberal sovietology.

An ahistorical approach

We recall that, according to the second liberal argument, Russia must gradually liberalize because of the imperative of economic modernization and the growing complexity of administering its economic system. The most optimistic representative of liberal sovietology, Jerry Hough, devoted a significant portion of his textbook, *How the Soviet Union is Governed*, written during the Brezhnev era to offering evidence that Russia was taking serious steps in the direction of liberalization.[15] Unfortunately, the most cursory glance at Russian economic history is enough to convince us that such optimism is groundless. Over the course of the 400 years that separate Ivan the Terrible's terror from Josef Stalin's, the complexity of administering Russia's economic system increased without interruption — yet did *not* lead to political modernization. Among the nations of Europe, Russia alone underwent *three* consecutive and tortuous attempts at industrialization and economic modernization — under Peter I, Alexander III and Stalin. According to the classic textbook on European economic history, Russia after the first of its modernizations, was economically the most advanced country in eighteenth-century Europe.[16] This, however, did not preclude the counter-reforms of Paul I or Nicholas I from again steering her into an era of historical and economic decline.

Hough would have had far greater grounds for optimism had he been a contemporary of Sharapov in 1901, after Russia's second economic modernization (although Sharapov, of course, himself drew very different conclusions.) Even so, the second birth of heavy industry in Russia in the 1880s and '90s did not by any means bring liberalization, but rather two cruel counter-reforms which landed the country in a new era of historical and economic decline. Thus, it would seem that the *inability* of economic modernization to influence the archetype of political change in Russia is another of the fundamental patterns of her political behaviour.

Our analysis of the arguments of liberal sovietology therefore leads us to the same conclusion as our analysis of the conservatives' theses in America's Soviet debate: that the argument lacks an historical dimension. To put it more precisely, the novelty of the Soviet political phenomenon causes it to lose sight of all earlier Russian history as a source of information for judging Russia's present-day· political potentialities. Liberal sovietology has deprived itself of the opportunity to register the long-established patterns of Russia's past political behaviour and cannot therefore offer a prognosis for her behaviour in the future. This is how the metaphor of the 'black box' would seem to have arisen.

A new crisis

For these reasons, participants in the Western debate are helpless when it comes to explaining the phenomenon of the Russian Idea's rebirth in the 1960s. While conservatives are inclined to view it as an alternative to Communism, liberals tend to neglect it as irrelevant to Russia's political future. For conservatives, it offers a solution to the fateful question: what would happen to Russia (and the world) if their policies were successful and the Soviet government fell? Liberals, on the other hand, cannot take the Russian Idea seriously because its very existence contradicts their postulate about the inevitability of Russia's gradual liberalization.

Suppose at the turn of the century America's Russian debate had been where it is now, would either conservatives or liberals of the time have believed that Russian tsarism's calamity would turn out to be Russian Marxism's triumph? For the same reasons they cannot believe in Dunlop's scenario today, with its threat of transforming Russian Marxism's catastrophe into Russian fascism's triumph. Neither the ideological approach of conservatives nor the liberals' geopolitical one can foresee and explain such a turn of events. It could, perhaps, be explained by conceiving of the Russian political dynamic, over the whole length of Russia's imperial existence, as a series of historical disasters. I call them counter-reforms; others may refer to them differently. But no matter what we call them, Dunlop's scenario would be quite at home within such a concept (just as the metamorphosis of Russian tsarism into a Marxist state would be). And this is by no means the only problem that cannot be solved by either of the two approaches that dominate the Western debate on how to deal with Russia. They cannot, for example, explain the reason for the — at first glance totally unexpected — renaissance of the Russian Idea in the Communist USSR. Only a concept of periodic imperial decline (as clearly seen on Figure 1), which no economic modernization or generational change can avert and which renders Russia particularly susceptible to counter-reform, is capable of explaining this rebirth, *as a symptom of new decline*.

Why has Russia proved to be the sole country in Europe where, over the course of centuries, not one reformist attempt (and among these were some truly great reforms) has led to political modernization? Why have all Russian reforms, without exception, been sooner or later reversed? Why was Russia the sole continental empire in Europe to remain intact after World War I, when all the others fell apart? Why, after World War II, when all the colonial empires in the world disintegrated, did Russia again prove to be the sole exception? How do the ideological or geopolitical approaches respond to these questions? They do not. These questions, central to an understanding of the Russian political system, it would seem, do not figure in the Western debate at all. Only Russian political history that poses these questions can answer them — if properly asked. Its answer puts the Russian challenge of the twentieth century into a grim and frightful relief.

Autocracy locked Russia into a kind of a historical trap from which she, as her entire past testifies irrefutably, *cannot* extricate herself on her own — without the intellectual and political support of the world community. Each of the three major sectors of her political establishment — the reformist, the conservative and the extremist (revolutionary—reactionary) — seems to be strong enough to neutralize the others. It was, one must assume, because of this that a Russia of reform, the only one capable in principle of unlocking the trap, has been unable to fulfil her historical mission to modernize the nation. Every time a reform was about to do this it was swept away either by forces of conservatism or by those of extremism. There is no other source for it to get the additional intellectual and political weight needed for a decisive breakthrough, except the international community.

Unfortunately, these lessons of Russian history have not yet found a place in America's Soviet debate. This is why neither the medieval passions of the conservatives nor the passive academic optimism of the liberals offers any kind of practical solution to the terrible problem of superpower nuclear confrontation. Negotiations have been tried as has refusal to negotiate. At times there have been agreements on arms control and at others there have been none. Detente has been tried as well as cold war. In essence, all the conservatives' recommendations have been tried over the past four postwar decades, as have all those of the liberals. Nothing has worked. The arms race and potential for confrontation have grown and put down deep institutional roots. Now the whole cycle is starting from its beginning again: the liberals prefer new arms control agreements if not a new detente; the conservatives counter with an intensification of the arms race under the guise of strategic defence. The Western debate grows more and more reminiscent of a broken record where the needle keeps skipping over the same section of music again and again. What, however, is the sense in repeating the same ineffectual strategies — on an ever growing level of technological complexity — thus prolonging the confrontation into infinity? Isn't it time to learn from our own experience, even if only the elementary lesson that, in order to resolve this confrontation, what is needed is quite simply another kind of approach toward Russia and another set of strategies altogether?

I am speaking about a set of strategies which would combine the activism of conservatives, though without its aggressiveness and militarism, with the optimism of liberals, yet without its passivity and detached scholasticism, one aimed at preventing a new systemic crisis in Russia at the end of the twentieth century. These strategies will be discussed in detail in my concluding chapter. Suffice it to say here that not to react to the Russian Idea's resurrection is a dangerous course. This rebirth marks, just as it did in the past century, the approach of the same systemic crisis for Russia in which, as we know from experience, 'there is no middle ground'. Whatever extremist ideology should win out in Moscow as the result of such a crisis and no matter which avenue of escape the empire takes, things would end, as they did in 1917 and always have in such instances in Russia, with a new counter-reform — this time, one capable of transforming the country into a fascist nuclear superpower.

In 1903, the world did not take notice of the formation of the Bolshevik Party in Russia. Afterwards, in hindsight, volume upon volume was written about it. Only later did it become evident that this had been a key event for all subsequent world politics in this century. Unquestionably, the liberals and conservatives in the contemporary

Western debate do not see the formation of the Russian New Right as a key event of our time. Are they repeating the same error their predecessors made in 1903?

Notes

1   Joseph S. Nye Jr., ed., *The Making of America's Soviet Policy*, Yale University Press, 1984, p. 4.
2   Ibid., p. vii.
3   *Dokumenty sovetskoi vneshnei politiki*, v. I, Moscow: 1957, p. 15.
4   V. I. Lenin, *Polnoe sobranie sochinenii*, 4th edition, v. 31, p. 274.
5   Leont'ev, *Sochineniia*, v. 6, p. 98.
6   *Russkii vestnik*, 1903, No. 4, p. 642.
7   Marshall Shulman, 'What the Russians Really Want', *Harper's*, April 1984, p. 69.
8   Ibid.
9   Timothy Colton, *The Dilemma of Reform in the Soviet Union*, Council on Foreign Relations, 1984, p. 99.
10 Ibid.
11 Ibid.
12 Ibid., p. 79.
13 Ibid. Testifying to the almost universal acceptance of this thesis by American liberals, S. Frederick Starr repeated it, quite independently but almost verbatim, a few years later: 'Soviet society is evolving in reformist directions through a momentum on its own. The old Stalinists are dying out, and their replacements are better educated and less insecure and dogmatic. The information revolution is proceeding slowly but making headway against the entrenched secretiveness of official life in Russia'. (*The Washington Post National Weekly Edition*, 30 June, 1986, p. 31.
14 See, for example, Alexander Yanov, 'The Drama of the Time of Troubles', *Canadian-American Slavic Studies*, vol. 12, No. 1, Spring 1978.
15 Jerry F. Hough and Merle Fainsod, *How the Soviet Union is Governed*, Harvard University Press, 1979.
16 Witt Bowden, Michael Karpovich, Abbot Payson Usher, *An Economic History of Europe since 1750*, American Book Co., 1937, p. 301.

7
My Hypothesis

As in the last century, contemporary imperial nationalism in Russia is composed of various different elements. Now as then, it has representatives in the official Russian establishment as well as among the dissidents who are irreconcilably opposed to that establishment. In the last century, dissident nationalism considered — and still considers today — establishment nationalism (in this case 'Russian/Soviet patriotism') an official lie. This none the less did not prevent Russian nationalism from itself becoming the regime's official ideology in the era of Alexander III's counter-reform. In other words, the interaction of the various components of imperial nationalism in Russia is governed by a dynamic all its own. Its evolution has a structure. Given this, can we formulate an hypothesis to include this dynamic and structure in a concise and schematic way? Can a single formula be found that would both explain the evolution of imperial nationalism and at the same time generalize the process of the degeneration of the Russian Idea in the last century to take in the analogous process that seems to unfold before our eyes today? Such a formula should not substitute analysis for a comforting but naive division of its elements into 'good nationalists' and 'bad nationalists', as Dunlop does. I shall now try to offer such a formula based on the following hypothesis:

I The Russian Idea arises as a meta-ideology, i.e., as a pair of sub-ideologies, one 'upstairs' and one 'downstairs' (let's call them the Establishment and the Dissident Right).

II These two begin in confrontation with each other: at the first stage, the ideological sisters do not recognize their kinship. The Establishment Right identifies itself with the establishment of the system, regarding its dissident sister not only as a competitor but also as a subversive ideology, and oppresses and silences its proponents. The Dissident Right, for its part, identifies with the anti-establishment dissident movement, accusing its establishment sister of profaning Russia's national feelings and of exploting patriotism for its own ends. But inasmuch as both of them have a common enemy — the West and its agents in Russia, the Westernizers — and see the intensification of 'Russianness' as the only solution to the same historical challenge (the decline of the empire), deep down they sense their kinship, and this leads them — via a series of painful ideological and political metamorphoses — to a state of mutual accommodation. (Elements incapable of adapting are simply weeded out or become insignificant marginal sects, as, for example, happened to Slavophiles of the 'immobile Aksakov cast' (or 'good nationalists', in Dunlop's language) who at the turn of the century were headed by Yu. Samarin, D. Shipov and V. L'vov).

III The driving motives of this adaptation differ for each of the two sub-ideologies according to different historical conditions. For the contemporary Establishment Right, the following are essential:

(a) The intensification of political struggle within the establishment as the system degenerates.

(b) Opposition to reform, which they see as undermining their privileges and as a threat to the empire, and a simultaneous unwillingness to reconcile themselves to the state of political stagnation that is leading the country into decline. Under these conditions, counter-reform may seem the least harmful, if not the only, means to enable the empire to halt its decline and begin a new spiral of historical ascendancy.

(c) Counter-reform demands a radical ideological shift to restore to the empire its former dynamic character, to gain the active co-operation and sympathy of the masses and parts of the intelligentsia, to justify an intensification of production, and of family and cultural discipline, and to resurrect the militaristic expansionist dynamic.

(d) Orthodox Marxism is on its last legs and is no longer capable of such a radical shift, and in no condition to justify the reinstitution of the ideological atmosphere of War Communism. It is also losing its international potency, as foreign Marxists are turning their backs on the Soviet model. It can no longer secure the expansion of Russia's power.

(e) A powerful and sophsiticated ideological strategy is demanded by counter-reform. Where is the Establishment Right to obtain this? As strong as it is in bureaucratic politics, it is helpless in the field of intellectual endeavour. In fact, its only resource is to be found in its oppressed and exiled dissident sister. In this sense, it is truly 'vulnerable to the arguments of the intellectually more sophisticated' dissident nationalists. However, it is selectively 'vulnerable', i.e., vulnerable only to those arguments which assist its own political strategy.

For the contemporary Dissident Right, completely different motives are essential:

(a)   The intensification of ideological struggle within the dissident movement and inability to cope on its own with its main opponent in the dissident camp (Westernism). Its intellectual defeat in this struggle can be converted into victory only with the help of the state (like the Orthodox church, unable to cope with heresy by the spiritual sword, for centuries resorted to calling for help on the state's physical sword, and so became dependent on it.) The contemporary Dissident Right feels increasingly out of place in the ranks of the dissident movement, which rebuts its demands for leadership and thus deprives it of a base of support among the incorrigibly 'westernized' dissident intelligentsia.

(b)   The lack of real means to influence the masses ideologically (means of mass communication, mass institutions and so on, which are controlled by its establishment sister).

(c)   A hatred for the 'rotten' West, i.e., for the values and morals of Western culture, which represent the tangible embodiment of decadence and historical degradation. This hatred the Dissident Right fully shares with its establishment sister.

(d)   A readiness to sacrifice (for the sake of 'Russia's salvation') political and intellectual freedom which is programmed into its political catechism. This helps the Dissident Right to overcome the emotional barrier of organic incompatibility with native autocracy common to all dissidents.

IV Finally, if for all these reasons the Dissident Right really manages to develop in the direction of mutual accommodation and adaptation and, eventually merges with its establishment sister, as happened in the last century, such an ideological evolution can be described in more or less strict terms.

For simplicity's sake, let's assume that the Russian Idea evolves through three main phases: from a liberal nationalism that confronts the regime (L-Nationalism), to an isolationist nationalism that strives for co-operation with the nationalist faction within the establishment

(I-Nationalism), and thence to a militaristic-imperial, Black Hundreds, fascist-style nationalism that blends with the official ideology in the process of counter-reform (F-Nationalism).

That is approximately how my hypothesis looked in 1975, when it was formulated for the first time in a paper 'Halfway to Konstantin Leont'ev: the Paradox of Solzhenitsyn', delivered at the 7th National Convention of the American Association for the Advancement of Slavic Studies (AAASS) in Atlanta, Georgia. It was then based mainly on Solzhenitsyn's letter to the Soviet leaders, on his articles in the collection *From Under the Rubble*, on my personal — and rather sad — experiences of discussions with Russian nationalists, and on the historical model of Slavophilism's degeneration. I understood that to identify Solzhenitsyn with the Russian Right at the moment of his greatest fame as a world tribune and fighter against totalitarianism meant making my hypothesis sound more like a sacrilegious prophecy than a dispassionate scholarly analysis. Since that time, however, I have collected enough documents to verify my hypothesis, which has been gradually fleshed out with facts and itself become a fact of life. As the reader will see, the momentum in the Dissident Right has indeed developed according to script, that is, from L-Nationalism to I-Nationalism. This process, however, is still incomplete. The evolution of the Russian Idea continues. Some of the contours of F-Nationalism, which, if one is to believe Dunlop, may be destined one day to become the new official ideology of the Russian empire, are already discernable. Yet it still does not exist as a complete doctrine like the one developed by the third pre-revolutionary Slavophile generation: 'The path to Constantinople leads through Berlin'; 'Russia as the sole bastion of Christianity in the struggle against the worldwide Free-mason—kike conspiracy', and so on. In this sense, my hypothesis remains an hypothesis.

8

Caught in the Crossfire

The fate of the Russian Idea in the last century has long been my specialty. At the end of the 1960s I defended a dissertation entitled 'The Slavophiles and Konstantin Leont'ev: the Degeneration of Russian Nationalism, 1856−91'. I shall not pretend that I was guided only by scholarly interest, though even from a purely academic standpoint the theme was an explosive one: Leont'ev had been taboo in Soviet historiography since the 1930s and the study of Slavophilism had remained at a standstill for decades. The most notable aspect of my subject, however, was not its academic potential at all; it was in Russian reality itself at the end of the 1960s, when history seemed to come to life before our eyes.

It was as though 'from under the rubble' of moss-covered official ideology, fresh new voices suddenly started to force their way through, proclaiming the need for a 'national rebirth', 'returning to national roots' and 'Russia's salvation'. A new spirit swept through Moscow like a whirlwind. It arose spontaneously from below, like a force of nature, not orchestrated by the authorities, but rather, at times, directly opposed to them. At literary gatherings in people's living rooms, at clubs and universities, nervous old men appeared from nowhere, as if risen out of the ground, calling for a 'return home' to 'the shrines of our national spirit', and sullen youths, solemnly held forth about the 'land' and the 'soil' — as if they were 1830s Slavophiles come back to life. One of the most popular Moscow magazines, *Molodaia gvardia* [*Young Guard*]' joined this chorus with a series of powerful articles. Suddenly the impending extinction of the Russian village (the very thing which had so appalled me when, as a journalist, I had travelled across virtually half of Russia and which led me to write my most bitter series of articles)[1] which was threatening to leave the cradle of the nation (the north-eastern part of Great Russia) horribly desolate, became a fashionable topic of conversation.

Suddenly, the intelligentsia began to spend their vacations in villages close to the graves of their ancestors instead of the popular resorts of the Crimea, Caucasus or Baltic. Young people started to wander around the dying villages collecting icons and very soon there was almost no intellectual's home in Moscow that was not decorated with symbols of Russian Orthodoxy. The writer Vladimir Soloukhin turned up at the House of Writers wearing a signet ring carrying the image of the late emperor Nicholas II. A fervent demand arose on the black market for books written by 'counter-revolutionaries' and 'White Guardsmen' who had died abroad. Solzhenitsyn later summed up the mood of the time: 'It is a thoughtless delusion to consider the Russians the "ruling nation" in the USSR . . . Russians are the main mass of that state's slaves. The Russian people are emaciated and biologically degenerating, their national consciousness is humiliated and suppressed.'[2]

This natural concern for the suffering of one's own people would not have elicited anything but sympathy if strangely familiar and ominous voices had not suddenly broken into the general nationalist chorus. There passed from hand to hand a leaflet — one of the first 'swallows' of samizdat — entitled 'A Code of Morals', which had come out of the depths of the Moscow City Committee of the Komsomol. It was written by a noted Komsomol functionary named Valerii Skurlatov and contained such assertions as 'there is no baser occupation than to be a thinker, an intellectual'. It called for 'orienting our youth toward the mortal struggle' connected with 'the cosmic mission of our people' along with 'introducing corporal punishment for women who give themselves to foreigners, branding and sterilizing them'.[3] At first, this seemed a sinister curiosity. But in the spring of 1968, when the arrest of the nationalist Fetisov group (whose ideas represented 'criticism of the Soviet system from a position of extreme totalitarianism and chauvinism')[4] became known, there were no longer any doubts that the reborn Russian Idea was casting its dark chauvinist shadow. In the words of these dissident nationalists 'mankind's historical development was represented as a struggle between order and chaos, embodied in the form of the Jewish people, who had been creating disorder in Europe for two thousand years, until Germanic and Slavic principles — the totalitarian regimes of Hitler and Stalin — put an end to this.' Furthermore, A. Fetisov and his confederates saw 'these regimes as historically inevitable and positive phenomena'.[5] (It is worth pointing out that these people — just like their role models N. Markov and Yu. Odinzgoev — were Russian Orthodox, i.e., *vozrozhdentsy* in Dunlop's present-day terminology, and therefore 'good nationalists'.)

Anti-Westernism

Thus, already at the end of the 1960s, the regenerated Russian Idea, in its most embryonic form, was clearly demonstrating that it had two roots. One of these was descended from Konstantin Aksakov's liberating anti-despotic utopia, while the other was from Sergei Sharapov's militant imperial fantasy. Despite their differences, however, both these tendencies were to find a common devil. Indeed, the origins of Solzhenitsyn's devil, as events soon showed, in no way differed from those of Fetisov's. Both blamed Western ideology, rather than the Russian empire, for the Russian people's misfortunes. Some blamed the Western ideology of Marxism and the Bolshevik conspirators who managed to conquer Russia with its help. Others blamed Western 'Judaization', which threatened to visit chaos upon the world. Neither, however, noticed the logical flaw in their main argument.

In fact, they had as little reason to blame the West or the Jews for the plight of the Russian peasantry as, say, Turkish nationalists at the turn of the century had to blame the Armenians for the impoverishment of the native population of the Ottoman Empire. After all, wasn't the Turkish peasantry, like the Russian peasantry, 'that state's main mass of slaves'? Certainly, its situation was dire, and it was far worse off than the other peoples of the empire, particularly the enterprising Armenians. Turkish nationalists at the turn of the century had every reason to say, anticipating Solzhenitsyn, that the Turkish people within the Ottoman Empire are 'emaciated and biologically degenerating, their national consciousness is humiliated and suppressed'. But they would hardly be justified in asserting on the basis of this that 'it is a thoughtless delusion to consider the Turks the 'ruling nation' in the Ottoman Empire'.

Herein lies the very insidiousness of the traditional Eastern European continental empires: while the elite of the imperial nation dominates the empire, its peasantry is forced to shoulder the 'burden of empire'. It would be just as absurd to blame Western ideologies for this as it is to blame the Jews or the Armenians: it wasn't they who created either the Ottoman or the Russian empires. These empires were founded by Turks and Russians. The truth is something quite different: the Ottoman Empire disintegrated as a result of World War I, whereas the Russian one managed to prolong its existence after the destruction of tsarism.

This is why I speak of the political system of autocracy as an 'historical trap'. Still it is incomprehensible why the West or the Jews should be blamed for this. Were they the ones who created Russian political tradition? Was it they who founded autocracy? The hollow-ness of the argument for shifting the guilt for Russia's misfortunes on to others makes it scarcely credible. At first glance, it might seem to be a logical error, if not an aberration. But studying it more closely, the observer uncovers a method: the Russian empire and Russian political tradition are thereby relieved of responsibility for what has happened to Russia. With the aid of such a logical sleight of hand it becomes possible to justify the ideological nucleus of the Russian Idea (that which unites the 'good nationalists' like Solzhenitsyn, and the 'bad', like Fetisov): a return of the nation 'home', that is, a return to the age-old isolationist and imperial political tradition represented as the ideal of true Russian civilization.

It is therefore by no means a logical error to blame the West or the Jews for Russia's misfortunes. On the contrary, it is the foundation of the Russian Idea. Without this, Russian nationalism, as any other imperial nationalism, simply could not exist. It cannot be anything but anti-Western and anti-Jewish; it must be sure of Russia's golden age, of her blessed utopian 'home', which was destroyed by certain alien and foreign elements, but to which Russia may return if she casts off the foreign yoke. For these reasons, Russian nationalism is incapable of fighting against Russian autocracy, despite all its rhetoric of liberation. In the final analysis, it must turn into a justification for autocracy and an apology for empire. From the very beginning it was a 'new chain laid on thought', and in the 1960s, that very same 'duality', which the classic critique of the Russian Idea identified, was right in front of us.

Scholarly crossfire

However, even to come close to analysing of these enigmas of Russian nationalism was unthinkable without first clearing away the obstructions presented by the dogmas of the Marxist 'class approach'. Over the course of decades this dogma, presented like Moses' tablets, had transformed the study of Russian nationalism into an intellectual wasteland. According to the dogma, 'The Slavophile movement arose among landlords who wanted to prolong their rule based on old patriarchal foundations, serfdom and all those privileges which the existing order had given them.'[6] This theory seemed indisputable —

so much so that when I started the debate on Slavophilism in May 1969, at first I seemed to my adversaries of the Marxist old guard to be just a whipping boy who had foolishly stuck his head under the implacable axe of Marxist logic. 'Sham enigma' was how the first of my opponents' articles was entitled. Others accused me of defending a 'landlord serf-owner' ideology, implying that I was not a good Soviet citizen (to whom else would it occur to defend such an obvious heresy?).

Victory over this scholarly anachronism was not simple. I shan't dwell on it here, other than to say that when the debate was over only fragments remained of the fossilized dogma that had imagined itself alone capable of interpreting Russian nationalism. Of course, my efforts by themselves were not enough to achieve this. A whole group of experts who had long ago begun to doubt the dogma's scholarly merits picked it apart piece by piece and proved its falsity. What I did not understand then, however, was that by destroying the old dogma I was at the same time calling down on myself the fire of the new. So from that point on I was trapped in a crossfire. The representatives of the new dogma attacked me for just the opposite sin: because, in the process of fighting to destroy the old dogma, I had challenged their newly obtained harmony; because I had resurrected the spirit of the classical critique of Russian nationalism; and because, finally, I had returned to the 'duality formula', from which the degeneration of the Russian Idea logically followed.

I enjoyed the fate of all those whose views do not fit neatly into any of the conflicting canons of the contemporary world. The Marxists accused me of Russophilism and the Russophiles of Marxism. For the 'left' I was 'right' and for the 'right' I was 'left'. This situation of being caught in the crossfire continued right up to the time I left Moscow — never to return.

The heat of the kitchen

Arrived in the United States, however, I did not have to wait long before I was again being called names — up until the publication of *The Russian New Right* in 1978, that is. This was a completely different kind of crossfire. On the one side were the representatives of the emigre faction of the Russian Idea and on the other were their academic fellow-travellers. Ironically, the former, unlike my Soviet critics, accused me of not being a good anti-Soviet citizen, while the latter accused me of, so to speak, academic insufficiency. The polemics of the 1970s, much more crude than the discussions of the 1960s, were none the less, in terms of content, unproductive. Not one of the principal questions of the Russian Idea's degeneration was even touched on. Let me cite a few examples.

Here's how Solzhenitsyn replied to my hypothesis on the structure of Russian nationalism's evolution:

> Think about it: those who collaborated with the National Socialists were condemned, but those who for decades collaborated with the Communists . . . those the West receives as best friends and experts . . . Here's Yanov. He was a Communist journalist for 17 years, unknown to anyone — published in [the magazine] *Molodoi kommunist* and still lesser ones. And here, all of a sudden he is a university professor. He has already published two books analysing the USSR with a most hostile attitude toward everything Russian . . . The message of his books is: prop up Brezhnev with all your strength, support the Communist regime![7]

As the reader sees, Solzhenitsyn responded to my arguments in exactly the same way as the Soviet press responded to his own, only in his case it was called — and justifiedly so — a smear campaign, while in mine it was used as a substitute for ideological discussion. Apparently, those representatives of the Russian Idea had nothing of substance to contribute to the discussion. Thus it was left to the academic fellow-travellers to attack me. Here is an example of how this was done:

> [Sidney] Monas seems to adhere to the view, first articulated by the historian P. N. Miliukov and lately resurrected (without attribution) by Alexander Yanov, that Slavophilism must degenerate, evolving in the direction of the Black Hundreds . . . The Miliukov—Yanov model is obviously inadequate.[8]

Considering that Miliukov, as we know from our study of the critics of the Russian Idea, was one of the last to join the general chorus of the liberal press at the time, and that the very term 'Black Hundreds' only appeared twelve years after Miliukov's lecture (so that he could not possibly have been the author of any model), it is obvious that this particular academic fellow-traveller has, unfortunately, intervened in the argument without having famailiarized himself with the facts beforehand. Even so, he has at least remained within an academic framework. Others did not.

'Yanov is an obliging propagandist of bankrupt socialist circles,' declared another fellow-traveller, 'and, apparently, a lobbyist for the so-called "Dnepropetrovsk group".'[9] A third proposed that Yanov 'is trying to revise the usual Western view of Soviet dissidence [because] he is a Jew'.[10] 'It looks as though', a fourth wrote, 'Yanov is lobbying for some group within the Soviet leadership (apparently the so-called "Dnepropetrovsk group"!) which fears that it will be swept aside after Brezhnev leaves . . . Enough. Enough of Yanov.'[11]

Life, however, continued to take its course. It subjected my hypothesis to the critical test which my opponents had refused it. The degeneration of the Russian Idea becomes more obvious with each passing year. Only now I am wiser than I was fifteen years ago. Now I know in advance that, with the publication of this book discussing the degeneration of the Russian Idea within the context of the Western debate on Russia, I shall, once again for the third time, be caught in a crossfire. Once again my views will not fit neatly into any of the conflicting canons. Conservatives will criticize my book because they still value the Russian Idea as an ally against Communism (and as a substitute for the answers they lack to the fundamental questions in their own political strategy). Liberals will hold it against me because their abstract faith in progress and enlightenment cannot accommodate my hypothesis of the inherently catastrophic nature of the Russian imperial dynamic. Well, as they say in Russia, 'If you're afraid of wolves, don't go into the forest' (or as they say in the West, 'If you can't stand the heat, stay out of the kitchen').

Notes

1   See, for example, 'Trevogi Smolenshchiny' (*Literaturnaia gazeta*, 23 and 26 June 1966); 'Kostromskoi eksperiment' (*Ibid.*, 17 December 1967); 'Kolkhoznoe sobranie' (*Komsomolskaia pravda*, 5 June 1966). All these articles have been reprinted in English (*International Journal of Sociology*, Summer—Fall 1976).
2   'Kommunizm u vsekh na vidy, a ne ponyat', ['Communism is there for all to see, but isn't understood'], *Novoe russkoe slovo*, 17 February 1980.
3   *Politicheskii dnevnik*, No. 18, March 1966.
4   *Khronika tekushchikh sobytii* [Chronicle of Current Events], No. 7, p. 17.
5   Ibid.
6   *Trudy biblioteki imeni V. I. Lenina, Sbornik IV* [Works of the Lenin Library, Collection IV], Moscow: 1939, p. 199.
7   *Posev*, 1979, No. 4, p. 25.
8   *Slavic Review*, Fall 1981, p. 458.
9   *Novyi zhurnal*, No. 139, p. 265.
10   New Oxford Review, Dec. 1979.
11   *Novyi zhurnal*, No. 137, p. 173.

II

In Anticipation of the Year 2000

9
VSKhSON – Beginning of the Dissident Right

The Liberalism of the VSKhSON

The VSKhSON was the first and, to date, only[1] relatively large underground organization in the post-Stalinist period to set itself the goal of overthrowing by force the existing state structure in the USSR.[2] As one would expect of conspiratorial organizations in general, the VSKhSON had its own set of by-laws, its own programme and its own methods of agitation and recruitment. It is not, however, the details of its day-to-day activity that interests us here (in fact, there is already a book in English devoted to the history of the VSKhSON).[3]

As to the organization's programme, it was based, as one might have expected, on irreconcilable hostility toward both traditional 'devils' of the Russian Idea: the 'soul-destroying despotism' of the native government and Western 'parliamentarism.' Yet, although the ideological thrust was the old one, the tactics differed. The VSKhSON proceeded from the assumption that 'the Communist world is disintegrating. The peoples have found from bitter experience that it [Communism] brings poverty and oppression, falsehood and moral decay.'[4] But the VSKhSON programme was not only a propaganda document. It also called for 'a revolution of national liberation, directed toward overthrowing the dictatorship of the Communist oligarchy.'[5]

Inasmuch as the VSKhSON considered Communism a phenomenon that was inherently anti-national and non-Russian, just as the 'Petrine governmental system' was for the Slavophiles, it assumed that the regime 'hangs in the air', without real roots in Russian society. 'The dogmatic grouping of the Communist class', it claimed, 'does not possess a broad social base among the people on which it could draw to organize serious resistance. Its utter defeat is predetermined.'[6] Hence the VSKhSON conceived of the revolution as essentially a military coup: 'For total victory the people need their own underground army of liberation which will overthrow the dictatorship and rout the oligarchy's security forces.'[7]

Moreover, because Communism is presented as the main threat to Christian civilization and the heart of Communism lies in Russia, obviously civilization can only be saved from within Russia. Since 'the fate of the world Communist movement will be decided in Russia',[8] the future of the human race will be determined there as well.

After victory, 'the direct participation of society in the life of the country must be realized by means of local self-government and the representation of peasant communes and national corporations — major unions of blue- and white-collar workers — in the highest legislative organ of the country[9] . . . The state must be constituted as theocratic, social, representative, and popular.'[10]

The theocratic character of the new state will be ensured by the creation of a special 'supervisory' organ — the Supreme Synod, which 'must consist of one-third members of the upper hierarchy of the church and two thirds of prominent representatives of the people, chosen for life.'[11] The Supreme Synod will have 'the right of veto over any law or action which does not correspond to the basic principles of the Social-Christian order.'[12] In addition, as the 'spiritual authority of the people', the Supreme Synod shall elect a Head of State — 'the representative of national unity'.

The theocratic Social-Christian state so constituted must provide 'basic human rights and civil liberties', among which the following are prominent:[13]

. . . Point 53:   The life and dignity of the person are inviolable.
. . . Point 56:   All citizens are equal before the law.
. . . Point 58:   Freedom of labour is provided for everyone by the right of each citizen to land and to credit for the acquisition of means of production.
. . . Point 62:   No form of compulsory labour can be permitted in regard to free citizens.
. . . Point 63:   Personal freedom is inviolable.
. . . Point 64:   All means for the dissemination of thought are free.
. . . Point 67:   There is freedom of assembly and to hold demonstrations.
. . . Point 79:   The secret political police must be disbanded.

It seems that everything Russian political thought had developed over the course of a century and a half, in its attempt to construct a specifically Russian and fundamentally non-European state, was brought together in this remarkable document. Here we find the romantic conviction of Pavel Pestel' that 'freedom of labour' and, more importantly, freedom from unemployment can be provided by giving each citizen the right to land. Here too are to be found: the passionately held tenet of Ivan Aksakov that 'parliamentarism' is a means for professional politicians to usurp power; the postulate of Petr Tkachev that the Russian state has no roots in Russian society and that therefore the people can be liberated by a military *putsch*; Vladimir Solov'ev's notion that the theocratic organization of society is the political embodiment of the Biblical commandments; Nikolai Berdiaev's declaration that both Western capitalism and Soviet Communism represent to the same degree fatal blind alleys in the history of humankind — paths to the triumph of the Antichrist; Fedor Dostoevskii's abiding faith that the world's salvation will come from Russia. Yet just as revealing as what this encyclopedic collection of Russian liberal anti-Europeanism contains, is what it fails to address.

In particular, it does not mention the nationalities' question (which is especially surprising in a political programme for establishing the state structure of a multinational empire). Even worse, there's no mention of the need for a working mechanism capable of ensuring the actual realization of all the civil liberties cited earlier. After all, these basic freedoms are fully specified in the Soviet constitution too. However, without a working mechanism to realize them, in the form of an institutionalized political opposition, historically they have proved to be no more than fictions, empty promises. Where is the guarantee that the same thing will not happen with the promises of the 'new Russian revolutionaries'? In other words, what guarantees their liberalism? I stress that I do not doubt the liberal *intentions* of the authors of the VSKhSON programme — merely whether they were capable of carrying them out. Given that the VSKhSON already has a kind of official interpreter in the West — John Dunlop — it is worth examining his views more closely.

What do the Russian people want?

Briefly, Dunlop believes that the VSKhSON represented the most promising wing of the Soviet dissident movement and carried within it the seed and prototype for a future anti-Communist revolution in the USSR. 'While the VSKhSON,' he writes, 'like the Decembrists, did not constitute a serious military threat to the existing order, the ideas it propagated — and continues to propagate — represent a formidable danger indeed.'[14] For this reason Dunlop is certain that the further development of the dissident movement in the USSR will follow the model of the VSKhSON. He even goes so far as to predict this.[15] As proof he cites 'the great similarity of the VSKhSON's views to those of Solzhenitsyn and his friends'.[16] Furthermore, Dunlop feels enormous personal sympathy for the VSKhSON, which serves him as a basis for yet another prediction. Although 'the VSKhSON's society would be more "authoritarian" than the Western democracies', it would nevertheless 'inevitably represent a marked improvement over the Soviet system', and 'that may very well be what the populace *wants*'.[17]

I haven't the slightest idea how Mr Dunlop arrived at this discovery. My personal observation has been that different people out there want different things. What interests us here is what the authors of the VSKhSON programme wanted. They, judging by the articles of their projected constitution cited earlier, wanted freedom, not authoritarianism. Just like the Bolsheviks, they were sure that a society built according to their plan would be *much freer* than Western democracy, which they, again as the Bolsheviks, considered 'an unconditional evil', and not in the least free. The question then becomes, whether the new Russian revolutionaries were not just as mistaken as the Bolsheviks, and whether their programme would not doom Russia to new authoritarian slavery instead of the freedom they promised. Unfortunately, Mr Dunlop doesn't tell us anything on this crucial question.

The Russian Path

The programme of the VSKhSON is divided into two parts, one critical, the other constructive. The critical part, which takes up the bulk of the document (30 out of 48 pages) is of no interest to our analysis. Mainly it just rephrases Milovan Djilas's *The New Class*. However, the constructive section raises a fundamental question: namely, for the sake of what is the 'Communist oligarchy' in the USSR to be overthrown? The programme makes it clear that this is necessary in order to save humanity from both Communism and capitalism, which it sees as the immediate source of Communism.

> Being a sickly child of materialistic capitalism, Communism has developed and perfected all of the harmful tendencies which were present in bourgeois economics, politics, and ideology . . . The component parts of Marxist-Leninist teaching were borrowed from

Western bourgeois theories . . . Communism brought to its limit the proletarianization of the masses begun by capitalism.[18]

In a word, to paraphrase Lenin's classic remark, Communism is the highest stage of capitalism.

What interests us, though, is not so much this remarkable similarity to Bolshevik dogma as the belief that the primary source of evil in Russia is of Western bourgeois origin. This fundamental feature of the VSKhSON programme entirely conditions its further development. Not only the economic structure of capitalism — its 'base', to use the Marxist terminology — but also its 'superstructure' prove unacceptable to the VSKhSON:

> The Social—Christian doctrine of the state regards as an *unconditional evil* an organization of authority in which power becomes a prize to be competed for between parties or is monopolized by a single party. The party organization of power is in general unacceptable from the point of view of Social-Christianity.[19]

Why is the multi-party system, which, for all its drawbacks, is none the less still the best guarantee of personal freedom known to humanity, an 'unconditional evil'? The reason is obvious: because *all* the products of Western capitalism contain within them the immanent danger of Communism. It is for just this reason that the 'new Russian revolutionaries' feel that their vocation is to lead humankind on to a fundamentally different, Russian, path. The Russian essence of this path derives from the belief that, contrary to the assertions of Western theoreticians, the centre of gravity for all conflicting forces in the world lies not in the realm of the struggle of democracy against authoritarianism, but in that of the struggle of metaphysical forces: God vs. Satan.

> The cause . . . of the dangerous tension in the world lies much deeper than the economic and political spheres . . . a spiritual battle for the individual is going on. Two paths are before mankind: free communion with God . . . or the denial of God, and then Satanocracy.[20]

The Corporate State

The philosophical premises of the VSKhSON programme inevitably had to lead it to the right in the area of socio-political planning as well.

Thus, in proposing to replace 'the party organization of power' with 'representation by corporations', the authors of the programme are, of course, only echoing the central idea of their teacher, Nikolai Berdiaev in his book *The New Middle Ages*. If it was Djilas who inspired the critical portion of their program, it was Berdiaev who inspired its constructive part.[21] It was he who in 1923 contrasted Western parliaments — 'these outgrowths on the body of the people, with their fictive vampire-like lives, no longer capable of fulfilling a single organic function . . . [these] degenerative talk-fests' — with 'representation by real corporations'.[22]

The matter is somewhat complicated by the fact that Berdiaev's fierce contempt for Western parliaments is reminiscent of Mussolini's pronouncements on the subject.

> No one any longer believes in any juridical or political forms; no one gives a damn for any constitutions . . . We, especially Russia, are moving toward a unique type [of state], which could be called 'Soviet monarchy', syndicalist monarchy . . . The regime will be strong, often dictatorial. A elemental grass-roots force shall invest elective individuals with the sacred attributes of power . . . features of Caesarism shall predominate in them.[23]

Even if Berdiaev hadn't directly referred to Mussolini, it would still be obvious who was his inspiration, but he goes on to make this quite clear: 'Fascism is the sole creative phenomenon in the political life of contemporary Europe[24] . . . Only people like Mussolini, perhaps the sole creative statesman in Europe, shall have meaning [in the future].'[25]

Even if the new Russian revolutionaries, did not understand that they were repeating Mussolini's Fascist rhetoric directly (although, as we have seen, references to it are given openly in their textbook), at least they were consciously using Berdiaev's ominous interpretation of it. Dunlop ought, therefore, to have known what a fatal role Berdiaev's most reactionary book played in the formation of the opposition consciousness of the VSKhSON. Indeed, he seems well aware of it. *'The New Middle Ages'*, he writes, 'is a provocative work that has surprisingly never been translated into English . . . It contains Berdiaev's program for Russia's emergence from the Bolshevik yoke . . . A number of Berdiaev's ideas . . . were incorporated into the "constructive section" of the VSKhSON program.'[26]

I must admit that of all Dunlop's commentaries this is the one which is the most bewildering. First, are we to understand from it that not only 'the new Russian revolutionaries', but also Dunlop himself, seriously views Fascism as a programme for Russia's emergence from the 'Bolshevik yoke'? Secondly, could Dunlop have failed to notice that Berdiaev, in his 'provocative' book, flatly contradicts all the liberal promises of civil rights contained in the VSKhSON programme? 'I assert', writes Berdiaev, '[that] the Russian people . . . *do not want a Rechtsstaat* [a state based on the rule of law] in the European sense of this word. [Russia] would sooner give birth to the Antichrist than to humanist democracy.'[27] For better or worse, humankind knows no other sense of the expression 'a state based on rule of law' than the European one. Moreover, if the categorical denial of a state based on rule of law is, in Dunlop's opinion, merely 'authoritarianism', then what is Fascism? Third, and finally, inasmuch as *The New Middle Ages was* translated into English (and reprinted three times!) even if under a different title,[28] it is unclear why Dunlop should deny it. Whatever the reason, the fact remains that 'the new Russian revolutionaries' in their programme preferred the principles of the Fascist corporate state to those of the 'unconditional evil' of Westrn democracy and so revealed their projected revolution in a somewhat unexpected light.

Great Russia

Suppose for a moment that the Russians really can be saved from the threat of 'satanocracy' only by the Orthodox corporate theocracy which the VSKhSON intended to bestow upon them. It should not be forgotten, though, that Russians make up only half the population of the USSR. Among the dozens of other nationalities included in the empire are some which are not Russian Orthodox, or even Christian. No plebiscite has ever been set up to establish whether any of these nations are especially inclined toward Orthodox theocracy. What fate awaits them in a 'society built according to the VSKhSON's plan' (so appealing to Mr Dunlop)? The programme gives no answer to this question at all. It doesn't even go through the formality of promising that the empire's non-Russian nations will have the right not to follow 'the Russian path', if they so choose. Point 73 merely states that the VSKhSON 'acknowledges itself as a patriotic organization of selfless representatives of all the nationalities of Great Russia.'[29]

Where are the boundaries of this 'Great Russia' conceived of by VSKhSON; within those of the present Soviet empire? What if the Muslims, Catholics, Protestants, Jews and Buddhists living within its territory should not wish to recognize Orthodoxy as the ideology of universal salvation, and theocracy as the mandatory form of political organization? According to Point 83: 'countries in which Soviet troops are temporarily stationed can be helped to national self-determination on the basis of Social-Christianity.'[30] But what if these countries should desire self-determination on some other basis? Since the programme doesn't address these questions, we must seek out other sources of information to help shed light on those issues about which the programme is obscure. In particular, we want to know about the attitude of key VSKhSON leaders toward certain national minorities. In the memoirs of B. Karavatskii, a fellow-traveller, there is a revealing passage on the views of the organization's 'head of personnel', Mikhail Sado: 'It is difficult for me to reconcile myself to the fact that anti-Semitic overtones slipped through in this man's conversation. Probably, this deeply rooted flaw in this uncommonly interesting individual was absorbed by him with his mother's milk.'[31]

We find other evidence in the recollections of A. Petrov-Agatov, a highly controversial personage who has spent the greater portion of his life in Soviet camps. There he met members of the VSKhSON whom he — like Karavatskii — considered 'the salt of the Russian nation' and 'the flower of Russian youth', and there he encountered virulent anti-semitism.

> The Jewish question was sharply posed . . . Having become acquainted with the Zionist Solomon Borisovich Dol'nik . . . I suggested to Andrei Donatovich (Siniavsky) that we go visit him. 'Fine with me; Solomon Borisovich is a nice person. But I ask you to bear in mind that the attitude toward Jews here is especially intolerant.' A rumour was even going around camp that Andrei Donatovich was a Jew. Incidentally, it wasn't just Siniavsky who was considered a Jew. Having seen my friendly relations with Dol'nik, people also began to say' 'Kike! What kind of Petrov is he? Some kind of Freierman or Zilberstein. The scum have all taken Russian surnames.' Hatred of Communism was also identified with Jews. 'Lenin, Khrushchev, Brezhnev, and Kosygin — all kikes', could be heard everywhere.[32]

This is a very strange situation indeed, where even hatred of the Soviet regime is based on a profound, instinctive, almost bestial ethnic hatred. Whereas the members of the VSKhSON saw the roots of Communism in 'materialistic capitalism', the mass of prisoners invariably saw them in 'Jewish oppression', in 'the kikes'.

In such a poisoned atmosphere, what would be the logical position of the leaders of a 'patriotic organization' claiming to represent 'all the nationalities of Great Russia'? Obviously, the least they could do would be to distance themselves from street anti-semitism; after all, they did want to become the leaders of 'Great Russia'. Here, in the Gulag, they encountered a kind of microcosm of the society they intended to lead along 'the Russian path'. If, even here, hatred of Communism was so closely intertwined with chauvinism and the pogrom-mentality of the Black Hundreds, think of the potential for an anti-semitic explosion if they tried to install a theocratic Russian Orthodox state. For just this reason their reactions here are especially significant. Judging from the evidence at our disposal, they not only failed to come to the defence of the 'insulted and injured', which would be their Christian duty, and to distance themselves from the persecutors, but even the 'director' of their 'ideological department', Evgenii Vagin, persuaded Petrov-Agatov that 'all Russia's misfortunes come from the Jews.'[33]

An analogous, even more ominous, story was recounted to me by Andrei Siniavsky, who also served his prison term together with members of the VSKhSON and those 'close to them in spirit'. Once he put the following question to one of them: 'What would you do with the Jews if you won?' The answer was easy: 'We would send them to Israel.' 'But what about the ones who didn't want to go?' Again the answer was simple: 'We would exterminate them.' 'What? Along with their children?' gasped Siniavsky. 'Well, after all, Andrei Donatovich, who, when he is exterminating rats, thinks about their babies?'

A Marked Improvement over the Soviet System?

The VSKhSON programme includes among its liberal provisions that: 'The information media . . . must not be a monopoly of the state. Censorship must be abolished.'[34] Further: 'All known religions must enjoy the right to preach and worship unhindered.'[35] Thus, the programme promises cultural and religious freedom of thought. But what about political freedom of thought? What would a VSKhSON government do with people such as Siniavsky or myself or, generally, with the traditionally 'heterodox' and — alas, equally traditionally — 'Westernizing' Russian intelligentsia? It's clear that this problem is no less poignant for the planners of 'Great Russia' than the problem of nationality. Essentially, it is the problem of the intellectual elite's position in the social order, of how new ideas are to be generated and the state's errors corrected. In short, it is the problem of the need for a political opposition, without which, as history has shown, the rational development of society is impossible. The authors of the VSKhSON programme did not yet call this intellectual elite 'educated shop-keepers', 'smatterers' or 'civilized savages', as their successors will. They promised merely 'not to take a hostile attitude toward those close in spirit [to the VSKhSON] but possessing a variety of different programmes. The final choice ought to be made after the overthrow of the Communist dictatorship.'[36]

Since it is more than likely that Siniavsky and I, along with thousands upon thousands, if not millions, of others, would not be judged close in spirit to the VSKhSON, what would the new military government propose to do about it? Would it apologize for causing a disturbance and go home in peace? Would it not, more naturally, place some of those who were 'more distant in spirit' in camps or exile them abroad as other military governments have done in similar circumstances?[37] A discussion broadcast over Radio Liberty, in which Evgenii Vagin explained his credo more precisely, sheds some light on this question, albeit indirectly.

Asked about a certain quotation from Dostoevskii, Vagin replied, 'As to the quotation you have cited, whether a Russian can be an atheist and to what extent the Russian nature is compatible with this, yes, in this sense I share Dostoevskii's belief that to be Russian is to be Orthodox, and that religion is, of course, the profound essence of the Russian person.'[38] But Dostoevskii, unlike Vagin, was not involved in devising plans for Russia's future political order nor did he intend to become one of its leaders, as Vagin did. For this reason we must be interested in the political meaning attached to his definition of 'the profound essence of the Russian person'. For myself — unlike Dunlop — this issue is not merely an academic one, but bears directly upon my fate. What would Vagin's government do with me and those close to me in spirit — not Russian Orthodox (and consequently not 'Russians'), and politically heterodox to boot? Would it not be natural for this government — in the best of circumstances — to send me into permanent exile abroad? But that's where I am already!

I was just paraphrasing a story told to me by Siniavsky. When he replied to his camp inmate ('who was close in spirit' to the VSKhSON) that he would protest against the genocide of those Jews unwilling to leave the VSKhSON's 'Great Russia', his fellow prisoner told him, 'And we would stick you in prison, Andrei Donatovich.' So how woud Dunlop's promise of a 'marked improvement over the Soviet system' benefit Siniavsky either?

The Utopia of L-Nationalism

I hope I have now provided enough evidence to convince the reader that the born-again Russian Idea was at its very inception permeated with anti-Europeanism, medieval dreams of theocracy, and the fascist principles of a corporate state. But if so, how are we to explain all the liberal provisions in the VSKhSON programme: its declarations concerning the abolition of censorship and freedom of religion; how 'judges must be irremovable and answerable only to the law';[39] how 'the cultural policy of Social-Christianity proceeds from the recognition that living culture . . . can blossom only under conditions of freedom'?[40] In short, how can we explain all the things which compelled Dunlop to believe in 'the new Russian revolutionaries'?[41] Is all this simply hypocrisy and political demagoguery? If not, how else are we to interpret this combination, in one and the same ideological concept, of 'freedom' and 'theocracy', of liberalism and anti-Europeanism, and of modern terminology and medieval ideas?

But exactly the same question could have been asked with regard to the political doctrine of the original Slavophiles, which in the same way — 130 years ago — combined a sincere and self-sacrificing struggle against 'soul-destroying despotism' with a no less sincere revulsion for 'Western constitutions' and 'the party organization'. My answer is that the inexplicable can be explained and the irreconcilable reconciled, but only within the framework of a *utopia* — an ideological construct unrealizable in practice. Thus my argument with Dunlop concerns not what Russia would be like if the VSKhSON programme were to be implemented (since it could not be in the form in which it was conceived), but rather what was the real social *function* of this nationalist utopianism in the ideological struggle unfolding in the USSR. The function was obviously a dual one. On the one hand, the VSKhSON programme was conceived in all sincerity as an anti-Communist manifesto, as a passionate appeal for 'Russia's rebirth from under the yoke of Bolshevism'. As an open and unyielding opponent of the Soviet system, its function was to stimulate the oppositionist, dissident movement in the USSR. On the other hand, permeated as it was with anti-Europeanism and medieval political attidudes, the VSKhSON programme inevitably stimulated the Right opposition, which is the main interest of this book.

Five ideological events have conditioned the development of this utopia:

(1) Khrushchev's revelations of the totalitarian nature of the Stalinist regime at the XXth Party Congress.

(2) The defeat of Khrushchev's reforms, leading to the conclusion that national regeneration 'from above' is impossible.

(3) The lessons of the Hungarian uprising of 1956, which seemed to demonstrate that a Communist regime is a form of latent civil war between the government and the people. (From this it followed that Communist governments 'hang in the air' and that a slight revolutionary push is all that is needed to topple them.)

(4) Milovan Djilas's book *The New Class*, which provided a theoretical basis for the practical lessons of the Hungarian uprising.

(5) Khrushchev's liberalization, which created the conditions under which young Soviets could for the first time become familiar with the books of Berdiaev, among these *The New Middle Ages*, which opposed to the Western (democratic) path of struggle against 'soul-destroying despotism' a fundamentally different 'Russian path'.

In fact, as history has shown, no such 'Russian path' exists. But the group of young people who gathered around the banner of the VSKhSON sincerely believed in it. However, this did not make them 'new Russian revolutionaries', as Dunlop would have it, but merely run-of-the-mill Russian utopians.

Summary of the VSKhSON

In conclusion, here is a summary of the ideas which the VSKhSON contributed to the formation of the doctrine of the Russian dissident Right in the twentieth century:

(1) Rejection — along with 'Communist totalitarianism' — of the Western parliamentary model. Belief that a special and primary place belongs to Russia in the sphere of the 'real liberation' of humankind.

(2) The definition of this 'real liberation' as the transfer of freedom from the sphere of political guarantees against the arbitrary use of power, to that of the struggle of absolute good against absolute evil (so linking it not with the tradition of promoting cultural and institutional limitations on power, but rather with that of

the Russian Idea, a tradition of 'free communion with God and the acceptance of His commandments'). Accordingly, the political struggle is described as 'a spiritual struggle for the individual'.

(3)   Abandonment of the idea of revising the imperial structure of 'Great Russia', which is equivalent to an oblique recognition of imperial nationalism.

(4)   Political intolerance, connected to the maximalist character of a doctrine which is tantamount to ruling out political opposition in future Russia.

(5)   Latent anti-semitism, not obvious on the level of the official programme, but established by the evidence of eyewitnesses.

Notes

1   Unless one counts the emigre People's Labour Alliance [Narodno-Trudovoi Soiuz — NTS].

2   In February, 1967, just before it was decimated by the KGB, the All-Russian Social Christian Union for the Liberation of the People [VSKhSON] had 28 members and 30 candidate members.

3   John Dunlop, *The New Russian Revolutionaries*, Nordland Press, 1976.

4   'Vserossiiskii Sotsial'no-Khristianskii Soiuz Osvobozhdeniia Naroda' ['All-Russian Social Christian Union for the Liberation of the People'], Paris: YMCA Press, 1975, p. 33.

5   Ibid., p. 34.

6   Ibid., p. 61.

7   Ibid., p. 34.

8   Ibid., p. 61.

9   Ibid., p. 64.

10   Ibid., p. 74.

11   Ibid., p. 75.

12   Ibid.

13   Ibid., pp. 76—8.

14   Dunlop, op. cit., p. 223.

15   'One feels safe in predicting that in the coming decade we will witness new variants of VSKhSON's "Program" emerging in Soviet Russia', ibid., p. 198. This prediction has been published precisely a decade ago. Nothing of the sort emerged, however, in Soviet Russia.

16   Ibid., p. 198.

17   Ibid., pp. 197—8. Emphasis in original.

18   VSKhSON, pp. 32, 35—6.

19   Ibid., p. 63. Emphasis added.

20   Ibid., pp. 32, 61. It is true the programme contains the assertions that 'the non-Communist world will come out of the crisis by an evolutionary process' (p. 33) but this is in such flagrant contradiction to the remaining content that it appears to be an alien element in the programme. How

can "materialistic capitalism", while it still remains capitalism — i.e., 'refuses God', and does not accept the VSKhSON programme's demand for a 'spiritual struggle for the individual' — provide the world with a 'spiritual rebirth' instead of the satanocracy which logically derives from it?

21   Nikolai Berdiaev, *Novoe srednevekov'e* [*The New Middle Ages*], Berlin: Obelisk, 1924.
22   Ibid., pp. 50—1.
23   Ibid., pp. 27, 53.
24   Ibid., p. 28.
25   Ibid., p. 78.
26   Dunlop, op. cit., p. 62.
27   N. Berdiaev, *Novoe srednevekov'e*, p. 62.
28   N. Berdiaev, *The End of Our Time*, London: Sheed and Ward, Aug. and Nov. 1933, Feb. 1935.
29   VSKhSON, p. 61.
30   Ibid., p. 73.
31   Ibid., p. 208.
32   A. A. Petrov-Agatov, 'Arrestantskie vstrechi' ['Prisoners' Encounters'], *Grani*, No. 83, 1972, p. 65.
33   Ibid., p. 64.
34   VSKhSON, p. 71.
35   Ibid., p. 73.
36   Ibid., p. 61.
37   The 'civil and human rights' promised in the programme are by no means intended to be introduced immediately after the victory of the VSKhSON. Point 74 states that, 'state power, after the overthrow of the Communist dictatorship, shall pass over to a people's revolutionary government which will immediately effect the radical reforms whose time has come'; only then 'shall the normal order of the state come into force' (ibid. p. 77). But what will become of the intelligentsia in this fateful interval — in the period of dictatorship of a 'people's revolutionary government'?
38   Quoted from the transcript of 'A Conversation about Dostoevskii' between Kiril Khenkin and Evgenii Vagin over Radio Liberty.
39   VSKhSON, p. 73.
40   Ibid., pp. 65—6.
41   'While the society brought into existence [by VSKhSON] would undoubtedly displease some Western libertarians . . . [nevertheless] were the Program put into effect, Russia would be able to breathe once again. The individual citizen would be free to select his profession, write and publish what he wants, move freely about the country, and travel abroad. He would be eligible for public office and could even, without hindrance, attend meetings and demonstrations and form unions, associations, and societies. In his family life, he would be free from the long arms of the state . . .' (Dunlop, op. cit., pp. 197—8).

10
'Young Guardism': The Beginning of the Establishment Right

John Dunlop is perhaps correct when he says that 'the debate among contemporary Neo-Slavophiles . . . could be deciding the future shape of Russia's society and government'. He is probably also right when he says, 'VSKhSON has encountered *Veche*. Their meeting may yet bear unexpected fruit.'[1] I only wish to add that one should not omit the fact that the debate surrounding contemporary Slavophilism was by no means confined to the underground samizdat, but extended to the official press — to magazines, journals and newspapers with circulations of many millions. These public debates were at times no less stormy than those in the samizdat, and their influence on thinking young people may have been just as important as that of the VSKhSON or *Veche*. In other words, before the VSKhSON 'encountered' *Veche*, it encountered the phenomenon of Young Guardism. This encounter may also yet bear 'unexpected fruit'. In any case, the historian of the Russian New Right cannot afford to ignore it.

The first — and most significant — essay in *Molodaia gvardia* [Young Guard], marking the start of the Establishment Right in post-Stalinist Russia, occurred at the time of the trial of the members of VSKhSON. This was Mikhail Lobanov's 'Educated Shopkeepers',* published in April 1968. It was followed in September of that year by Viktor Chalmaev's essay 'Inevitability'.

*[Translator's note: The Russian term *meshchanstvo*, translated here as 'shopkeepers' (as in Napoleon's description of England as 'a nation of shopkeepers'), is taken from the name of one of the estates into which the population of tsarist Russia was divided. As now used in the Soviet Union, it connotes a narrow, conventional, money-grubbing mentality — not unlike 'babbitry' in the American context.]

'Educated Shopkeepers'

To say that the appearance of Lobanov's essay in the official press — indeed in such an influential and popular journal as *Molodaia gvardia* — was surprising is an understatement. It came as a great shock. The level of malice, venom and wrath which the Soviet press usually reserves for discussions of 'imperialism' or similar 'external' themes was now directed, so to speak, inwardly. Lobanov had unexpectedly uncovered a rotten core at the very heart of the first socialist state in the world — and at the very height of its triumphant transition to Communism. He had discovered an ulcer certainly no less frightful than imperialism — in fact, much worse. It consisted in 'the "educated" person's spiritual degeneration, in the decay of everything human in him'.[2] What is involved here is not just an isolated psychological phenomenon, but a *social* one on a mass scale — the 'masses (all with advanced degrees) [being] infected with a shopkeeper mentality'.[3] These masses, Lobanov claimed, were being churned out by the 'flood of so-called education', which 'like a bark borer . . . is gnawing away at the healthy trunk of the nation.'[4] They are 'shrilly active in negating', and are thus 'threatening to disintegrate'[5] the very foundations of national culture.

In short, unforeseen by the classical Marxist theoreticians and unnoticed by the ideologists of the regime, there had already developed in socialist Russia an established stratum of 'educated shopkeepers' which now represented the nation's number one enemy. Such was Lobanov's fundamental sociological finding.

He attacked this enemy of the nation with all the passion an official journalist could bring to bear. True culture, he wrote, does not come from education, but from 'national* sources', — from 'the grass-roots of the people'. It is not the educated shopkeepers but the 'suppressed . . . uneducated folk who gave birth to . . . the imperishable values of culture'.[6] As for the shopkeepers, 'They have a mini-language, mini-thoughts, mini-feelings — everything mini. And', he solemnly intones, '[the] Motherland is mini to them [too].'[7]

---

*[Translator's note: the Russian adjective *natsional'nyi* is used to express many more ideas than its English cognate 'national'. It can be used to refer to the people of a nation, nationalism, nationality, or even ethnic identity all at the same time. For example, the issue of the Soviet Union being made up of people of many different nationalities is expressed in Russian as *natsional'nyi vopros* and usually translated as 'the national question' or 'the nationalities question', though ethnicity is clearly an important part of it as well.]

In the best traditions of journalistic toadyism, Lobanov goes on to illustrate his point by denouncing people (both living and dead): the stage director Meyerhold, shot by Stalin, and the contemporary stage director Efros. For some reason all of Lobanov's illustrations — all his 'corrupters of the national spirit' — bear unmistakably Jewish surnames. It is these Jewish elements that 'latch on to the history of a great people',[8] which play the role of kind of enzyme among 'the diplomaed masses infected with a shopkeeper mentality'.

As we try to analyse Lobanov's 'findings', we must not fail to take account of the fact they were made at the height of the 'Prague Spring', which was seen 'upstairs' as the result of the seizure of key positions in the Czechoslovakian mass media by Jewish intellectuals. Nor must we forget that the 'signature campaign' (in the course of which hundreds of Moscow intellectuals, in large part Jews, signed their names to protest against re-Stalinization and the trials of Siniavsky and Ginzburg) had yet to die down in the USSR. From this standpoint, Lobanov's unexpected sociological revelations can to some degree be explained. The regime suddenly saw itself faced with an acute threat from the educated strata of the population. A journalist eager to score points with his higher-ups therefore denounced this threat in an effort to win the support of youth for his bosses.

But what is so striking about Lobanov's defence of the regime is its odd appearance. He does not appeal to Marx or to 'proletarian internationalism'; on the contrary, he appeals only to 'the national spirit' and to the 'Russian soil'. His article does not have the cliche-ridden look of a 'refutation' by a Marxist hack, but rather resembles the anguished cry of a Russian terrified of what is happening to his country, to his *nation*. Moreover, it indirectly accuses the regime of not only allowing the formation of such a sinister social phenomenon as a stratum of 'educated shopkeepers', but of bringing matters to such a dangerous pitch that, as Lobanov exclaims despairingly, 'the mini is triumphing!'[9] In the Aesopian language which Lobanov uses, this means the bosses have gone blind: they do not see that the 'mini' exists not just as a thing in itself but also as a kind of 'lobby' for the 'bourgeois spirit' which has conquered Europe and is now laying siege to Russia. Interestingly, as Lobanov sought to explain why the bourgeois 'mini' was so powerful and attractive to Soviet youth, he openly asserted, 'there is no fiercer enemy of the people than the *temptation of bourgeois prosperity*.'[10] Following this up, he exclaims (quoting Herzen), 'A bourgeois Russia? May Russia be spared this curse!'[11] An 'Americanism of the spirit' was what was conquering Russia, not just with the help of the seductive 'minis' with their refined manners and Jewish surnames, but also aided by the 'temptation of bourgeois prosperity'. (In place of this read 'the material well-being of the working people', which is the fundamental bulwark of post-Stalinist Soviet ideology.)

In other words, the Soviet leaders themselves, by their orientation toward material prosperity and their promises that Communism will bring physical as well as spiritual 'satiety', are helping the bourgeois spirit to conquer Russia. They engage in flirtation with America. They think their ICBMs will be able to defend them from the mortal threat radiating from that country. They will not, Lobanov admonishes. The real threat is not American missiles, but rather the 'bourgeoisness' of the 'American spirit'. This 'bourgeoisness' is not 'man's exploitation of his fellow man', but the lure of satiety. That is Lobanov's second 'finding'. 'Spiritual satiety — is the *psychological* [my emphasis] foundation of the bourgeois.'[12] But the *social* foundation of the bourgeois nature, of course, is material satiety — 'existence within the limits of the pleasures of the stomach'.[13] Lobanov launches a powerful invective against these 'gastric pleasures', against 'the pot belly,' drawing on quotations from Hugo and Gogol' and devoting almost an entire page to them.[14]

If the real threat to Russia is not missiles but 'satiety', then Lobanov's third — and most important — 'finding' starts to appear rational: namely that the *Americanization* of the spirit can be combated only by its *Russification*. Here begins the, so to speak, 'constructive section' of Lobanov's program. This is also where his inevitable encounter with the VSKhSON programme occurs. Just like the VSKhSON, he starts from the assumption that 'the reason . . . for the dangerous tension in the world lies much deeper than the economic or political spheres'. It derives from the fact that 'a spiritual struggle for the individual is going on'. In other words, Lobanov also transfers the centre of the world drama from the struggle of socialism vs. capitalism to the metaphysical realm of spiritual confrontation. In the same way as the VSKhSON, he too predicts that 'sooner or later these two irreconcilable forces will collide with one another'. But he gives the actors in this approaching mortal conflict different names: 'moral uniqueness and Americanism of the spirit'.[15] (Incidentally, isn't Lobanov's 'Americanism of the spirit' the exact counterpart of the VSKhSON's 'satanocracy'?) It is true that Lobanov's 'moral uniqueness' is nothing like the VSKhSON's 'theocracy' (Lobanov believes in the potential effectiveness of the Soviet regime), but what interests us here is that Lobanov, like the VSKhSON, sees the only alternative to the world's ruination in a third, 'Russian', path.

Of course, noblesse oblige (and the censor too!), Lobanov's constructive recommendations do not go beyond suggesting that the regime seek its social power base (a constituency, so to speak) not among the 'educated shopkeepers', but among *simple Russians*, peasants unspoiled by either satiety or education, unique — and in their uniqueness not subject to the temptations of world evil. 'These are the people', Lobanov concludes, 'who have saved Russia. Are they not the embodiment of the historical and moral potential of the nation? Is not our faith and hope to be found in them?'[16]

Cutting through Lobanov's rhetoric and emotional outbursts, we can reduce the 'constructive section' of his programme to the three main propositions:

(1)   The regime's social orientation should be Russified. (Reliance on the 'educated strata', on the 'diplomaed masses', represents the ruinous Western path, leading to the bourgeoisification of Russia; hence the regime's orientation toward universal secondary education and broadening the system of universities runs counter to the 'Russian spirit' and will lead to a deepening of the crisis.)[17]

(2)   The regime's domestic political strategy should be Russified. (It is not 'material prosperity', which inevitably leads to 'Americanization of the spirit', but spiritual Russification, that is the key to the nation's salvation.)[18]

(3)   The regime's foreign policy should also be Russified. The country must be closed to alien cultural influences. Detente, from this point of view, appeared very much like a one-way street, an instrument for the 'Americanization of Russia's spirit'.

'Inevitability'

Lobanov spoke mostly of the 'national spirit' and of its 'corrupters'. However, the conclusions which seemed to follow from his article were so fundamentally opposed to the basic attitudes of the regime and the interests of a considerable part of the establishment that in practical terms no discussion of them was possible in the official press. Even in living rooms his article was spoken about for the most part in whispers. This torpid silence encouraged *Molodaia gvardia* to new exploits. Viktor Chalmaev's essay 'Inevitability' was met with a storm of indignation, not because it was less bold than Lobanov's, but because it seemed less immediately relevant — because arguments about it could be portrayed as arguments about history rather than about the need for change in the current regime's social and political strategy. In fact, Chalmaev was attempting to lay the historiographic groundwork for Lobanov's conception of the Russific- ation of the spirit. His aim was to persuade Russian youth of the historical inevitability of global confrontation between aggressive 'Americanization' and the only force in the world capable of resisting it — Russia.

The tone of Chalmaev's article is the same as Lobanov's, but his vision of the future confrontation is even more apocalyptic. He tells horrifying stories about 'the loss of many wonders of human civilization in the bourgeois world'. He argues (with the help of Ivan Bunin) that 'America is the first country . . . which, although enlightened, lives without ideas'.[19] He also inveighs against 'vulgar satiety' and 'material prosperity'.[20] But when he speaks with elation of the Archpriest Avvakum, (who, in the Muscovite tsardom, performed the same function that Aksakov did in the Petersburg empire and Solzhenitsyn in the Soviet) as a 'Russian herald of the word of Christ, humbled before no one',[21] when he speaks of the 'fluidity of the Russian folk spirit which in its development often runs ahead of the outward forms of the people's daily lives',[22] and — if that wasn't going far enough — adds that the 'official regime and the canons of the state . . . by no means take Russia to her limit'[23] — it must have tried the patience of the 'official regime'. It was not at all clear whether, in Chalmaev's view, the 'fluid Russian spirit' had not already surpassed those very 'outward forms' it was not supposed to, and had thereby 'run ahead in its development' of the 'canons' of the current 'official regime'.

Chalmaev was attacked — ferociously. 'The canons of the state' represented by a powerful clique of Marxist dogmatists (Soviet Preasthood, as I call them) gave the 'folk spirit' (in the person of Chalmaev) to understand that it was they who were still firmly in the saddle and had no intention of yielding that position to any 'herald of the word of Christ' — even a 'Russian' one. This was a kind of declaration of war between canonical Marxism and the Establishment Right — a fight to the death whose finale even now is far from clear.

Indeed, Chalmaev's interpretation contradicts all the Marxist canons. To him, Russian history is essentially that of the development and maturation of the 'national spirit' — its preparation for the last decisive battle with Americanism, for another, more glorious Stalingrad where the Russian spirit will finally triumph over the bourgeois devil. No gulf exists between Soviet and tsarist Russia for Chalmaev. It is not revolutions or reforms which are the landmarks of his history, but rather the battles in which the 'Russian spirit' came of age: from Lake Chud, where Prince Aleksandr Nevskii routed the Germans, to the field of Kulikovo, where Prince Dmitrii Donskoi defeated the Tartars; from Poltava, where Peter I routed the Swedes, to Borodino, where Alexander I laid the beginning of the end for Napoleon; from Stalingrad, where Stalin routed the Germans — to an unknown but impending new Stalingrad. From his standpoint, the October Revolution was just another stage in the maturing of the Russian spirit, and thus by no means the epoch-making date of the birth of socialism. To him, the actions of Ivan the Terrible or Patriarch Germogen, for instance, were just as important as those of Lenin — all of them led the 'national spirit' to feats of greatness on behalf of the state. 'This is the history of the people', writes Chalmaev, 'who, sometimes by evolution and sometimes by means of revolutionary explosions, pass from one form of state and societal consciousness to another, more progressive one.'[24]

Even more important than any political event is the role of the church and of Russian Orthodoxy as an organizing and indoctrinating force in the triumphal progression of the 'Russian spirit'. Everything which for decades Marxist historiography had dismissed as the accursed tsarist past and opium of the people, and passionately attacked as 'reactionary' and 'backward', with Chalmaev now emerged into the foreground as the harmonious creative collaboration of Russia's tsars and her church for the good of the nation and, ultimately, the Communist Party.

'The contemporary young person', writes Chalmaev, 'will probably be surprised at the fact that in the historical novels of recent years, such a large place has come to be taken by tsars and Grand Dukes, and along with them, but by no means inferior to them, patriarchs and other princes of the church, schismatics and anchorites.'[25] He explains that the 'greatly poetic' Patriarch Nikon, the 'anchorite patriot' Sergii Radonezhskii, and the 'patriot Patriarch' Germogen, together with others, embodied the 'spiritual power' of the Russian nation, its 'fiery transports and dreams', from which it 'forges . . . the foundation for feats on behalf of the state.'[26] 'A great country', he adds, 'cannot live without deep pathos, without inner enthusiasm — otherwise it is seized by flaccidity and torpor.'[27] Moreover, inasmuch as the actual bearer of Russian history — the people — 'only once in a hundred years . . . [is required to] rise to the occasion of a battle of Poltava or defence of Stalingrad',[28] someone must in the meantime keep alive their 'deep pathos' and 'inner enthusiasm'. The intelligentsia, the 'educated shopkeepers', are, of course, unsuited to this role. But who does that leave, except tsars and princes of the church?

> In the efforts of Peter I and Ivan the Terrible, and in the attempts of the church reformers to modify for the good of the motherland the Byzantine idea of denial of the earthly world as man's greatest achievement, there is something majestic, which is an inspiration to our thought too.[29]

As we can see, there is really no great difference between Lenin and Ivan the Terrible, or between socialism and the reformers of the church — contrary to everything Marxist ideologists had been teaching Soviet youth for half a century. Suddenly — in 1968 — the organ of the Central Committee of the Komsomol starts to exchange optimism for the sombre rhetoric of the church, trying to persuade Soviet youth that, all along, both of them have been working toward one and the same goal. But which goal? Where is the common denominator between Poltava and Stalingrad, between Lenin and Ivan the Terrible? Who would, even in jest, count Peter I among the builders of Communism, or Lenin among the anchorites?

Here is where the grandiose vision of the 'Byzantine Idea'[30] enters in. It is this, it turns out, that all the titans of Russian history — its patriot-anchorites and its patriot-Communists — have jointly been working towards. Now we can understand Chalmaev's programmatic declaration that, 'the measure of true intellectuality and progressiveness in our day is the struggle against the ideological opponents of *our Motherland*';[31] and that, 'Awareness of this uncompromising ideological divide is the historical inevitability of our time.'[32]

According to Lobanov, 'the ideology of our country' is derived from the 'moral uniqueness' of the Russian nation. History helped Chalmaev to formulate this derivation more precisely. It proved to be 'Byzantinism', through whose prism Russian history is transformed into a preparatory school for the next Stalingrad; and Byzantinism that helps to rekindle 'deep pathos' and 'inner enthusiasm', without which Brezhnev's Russia 'is seized by flabbiness and torpor.'

'Chalmaevism'

Lobanov's and Chalmaev's essays, accompanied in *Molodaia gvardia* by dozens of poems and short stories all devoted to the same resurrected 'land and soil' and 'national spirit' themes were an open challenge to the Brezhnev regime and its ideologists. The regime responded — not only with a hail of indignant articles, but also with a number of actions undertaken by the Propaganda Department of the Central Committee. There was even a special session of the Central Committee Secretariat devoted to 'Young Guardism'. (Brezhnev himself, according to authoritative sources, complained at this meeting that whenever he turned on the television, he heard only the ringing of church bells and saw nothing but onion domes. 'What's the matter, comrades?' he asked. 'What time are we living in? Before the Revolution or after it?') Finally, the regime responded by ousting the editor-in-chief of *Molodaia gvardia*, Anatolii Nikonov. A special term — Chalmaevism — was coined and began to be used in ideological propaganda attacks.

However, nothing changed. The mountain had laboured and brought forth a mouse. Almost contemptuously, Nikonov was appointed editor-in-chief of the 'cosmopolitan' magazine *Vokrug sveta* [Around the World] — in the same publishing house as *Molodaia gvardia* but one storey higher. His place was ultimately taken by his former deputy, Anatolii Ivanov, an even more faithful henchman of Chalmaev's. Brezhnev's patience continued to be tried by the church bells and onion domes on TV. 'Chalmaevism' in poetry and prose continued to dominate *Molodaia gvardia*, and a new magazine of the 'Chalmaevist tendency' — *Nash sovremennik* [Our Contemporary] — appeared. Its editor-in-chief, Sergei Vikulov, did not even try to disguise his sympathies. More importantly, *Molodaia gvardia* dared to hit back — and was supported by *Moskva* and *Ogonek* [Little Fire].

Something totally unprecedented was happening: the impeccably obedient journalistic machine, which had worked faultlessly for decades, this time balked. The Propaganda Department of the Central Committee proved powerless to enforce the Secretariat's decisions. Everything seemed to be taking place in a kind of Kafkaesque world. The Cultural Department of that same Central Committee impudently denied that any decision on 'Chalmaevism' had been taken at all. No terrible vengeance was visited upon them. Instead, a half-hearted, though noisy quarrel dragged on for years between two departments at the very top of the ideological tree. What this led to, we will see later.

The Defeat of a Marxist

The chorus of Marxist voices which attacked *Molodaia gvardia* was ultimately joined by the liberal *Novyi mir*. For fifteen years this journal had fought bravely with the orthodox Stalinist *Oktyabr'*, but now found itself in the same camp. In truth, everything went topsy-turvy when the black cloud of Russophilism appeared on the horizon. In place of their good old enmity, familiar as the daily paper, seemingly irreconcilable opponents suddenly finished up on the same side of the barricades. What's more, they began to speak almost the same language — the language of dogmatic Marxism. Aleksandr Dement'ev, in a lengthy essay, accused *Molodaia gvardia* of what it should have been accused of long before. He wrote:

> Chalmaev speaks of Russia and the West in the language of Slavophile messianism rather than that of our contemporaries . . . Our scholarship . . . treats [this problem] above all as a struggle between the world of socialism and the world of capitalism . . . Underlying today's struggle between 'Russia' and 'the West' are not national, but social and class distinctions . . . [From Chalmaev's essay] it is but one step . . . to the idea of national exclusiveness and the superiority of the Russian nation over all others, to an ideology incompatible with proletarian international-ism . . . The meaning and goal of life [for Chalmaev] are not in the material, but in the spiritual . . . [which] is an obstacle to the material and spiritual advancement of the Soviet peasantry.[33]

All of this reinforced-concrete phraseology sounded impeccable, albeit trivial. Dement'ev overlooked just a single blunder — so small that an outsider would not have even noticed it. The long essay contained a short passage with which Dement'ev effectively condemned himself — himself and not Chalmaev, a Marxist and not a heretic — to ideological extinction.

'Chalmaev and Lobanov', he wrote, 'point to the danger of alien ideological influences. Will we be able to stand our ground, say, against the temptation of "bourgeois prosperity"' . . . 'In today's ideological struggle the temptation of "Americanism" . . . must not be underestimated', Chalmaev asserts. Correct. But neither should it be overestimated . . . Soviet society, by its very . . . nature, is not predisposed to bourgeois influences.'[34]

That was it — and the death sentence was pronounced — not only for Dement'ev, but also for *Novyi mir*, which had heroically withstood the rabid attacks of all the Stalinist hacks, had published Solzhenitsyn and Siniavsky, and had apparently stood unshaken as the sole bastion of liberalism in a stormy sea of reaction. Now it fell. It fell (what irony!) not because of Solzhenitsyn or Siniavsky, but because of an orthodox Marxist essay which sought to defend the purity of the Party's ideological vestments.[35] Dement'ev himself involuntarily prophesied this distressing finale when he noted that, 'it is . . . dangerous to find oneself in the hands of the violent, unrestrained enemies of "the educated shopkeepers" and passionate zealots of "the national spirit".'[36] Yea verily, as it turned out, it is quite dangerous — even for Marxists in Moscow.

Doesn't this mean that by protesting against the Russian Right *Novyi mir* struck the regime's most sensitive nerve (considering the balance of forces in it at the time)? This is perhaps most clearly to be seen from the furious collective letter signed by eleven writers — including representatives of both orthodox Stalinism and the Russian Right — printed in *Ogonek* under the title 'What Is *Novyi mir* Speaking Out Against?'[37] Their argument was simple and devastating:

Contrary to the zealous appeals of A. Dement'ev not to exaggerate 'the dangers of alien ideological influences', we continue to maintain that the penetration of bourgeois ideology among us was, has been, and remains a very serious danger . . . [which] may lead to the gradual replacement of the concepts of proletarian internationalism with the *cosmopolitan ideas* so dear to the hearts of certain critics and writers grouped around the journal *Novyi mir*.[38]

The ominous word 'cosmopolitanism' had been pronounced.[39] To someone who is aware of the internal balance of ideological forces in the Soviet establishment (or one who merely knows who's who), this explains how representatives of the orthodox Stalinist right, such as M. Alekseev and V. Zakrutkin, came to unite with apologists of the new Russian Right, such as A. Ivanov or S. Vikulov. It also explains how *Novyi mir* had been able to stand up to *Oktyabr'* for so long. It was because the two factions of the right were divided. Up till then, the Russophiles had only stood by in amusement as the Stalinists and the liberals quarrelled and paid no attention to their ideological expansion. Only when they joined forces did they begin to sense their real power. This was the first action in the post-Stalinist era by a *unified* Establishment Right — a kind of historical experiment which demonstrated its extraordinary political potential.[40]

It was now a matter of carefully and tactfully bridging the gap that separated the Russophiles from the Stalinists — of transforming the alliance of right-wing factions from an ad hoc tactical union into a stable political force able to exert a continuing influence on the strategic goals of the regime.

After the enraged invective of the 'old guard' (*Oktyabr'*) against Young Guardism, such an operation had seemed, in principle, impossible. *Oktyabr'* would never commit itself to such heresy as to say that the foundation and life-blood of the Soviet state was not the working class but the peasantry, or that the 'national spirit', rather than 'proletarian internationalism', should serve as its guiding star — never in a million years. But *Ogonek* was more compliant. It suddenly discovered that Lobanov's 'diplomaed masses' were essentially the same as Sofronov's 'rootless cosmopolitans' by another name. In other words, it seemed for a time that both factions of the Establishment Right at last understood that they had *one common enemy*.

But very shortly they came under attack. So long as it was a matter of common struggle against the liberal intelligentsia, epitomized by *Novyi mir*, they were allowed to have their head. But the term 'diplomaed masses' did not include just liberals. A significant part of the powerful ruling faction of the Centre was also 'diplomaed' — and furthermore, considerably more interested than liberals in contacts with the West (to say nothing of the fact that its 'cosmopolitanism' — its opportunities, so to speak, for the importation of 'world evil' — were incomparably broader).

Thus what began as a relatively innocent coalition against *Novyi mir* had to grow if it was to stabilize into a *political opposition* to the 'cosmopolitanism' of the Brezhnev regime itself (which was infected to the marrow by bourgeois ideas of 'satiety'). The struggle against liberal 'cosmopolitanism' was related logically to the struggle against governmental, Brezhnevist, 'cosmopolitanism'.

I do not claim that the leaders of Russophilism necessarily had any clear conception of this. I only wish to note that when *Molodaia gvardia* published its third programmatic declaration in 1970 (Sergei Semanov's essay 'On Relative and Eternal Values') it did precisely what we have just been talking about: it took a bold step toward meeting the old guard half-way. However, it made the tactical mistake of executing this very clumsily.

Young Guard's Mistake

Certainly *Molodaia gvardia* was no stranger to, so to speak, sentimental Stalinist motifs. Dement'ev noted, for example, the extraordinary nature of Feliks Chuev's poem about Stalin.[41] But whereas Chuev's poem was a sinister but still minor episode in the evolution of Young Guardism toward Stalinism, Semanov's article was intended to lay the ideological groundwork for this evolution. It contained no fewer odes to the national spirit, songs of praise for the Russian soil, or denunciations of the educated shopkeeper mentality than Chalmaev's article. In it the October Revolution was described as a Russian national (in the sense of ethnic) achievement.[42] Semanov declared that, 'in our society, services to the Motherland are valued more highly than anything else',[43] and that the chief sin of Trotskyism was 'its profound revulsion for our people, their . . . traditions . . . their history'.[44] But the main point of the article was its unprecedented assertion that, 'the turning point in the struggle against wreckers and nihilists took place in the middle of the 1930s', and that, 'it was precisely after the adoption of the new Constitution that . . . all honest working people of our country were once and for all welded into a unified and monolithic whole.'[45]

After Khrushchev's revelations at the XXth Party Congress, the time about which Semanov is speaking ('the epoch of 1937') was pronounced anathema and condemned to oblivion. Even according to official historiography, this was the era of the Party's devastation. Here Semanov declared it the main part of the Revolution, which put an end to the 'wreckers and nihilists' and marked the beginning of 'the monolithic unity of our people'.

This was truly the kind of help the Stalinists could do without. By declaring that 'these changes exercised a highly favourable influence on the development of our culture',[46] Semanov was revising the decisions of the XXth Party Congress and trying to rehabilitate Stalin. His intentions in this sense were — from the Stalinist standpoint — for the best, but their execution was terrible. A romantic, virtually Napoleonic, legend about 'our Generalissimo' is one thing. Open praise for the era of the 'old Guard's' mass murder is quite another. Semanov reminded people of precisely what needed to be forgotten. With one blow he destroyed everything that had so successfully been started a year earlier by *Ogonek*, and put an end to the rightist alliance. He thus played right into the hands of the Propaganda Department. It is no coincidence that shortly after Semanov's article appeared, the Secretariat of the Central Committee held the session at which Brezhnev complained about the church bells, and Nikonov was fired.

In fact, it was through Semanov's article that the ideologists of the Establishment Right revealed the bankruptcy of their situation: their inability to develop either a common ideological platform for a right-wing coalition or a common strategy for struggle against the 'diplomaed masses' and the 'cosmopolitan' Brezhnevist centre.

From the Propaganda Department's point of view, the situation was extremely simple. First *Novyi mir* had made a slip (with the Dement'ev article), as a result of which it became necessary to sack its entire editorial board. Now, *Molodaya gvardiya* too had made serious error, and the time had thus come to get rid of its editorial board. This was logical. It was in the spirit of the Brezhnev regime of 'stabilization', which dealt blows equally to the right and to the left. The blow was dealt. The journal *Kommunist* fired its long-awaited salvo. The reader should understand that *Kommunist* never repeats itself. It does not deliver lectures or parcel out reprimands. It pronounces sentences — final and not subject to appeal. Its sentence was as follows:

> V. Chalmaev's essay 'Inevitability' . . . attracted attention to itself at once by its, if you will, utterly unprecedented . . . extra-social approach to history, its mixing together everything with everything else in Russian history, its attempt to place in a favourable light everything reactionary, right up to the statements of even such arch-reactionaries as Konstantin Leont'ev.[47]

These lines sounded like a death knell for Chalmaev, but *Kommunist* went on to speak of 'Chalmaevism' and of how,

> these kind of authors, who have appeared primarily in the magazine *Molodaia gvardia*, ought to have listened to the rational and objective things that were contained in [the] criticism of the article 'Inevitability' and several others in a similar vein. Unfortunately, this did not happen. Moreover, individual authors went still further in their delusions, forgetting Lenin's direct instructions on the issues which they have undertaken to judge.[48]

Later in the article, following all the rules of Party inquisition, the writings of those afore-mentioned 'individual authors' (including, of course, Semanov) were drawn together by *Kommunist* to describe the magazine's 'line', and it was stated that this line 'lends the magazine a clearly *mistaken slant*'.[49] The same approach had been tried a thousand times, and a thousand times it had meant the end — whether of a writer, an editorial board, or an 'anti-Party group'. This time, as we have seen, it did not work. No end came — not for Chalmaev, nor the editorial board of *Molodaia gvardia*, nor even the mistaken slant.

The Melent'ev Affair

The Melent'ev affair concerns an episode connected with Young Guardism for which — as distinct from the cases of Chalmaev, Dement'ev and Semanov — I do not have any documentary evidence.

Indeed, such evidence could not exist because of the very nature of the case. It is based solely on talk, but talk originating with persons directly concerned with the affair.

Yu. Melent'ev was the director of the *Molodaia gvardia* publishing house (the magazine *Molodaia gvardia* was under his immediate supervision). At the height of the *Molodaia gvardia* campaign, the head of the Cultural Department of th Central Committee, Vasilii Shauro, assigned Melent'ev to conduct the difficult negotiations with the Propaganda Department regarding Chalmaevism and the reorganization of *Novyi mir*. When there began to be signs of a convergence between the two factions of the Right, someone 'higher up' apparently decided the time had come to feel out 'the Boss' himself. For this unprecedented assignment a person of great courage and devotion to the rightist cause was needed. He would be risking, if not his head, at least his career, because it was known that in personal matters Brezhnev was merciless and somewhat vindictive. The assignment was given to Melent'ev, who was then at the height of his career.

He obtained an audience with Brezhnev and spoke with him for an hour. More properly, it was not so much a conversation as a monologue; Brezhnev just listened. Melent'ev spoke of how the mood among Soviet youth, the military and the patriotic intelligentsia was one of alarm. The penetration of Western ideology had reached dangerous proportions. It was already being reflected in the quality of recruits and the morale of the officer corps. The country was losing its military readiness. Many people felt that decisive measures needed to be taken. First, the whole programme of ideological work with Soviet youth had to be changed to introduce a truly 'patriotic' indoctrination programme, like the one which helped win the war against Hitler. Failure to do this could have catastrophic consequences. Second, all contacts with the West had to be minimized. Third, more rigid ideological control had to be established over both the intelligentsia and some of the central staff of the Party, who were deeply infected by alien ideological influences. In general, Melent'ev proposed a programme of political isolationism and intellectual protectionism based on the struggle of the 'Russian spirit' against 'cosmopolitanism'. It was the programme of the *Molodaia gvardia* — *Ogonek* alliance laid out in formal party terms.

We can assume that this was the time Brezhnev was considering his epoch-making turn toward detente. It may be that those who sent Melent'ev to him did not know this. On the other hand, perhaps they did know and were trying to prevent such a turn by offering Brezhnev an alternative. We have no way of knowing.[50] In any case, in its unfortunate timing and ill-conceived tactlessness, Melent'ev's visit can be compared only with Semanov's article; it was, its, so to speak, organizational equivalent. Brezhnev's reaction was harsh. After hearing Melent'ev out, he spoke only a few sentences, but among these was the following: 'There is no place for you even in the Party, let alone the Central Committee.' Coming from Brezhnev, those words meant the end of Melent'ev's career or — more accurately — should have meant that. The next day Melent'ev was removed from the Central Committee.

However, here we find ourselves once again in the bizarre Kafkaesque world of the Brezhnev establishment. The General Secretary's condemnation not only failed to put an end to Melent'ev's party career, but gave it new impetus. Melent'ev became Deputy Minister of Culture for the Russian Republic, and later Minister. Who was behind him? We can only surmise that if a person for whom, in Brezhnev's opinion, there was no place in the Party, none the less rose to the post of Minister, then there must have been someone so powerful behind him that even Brezhnev did not find it worth his while to quarrel.

Melent'ev's fate seems especially odd in comparison with that of another official of the Central Committee, who in his day soared even higher. I have in mind A. N. Yakovlev, who for several years was the acting head of the Central Committee Propaganda Department — that is to say, was the Party's chief ideologist.

The Yakovlev Affair

Yakovlev, who stood on the left flank of the Brezhnevist Centre, was concerned not only with ideological considerations, but also, one must assume, with personal matters. He was in effect performing the functions of a Department head though he did not carry that title. He was too far to the left for that. His reputation carried along with it certain obligations. In order to justify his 'leftism', Yakovlev tried to move the centre of gravity of the Brezhnevist faction to the left. The most handy political lever for doing this was the struggle against Russophilism. As far back as 1968, Yakovlev had been trying to transform Russophilism into an object of political struggle higher up. He was behind the critical salvo fired at Chalmaevism; he was behind the article in *Kommunist*; he was behind the session of the Secretariat at which the fate of *Molodaia gvardia*'s editor was decided.

However, at this point he ran into a brick wall. Resistance to the attack on *Molodaia gvardia* was coming from the Cultural Department of the Central Committee itself. Shauro was clever enough to deflect Yakovlev's attacks so that they did not pass from the realm of permissible ideological debate to the fatal realm of political deviation.[51] After several years of unsuccessful manoeuvring and intrigue, and having tried all of the behind-the-scenes approaches and methods of indirect attack, Yakovlev was compelled to stake everything on a single card. Like Melent'ev, he too put his career on the line; but unlike Melent'ev, he was well and truly burned.

The moment he chose for his attack seemed appropriate. On the one hand, the 50th anniversary of the multinational Soviet Union was due shortly; on the other, detente with the West was in full swing. It was a matter of proving, first, that contrary to Shauro's assertions, Russophilism was not a lyrical nostalgia for the rural past but a wholly political, anti-Marxist and even 'counter-revolutionary' phenomenon; second, that Russophilism stimulated nationalist sentiments in the non-Russian republics of the USSR; and third, that it was incompatible with the 'course of the XXIVth Congress' — the Congress of Detente.

On 15 November 1972, an enormous article by Yakovlev, taking up two newspaper pages, appeared in *Literaturnaia gazeta* under the title 'Against Anti-Historicism'. 'In essence,' Yakovlev wrote, 'there is behind all this an *ideological position* which is dangerous in that objectively it *contains an attempt to bring back the past*.'[52] As if this didn't go far enough, Yakovlev added, 'The polemics [of the Russophiles] deal not only with Chernyshevskii, but also with Lenin.' No one in the USSR — not even Stalin — had ever permitted themselves to argue with Lenin (or with Chernyshevskii for that matter) — except the Russophiles, that is. It follows therefore that Russophilism must be an extraordinary phenomenon, by no means confined to the limits of permissible debate. One has to have lived one's life in the Soviet Union to understand how ominous accusations such as Yakovlev's sounded — even in 1972.

To support his case, Yakovlev laid out a vast, truly alarming, panorama of the penetration of Russophilism into all fields of literature and the social sciences — from 'Shevtsov's hysterical writings' to the *Soviet Encyclopedia*. He uncovered Russophilism in historiography, in *belles-lettres*, in poetry, in literary scholarship — everywhere. Very carefully, but persistently, he tried to present Russophilism as a diversionary alien ideology, of a kind unheard of since the destruction of all the Party opposition groups, which was especially dangerous in that it helped 'bourgeois propaganda' to spark off conflicts between the nationalities of the USSR. 'It is well known', wrote Yakovlev, 'what an active campaign is being waged by our class antagonists in connection with the 50th anniversary of the multinational Soviet state.'[53] Furthermore, unlike Dement'ev's, there were no slip-ups in Yakovlev's article; it was one huge, smooth, dogmatic monolith.

The Party's chief ideologist is not a *Novyi mir* author. One cannot reply to him by a letter in *Ogonek*. No one dared indulge in polemics with Yakovlev — no one, that is, except the samizdat journal — *Veche* (Assembly). In an editorial entitled 'The Struggle Against So-Called Russophilism, or the Road to Suicide for the State', it subjected Yakovlev to a devastating critique. Only the Dissident Right could permit itself a critique whose methodology was so elementary: You rely on Lenin? All right. Then be consistent. Lenin wrote about national self-determination, about the 'smothering of the Ukraine'. So why don't you suggest, along the lines of Lenin, that we stop 'smothering the Ukraine' right now? And further: 'If comrade Yakovlev doesn't like the union of Central Asia with Russia, then why, on the occasion of its anniversary, doesn't he propose the dissolution of the Soviet Union?'[54] In other words, quoting Lenin as Yakovlev does can lead in *Veche*'s opinion to 'suicide for the state,' and hence outright *anti-Sovietism*. 'In 1918,' accuses *Veche*, 'the Soviet Republic was reduced to the dimensions of the Muscovite kingdom during the time of Ivan III. This is what the Russophiles' persecutor dreams of.'[55]

One would think the chief Party ideologist could hardly be toppled with arguments like this — let alone arguments that issued from a semi-underground samizdat journal. Nevertheless, toppled he was. Like Dement'ev, he suffered for having written an orthodox Marxist article, a 'refutation' of anti-Party ideology. Who was behind the fall of this high-flying ideologist, suddenly demoted to the rank of ambassador (and sent off to Canada)? Once again, we can only guess.[56] We know one thing though: with his fall the campaign against Russophilism not only ceased being a political arena, but the arena was totally closed off. Clearly, very powerful forces on high were concerned not to let the editorial board of *Molodaia gvardia* go under (the way the editorial board of *Novyi mir* did) and to assure that the Establishment Right retained its forces intact for better times. These forces however, could not be allowed to remain a threat to the Brezhnevist Centre. The highly placed patron of *Molodaia gvardia*, Polianskii, was quietly dropped from the Politburo and ultimately shared the fate of Yakovlev (he was sent to Japan).

The true lesson of the 'Yakovlev affair' was something entirely different. It was that someone would not allow the Establishment

Right to share the fate of the Establishment liberals, or let the Melent'ev affair end in the same way as the Yakovlev affair. Somehow, the editorial board of *Molodaia gvardia*, which was politically defeated, nevertheless retained its personnel, its position and its ideological ammunition. What for? Only the future can answer that.

Summary of 'Young Guardism'

(1)   Bringing to the centre of the contemporary world drama — in place of the struggle of 'socialism' against 'capitalism' — the conflict of 'spirits': the Russian vs. the bourgeois (which is embodied in 'Americanism').

(2)   Bringing to the centre of the contemporary Russian drama the conflict of 'the people' versus the 'diplomaed masses' of 'cosmopolitan shopkeepers'.

(3)   Recognition in principle of the Soviet system as potentially 'Russian' in spirit.

(4)   Latent recognition of the Brezhnevist regime as oriented toward the 'diplomaed masses' and the bourgeois values of 'satiety' and 'education', as 'cosmopolitan' and 'non-Russian' in spirit, therefore not Soviet and the embodiment of 'flabbiness and torpor'.

(5)   An apocalyptic vision of the 'inevitability' of a final showdown between the 'Russian spirit' and 'Americanism', which will complete the world's pre-history.

(6)   The necessity of completely changing the orientation of the regime, which is now 'flippant in its attitude toward the Motherland'.

(7)   An agreement to return to at least some of the values of the 'lost paradise' of Stalinism as the embodiment of the Russo-Byzantine tradition.

(8)   A distinction made for the first time, and in Aesopian language, between the Soviet *system* (positively 'Russian') and a particular Soviet *regime* ('non-Russian' in its basic orientation). Hence the gulf in strategies recommended by the Dissident and Establishment Right from the outset: whereas VSKhSON proposed replacing the Soviet system with a 'corporate state' via 'revolution from below', Young Guardism essentially proposed replacement of the pseudo-Soviet, in its view, Brezhnevist regime by a genuinely Soviet 'Russian' one via 'revolution from above'. (That is, in my terms, via a counter-reform).

Notes

1   John Dunlop, *The New Russian Revolutionaries*, p. 221.
2   *Molodaia gvardia*, 1968, No. 4, p. 297.
3   Ibid., p. 299.
4   Ibid., p. 303.
5   Ibid., p. 296.
6   Ibid., p. 299.
7   Ibid., p. 296.
8   Ibid.
9   Ibid.
10   Ibid., p. 304. Emphasis added.
11   Ibid.
12   Ibid.
13   Ibid.
14   If my analysis of the structure of the Soviet Establishment in *Detente after Brezhenev* (Berkeley, 1977) is even partly correct, and if within the Establishment there are powerful groups (aristocratizing elites) who consider their 'pleasures of the stomach' (primarily Western in origin) as the highest value in life, then Lobanov's philippics probably reflect the reaction of their puritanical Stalinist opponents.
15   *Molodaia gvardia*, 1968, No. 4, p. 304.
16   Ibid., p. 306.
17   Strange as it may seem, the politically stagnant regime of the last two decades may have actually taken some of the Young Guard's advice. Whereas at the start of the 1960s, under a regime of reform, 57% of the graduates of Soviet secondary schools were allowed to matriculate at institutions of higher education, a decade later the figure had fallen to only 22%. (See Murray Yanowitch, 'Schooling and Inequalities', in Leonard Schapiro and Joseph Godson ed. *The Soviet Worker: Illusions and Realities*, Macmillan, 1981.)
18   A regime of stagnation could not have taken this advice without denying its own fundamental tenets. Only a dictatorial regime, in a counter-reform situation, would be able to implement Lobanov's ascetic recommendation — yet another piece of evidence to support the view that the Russian New Right is oriented toward counter-reform.
19   *Molodaia gvardia*, 1968, No. 9, p. 271.
20   Ibid., p. 270.
21   Ibid., p. 266.
22   Ibid., p. 268.
23   Ibid.
24   Ibid., p. 266.
25   Ibid., p. 265.
26   Ibid., pp. 267—8.
27   Ibid., p. 256.
28   Ibid., p. 268. And on p. 264: 'Once in a hundred years — the ice of Lake Chud, the lush grasses of the fields of Kulikovo, Poltava, Borodino.'
29   Ibid., p. 266.

30   The 'Byzantinism' of Russia is an idea of Konstantin Leont'ev. According to this concept, Russia is not merely a state: Russia is a separate world, a special civilization, which has inherited the world task of the Eastern Roman Empire — that of resisting the bourgeois West; or, as Lobanov would put it in the terms of the contemporary Russian Right, the task of crushing 'Americanism of the spirit'.

31   *Molodaia gvardia*, 1968, No. 9, p. 262. Emphasis added.

32   Ibid., p. 263.

33   *Novyi mir*, 1969, No. 4, p. 226.

34   Ibid., pp. 225—6.

35   I have heard more than once from members of the Central Committee staff that Dement'ev's essay was, if not the cause, then the pretext for the removal (in 1970) of Tvardovskii, the liberal chief of *Novyi mir*.

36   *Novyi mir*, 1969, No. 4, pp. 221—2.

37   These 'signatories', who not only were not punished for their joint letter — unlike in dozens of analogous cases which occurred at the same time — but even managed to topple Tvardovskii from his position were: Mikhail Alekseev, Sergei Vikulov, Sergei Voronin, Vitalii Zakrutkin, Anatolii Ivanov, Sergei Malashkin, Aleksandr Prokof'ev, Petr Proskurin, Sergei Smirnov, Vladimir Chivilikhin, and Nikolai Shundik.

38   *Ogonek*, July 1969, No. 30. Emphasis added.

39   Of course it is no coincidence that the letter was published in *Ogonek*, which was headed by the chief witch-hunter of the 'cosmopolitan' campaign of the late 1940s, A. Sofronov. Sofronov has an excellent feel for such things, and the fact that he considered it possible to intervene openly in the conflict suggests that a showdown was in the air in 1969.

40   The Western observer should take careful note of this episode, which clearly indicates how effective a coalition of the right-wing factions within the Soviet establishment can be under certain conditions, and not only in the struggle against 'liberalism'. It is clear that establishment 'liberalism' can exist only as long as the ruling centrist faction finds it convenient and politically safe to support it. We can therefore tentatively suggest that the rout of the old editorial board of *Novyi mir* to some extent represented a retreat by the centrists. It may be that Sofronov's feelings did not deceive him: it may be that he was not mistaken in thinking that his hour had come once again. Perhaps the rout of *Novyi mir* could — under the right circumstances — have served as a signal for a new 'anti-cosmopolitan' campaign.

41   This poem (a very sincere one, incidentally) speaks of a day when a Museum of World War II will be erected in Moscow: 'Let all who come in feel their dependence/On the Motherland, on everything Russian/There in the middle — is our Generalissimo/And his Marshals great.' Dement'ev commented venomously: 'Here we already have a notable attempt to combine an appeal to the "sources" with dreams of the future' (*Novyi mir*, 1969, No. 4, p. 230) It is true that a motherland unconditionally tied to things 'Russian' (and not things 'Soviet') is Young Guardism, but 'our Generalissimo' in centre stage is already something out of another 'old guard' opera.

42   *Molodaia gvardia*, 1970, No. 8, p. 317.

43   Ibid., p. 316.

44   Ibid., p. 318.
45   Ibid., p. 319.
46   Ibid.
47   *Kommunist*, 1970, No. 17, p. 97.
48   Ibid., p. 98.
49   Ibid., p. 99. Emphasis added.
50   The Melent'ev affair, which became partially known through Melent'ev himself, was for a long time a favourite subject of discussion in the corridors of the Central Committee and in circles close to it. However, to get an authoritative and unambiguous answer from the inhabitants of these corridors to the question, precisely who gave Melent'ev the authority for such an unprecedented move, proved impossible.
51   Shauro's tactics were constructed on the principle of hiding the political nature of Russophilism and depicting it as an exclusively cultural phenomenon. After all, what's so bad about young people being interested in their nation's past, or enthusiastically paying tribute to their roots in the Russian village? Shauro's position can best be described in the words of an authoritative scholar: 'In some Russian circles . . . there has been within the last decade something akin to a cult of the Russian past — the village tradition, Russian folk customs and art, and so forth . . . mainly cultural in character' and 'on the emotional level' (*Commentary*, August 1977, p. 42). If Yakovlev read this passage he would probably be convinced that it had been written by someone prompted by Shauro. One can imagine how surprised he would have been had he found out that this was written not by one of Shauro's minions from the CPSU Central Committee Cultural Department, but by Walter Laqueur (whom I cited earlier for his penetrating explanations of the intricacies of 1920s emigre Russian nationalism). Unfortunately, as happened later with Pipes and Hough and virtually every other American expert, all his subtle political insight left Mr Laqueur as soon as he encountered the phenomenon of contemporary Russian nationalism.
52   Emphasis added. Twenty years before this sentence would have sounded like a direct accusation of counter-revolution. In Brezhnev's Russia such things had gone out of fashion. But how else can a Soviet ear, trained to associate 'the past' with either tsarism or Stalinism, interpret it, even now?
53   One must not forget the precariousness of Yakovlev's own position. As the official party ideologist, he bore personal responsibility for everything that happened on the ideological front. Therefore, by laying his colours on thick, he *ipso facto* exposed himself to attack (which was probably successfully exploited by his opponents), but the fact that he went this far — even risking his position — indicates how seriously he regarded the matter.
54   Vol'noe slovo, No. 9—10, p. 44.
55   Ibid.
56   Yakovlev was returned from exile by Andropov during his short reign. In July 1985, almost a decade and a half after his defeat, he finally managed to achieve what he could not under Brezhnev. At the XXVIInd Party congress, in February—March 1986, he was made a Secretary of the

Central Committee in charge of Propaganda. Shauro was, needless to say, fired — another indication that the centre of gravity of the ruling coalition *is* moved to the left by what Gorbachev calls his 'revolution' and which is in effect a repetition of Khrushchev's desperate attempt to revitalize the nation and undermine the Stalinist foundations of Soviet economy and culture.

11

Veche: Loyal Opposition to the Right

The existence of *Veche* was undoubtedly a landmark in the history of the Dissident Right of post-Stalinist Russia. 'Fat' journals of public affairs, politics and *belles-lettres* are an old Russian tradition, but being a fat typewritten journal of an oppositionist persuasion — with the editor's name and address on the cover and a more or less regular distribution in the USSR for almost four years — made *Veche* something truly phenomenal.[1]

From the very beginning its editorial board enunciated the principle of free and open discussion. Everything that had been accumulating over the course of decades in the minds and souls of those of a 'patriotic Russian' persuasion poured out in its pages. In this sense — as an barometer of the mood of the 'patriotic masses' — *Veche*'s contribution was priceless. On the other hand, it was a sophisticated journal, published at a highly professional level and so demanding of the Russian intellect that the historical excursions of the VSKhSON and the Young Guards seem amateurish by comparison. Danilevskii and Khomiakov, Leont'ev and Skobelev, as well as all the other luminaries of the nineteenth-century Russian Right were subjected by *Veche* to exacting analysis and interpretation in terms of current perspectives. The ecological, economic, architectural, city planning, demographic and literary issues that faced the country were all examined in depth.

Thus, *Veche* as an historical source that offers roughly 2,000 pages of very serious material touching on virtually all aspects of Soviet life, deserves a special study in its own right. It cannot be exhaustively dealt with in the space of this chapter. What interests me here is *Veche*'s importance as an indicator of the political evolution of the Russian Dissident Right and as a remarkable, if unsuccessful, attempt to avert the movement's slide from L-Nationalism to F-Nationalism.

I have no doubts that the editorial board of *Veche* and, in particular, its editor-in-chief, Vladimir Nikolaevich Osipov, were liberals (that is, representatives of L-Nationalism) so far as this is possible for imperial nationalists.[2] They fought honestly and bravely for their liberal values against all the manifestations of the Black Hundreds' mentality — its anti-semitism, and chauvinism — which weighed heavily on them. Nevertheless they were defeated — and this is what seems to be the most significant point about *Veche*'s four-year history. From its very inception it was forced to fight on two fronts — not only against the KGB (as is clear from the many declarations of Osipov and noted by all those who have written about the journal), but also against its own constituency, the 'patriotic masses' (a point which, to my knowledge, has so far not been noted by anyone). It is hard to say which of these fronts was the more difficult — the police persecution from 'above' or maintaining their liberal positions under very powerful pressures from 'below' (at least, the split in the editorial board preceded Osipov's arrest). In this sense, *Veche* is an excellent indicator of the very severe crisis through which liberal nationalism passed in the first half of the 1970s. For, despite the liberalism of its editorial board, many of the prerequisites for a transition to F-Nationalism became rather clearly formulated on its pages. Moreover, the gloomy nostalgia that gripped its audience, 'the patriotic Russian masses', and the yearning for the restoration of dictatorship, for crude restraint of 'non-Russians' and for a new Stalinist campaign against 'cosmopolitanism', found expression there as well.

In this sense *Veche*'s experience is unique. Neither before nor since has there been a publication which offers us such an opportunity to look at what is really going on 'down there' among the 'patriotic Russian masses', what they felt and how they reacted to a regime of stagnation, and how they themselves pictured the Russian Idea. It was a window on something otherwise totally obscure — a point which no Western commentator has noted. Likewise, they have failed to note the principle paradox of *Veche*: it had two faces, its liberal one having been gradually but inexorably squeezed out by a savage chauvinist twin.

Veche's Conception of Isolationism

In the 1960s, in the period of the VSKhSON and Young Guardism, the Chinese threat was not yet perceived as something of decisive importance for Russia's national survival. Therefore, the critical edge of rightist doctrine was directed against either 'Communism and capitalism' or 'Americanization of the spirit'. Nationalist thought was dominated by the problem of 'Russia and the West'. The world drama it sought to describe was that of the salvation of mankind from the poisonous products of the Western spirit, which were seen to be leading humanity into an abyss. Russia, with her Orthodoxy on the one hand and her 'moral uniqueness' on the other, was assigned the active, saving, messianic role in this drama.

There simply was no room for a Chinese threat in this carefully constructed picture: it had nothing to do with 'bourgeois satiety' or 'Americanism of the spirit'. With the emergence of the Chinese threat, however, this portrait had to be redrawn.[3] The same series of historical events that had prompted the ruling Brezhnevist Centre to develop a policy of detente toward the accursed West, prompted the Russian Right to develop an ideological alternative to that policy. This was a task of colossal intellectual complexity for which the ideologists of the Establishment Right, with their secondary-school level knowledge of history, were quite unsuited. Genuinely talented people were needed — real intellectuals, who in Russia have traditionally been found in opposition to the regime.

Inasmuch as *Veche* had declared itself an organ of a loyal opposition, it was compelled to observe certain time-honoured rules of the game practised in all the legal 'fat' journals, and to use the traditional style of analysis. This style, of course, was the technique of historical analogy, developed over the course of centuries by the Russian loyal opposition press to a point of supreme craftsmanship and filigree delicacy. Thus the main contribution of *Veche* to the development of an alternative strategy was made in the form of historical-philosophical essays, among which the most notable was the unsigned article 'N. Ya. Danilevskii's Role in World Historical Philosophy'.

As the reader may recall from Chapter 3, Danilevskii was classical Slavophilism's first revisionist. His fundamental work, *Russia and Europe*, first published in 1871 during a period of crisis for the pre-revolutionary liberal nationalism, laid the basis for the strategic re-orientation of the Russian Right in the nineteenth century. Danilevskii was a liberal nationalist, like Osipov himself. Obviously, for all these reasons, an interpretation of Danilevskii must have seemed to the ideologists of *Veche* to be the most suitable vehicle for starting up a dialogue with Soviet leaders.

Danilevskii's main thesis, you may remember, was that there is no such thing as world civilization. There are only individual 'cultural-historical' types which have no more in common with one another than do different biological genera, such as fish and lizards, for example. At the core of each of these types are 'historical nations', which differ from non-historical ones in that, 'they have their own tasks . . . their own ideas.' For this reason, the 'political formulas worked out by one people are suited only to that people.'[4]

If Danilevskii had been consistent, he would have had to concede the right of every nation to self-determination. 'Unfortunately,' *Veche* condescendingly notes, 'Danilevskii was far from sympathetic to every kind of uniqueness. Peoples who found themselves within Russia's state borders could not count on his tolerance.'[5] Danilevskii explains this position in theoretical terms by claiming that, besides historical nations there are also, so to speak, ne'er-do-well peoples who for various reasons lack their national ideas and as a result wind up as merely 'ethnographic material'. In addition, there are nations who have already fulfilled their historical task and have died 'a natural death, by senile weakness (China)'[6] and have thereby also become ethnographic material.

One of the main points in Danilevskii's revision of Slavophilism was his denial of the principle of universal morality (which *Veche* mildly calls 'pragmatism'). Specifically, he considered it inappropriate to apply rules of morality to international relations: 'An eye for an eye and a tooth for a tooth . . . that is the law of foreign policy, the law of relations of one state toward another. The law of love and self-sacrifice have no place here.'[7] Thus, indifferent coexistence between nations — or, in the case of conflicting interests, open enmity ('cold war', as we would say these days) — was raised by Danilevskii to the level of natural law. Under these circumstances it was, of course, permissible to treat 'ethnographic material' like . . . well, material. By denying the existence of such a concept as 'the interests of all mankind'[8] and, instead, asserting that 'the real and profound danger is precisely the enthronement . . . of the idea of world civilization',[9] Danilevskii advanced 'a complete program for a kind of isolationism'.[10]

Thus the conclusion that *Veche* led its readers to was that the Slavophiles were wrong (as was the VSKhSON) in considering Russia a tool for saving humankind from 'satanocracy'. Humankind is a phantom and there is nothing to save in it. What must be saved is Russia as an 'historical nation' which is destined to implement her 'idea'. What is this idea? Danilevskii had provided the answer: 'Russia cannot occupy a place in history worthy of herself and of the Slavs except by becoming the head of a special autonomous political system of states . . . [and] serving as a counterweight to Europe.'[11]

How did the political universe during the era of Danilevskii (and particularly of his epigones Nikolai Strakhov and Konstantin Bestyzhev-

Riumin) appear from the perspective of their 'pragmatic isolationist' doctrine? Basically, it was made up of three elements: Russia, which must fulfil her historical mission; Turkey, 'the living corpse' which had long since become ethnographic material but refused to accept the fact, and was threatening to interfere with Russia's fulfilment of her historical role (unless she defeated Turkey, Russia could not become 'head of an autonomous system of states' or serve as 'a counterweight to Europe'); and the rotting cosmopolitan West, which, though doomed to become ethnographic material eventually, was nevertheless for the time being hindering Russia from crushing Turkey.[12]

Proceeding from this picture of the world, Danilevskii's political doctrine implied a very simple strategy: Russia must become strong enough that the West cannot prevent it from routing Turkey; on the ruins of Turkey, Russia must build an 'isolated' empire extending from the Adriatic to the Pacific Ocean; after sealing off the borders of this gigantic empire, Russia can wait patiently until the West, its boundaries greatly shrunken, finally rots away under the pressure of its own internal decay.

If we compare how the contemporary political universe appeared to *Veche*, we find that it consisted of three elements: Russia, China, and the West. Moreover, the functions of these elements are the same as the earlier three. Specifically, the 'living corpse' China threatens to disrupt not only the execution of Russia's historical mission but also her Orthodox renaissance, while the decaying West is preventing Russia from ridding herself of this threat. What is the strategy that logically follows from such a view of the world? Is it not exactly the same as the one that emerged from Danilevskii's doctrine? *Veche* proposed, it seems, not the pursuit of detente, but the acquisition of strength sufficient to prevent the West from interfering with the destruction of China and allow Russia an isolated and 'self-contained' existence apart from the rest of the world. (Certainly, this appears to be the strategy proposed, based on the most significant historical-philosophical essay published in *Veche*.)[13]

According to Danilevskii, Russia could not become Russia — that is, realize her 'idea' — without first disposing of the Ottoman empire. According to *Veche*, Russia cannot become Russia without disposing of the 'living corpse' of China. Thus it proved possible *to combine traditional Slavophile hostility toward the West with an anti-Chinese orientation*.[14] To transform Russia into a gigantic, 'closed', 'isolated' empire where no outsider would dare to meddle, an empire that would live by its own 'political formulas' as it patiently waited for the West to turn into ethnographic material suitable for acquisition —

such was the alternative to 'Europeanization' envisaged by the Old Russian Right in the 1870s. This could also be the Russian New Right alternative to detente in the 1970s, at least, that seems to be the meaning behind its essay on Danilevskii once it is decoded according to the traditional rules of the loyal opposition press in Russia.[15]

Imperial Liberalism

The Western reader may be shocked to learn that such a rigidly isolationist—imperialist plan for foreign policy could be put forward (even in coded form), not by the hawks of Russian nationalism but by its doves — people whom I sincerely consider the liberals of the 'patriotic' camp, and, more importantly, people who consider themselves liberals.[16] To understand this paradox, one must first understand the paradoxical nature of the liberal nationalist consciousness. It does not include the same parallels between foreign and internal policy which characterize the European way of thinking. We have already seen how *Veche* sharply distinguished these policies from one another; we shall further see how it also counterposed them to each other. This is not a distinction that has been introduced by the twentieth-century Russian Right: it is a tradition in which *Veche* once again follows Danilevskii's lead.

This tradition proceeds from the concept (here we are following *Veche*'s interpretation) that, in and of themselves, 'the political demands, or more accurately, the hopes, of the Russian people are extremely moderate, since . . . they do not see authority as an enemy but relate to it with complete trust.'[17] In other words, the character of the Russian people renders a political opposition out of the question. If, nevertheless, such opposition does exist, then it could only have come from abroad: 'everything we have which could be called parties depends on the intrusion of foreign and alien [*inorodcheskikh*] influences.'[18] The only conclusion that can be drawn from this is a recommendation to the government to close the country to foreign influence and eliminate those alien influences already there. When this is accomplished, it will immediately become evident that in Russian society 'no anti-state or anti-governmental interest whatever exists.'[19] Under these conditions, some relaxation in the areas of 'open government' and civil rights not only would be safe for the state, since (according to *Veche*'s interpretation of Danilevskii) it could never lead to political opposition, but would also be extremely useful to it, since 'lack of openness in government and of constitutional guarantees of human rights hinders the realization of national goals.'[20] In other words, the greater the degree of isolationism in foreign policy, the more liberalism can be permitted in Russia's internal policy; or, to put it another way, behind an Iron Curtain the Russian government could have absolute trust in its people. More importantly, 'the Russian periodical press, a power for good, is [under these circumstances] quite incapable of evil.'[21] These conclusions, we are told, are 'based on the following properties of the Russian person: his capacity for and habit of obedience, his respect for and trust in authority, his lack of a lust for power, and his distaste for interfering in matters where he does not consider himself competent.'[22]

As for inter-ethnic relations within the isolated empire, these too, according to *Veche*, could be liberal, because of the special and exceptional traits of the Russian people as an 'historical nation' and the nucleus of the Russian empire. Quoting Vladimir Solov'ev, *Veche* asserts, 'Russia is more than a people . . . The supra-ethnic significance of Russia can only flow out of the essence of the Russians as a people',[23] and, further, quoting Berdiaev, 'In the Russian nature there is, in fact, some kind of national unselfishness and willingness to sacrifice unknown to Western peoples.'[24] This explains why the Russian empire had nothing in common with despised Western colonialism:

> Russian history has been characterized by the voluntary union of peoples with Russia . . . If it can be said that the Russian empire was maintained by bayonets, this was true only in the sense that Russian bayonets defended the outlands from the claims of cruel neighbours. Russia knew how to instil love for herself and this was the secret of her power.[25]

In conclusion, 'whatever can be said about the role of non-Russians in the Russian Revolution', says *Veche*, 'or about the triumph of the non-Russian element in October . . . one thing can be firmly believed: the new Federation of Peoples [the USSR] was set up *in Russian style*.'[26]

Once again, we find the two negative models of multinational societies characteristic of all *Veche*'s thinking — the American and the Chinese — and the one positive model: the Russian. What is the American model? asks *Veche*, making use of Faulkner:

> A new nation? No, only 'a mass of people who no longer have anything in common save a frantic greed for money and a basic fear of a failure of national character which they hide behind a noisy lip-service to a flag'.[27]

What is the Chinese model? It is 'the destruction of every other [national] origin entirely',[28] and 'the compulsory Sinicization of the whole population of the country, by means of forced marriages.'

The Russian empire, however, is something altogether different. The dominance of the Russian historical nation is based on its moral supremacy over the 'ethnographic material' of the 'outlands'. If the outlands correctly understand their 'ethnographic' nature, they will feel themselves drawn toward the Russians as their historical centre and source of higher values: 'If the outlands see in the centre a concentration of culture higher than theirs, of higher . . . morality, national tolerance, kindness, and generosity, then they will be attracted to it voluntarily.'[29] In other words, so long as the opposition of the outlands does not take on a political coloration (and it will not be able to do so if 'foreign influences' at the centre are eliminated), *Veche* recommends the broadest possible cultural liberalism.[30]

As we see, *Veche* somehow succeeds — at least in theoretical terms — in reconciling the irreconcilable, preaching a rigid isolationism in foreign policy, combined with liberalism in internal affairs.

The Siberian Gambit

The liberal imperialist strategy of *Veche* rested on a profound faith in the potential supremacy of the Russian nation over the entire world.[31] Therefore, in *Veche*'s opinion, the Iron Curtain between Russia and the West is not an end in itself, but rather a means toward a social, moral and religious renaissance within Russia.

Veche's 'renaissance' plan, insofar as it can be assembled from isolated fragments, proceeded from the following postulates:

(1) 'A nation resettled into cities is doomed to extinction.'[32] 'All patriotism is inseparably linked to love for the land, for the sower and protector of the land, the peasant. All cosmopolitanism is equally inseparably linked to hatred of the peasantry — the creator and preserver of national traditions, the national morality and culture.' 'The peasant is the most morally unique type (M. Lobanov).'[33] From this viewpoint, the hopelessly urbanized West is doomed, but for Russia, 'where everyone has, if not a peasant mother, then at least a peasant grandmother', all is not yet lost. In Russia, *reverse migration*, or the ex-urbanization of society is still possible.

(2) 'Russia is to be saved by Orthodoxy. Russian Orthodoxy is indestructible. It is the work of God, and a Russian can only be Orthodox.'[34] In this respect too, the West is doomed, of course, but for Russia all is not yet lost: it is still possible to render her society Russian Orthodox — if not juridically, then at least *de facto*.

(3) The restoration of peasant and Orthodox Russia is what will finally eliminate 'cosmopolitanism' within the country and create an effective screen against the West, with its corrosive urbanization and faithlessness. But is this possible in authoritarian Soviet Russia — and if it is, then how? 'The Soviet regime, as history shows, is capable of making concessions when military or economic circumstances demand it, but is organically incapable of sacrificing itself for the sake of moral principles. It makes concessions only to preserve the main thing — power.'[35] Is it then possible to combine 'moral principles' with 'military circumstances'? These are the lines along which *Veche* was thinking. What could compel the Soviet regime to make such very difficult and far-reaching concessions? *Veche* could see only one such opportunity: preparation for war with China.

When Stalin formulated his five essential conditions for military victory, he ranked strengthening the home front number one, the *decisive* condition. Why this and not improving the quality of weapons, for instance, or increasing the number of divisions? Because Stalin was dominated by a fear of his own people — and fear continues to dominate the present Soviet leadership, who are graduates of the Stalinist academy. This way, 'strengthening the rear' is turned into a magic formula which *Veche* sought to use as a stimulus for the realization of its programme. When the most difficult war in Russian history begins, the Soviet army must have at its back, not a Siberian desert, but a strong home front united by a single faith — a rearguard that can transform Siberia into a Russian fortress, capable of withstanding the onslaught of the Chinese 'human sea', as it tries to 'roll in a dense wave over the empty spaces of Siberia', one that will be reinforced by the traditional patriarchal solidity of the Russian peasant soldier and his Orthodox religion. This is where the interests of all Russian patriots coincide.[36]

From this point of view, *Veche*'s proposal for creating a 'second Russia' in Siberia appears quite realistic. The need to create a strong rear will compel the regime, which is powerless to establish it by bureaucratic Soviet methods, to bring about the voluntary colonization of Siberia. 'Millions of zealots' led by 'priests deprived of their status, dissenters deprived of work and public careers'[37] would move on to unsettled lands in Siberia and transform them into a new Slavophile Atlantis; 'only Siberia can safeguard freedom, and the Fatherland, and Soviet aspirations.'[38]

(4) Hence, the division of Russia into urbanized European and peasant Siberian, Marxist European and Orthodox Siberian, forms the basis of *Veche*'s liberal utopia. It is a deliberate gambit. The new Asiatic Russia was supposed to sacrifice — if only for the time being — its European ancestor: 'Siberia can be settled only if there exists a rigid political counterweight in European Russia.'[39]

(5) The gradual influence — and success — of the 'second Russia' will one day change the situation in the European part of the country. A truly Russian renaissance — the creation of hitherto completely unknown forms of peasant Russian Orthodox civilization — would lead to the transformation of the whole country and ultimately to the triumph of the Russian 'cultural-historical type'.

All that would be needed, to make this happen, would be to awaken the Russian Orthodox peasant soul in the Soviet leaders, who, after all, also had 'if not a peasant mother, then at least a peasant grandmother' (and an Orthodox one at that). 'I do not think', Osipov declared, 'that there are no sobre minds within the Soviet state apparatus.'[40]

The Other Face of *Veche*

Experts may object that it was by no means only the isolationist doctrines of Danilevskii that inspired *Veche*, but also the messianic ideal of the Slavophiles and of Dostoevskii, and that the journal contains plenty of aggressive chauvinism and Black Hundreds material in the spirit of 'Chalmaevism', or even the National Socialism of Ivan Shevtsov.[41] All this is true, but these are objections that should be raised with *Veche*, and its 'liberal' face. The liberal nationalist plans of *Veche* which have been considered up to now not only did not constitute the whole of 'patriotic Russian' public opinion of the early 1970s, they were not even dominant in it. The most interesting statement of the 'messianic' point of view is Mikhail Antonov's article,

'The Slavophiles' Teachings — The Highest Flight of Popular National Self-Awareness in the Pre-Leninist Period', which *Veche* used to open its debate with its allies 'to the right'.[42]

Antonov saw it as part of his object to demonstrate the 'opposition between Western and Russian views . . . in all spheres of life'[43] and to expose the 'rootless cosmopolitanism' of the Russian (and Soviet) intelligentsia which acts as a harmful lobby for 'Western views'. He intended to show that, 'Leninism has incomparably more in common with Russian Orthodoxy and Slavophilism than with Marxism and Catholicism',[44] and therefore 'only *a union of Russian Orthodoxy with Leninism* can yield an adequate world-view of the Russian people which will synthesize the whole, centuries-long life-experience of the nation.'[45]

As we have seen, the liberal wing of *Veche* — following Danilevskii — regards the West as, so to speak, another species of the genus mankind. Therefore, provided there was an Iron Curtain, Russia would react to the West's 'decay' and its gradual transformation into 'ethnographic material' in a mainly contemplative way, with almost total indifference. Antonov relates to the West (and to the 'cosmopolitans' who represent it within Russia) with the undisguised hatred of a fanatical missionary calling for a crusade against infidels. For him, 'the people and states of the West have outlived their age and are dying . . . they shall inevitably soon perish; moreover, not by a sudden attack, but because its vital forces are drying up. They are tired of living; the whole West is in a blind alley.'[46]

The liberals of *Veche* (together with Danilevskii) would reply to it thus: if Antonov thinks that the Western peoples have a 'false world view . . . and they cannot in principle correctly conceive of the way out of their dead end',[47] such is the law of nature; we haven't the power either to help or to prevent it. Amen. Antonov, however, draws a very different conclusion. The 'false world-view' of the West seems to him so dangerous and infectious (almost like religion was for Lenin) that it draws the Russian people to the edge of the abyss as well. Why? He speaks of the 'organic properties of the English character, which render Anglican—Puritan circles eternal, incorrigible and sworn enemies of the Russian people.'[48] But the main danger — insofar as Antonov's rather incoherent article lends itself to rational interpretation — lies in the fact that these Anglican—Puritan circles are only a kind of executive organ for the 'false world-view', while its essence is to be found elsewhere. It is no coincidence that, 'the founder of all contemporary Western philosophy — that religion without faith — was the Jew Spinoza.' It is also no accident that, 'the roots of the materialistic tendency in philosophy go back to the depths of the Jewish ethnic character.'[49]

If one were to say that Danilevskii looked at the West as a 'dual foundation Romano-Germanic cultural-historical type', then Antonov regarded it as a 'dual-foundation Jewish-Puritanical cultural-historical type'. The trouble is that one of these types — the Jewish — has wormed its way into the very heart of Russia. It makes up the soul of the 'lumpen' whom Antonov despises (that is how, for some reason, Antonov refers to Russia's westernized intelligentsia, whom Lobanov before him called 'educated shopkeepers' and Solzhenitsyn after him called 'smatterers'). This 'lumpen' stubbornly destroys mother Russia day in and day out, before everyone's eyes. Thus she must begin ridding the world of this devil's seed by eliminating it first at home.

To initiate this process, Antonov needs not Osipov's feeble kind of loyalty, but an active alliance with the state — for the immediate restitution of the 'cosmopolitan campaign' that was interrupted by Stalin's death. A union of Leninism with Russian Orthodoxy is needed to form the foundation for a restoration of Stalinism in order to deal once and for all with the 'lumpen':

> At the present time, the same task arises in all areas of the life of the Russian people: to beat back the attack of rootless and cosmopolitan elements, to repel the Western forms, alien to its spirit, which have been foisted upon the people, and to return to age-old Russian origins, while assuring their further development.[50]

He says, along with Khomiakov, 'History calls upon Russia to take the lead in worldwide enlightenment.'[51] But this will come later, after Russia has put its own house in order and 'the idea of Moscow as the Third Rome, a New Jerusalem, the embodiment of Leninist higher Truth and Justice on earth' has become central in Russia's world view.[52] Then will come the turn of her world mission — to deal with the entire Jewish—Puritan 'lumpen' on a global scale.

All this theorizing and polemic must be gathered up, crumb by crumb, from a boring 99-page long article, overloaded with quotations, which unrelentingly revises the classic postulates of Slavophilism, transforming it from a peaceful, liberal utopian doctrine into a science of hatred. Antonov does not call for any intellectual sophistries, any civil rights, any 'second Russia'; he brings not peace, but a sword. Such was the other — Antonovist — face of *Veche*.

The Capitulation of National-liberalism

When we look at *Veche* from the point of view of this internal conflict, we discover quite a paradoxical situation. While a group of 'staff' political writers — highbrow liberals of the Osipovist school — were writing long, coded essays, skilfully formulating sophisticated historical analogies and developing complex plans for imperial liberalism and the 'Siberian gambit', their political constituency — i.e., their readership (and presumably followers) — were moved by quite different, 'Antonovist' visions and passions. It was not the idea of the Siberian gambit, but the problem of the 'aliens' that excited the reader who wrote the following: 'We Russians have become too used to hanging back, showing timidity, and effacing ourselves before *foreign ruffians*.'[53] It was not civil rights, but quite the contrary — nostalgia for Stalin — that prompted another reader to ask: 'Have you ever wondered why the Russian Orthodox Church was freer under Stalin? It is said that he even liked to talk to the Patriarch. Have you ever wondered why all the churches held services for Stalin? They didn't hold services for the others, but they did for him.'[54] It wasn't the idea of imperial liberalism, but a fanatical hatred for 'cosmopolitanism' that agitated a third reader: 'Cosmopolitanism is spiritual slavery . . . Cosmopolitanism prepares the way for the Antichrist.'[55] A fourth reader called not merely for loyalty to the Soviet regime, but for close alliance with it: 'Are Russian patriotism and a Marxist-Leninist world-view really incompatible? Didn't the soldiers ask to be considered Communists before giving their lives for the Motherland? Who would dare call them non-Russians?'[56] A fifth reader's letter, far from Danilevskii's contemplative view of the 'sick' West, proclaimed 'Europe is an incorrigible harlot, and America represents its final, most insane, nocturnal orgy, after which there can only be disillusionment and ruin.'[57]

Veche's own constituency was rebelling against its national-liberal course. It was calling openly and passionately for a Russo-patriotic Antonovist course of action: Bash the aliens and unite with the regime! In short, the constituency of 'Osipovist' *Veche* turned out, in fact, to be 'Antonovist'; the mood of the 'patriotic masses' had gone beyond the intellectual L-Nationalism it evinced.

Perhaps the saddest aspect of all this was that Osipov and his liberal collaborators blindly refused to recognize what was going on. When Osipov wrote that, 'Solzhenitsyn's letter, in its Slavophilism and patriarchal mood, will perhaps strike a deeper chord in the Russian heart than the democratic alternatives of the intellectuals',[58] he was unaware that he was signing his own death warrant. The Osipov who stated that, 'even the problem of civil rights in the USSR is less important . . . than the problem of the dying Russian nation'[59] was vanquishing the Osipov who, as ideologist of the loyal opposition, had generously extended his hand to Sakharov. The time of the VSKhSON had passed. Liberalism and nationalism were no longer compatible within the 'patriotic' heart. A choice had to be made one way or the other, the same choice Ivan Aksakov had been compelled to make a century earlier. There was still 'no middle ground' for a Russian nationalist in a critical situation. The Old Slavophiles learned this the hard way in the 1870s. In the 1970s, it was the new generation's turn. Those who could not make this choice were doomed politically — as Osipov discovered. He had perished — along with *Veche*'s liberal wing — even before the KGB arrested him.

The best evidence of his coming demise is to be found in readers' letters to his own journal. But these were only the mild examples of criticism from 'below'. The truly big guns are to be found in an article entitled 'Critical Notes of a Russian Man', which Osipov didn't even dare to print and whose anonymous author, in the course of attacking the contradictions of national-liberalism, openly accused *Veche* of 'anti-patriotism' and 'treason against all that is truly Russian and Slavic'.[60]

The 'Critical Notes of a Russian Man'

The main thing the author of the 'Notes' demanded of *Veche* was logical consistency. If cosmopolitanism truly is the worst crime against the Russian people and humanity, then how can one fail to point out that its source is the cosmopolitan nature of Christianity itself? How can one demand a rehabilitation of Russian Orthodoxy if Orthodoxy itself has historically 'played the role of Judas in relation to both *Autocracy* and the Russian nationalist consciousness or, as the Slavophiles called it, *Nationality* [narodnost']'?[61] How can one forget about the 'traitorous role of Russian Orthodox cosmopolitanism, which paved the way for the Zionist cosmopolitans of our day'? 'If anyone now needs to rehabilitate Russian Orthodoxy', the argument proceeded, 'then first and foremost it is those who created it — the Zionists.'[62] Here, of course, the author trots out ideas from the

Protocols of the Elders of Zion and presents them as irrefutable documentary support for his position.

> For themselves, they created Judaism, according to which mankind is divided into people (only the Jews) and Goys . . . For the Goys, Christianity and Islam were created — sister subsidiaries of Judaism Ltd., called upon to keep all other peoples obedient before a master race or people, chosen by God (i.e., the Jews). The Goys, according to the Old Testament, are supposed to become slaves of the Jews by the year 2000.[63]

From this vantage point, it naturally follows that:

> One's attitude toward Zionism is the litmus test which reveals either patriotism or treason. There is no in-between! Who is not with us is against us! Who is not against Zionism in all its manifestations is against the Russians, against the Slavophiles, and against everything honest on this earth. In light of this, a journal, if it really wants to make itself *Patriotic* and *Russian*, rather than a bath-house dressing-room for Zionist dissidents, their unpaid agent, must seek to clarify that the main link in the entire chain of problems facing the Russian people is the struggle against Zionist domination. Once we have taken hold of this link (and only this one) it will be possible to pull the whole chain of problems straight. If we do not do this, by the year 2000 the Zionists will *physically* exterminate the Russian people along with all our problems.[64]

From the author's point of view, the dilemma is simple: a dramatic, mortal confrontation is going on in the world between Russia and Zionism. They cannot coexist on the same planet. A Russian patriotic journal, worthy of the name, cannot maintain its neutrality in this conflict. *Veche*, in the author's viewpoint, is trying to do just this.

> How can a Russian [believe in *Veche*'s patriotism] when this journal offers its pages to such sworn enemies of the Russians and Russia as A. Sakharov and A. Solzhenitsyn? . . . This journal mourns, together with the Zionist samizdat, for Yurii Galanskov . . . But who was Galanskov fighting for? For the same wicked enemies of Russia and the Russians — the Zionists, [he was fighting to get hold of] the records of the trials of Zionist agents clad in the sheep's clothing of dissidents — Siniavsky and Daniel. It is a disgrace to the journal to reprint the declarations of A. Sakharov, Shafarevich and the other assorted Zionist packs of scientists and pseudo-scientists who wail for freedom of the press . . . There, where this has been formally achieved (the US,

England and other Western countries) the press is fully monopolized by
Zionists. What kind of freedom of the press is that? No, better our
Glavlit [Soviet censorship office] than that kind of freedom![65]

For whom is *Veche* working, the author goes on to ask. For Russia or
her enemies?

The Zionist dissidents, with the state sponsorship of the US Congress
and the governments of the other Western countries infected by Zionism,
try by various means to undermine us from within, in order to pave the
way for the children of Israel's world domination. Is this *Russian
Patriotic* journal on the same path as them? *Communism* and the *Soviet
Regime* (the whole socialist system) are now the only powerful barrier
standing in the way of Zionism's march to its year 2000. The Russian
people go their way, in the vanguard of the USSR and, consequently, of
the whole socialist system. Without question, it is difficult for Russians
to accept the chains of Zionist domination, but it is still harder for them
to accept other Russians who stab them in the back . . . still harder
when Russians professing the best of motives endeavour to put together
a samizdat journal and then beat the trusting Russian folk over the
head with a rock.[66]

The hysterical tone of the passage is unimportant. What matters is
that it clearly demonstrates how, in the 1970s, 'Russian patriotic
consciousness' proved a Procrustean bed for liberalism (even the
imperial sort). Neither naive faith in the possibility of freedom of
speech behind the Iron Curtain ('the drive for objectivity and so-called
freedom of speech leads to granting pages to full- as well as half-breed
Zionists'[67]), nor the idea of de-urbanization and de-industrialization
('We are not alone on the planet. If the Russian people reduce
production, the Zionists will smother them'[68]), nor liberal Slavophilism
('had they [the Slavophiles] lived in our time, they wouldn't have
sought to rise up against the existing ideology and form of rule, but
probably would have tended to defend them for the good of the
Russian people'[69]) — none of these find room here. The 'patriotic'
reader has to be given a completely different idea of what constitutes a
truly Russian journal.

[It ought] to publish materials about the worthlessness of the scientific
works of Zionist pseudo-scientists. (Such efforts are already underway.
The theoretical physicist Tiapkin is in the process of proving that the
Einstein cult was created by the talentless Jews in order to raise their
scientific prestige. The same has been supported by Shevtsov.) To
publish materials about Zionist attacks against honest Russian people

. . . materials about the corruption and decadence of Zionists, materials about their mob gatherings outside synagogues . . . letters from the provinces about the outrages committed by internal emigres, about the usurpation of housing in cities . . . demand the just distribution of apartments for the benefit of the native population, pose questions to the organs of the office of the public prosecutor about the money Zionist elements use to acquire cars, dachas and so forth, pose questions about why in this or that office 70 or 90 per cent [of the employees] are Jews, demand that the percentage of Jewish youths admitted to institutions of higher education be in accordance with the percentage of Jews living in the country (about one per cent).

Demand that this one per cent be dispersed among all institutions and enterprises and under the slogan of equality for all, no advantages for those who could end up in Israel tomorrow.

Recognize that the journal [Veche] . . . had a vague and objectively pro-Zionist platform. Materials of an anti-Zionist character lent the journal merely the appearance of objectivity . . . Therefore against its will the journal compromised itself as an accomplice of the Zionists.

Set out under the banner: 'Death to the Zionist Invaders!' or 'All Hands to the Struggle Against Zionism!'

The journal ought to be oriented not toward the religious believers, who will not save Russia from Zionism by their prayers, not toward scum like Sakharov and Solzhenitsyn who need cosmopolitanism more than [they need] the Russian people . . . [but] toward honest party and Soviet workers and members of the military, toward patriotically-minded cultural and artistic figures . . . and other Soviet people, Communists and non-party members [alike] who carry weight with the administration.[70]

Isn't it obvious that, with such a programme, the 'patriotic' reader would need, not a *Veche*, but a *Russkii golos*, not Vladimir Osipov, but Sergei Sharapov, not opposition to the regime, but alliance with it, not national-liberalism, but a call for pogroms? To its misfortune, *Veche* had opened a Pandora's box. Among the savage winds that issued forth, none was sympathetic. They all blew hard against *Veche*. They beat it to ground and condemned it to death — even before the KGB intervened.

Orthodox and Heathens . . .

A fellow-traveller of the Russian nationalists, M. Agurskii, who published the 'Critical Notes of a Russian Man' in an emigre journal, prefaced them with his own critical remarks under the title 'The Neo-

Nazi Danger in the USSR'. He wrote: 'Soviet racism comes out not as atheism, but as a new form of heathenism, like [the way] National Socialism appeared . . . It seems utterly obvious that the sole realistic alternative for those who really do wish to regenerate Russian life on a new basis would be the acceptance . . . of that humanitarian program which Solzhenitsyn proposed in his *Letter to the Leaders*.'[71] In other words, Agurskii counterposes the good Christian nationalists to the bad 'heathen' ones. We have heard this argument already from Dunlop. To his misfortune, Agurskii tries to be a little more precise. As an example, he names, along with Solzhenitsyn, 'such Russian Christian nationalists as . . . the Archdeacon Varsonofii'.[72]

We will discuss Solzhenitsyn's programme a bit later. As for the archdeacon, he appears to be a co-author of the so-called 'Letter of the Three'. In terms of its Black Hundreds-style ferocity, this letter was fully comparable with the 'Critical Notes of a Russian Man', but, in contrast to the latter, it was published by Osipov himself, at *Veche*'s very beginning (issue No. 3, 1971).[73]

Before discussing the content of this letter however, it is worth relating one episode connected with it which shows to what degree the editors of *Veche* — or at least its liberal wing — failed, until the very end, to understand both how far they were estranged from their constituency and the dramatic nature of the warning they received. In his article 'The Rebirth of Russian Nationalism in Samizdat',[74] Pospelovsky described the 'Letter of the Three' as a sinister document, a deviation in the direction of nationalistic and religious racism. The editors of *Veche* responded. They repudiated Pospelovsky's judicious criticism (or even, if you will, the tactful concern he showed for them). They ridiculed him unrestrainedly, assuring not only their readers but also (it would seem) themselves that this foreign observer was talking about trifles not worthy of attention: 'A single phrase provoked the indignation and all the accusations directed at the journal: in the preamble of the letter, the word "Zionism" is connected by the conjunction "and" with the word "Satanism".'[75] A venial sin! It is not surprising that over the course of two years the journal found no opportunity to distance itself from such a trifle — a mere slip of the pen. However, I shall let my reader judge for him- or herself who was right in this argument, and how good a Christian nationalist Agurskii's hero is, from the following extract from the Letter:

We must not be silent when the growing danger from the organized forces of broad Zionism and Satanism have become obvious to all. . . . The agents of Zionism and Satanism . . . are artificially creating friction

between the Church and the State with the aim of weakening both . . .
and are trying to poison society, particularly the intelligentsia and the
young people, with ideas of anarchic liberalism and amoralism, and to
destroy the very foundations of morality, the family, and the state.[76]

Thus it is not disagreement in principle, much less antagonism,
between the atheistic state and the Russian Orthodox Church which
creates the conflict between them, but the machinations of an *external
force*. (It should be noted that 'conflict' is not spoken of in the letter,
but is replaced by the euphemism 'friction' — and that even this
friction is created 'artificially.') This external force is called by name:
'Zionism and Satanism'. Even if there were no conjunction 'and',
would this actually make such a difference? This sinister force, by
nature anti-Orthodox, simultaneously wages a 'hidden struggle against
our state from within and without'.[77] In other words, the Soviet state
and the Russian Orthodox Church have a common enemy.

But the authors of the letter assert that there is also a more positive
reason for the proposed alliance between church and state: they share
common goals. The goal of the church ('the salvation of mankind from
sin and its consequences') is essentially the same, in their view, as
that of the Soviet state ('the struggle against the forces of destruction
and chaos'). If, however, the goals of the Soviet state (which is
represented in its 'struggle against the forces of destruction and chaos'
by a special agency commonly known as the KGB) coincide with those
of the Russian Orthodox church, and if they have a common enemy,
then does not their alliance amount to a kind of division of labour
between them? What cannot be done by the physical sword of the
KGB can be done by the church, as the 'moral force and bulwark of
the state in its noble struggle'.[78]

The letter also considered what might happen if the state and the
church do *not* unite in this struggle. Here the authors present a
hideous picture of wild excesses by 'agents' both inside Russia and 'in
the Zionist centres of the countries of the West, primarily the USA,
where the church of Satan functions'.[79] These 'agents', of course, 'are
trying to corrupt our people.' Not only are they poisoning people's
minds with 'cosmopolitanism' and 'doubts regarding all spiritual and
national values' (as reported by the Young Guards and Antonov), but
in addition they are responsible for 'spreading perversion and
drunkenness' and even for 'the increase in abortions'. But the list of
their offences does not end there: they also encourage 'indifference
towards the execution of family, parental and patriotic duties' as well
as promoting 'hypocrisy, faithlessness, lies, money-grubbing and all
other vices'.[80]

Clearly, absolutely everything bad that takes place in the USSR results from the fact that the KGB has not exercised adequate surveillance over the 'agents' of Zionism and Satanism. This is not because the KGB is not vigilant enough (perish the thought!), but because it does not have the church as a reliable and faithful ally and to act as a 'bulwark'. Hence it is as clear as day that, 'one of the primary tasks of our time is to search *for practical means of convergence* [of the church] *with the state*'.[81]

How far the Russian Right had come in less than a decade! It no longer called, as VSKhSON did, for 'the destruction of the oligarchy's security forces'. On the contrary, the authors of the 'Letter of the Three' publicly offer themselves as assistants to those same secret police. But most importantly, this letter came from people who are by no stretch of the imagination heathens, but good servants of the Russian Orthodox church, and it was signed by the same Archdeacon Varsonofii whom Arguskii contrasts with the 'heathen' author of the 'Critical Notes'.

All these views were taken up by the editors of *Veche*, who, in one of their *last* issues, rebuffed Pospelovsky and excused the letter's invectives against 'Zionism and Satanism' as a slip of the tongue, or at worst a grammatical error. But it was no error; it was policy — the militant policy of the Black Hundreds, the alternative to the national-liberal programme of *Veche*. This was now the policy within *Veche* — no longer outside it. Verily, two souls lived in the soul of one: its rebuttal of Pospelovsky was *Veche*'s testimonial to its own capitulation.

Summary of *Veche*

(1) The transition from an open political confrontation with the regime (possible in the USSR only in the form of an underground anti-governmental organization — e.g., the VSKhSON) to the status of a loyal opposition, i.e., the first revision of L-National-ism.[82]

(2) The adoption as the basis for this revision of the postulate that the USSR is potentially in the same situation as Nazi Germany, that is, facing struggle on two fronts — against the West and China.

(3) The consequent division of *Veche*'s political position into two parts: passive opposition to the regime's internal policy and active support of it 'in the face of the external threat'.

(4) An attempt to work out a 'Siberian gambit' as an imperial-isolationist strategy alternative, combining the anti-Western

tendencies of the Russian New Right with an anti-Chinese orientation.

(5)   An attempt by means of this isolationist strategy to preserve the basic values of national liberalism. This effort ended in the split of the editorial board into a liberal 'Osipovist' faction, which limited its support of the regime to the area of foreign policy, and a 'Russo-patriotic' one, which strove to develop the pre-conditions for total collaboration with the regime.

(6)   The realization by the Russo-patriotic faction of the impossibility of combining nationalism with liberalism and a call for the renewal of the 'cosmopolitan campaign' as the ideological basis for restoring dictatorship.

Notes

1   Of course *Veche* declared itself an organ of the 'loyal opposition' and promised not to touch upon political matters. It proceeded from the premise that, 'we must convince the administration that the existence of a loyal opposition does not harm the Soviet state, but is of benefit to it.' *Veche* was supposed to be of benefit to the regime for the following reasons: 1. 'A loyal opposition is a defence against the self-perpetuating bureaucracy from whose arbitrary action the leaders' suffer no less than working people . . .' 2. '[This opposition] guards against the possibility of the emergence of a personal dictatorship.' (*Vol'noe slovo*, Posev publishers, No. 17 – 18, p. 6). Nine issues of the journal under the editorship of Vladimir Osipov appeared between January 1971 and March 1974, after which a bitter struggle within the editorial board resulted in a split accompanied by strident accusations and counter-accusations. Osipov and V. Radionov issued two numbers of a new journal, *Zemlia* [Soil], while A. Skuratov and I. Ovchinnikov put out the tenth issue of *Veche*. By the end of 1974, *Veche* and *Zemlia* had ceased to exist. At that time Osipov was arrested, and later sentenced to eight years detention. There is an interesting coincidence here that, to the best of my knowledge, has gone unnoticed by Western observers: the KGB embarked upon its suppression of *Veche* in 1973, at the same time as the influence of Polianskii and the Establishment Right began to decline.

2   Hardly any Western observer doubted the liberal nationalism of Osipov. See, for example, the article by D. Pospelovsky (*Survey* 1, 1973, p. 64). See also the statements by Osipov himself in *Veche* No. 1 (*Arkhiv Samizdata* [hereafter cited as AS], No. 1013) and No. 7 (*Vol'noe slovo*, No. 17 – 18) or his protest against the accusation of anti-semitism in an interview with Dean Mills, Moscow correspondent of the *Baltimore Sun* (*Vestnik RKhD*, No. 106, 1972).

3   Osipov started in on this task with the following graphically eloquent passage: 'The specific character of the Chinese threat consists not in its

military potential, but in the enormous advantage of geographical position and human reserves. Our surplus military potential shackles our own feet. We cannot make a move in an Eastern war. When the Chinese say that they will drown the enemy in a human sea, they are by no means bragging. This sea is always increasing, and with each year the hour comes closer when it will overflow and come rolling [towards us] in a dense wave across the wide open spaces of Siberia' (*Vol'noe slovo*, No. 17—18, p. 9). On 25 April 1972, in an interview with Associated Press correspondent Stevens Browning, Osipov spoke of the necessity of 'the appeal to a national ideology': 'In the face of the advancing threat from Communist China and the unceasing enmity of cosmopolitan capital, Russian society does not wish to show itself ideologically impotent' (*AS*, No. 1599, p. 14).

4   *Vol'noe slovo*, No. 9—10, p. 9.

5   Ibid., p. 31.

6   Ibid., p. 11.

7   The denial of universal morality flowed directly from the rejection of the concept of world civilization. Why should lizards sacrifice themselves for the sake of fish? Danilevskii's pupil Konstantin Leont'ev spoke of this even more openly: 'There are no humane states . . . They are ideas, embodied in a certain social structure. Ideas do not have humane hearts; they are merciless and cruel' (K. Leont'ev, *Sobranie sochinenii*, v. 5, p. 38). I do not contend that in their day-to-day activities states are guided by philanthropic principles, but they at least do not try to make a virtue out of necessity.

8   *Vol'noe slovo*, No. 9—10, p. 18.

9   Ibid., p. 22.

10 Ibid., p. 36.

11 Ibid., p. 37.

12 It is significant that it was not until the fourth edition of *Russia and Europe*, in 1889, that the book became really popular. This was after the 1878 Congress of Berlin (as well as Alexander III's nationalist counter-reform in 1881), when Europe had, so to speak, robbed Russia of the fruits of her victory over Turkey in the Russo—Turkish War (1877—8) — thus repeating by diplomatic means the outcome of the Crimean War (1853—6). That would also explain the unusual popularity of Danilevskii in the 1880s — he had proved to be a prophet, essentially predicting the results of the Berlin Congress.

13 The importance *Veche* assigned to the essay on Danilevskii was clearly emphasized in its response to Pospelovsky's article in *Survey* (1973, No. 1): 'As to national messianism, we would like to note the following. Besides the early Slavophiles and Dostoevskii, who really preached this idea, there was also in Slavophilism N. Ya. Danilevskii, who repudiated any [form of] national messianism . . . In issue No. 6 of *Veche*, there was an article on the views of Danilevskii which Pospelovsky, unfortunately, did not read' (*Vol'noe slovo*, No. 17—18, p. 169). There can hardly be any doubt that in this passage the 'isolationist-pragmatic' ideologists of *Veche* are defending their position, not so much from Pospelovsky as from the pressure of their own 'messianist' readers. Answering Pospelovsky could only be an excuse for them to respond to forces much

more dangerous to *Veche* than *Survey*. In any case, it is clear that *Veche* did not want to identify itself with the 'messianists'.

14   It is interesting to note that *Veche*'s interpretation of Danilevskii was entirely original. In any event, it decisively differs from the generally accepted Western academic interpretation expressed by Robert E. MacMaster in his *Danilevskii: A Russian Totalitarian Philosopher* (Harvard University Press, 1967). MacMaster focuses on the 'war element' in Danilevskii's teachings and downplays the decisive 'isolationist element', thereby depriving himself of the opportunity to reconcile Danilevskii's 'liberalism' with his 'totalitarianism'. MacMaster fails to see even the existence of 'imperial liberalism'. It is true that Danilevskii predicted a ferocious struggle between Russia and Europe over Constantinople. For *Veche*, of course, the problem of Constantinople no longer existed. Therefore they shifted the 'war element' to the Sino—Soviet border and thus depicted it as only a fragment in Danilevskii's overall isolationist strategy. There is a certain irony in the fact that *Veche*'s interpretation, in spite of its openly political and clearly non-scholarly goals, is in a position to explain Danilevskii's liberalism much more logically — and convincingly — than MacMaster's purely academic approach.

15   I, for one, who for many years worked in this press and wrote dozens of articles in its Aesopian language, cannot find any other meaning in this essay. Furthermore, the same thing can be proved by purely deductive methods. In an important programmatic declaration, Osipov promised, on the one hand, 'loyalty to the existing system', and on the other, 'support for the state in the face of external threats' (*Vol'noe slovo*, No. 20, p. 6). As we can see, in the field of foreign policy he did not intend to confine himself to passive loyalty. In another programmatic declaration, Osipov stated: 'Whether the existing system is viable or whether it is doomed to a transitory role . . . the position of Russian patriots remains unchanged, since we will not take upon ourselves the boldness or the impudence to oppose our own social plan to that of the existing system . . . We remember that no matter how the political destiny of Russia may have developed, national interests are primary, supra-social, and eternal' (ibid., No. 17—18, p. 15). This means that, unlike VSKhSON, *Veche* did not intend to propose an alternative to the Soviet order (as a social system). Nevertheless, Osipov's declaration leaves open the field of strategic recommendations — i.e., the proposal of foreign policy alternatives which might promote the realization of the 'primary' national interests. From this standpoint, three possible alternative strategies emerge in the concept advanced by the author of the article on Danilevskii: (a) Russia may agree to stay just one among the great powers of the contemporary world (in the final analysis, this is what detente with the West leads to); (b) Russia may seek world domination (this is what the founders of Marxism suspected Russia of seeking: 'Panslavism', wrote Engels, 'is a fraudulent plan of struggle for world domination' [Marx and Engels, *Sochinenia*, v. I, p. 185], and it is why — such are the ironies of history ! — Marx and Engels were fanatical proponents of a general European crusade against Russia; in the modern parlance, they were certainly hawks); (c) Russia may seek to establish an 'isolated' empire

over most of the Eurasian mainland, as Danilevskii suggested (this empire — a federation, according to Danilevskii — 'must embrace all countries and peoples from the Adriatic to the Pacific Ocean and from the Arctic Ocean to the Archipelago . . . under the leadership and hegemony of an integral and unified Russian state' (*Vol'noe slovo*, No. 15, p. 38)). With which of these alternative strategies does *Veche*'s sympathy lie? It rejects (a), following Danilevskii's argument that, 'Russia is too great and mighty to be only one among the great European powers' (ibid., p. 37). It considers (b) (again following Danilevskii) to be unnatural — that is, not in accordance with the theory of 'cultural-historical types'. What is left then but the imperial—isolationist strategy (c)?

16 In the same interview with Stevens Browning, to the question 'What is your attitude toward the "democratic movement"?', Osipov replied, 'Very sympathetic. *Veche* and the "democrats" jointly embody the Slavophile principles on internal policy — national and liberal.' (*AS*, No. 1599, p. 16).

17 *Vol'noe slovo*, No. 15, p. 27.

18 Ibid.

19 Ibid.

20 Ibid., No. 20, p. 5.

21 Ibid., No. 15, p. 27.

22 Ibid., p. 28.

23 Ibid., No. 17—18, p. 27.

24 *AS*, No. 1599, p. 7.

25 *Vol'noe slovo*, No. 17—18, p. 26.

26 *AS*, No. 1599, p. 6. Emphasis added.

27 Ibid., Unable to find this quotation from Faulkner, I asked my readers, in the footnotes to *The Russian New Right*, for assistance. Josef Skvorecky from Toronto informs me that it comes from the novel *Intruder in the Dust* (Modern Library College Edition, p. 156) and is spoken, not by Faulkner, but by one of his characters, the lawyer Gavin Stevens. I would like to take this opportunity to thank Mr Skvorecky as well as the many other readers who responded to my request.

28 Ibid.

29 *Vol'noe slovo*, No. 17—18, p. 27.

30 As far as traditional 'Great Russian nationalism', which could serve as a barrier to such liberalization, is concerned, in *Veche*'s view, it simply does not exist nor ever did. The Russian empire never was a 'prison of peoples', as the liberal and Marxist myth holds. On the contrary, it was always a fraternal union of nations which were attracted to Russia because of the protection she offered them against their greedy neighbours. The only basis for the myth about Russia as a 'prison of peoples' were the 'foreign admixtures' — the Germans, Poles and Georgians, who ruled the empire from time to time: 'Is it appropriate to speak of a Great Russian nationalism? Is it truly Russian? Who were its bearers? The bureaucratic apparatus of the post-Petrine monarchy, saturated through and through with Germans? Djugashvili and Dzerzhinskii?' (*AS*, No. 1599, p. 9).

31 The discussion is once again about the old Slavophile conviction that the

moral superiority of the Russian people consists in their apolitical character.

32   *Vol'noe slovo*, No. 17−18, p. 30.
33   Ibid., p. 29.
34   *AS*, No. 1013, p. 51.
35   *Vol'noe slovo*, No. 17−18, pp. 10−11.
36   I have no doubt that *Veche*'s fear of China was absolutely sincere. One of the members of the editorial board grimly told me in private how he dreamt at night of the Chinese in Siberia. Thus, did *Veche* not only try to manipulate the Soviet leaders' fear of the Chinese menace, but they themselves were scared to death of it.
37   *Vol'noe slovo*, No. 17−18, p. 9.
38   Ibid., p. 10.
39   Ibid. Subsequently, as the reader will see, Alexander Solzhenitsyn was to borrow this pivotal proposal of *Veche*'s and publish it (without citation, unfortunately) in his well-known *Letter to the Leaders* — a fact which, as far as I know, has not been noted by any of his biographers.
40   *Vol'noe slovo*, No. 17−18, p. 10.
41   To cite only one example: 'You can argue with Shevtsov about the evaluation of the force and role of Zionism in the USSR, but what does hostility toward the intelligentsia have to do with it? Are Zionists the only intellectuals in present-day Russia? Isn't Shevtsov himself the same kind of intellectual as . . . the active membership of the Communist Party, or the Soviet government?' (ibid., p. 46). For more detail on the doctrine of I. Shevtsov, see my *Detente After Brezhnev* (pp. 51−5). See also the statement of the editors of *Veche* (in response to a letter by Mikhail Agurskii) in which 'the conquests of Peter and Catherine' are described as 'the restoration of Russian lands usurped by Sweden and Poland' (*Vol'noe slovo*, No. 17−18, p. 148). What is being referred to here is the seizure of the Baltic area and the partition of Poland. In addition, Soviet Jews are blamed for 'living under the best material conditions' and 'claiming a privileged position in . . . Russia' (ibid., pp. 149−50).
42   M. Antonov was a member of the so-called Fetisovist group, which was openly pro-Stalinist and pro-Fascist, and which was usually included by observers in the 'national Bolshevist' tendency. Antonov's lengthy article took up a considerable portion of the first three issues of *Veche*. At the end, the editors added the caveat that 'the personal opinions of the author differ to a considerable degree from those of the editorial board,' and printed an article entitled 'An Opponent's Opinion' which criticized certain of Antonov's conclusions. Nevertheless, the fact that the editors of *Veche* found it possible to give Antonov's article such prominence; that they did not raise any questions concerning the author's view of the 'West', which constituted the core of his analysis; and, finally, that they described Antonov as 'a follower and propagandist of the ideas of the remarkable Russian scholar and public figure A. A. Fetisov' (*AS*, No. 1013, p. 45), shows that the Antonov's views represented such a strong sector of 'patriotic Russian' public opinion that it was impossible for *Veche* to ignore. (Fetisov was a man who left the Communist Party in protest against de-Stalinization.)
43   *AS*, No. 1013, p. 25.

44 Ibid., No. 1108, p. 45.
45 Ibid., p. 39. Emphasis added. Lenin wrote the following about religion: 'Any idea about any godling, or any flirtation with a godling, is the most inexpressible rottenness . . . the most dangerous rottenness, the vilest kind of infection' (*O religii i tserkvi*, [On religion and Church.] Moscow: 1977, p. 31). On this basis I appeal to the reader to consider the mind-boggling complexity of the task which — through Antonov — the Russian New Right, for the first time, set itself, in seeking this union of Orthodoxy with Leninism. Personally, of course, Antonov met with complete failure, but his idea is alive and well in the 'patriotic masses' and in the minds of its ideologists. Who can know what metapmorphoses and forms of expression lay ahead for it? If its real essence lies in a detente between what I have termed the Soviet welfare system of economics and the Russian Orthodox Church, then why should this not be realizable? Serfdom is theoretically incompatible with Christianity; nevertheless, a functioning detente between the two managed to work in Russia for a few centuries.
46 *AS*, No. 1013, pp. 26—7.
47 Ibid., No. 1020, p. 18.
48 Ibid., No. 1013, p. 22.
49 Ibid., p. 23.
50 Ibid., No. 1108, p. 37.
51 Ibid., No. 1013, p. 19.
52 Ibid., No. 1108, p. 38.
53 Ibid., No. 1140, p. 168. Emphasis added.
54 Ibid., No. 1013, p. 15.
55 Ibid., No. 1020, p. 32.
56 *Vol'noe slovo*, No. 9—10, p. 184.
57 Ibid., p. 190. It would be possible to extract from a number of other readers' letters quotes ranging from simple information ('Dear Sir: I want to call the attention of the readers of your journal to the Catholic danger in Russia, which has been growing as the contemporary elements of cosmopolitanism more and more seduce the consciousness of the Russian Orthodox people' (*AS*, No. 1140, p. 166)) to something like a philosophical tract ('The theory of a state based on the rule of law is by its origins exclusively pro-Western . . . The essence of the theory is in the separation and opposition of legislative and executive authority, which, in the opinion of theorists, leads to the democratization of the state. In practice such a separation results not in democratization, but instability . . . [and] perfect nonsense . . . Such a dialectic is not in the spirit of traditional Russian jurisprudence . . . [which favours] the concentration in one state organ of both the legislative and executive functions' (*AS*, No. 1108, pp. 157—8)) to romantic reminiscences ('"For the faith, the tsar and the fatherland!" . . . this cry was the most sacred and most selfless. With it they died and hoped to receive the Kingdom of God . . . Remember the last war? "For the Motherland, for Stalin — forward!" And that too was sacred' (*AS*, No. 1013, p. 49)) and finally solemn prophecy ('It approacheth, the *Pax Russica* is already at the doors!' (*AS*, No. 1230, p. 159)). But the general tone and direction of *Veche*'s reader mail did not, as we see, vary very much.
58 *Vol'noe slovo*, No. 17—18, p. 3.

59 *Vestnik RKhD*, No. 106, p. 295.
60 *Novyi zhurnal*, No. 118, 1975, p. 227.
61 Ibid., p. 220. Capital letters are the author's throughout.
62 Ibid., p. 221.
63 Ibid.
64 Ibid., p. 223.
65 Ibid., p. 222.
66 Ibid., p. 227.
67 Ibid., p. 224.
68 ??
69 Ibid., pp. 221—2.
70 Ibid., pp. 223—4.
71 Ibid., p. 202—3.
72 Ibid., p. 202.
73 'Petition to the Regional Synod, 1971', signed by the Priest G. Petukhov, the Archdeacon Varsonofii Khaibulin, and the layman Fomin.
74 *Survey*, No. 1, 1973.
75 *Vol'noe slovo*, No. 17—18, p. 166.
76 *AS*, No. 1108, p. 63.
77 Ibid., p. 64.
78 Ibid.
79 Ibid., p. 64.
80 Ibid., pp. 63—4.
81 Ibid., p. 64.
82 Documentary confirmation of this is provided by Osipov's declaration: 'Having in the past been an active oppositionist, I have now abandoned political confrontation with the regime, at the same time hoping that the regime will not destroy me for my activity in the interest of national culture' (*Vestnik RKhD*, No. 106, p. 295).

12
Enter Fascism:
The Nation Speaks

The 'Deficiencies of "Our Wise Men"'

While *Veche* was agonizing under pressure from its own readership's 'patriotic' passions, *Slovo Natsii* [The Nation Speaks], a 'Russian patriots' manifesto',[1] appeared in the samizdat to sum up the mood of the 'patriotic masses' in the late 1960s and early '70s.

This manifesto not only attacked Osipov's liberal sympathies, but also ridiculed the theoretical basis of VSKhSON's programme. The anonymous 'Russian patriots' who were the signatories saw both as merely 'theatrical thunder and lightning addressed to the bureaucratic elite'.[2] The manifesto goes on:

> You say this elite neither represents the people nor any class of society, it represents only itself. But hold on there! Such thoughts have already been expressed at one time by someone who, admittedly, was not one of the best minds — P. N. Tkachev. This discovery worthy of Copernicus, that the Russian government supposedly hangs in the air and is supported by nothing but itself, by rights belongs to him. In his time, Engels justifiedly mocked this discovery, but perhaps now the situation has changed and what was untrue has become true? Alas, this has not happened. As before, in the reasoning of our wise men there are glaring deficiencies.[3]

The reader, who is already familiar with the VSKhSON programme will, of course, know which 'wise men' are being referred to. When we read further that, 'Democratic institutions do not carry with them the cure, but more likely the opposite, they aggravate the illness',[4] and compare this with *Veche*'s reader mail, we are forced to ask ourselves, Isn't the time of the ideologists of the VSKhSON and Osipov variety

— and, indeed, of imperial liberalism in twentieth-century Russia well and truly past? In reality, the 'patriotic masses' consistently supported the 'heathens' over 'our wise men'.

On the Path to 'Worldwide Disintegration'

'The main threat,' the manifesto said, 'as yet understood by hardly anyone, remains a general one: degeneration, caused by biological factors that act faster the less attention is paid to them, is persistently eating away at the threadbare pseudo-truth about the primacy of so-called social factors over biological ones.'[5] Moreover, 'Democracy, in its egalitarian form, is one of the consequences of degeneration and at the same time its stimulus.'[6] Spineless Western democracy has brought misfortune to the world. It has let the genie out of the bottle: the yellow and black races, whose liberation from colonial dependence 'indicates only the degeneration of once mighty peoples',[7] are threatening to engulf Aryan civilization. 'If we don't take timely measures,' the manifesto warns, 'we could live to see the day when we will become mere pawns or, at best, passive observers in the battle between the black and yellow races for world supremacy.'[8] 'Somewhere on the path to worldwide disintegration a rampart will finally have to be erected.'[9]

There is no point in arguing over what people should believe in. The only thing which the reader might demand of these 'Russian patriots', as they try to articulate the darkest fears of their readership, is that they be true to their own postulates and try to maintain some logical consistency between their assumptions and conclusions. Where and how could this 'rampart' against 'worldwide disintegration' be erected? Where will the news of salvation come from? Not from Europe. 'The European peoples' life-forces are failing them.'[10] France and Germany, we are told, are 'today squeezed between two super-giants, whose very names are for some reason encoded'.[11] Even without a key to the code, we know immediately who the super-giants are. One of them, the USA, is obviously completely unsuited to the role of building a saving rampart:

The representatives [of the Third World] sprinkled throughout American society plan pogroms ['pogroms' here means 'riots'] and acts of arson, they seize the platform which has been obligingly set up for them by liberals and firmly direct their efforts toward becoming the dominant class in America. When the Anglo-Saxons finally lose all sense of national pride and sink into the liberal slime, the whole enormous industrial potential of the USA could be transformed into a tool of the black race for achieving world supremacy.[12]

Compare this with the tirade in the letter to *Veche* cited earlier, in which Europe is declared 'an incorrigible harlot' and America 'her final, mad, nocturnal orgy' which 'can only end in death'. There can be no doubt who these 'Russian patriots' are speaking for in their manifesto.

So if Europe and America are hopeless, what resources does Aryan civilization have left to defend itself against new barbarian incursions? Why — Russia, naturally.

Thus, by a circuitous route — via crude racist speculation — these 'Russian patriots' return to their native soil and to the same theme that prophets of imperial nationalism, from the early Slavophiles to VSKhSON whom they despise, have never stopped repeating for a century and a half: Russia as the world's saviour. Is it not surprising that, however Russian nationalists have chosen to formulate the mortal threat to our poor world over the past 150 years, it has somehow always been 'the West's life forces [that] are failing it', while Russia has these in such abundance that she is prepared to save it? Regardless of whether this threat came from 'unbelief' or 'parliament-arism', 'shopkeeper mentality' or 'Americanization of the spirit', 'the metaphysical essence of Communism' or, finally, 'biological degener-ation', the sole hope for the world has invariably been focused on Russia.

Fortunately for the Russian nationalists, no one in the West has so far catalogued that long and ancient list of 'mortal threats', varying over the course of centuries, from which Russia was destined to save the world but never did. Why has no one ever posed this devastating question to the Russian nationalists? Yet, even if someone had said to them the obvious 'Physician, heal thyself!', it would scarcely have cured them of their parochial messianism. Dialogue, as we have seen, is something alien to them in principle. They believe only in monologue. For centuries they have listened only to themselves. Yet such a catalogue would at least show their good-hearted Western fellow-travellers what a precarious position they place themselves in by supporting this messianic fervour.

But that is an aside. Certainly, the 'Russian patriots' who signed *The Nation Speaks*, for all their biological and racial pretensions, remain within the mainstream of Russian extremist nationalist thought, with its provincial messianism, its faith in the unique salvation qualities of Russia and its slavish justification of the empire. 'Our slogan', they proclaim, 'is a United Indivisible Russia.'[13]

Hitler's Mistake

Yet here arises a logical contradiction in their racial concept. They are well aware that they are not pioneers in the business of saving Aryan civilization. That title must undoubtedly belong to Hitler. But Hitler, like the Russian 'patriots' of the civil war from whom they borrowed the slogan 'A United Indivisible Russia', suffered a resounding defeat. They cannot forget that they are the ideological heirs of failure. It is therefore imperative for them to find a rationalization for this failure — and they do.

These 'Russian patriots' portray Hitler's defeat as having been brought about by his betrayal of the righteous principle of race war. It is true that, 'he declared a merciless war on degeneration. But he was in no position to complete this task because he was by no means ruled by the racial principles he proclaimed, but rather by a narrow nationalistic egotism. He even declared as inferior, peoples on the same level as the Germans.'[14] However, if Hitler's main mistake, from the point of view of 'Russian patriots', was that he substituted nationalist principles for racial ones, then, above all, they should have tried to avoid doing the same thing themselves. Alas, as for Hitler, in the final analysis the salvation of the world is reduced to the creation 'of a powerful national state to serve as the centre of gravitational attraction for the healthy elements of all *fraternal* (sic!) countries'.[15] At the same time, 'in this state the Russian people . . . must necessarily become the dominant nation.'[16] In other words, like Hitler, the Russian racists turn out to be merely nationalists.

Russian Orthodox 'Heathens'

The logical problems in the 'Russian patriots', racial conception are compounded by their attitude toward Orthodoxy. As the national religion, Orthodoxy (not just Christianity) is declared by them to be indispensable to the Russian empire and thus to saving the world. 'Throughout Russian history, the Orthodox church has played an enormous positive role . . . the savage anti-clerical orgy [of the 1920s] was part of a campaign by the forces of chaos against Russian national culture. In a national state, the foundation of which we place as our goal, traditional Russian Religion must take its proper honoured place.'[17]

Statements such as these confuse the issue for Russian nationalism's Western fellow-travellers. How, one asks, should the authors of *The Nation Speaks* be categorized? Should they be written off as 'reactionary racists', or National Bolsheviks as Darrell Hammer prefers to call them?[18] If so, how can we square this with Dunlop's classification system according to which their very attachment to Russian Orthodoxy makes them good nationalists, quite distinct from the repulsive National Bolsheviks? As we have seen, 'Russian patriots' are far from being atheists or pagans. They are believers in the Russian Orthodox church. Moreover, Orthodoxy is, for them, not just the highly esteemed traditional Russian Religion (with a capital R), but the only branch of Christianity capable of saving the world. Christianity's other branches have betrayed the racial principle and are in essence aiding 'worldwide disintegration':

Today the spirit of evil, having disguised its horns under a Beatles haircut, is trying to conduct its demoralizing and disintegrative activity within individual branches of the Christian Church by other means, preaching the ideology of the Jewish diaspora, egalitarianism, and cosmopolitanism, thus aggravating the process of worldwide miscegenation and degradation.[19]

One has only to compare this passage with 'The Letter of the Three', published in *Veche* and signed by a priest and an Archdeacon of the Russian Orthodox church, to be convinced of the source of the Russian patriots' manifesto, *Nasha Strana* ['Our Country'] — a thoroughly Russian Orthodox newspaper with a Black Hundreds mentality — published *The Nation Speaks* for the first time in Russian outside the Soviet Union, calling it 'the beginning of a spiritual awakening' in Russia.[20] There can be no doubt, therefore, that the authors of *The Nation Speaks* were 'good Russian nationalists', *vozrozhdentsy*, in Dunlop's terminology — only at the same time they are also racists and, even worse, followers of Adolph Hitler. Not surprisingly, their Western fellow-travellers cannot explain this paradox. To them, it remains a theoretical problem with no solution. But there are other paradoxes and sources of confusion within the thinking of the 'Russian patriots'.

A Few Words about 'National Uniqueness'

'The struggle for national uniqueness is part of the great battle between the forces of life and death in the universe.'[21] Oddly enough, however, the 'Russian patriots' are concerned with just one type of national uniqueness in the context of Russia — imperial. They become cynical and bitter as soon as the discussion turns to the national uniqueness of other peoples within the empire. It disturbs them that 'for some reason the existence of the Belorussian nation is artificially supported, though the Belorussians have no sense of themselves as such, and the Belorussian language is merely a collection of western Russian dialects.'[22] They are honestly offended by the fact that, 'all the so-called union republics have their own Communist parties except Russia. The result is a disproportionate strengthening of the most powerful of the regional groupings — the Ukraine.'[23]

Two peoples provoke the greatest displeasure among 'Russian patriots': the Ukrainians and (who else?) the Jews. One would think that these peoples' active struggle to assert their own national uniqueness, it ought to place them on the 'correct' side of the barricades in the 'great battle between the forces of life and death in the universe'. Yet, the conclusions of the 'Russian patriots' in this regard, once again, do not follow from their own assumptions. They consider that 'entire provinces of the Ukraine by rights ought to be part of Russia', and complain of 'such crying injustices as the transfer to the Ukraine of the Crimea, where a predominantly Russian population is now forced to study Ukrainian'.[24] As for the Crimean Tartars, whom Stalin drove from their historic homeland, their national uniqueness is of so little concern to the 'Russian patriots' that they do not even receive a mention in their manifesto. Yet this is hardly surprising when we consider their views on the possible independence of even so powerful a nation as the Ukrainians.

> If the separate existence of the Ukraine really became an issue, its borders would inevitably need to be re-examined. The Ukraine would have to cede to Russia: a) the Crimea, b) the provinces of Kharkov, Donets, Lugansk, and Zaporozh'e with their predominantly Russian populations, and c) the provinces of Odessa, Nikolaev, Kherson, Dnepropetrovsk and Sumy, whose populations are to a *sufficient degree* (sic!) Russified . . . What would remain to the Ukrainians, having no access to the sea and no basic industry, let them figure that out for themselves. Let them also consider the [territorial] claims that might be

made by the Poles in the western provinces [of the Ukraine] whose populations are pro-Polish.[25]

The national uniqueness of the Moldavian people is declared to be 'laughable',[26] 'patriots' see fit to talk about it only in connection with 'foreign appetites for our territory'[27] (Rumanian, in this case). Just as allegorically, they refer to the right of Russia to put down rebellions in her eastern European empire (having in mind the suppression of the Prague Spring in 1968):

> Those who imagine they understand things, would wish to bridle our statesmen with their understanding. 'Hands Off!', they cry out in the event of any kind of *often necessary intervention in the affairs of other countries*. They are like a wife who, hearing a cry for help from the street, flings herself upon her husband and doesn't let him go out [to help] . . . What is the value of that kind of understanding? What is it that distinguishes an ideological liberal from a plain philistine? The courage of a deserter?[28]

I hope the reader recalls the formula of the Russian nationalists that became standard in their discourse after V. Mikhailov used it in his book *New Judea*. 'The Jewish yoke over the Russian folk,' wrote Mikhailov, 'is an established fact which can be denied only by either complete cretins or scoundrels who are completely indifferent to the Russian nation, her past and the fate of the Russian people.' In full accordance with this tradition of nationalist Russia, *The Nation Speaks* declares any struggle against the empire as 'either resulting from an inability to think things out or an insidious ploy by those who would seek worldwide demoralization and disintegration.'[29]

Once the conversation has turned to 'worldwide demoralization and disintegration', the Jews are inevitably next in the line of fire. Unlike V. Mikhailov, *The Nation Speaks* does not openly refer to a 'Jewish yoke over the Russian people'. After all, it was written half a century later. Nevertheless, being resourceful, the 'Russian patriots' manage to work it in somehow. Despite their contemptuous treatment of the Belorussians, Ukrainians, Moldavians and Czechs, still their most vicious lines were reserved — as befits any self-respecting followers of F-Nationalism — for the Jews:

> Lots of noise is made about anti-semitism in Russia. The Jews pose as a national minority oppressed by the Russians while at the same time conducting a policy of ethnic favouritism. They have virtually monopolized the fields of science and culture. The Russian soil has not

yet lost its capacity to give birth to Lomonosovs, but today their path is blocked by the next Germans in line,* while the poor 'priveleged' Russians meekly skulk off to the side. And God forbid they should be offended![30]

The manifesto's conclusion is also referring to Jews when it says, 'When we speak about the Russian people, we mean people who are genuinely Russian in blood and in spirit. We must put an end to disorderly hybridization.'[31]

To *The Nation Speaks*, Jews in Russia play the same role as the 'representatives [of the Third World] sprinkled throughout American society' do in the USA. They 'seize the platform which the liberals have obligingly set up for them and firmly direct their efforts toward becoming the dominant class.'

The New Russian Revolutionaries

VSKhSON and *Veche* considered imperial treatment of national minorities unseemly, as can be judged from point 83 of VSKhSON's programme or *Veche*'s critique of Danilevskii's imperial theories. For all L-Nationalism's contradictions, its adherents' critique nevertheless contained an element of protest against the unceremonious oppression of lesser nations. The 'Russian patriots', worried about 'biological degeneration' and 'worldwide miscegenation', openly denounced this protest as 'the courage of deserters'.

From their manifesto we can clearly see how hopeless liberal Nationalism's case had become by the early 1970s. It was the still-born product of high-brow intellectuals who were trying to reconcile the savage yearning of the 'patriotic masses' for pogroms with their own refined political schemata. Their audience had no need of such schemata. They thirsted, not for a 'revolution of national liberation', but rather for a new — massive and decisive — campaign against 'cosmopolitanism', overt suppression of national minorities and isolation from foreign 'Zionism and Satanism'. The 'patriotic masses' harboured a longing for dictatorship, for the iron hand that would put a stop to 'disorderly hybridization'. They found the genuine expression of their aspirations in *The Nation Speaks*, not in the equivocal *Veche*

---

* [Translator's note: The bigoted stereotype being reflected here sees the Germans of Lomonosov's time as the ones who 'nepotistically' dominated Russian scientific and cultural life. Today it is the Jews who are seen in this role.]

or the anti-Soviet VSKhSON. These 'patriotic masses', as *Veche*'s readers indicated, are Soviet through and through, only they are the people of Soviet dictatorship, not rotten Soviet conservatism. They were opposed not to the Soviet *system*, but to the corrupt Brezhnev *regime*. In this sense only, are they revolutionaries.

The Dictatorship's Ideological Reorientation

'Revolution is a transitional state', say the 'Russian patriots'. 'In mathematics such a state is denoted by zero and has neither a positive nor a negative sign'. . . . In history, such 'eruptions of the people's vibrant energy are natural phenomena . . . They accompany, as a rule, the periods of the nation's greatest vitality. If in some small portion of the contemporary world, taken by some to represent the whole world, we do not see such explosions, this indicates that that particular portion of the world has passed its peak period and is headed towards decline.'[32] In the West, we are told, 'the stormy currents of revolution . . . flow into stagnant pools of the shopkeeper mentality'. If, however, Russia manages to avoid such a fate, and 'we have every instinct to do so',[33] all our sacrifices shall be rewarded.

Of course, the revolution of the 'Russian patriots' is far removed from VSKhSON's anti-Communist 'revolution of national liberation'. They have no need of 'an underground army of liberation which will topple the dictatorship'. Their revolution is not *against* dictatorship, but *for* it: 'such a feat is only within the strength of a dictatorship';[34] 'there can be no talk of either the convergence or the ideological capitulation of Russia.'[35] 'Therefore what is important for us is . . . the dictatorship's ideological reorientation, a kind of ideological revolution in its own way . . . We are striving for a rebirth of the sense of nationality in a confused world, in order that each is aware of his personal responsibility to his nation and to his race.'[36]

Thus, the 'Russian patriots', capturing the exact mood of the 'patriotic masses', rejected the sham patriotism of the Brezhnev regime (as did the Young Guards, at the same time, speaking in the name of 'patriotic youth'). However, in contrast to Chalmaev and Lobanov, who had to work within the confines of state censorship, the authors of *The Nation Speaks* were able to articulate much more openly the sinister Black Hundreds mentality and the yearning of the 'patriotic masses' for Fascism.

Summary of *The Nation Speaks*

(1)   The centre of gravity in the battle between Good and Evil is transferred from the metaphysical heights of L-Nationalism to the totally earthly realm of the biological degeneration of human-kind. Its doctrinal thrust is directed at the struggle against non-Russians and 'disorderly hybridization' which threatens to undermine the position of Russians as the dominant nation (and race) within the empire.

(2)   Maintaining the empire is declared not only the sacred duty of 'Russian patriots' but also the main means of saving civilization from 'worldwide disintegration'.

(3)   Dictatorship is represented as the sole institutional structure adequate to this task.

(4)   The main goal of 'Russian patriots' is therefore the 'reorientation of the dictatorship' along the lines of a nationalist and racist 'ideological revolution', i.e., the creation of a Fascist state.

Notes

1   This is how the emigre *Veche* described *The Nation Speaks*, No. 3, 1981, p. 107.
2   Ibid., p. 115.
3   Ibid.
4   Ibid., p. 130.
5   Ibid., p. 107.
6   Ibid., p. 108.
7   Ibid., p. 113.
8   Ibid., p. 130.
9   Ibid., p. 126.
10 Ibid., p. 113.
11 Ibid., p. 117.
12 Ibid., p. 113.
13 Ibid., p. 125.
14 Ibid., p. 110.
15 Ibid., p. 130.
16 Ibid.
17 Ibid., p. 129. Capitalized in the original.
18 Darrell P. Hammer, 'Russian Nationalism and the "Yanov Thesis"', *Religion in Communist Lands*, Winter 1982, p. 313.
19 *Veche*, No. 3, 1981, p. 128.
20 *Nasha strana*, 18 April 1972.

21 *Veche*, No. 3, 1981, p. 116.
22 Ibid., p. 123.
23 Ibid.
24 Ibid., p. 124.
25 Ibid. Emphasis added.
26 Ibid.
27 Ibid.
28 Ibid., p. 118. Emphasis added.
29 Ibid., p. 114.
30 Ibid., p. 125.
31 Ibid., p. 131.
32 Ibid., p. 112.
33 Ibid.
34 Ibid., p. 111.
35 Ibid., p. 129.
36 Ibid., p. 130.

13

Solzhenitsyn:
From Under the Rubble

I am keenly aware that in touching on the subject of Solzhenitsyn in the context of the drama of the Russian Right, I touch upon an extremely subtle, intimate, and at the same time immense subject. First of all, Solzhenitsyn is not an Osipov or a Chalmaev, nor an anonymous 'Russian patriot': he is part and parcel of political reality in the West. Hundreds of articles and dozens of books have been written about him. More importantly, many people in the West as well as in the Soviet Union are bound to him by personal feelings: they have studied him, learned from him, been inspired by him, loved him, expected the ultimate truth about Russia from him, as well as been disappointed in him. I do not intend to draw a political portrait of Solzhenitsyn here — or even a sketch for such a portrait. My aim is very much more modest: to examine the intellectual contribution of Solzhenitsyn and his followers to the formation of the reborn Russian Idea.

But to attempt even this is rather painful for me, as someone who was raised on Russian culture and shared in everything good and bad it has given the world. For myself as for many in Russia, Solzhenitsyn was once the conscience of the nation. For us, Solzhenitsyn was a symbol of those things of which we ourselves were not capable. This is not only with reference to his artistic gifts and legendary courage, but also to the role he has played in the spiritual liberation of our country, and therefore also in my own liberation. The tragic aspect of the phenomenon of Solzhenitsyn is that he has turned up in the ranks of the New Right. But besides observing that this in itself is an indication of the enormous power which the right-wing tradition exerts in Russian culture, I am asking, Why? Why would a person who has done so much for me, afterwards betray me? And not only betray me, but damn me as a part of the Russian intelligentsia he curses?[1]

For this reason the chapters of this book on Solzhenitsyn are written as an argument, a confession, a search for an answer to a question which has been fateful for me — in short, as a critique of Solzhenitsyn's critique. This is a difficult role for me, but I cannot refuse it — if for no other reason than that Solzhenitsyn himself taught me this unyielding attitude. After all, he himself wrote his *Letter to the Soviet Leaders* with almost no hope of success. Can he now abandon his own ideology? If he made such demands of the leaders of the USSR, he must be capable of facing them himself.

Morality and Politics

What are the methodological roots of Solzhenitsyn's position? There are many. However, we are interested here in only one, which traditionally pertains to Russian writers who, just as traditionally, appear in the role of political prophets. Gogol, Dostoevskii and Tolstoy — however different their doctrines — have all proceeded from a single postulate. They measured *political* reality by absolute *moral* criteria, found reality wanting and — without even noticing how easy and fruitless their victory was — drew the conclusion that, from the point of view of the Lord's commandments and the moral perfection of man, there was essentially no difference between authoritarianism and democracy.

In much the same way as the thinkers of the French Enlightenment held that religion was a huge fraud lasting thousands of years and extending over the whole earth, that was perpetuated by a caste of professional clergy, so Russian writers have held that politics is all lies and in principle amoral, and was inculcated by a caste of professional politicians. For this reason, the special 'Russian' path to salvation which they have constructed has always consisted, not in the *control* of politics by society, but in the *removal* of society from politics, with its implied acceptance of authoritarianism. Utopianism was another result of this combination of political naivety and a passion for political prophecy. Invariably that utopianism was reactionary, presenting the traditional backwardness of Russian political culture as the summit and crown of human thought. Take, for example, the following quotations:

> You [the leaders of the USSR] will still have unshakable power, a single, strong, closed party, the army, the police, industry, transportation, communications, natural resources, a monopoly on foreign trade, and control over the value of the ruble — but give the people room to breath, think, and develop!

> The people desires for itself one thing only: freedom of life, thought and the word. Not interfering in the power of the state, it desires that the state not interfere in the autonomous life of its spirit. . . .[2]

Don't these sound as if they were written by one and the same hand? However, the first quotation belongs to Solzhenitsyn, while the second, as we already know, was addressed to completely different leaders at another time entirely. Konstantin Aksakov, 130 years ago, was saying to the head of the Russian Orthodox state exactly the same thing as Solzhenitsyn was telling the Soviet leaders: take all *power* for yourself, but give the people all the *freedom*. The people will not interfere in politics, Aksakov and Solzhenitsyn promise, they desire only 'to breathe, think, and develop' freely. For only by separating themselves from politics, they believe, can the people realize their moral essence. Yet alas, as history shows, where the people do not control the government, the government controls the people, not letting them either breathe, think, or develop.

The theme of both these letters is the same. The questions which both authors raise coincide, as do their answers. But Russia remains in the same situation it was a century ago — trapped by lies. I wonder whether the parallel occurred to Solzhenitsyn when he repeated the demands of his teachers — demands which have failed the test of history.

From Under the Rubble

As we saw in the last chapter, already in the early 1970s the liberal nationalists had turned out to be generals without an army. Yet the lessons of *Veche*, and of *The Nation Speaks* went unheeded. In the mid-1970s the authority of Solzhenitsyn and the courage of his adherents made possible yet another (and probably the last) bright flash of national-liberal thought. Moreover, the collection of samizdat articles *From Under the Rubble* without doubt represented, in terms of L-Nationalism, an intellectual advance over *Veche*. Since it did not have to observe the constraints of 'the loyal opposition', its authors were free of both the explicit pressure of Soviet censorship and of implicit dependence on the 'patriotic masses'. They had no need to resort to the traditional methods of allegory used by the loyal oppositionist Russian press or to speak to the reader through innuendo and association of ideas. Solzhenitsyn was right when he said, 'In fifty years there has not been in the Soviet Union an anthology of such scope and seriousness that sets out basic problems and is so decisive in its treatment of them, in complete contrast to their official formulation.'[3]

The 'From under the rubble' current of the national-liberal stream also had another characteristic. It aspired not only to independence from censorship (both 'from above' and 'below'), but also from its old teachers. Neither Danilevskii nor Khomiakov served as absolute authorities. The authors who published in *From Under the Rubble* were their own Aksakovs and Berdiaevs. They embodied the effort of the post-Stalinist Russian Right to stand on its own two feet and rid itself of the 'second-hand' character of VSKhSON and *Veche*. They created their own metaphysical, religious, social, and political concepts independently, and from square one. However, in so doing, they fell into the trap of what I would call 'the repetitive effect' in Russian history. For all its courage and literary vividness, the New Right did not re-invent gunpowder, as we saw from the comparison of Solzhenitsyn and Aksakov. All they did was to reach — on their own initiative and independently — conclusions analogous, if not identical, to those reached by their Slavophile predecessors a century earlier under what would seem to have been completely different historical conditions.[4] Hopefully, this will become clearer when we start to analyse the political views of *From Under the Rubble*'s chief author.

Evolution of a Doctrine

At the beginning of the 1970s, when Solzhenitsyn wrote his *Letter to the Soviet Leaders*, it seems that he was not at all convinced of the hopelessness of Western democracy or that authoritarianism should be Russia's eternal fate. Discussion was still possible with Solzhenitsyn while it seemed he was in the process of groping for a political doctrine of his own. He himself said in the *Letter*, 'I am prepared to retract right now [his practical proposals] if anyone at all will offer not a wry criticism but a constructive path, a better way out, and, most importantly, a completely real one, by earthly means.'[5]

It is true that Solzhenitsyn's *Letter to the Soviet Leaders* has a chapter entitled 'The West on Its Knees,' in which the author speaks of 'an impasse on all sides' and even 'the ruinous path' of Western civilization. Nevertheless, he still believes that, 'it is still probable that Western civilization will not go under. It is so dynamic, so inventive, that it will survive even the impending crisis.'[6] In other words, although the West lives by 'centuries-old false notions', its case is not hopeless. For that matter, the *Letter* speaks of authoritarianism in a restrained and even rather questioning way: 'Thus, perhaps we should recognize that for Russia this path [the struggle against authoritarianism] was mistaken and premature? Perhaps, in the foreseeable future, whether we like it or not, . . . Russia is nevertheless destined to have an authoritarian system? Perhaps this is only as far as she has matured?'[7] I would argue that this is an entirely reasonable and pragmatic point of view, in which three points that I consider indisputable are expressed in a manner unfamiliar to the Western ear:

(1)   Democracy is imperfect. It needs further development, and is capable of such development.
(2)   The transition from authoritarianism to democracy takes time. At present, Russia is not capable of it. Therefore, within the foreseeable future, she can be expected to remain authoritarian.
(3)   'Everything depends on *what kind of* authoritarian structure awaits us.'[8]

This last point seems to me the most important. In fact, even the militant Jeanne Kirkpatrick admits that various authoritarian political systems can critically differ from one another[9] and thus a typology of authoritarianism is possible. That Kirkpatrick, like Solzhenitsyn, reduces this typology to a black and white distinction between Communist and anti-Communist authoritarianism is another matter. There is, however, a healthy kernel in her analysis. Russian autocracy for example, unlike, say, English or French absolutism, did not harbour the potential for transition to democracy and, in a series of counter-reforms, has been closing off the transitional path. Therefore it can be termed 'anti-democratic' authoritarianism. Meanwhile, European history (as well as Asian) illustrates that the transition from authoritarianism to democracy is possible both in principle and in practice. Consequently, as well as 'anti-democratic' authoritarianism there must also exist an authoritarianism one could define as 'non-democratic' (i.e., in principle not blocking the path to democratic transition). If this is the case, then the real problem which now faces both the Russian and the world intellectual community is to find out what are the possible paths for Russia's transition from an anti-democratic to a non-democratic authoritarianism, capable, in principle, of becoming a democracy. To do this, it is necessary to study, for example, what happened in Russia during the decade Khrushchev was in power, and what is taking place in Hungary and China today, where the backbone of the Stalinist economic system (which is the essence of the Russian-Soviet model) is gradually being dissolved in the heat of constructive reforms.

Thus, if Solzhenitsyn did indeed begin the 1970s seeking 'a better way out, a completely real one, by earthly means', he had at his disposal the constructive experience of Russian (and Soviet) reforms, which, although they were not attempts to introduce democracy, did in fact offer strategies for moving the country in that direction.

Moving in the *direction of democracy* can thus serve as the *criterion* for evaluating any given oppositionist strategy, including Solzhenitsyn's own. Using this criterion, it would be relatively easy for us, having carefully examined European history, to discover where and how the actual process of limiting power and moving in the direction of democracy began. We would soon see that the motive force and principal agent behind this movement has always, and without exception, been the *middle class*, which is created in the turmoil of fundamental socio-economic change — that is, the very process that occupied Khrushchev in Russia and occupies Kadar in Hungary and Deng Xiao Ping in China today, even if this is not their intention. In any case, without a strong middle class there can be no transition to democracy — that is the main and indisputable lesson of world history. If Solzhenitsyn had mastered that lesson, it would have become clear to him that his own proposal (to start the transformation of centuries-old Russian authoritarianism by appealing to the Soviet leaders' mystical 'Russian souls') is the least 'earthly' and least 'real' of all possible paths.

All I wish to show by this is that the main question of Solzhenitsyn's *Letter* (What kind of authoritarian structure awaits us?) is entirely reasonable and that genuine dialogue with him may have still have been possible at the beginning of the 1970s. Unfortunately, this dialogue never took place. Consequently, in the Solzhenitsyn of the mid-1970s — the author of the 'Answer to Sakharov' published in *From Under the Rubble*[10] — we already encounter a completely different person, not the austere but well-meaning critic of the West who spoke of the prematurity of democracy in Russia and was open to opposing viewpoints, but the author of a precise and rigid conception that condemns Russia to the authoritarian yoke till the end of time. This Solzhenitsyn no longer seeks an answer to the questions which previously tormented him. He has found the truth. He has come to despise heterodoxy. In so far as he sometimes does not hesitate to slander his opponents, to lie openly in the name of the cause he considers right, he no longer differs from his Moscow opponents.[11] Unfortunately, the truth for which he is prepared to forsake even the most elementary norms of fairness, not to mention Christianity, turns out, as we have seen, to be no more than a repetition of old Slavophile maxims.

The Utopia of 'Enlightened Authoritarianism'

In repeating these maxims, Solzhenitsyn, of course, observes all the trappings of our time, fashioning the image of the era he needs. First and foremost, he introduces the theme of the internal equivalence of both systems — democratic and anti-democratic. It turns out that these are simply 'two societies suffering from vices'.[12] Their vices are different but their sentence is the same — death.

In other words, not only does 'anti-democratic authoritarianism' have no future, but neither does democracy. Hence he devaluates freedom — intellectual and political — as the historical goal of the nation: 'The West has supped more than its fill of every kind of freedom, including intellectual freedom. And has this saved it? We see it today crawling on hands and knees, its will paralysed, in the dark about the future, spiritually tortured and dejected.'[13]

So much for intellectual freedom. As for political freedom, with its multi-party parliamentary system, Solzhenitsyn sees in it only an 'idol'. He calls attention to its 'dangerous, if not mortal vices', which lead to a situation where 'the Western democracies today are in a state of political crisis and spiritual confusion',[14] and concludes that, 'a society in which political parties are active *does not rise in the moral scale*.'[15]

But that's not all. Along with his damning critique of the West, Solzhenitsyn plays up the moral value of authoritarianism. On this basis, the old Slavophile image of 'two freedoms' — one internal and one external — which Solzhenitsyn has discovered anew for himself, arises and resounds ever more strongly. Apparently, 'we can firmly assert our inner freedom even under external conditions of unfreedom'.[16] More than this, under authoritarianism 'the need to struggle against our surroundings rewards our efforts with greater inner success'.[17]

The implication is that, not democracy, but authoritarianism leads by the shorter path to inner freedom, which itself is declared to be the goal of the 'historical development of the nations'. From here it is but a single logical step to the statement, unexpected from Solzhenitsyn, that 'the state system which exists in our country is terrible, not because it is undemocratic, authoritarian, based on physical constraint — a person can still live in such conditions without harm to one's spiritual essence.'[18] However, if in democratic systems a person cannot live 'without harm to one's spiritual essence,' while in authoritarian systems one can, then which type of system is to be preferred? Which system is healthier for 'inner freedom' and 'moral elevation'?

This is the point to which Solzhenitsyn has come in the absence of any dialogue — to a justification of 'outward unfreedom'. Here, he repeats Aksakov's utopia of 'enlightened authoritarianism', according to which, on the one hand, the full range of powers over society are vested in the government, and, on the other, this is supposed to assist that society's 'moral elevation'.

The Historical Validation

So how can the capitulation to authoritarianism of a man with the reputation of a great fighter for freedom be explained? Like every self-respecting Russian writer, Solzhenitsyn must have for this purpose a sort of historical justification. Those who have read the old Slavophiles would not have great difficulty in deducing it. But let's go to Solzhenitsyn's texts.

On the one hand, he says, Western democracy is unsuitable as a pattern and model for Russia's future because it stems from the secularism of European culture: 'This is mainly the result of a historical, psychological and moral crisis affecting the entire culture and world outlook [of Europe], which were conceived at the time of the Renaissance and attained the peak of their expression with the eighteenth-century Enlightenment.'[19] On the other hand, the existing form of Communist authoritarianism in the Soviet Union is unsuitable as a pattern and model for Russia's future because of its non-Russian origin. The Soviet system is not, apparently, the product of Russian history, but the result of the fact that a 'dark whirlwind of Progressive Ideology [Marxism] swept in on us from the West'.[20] Solzhenitsyn tells us that 'Soviet development is not a continuation of Russian development but a distortion of it carried out in a new and unnatural direction, hostile to her people.'[21] Consequently, 'The terms "Russian" and "Soviet" . . . are not only . . . not equivalent . . . but irreconcilable opposites, completely excluding one another.'[22] In fact, 'For a thousand years Russia lived with an authoritarian order — and at the beginning of the twentieth century both the physical and spiritual health of her people were still intact.'[23]

'Who is to blame?' is a traditional Russian question. The whole Russian idea arose from the presumption of Russia's guiltlessness of her own misfortunes. In the seventeenth century the musketeers (strel'tsy) revolted because 'Germans are walking around in Moscow, spreading the habits of shaving and tobacco, to the detriment of all standards of common decency.'[24] Whoever has read Katkov knows that the Poles are to blame. Whoever has read Sharapov knows that the Jews are at fault. In our day, whoever reads Chalmaev or Antonov knows that it is the West. Even if we accept this mode of thought — profoundly humiliating for the Russian people, depicting it as helpless, blind and ready to follow any foreign influence — a key question remains unanswered: Why did that 'dark whirlwind' attack, not the West, which as we know has lived in uninterrupted 'historical, psychological, and moral crisis' since the sixteenth century, and where there is 'a passive feeling of doom in the majority', 'weakness of governments and paralysis of society's defensive reactions' and 'spiritual distress passing over into political catastrophe,'[25] but rather Russia, which did not pass through any fatal Renaissance, has not been in crisis, and in which 'at the beginning of the twentieth century both the physical and spiritual health of her people were still intact'? Why has not one putrid democracy in the world succumbed (apart from those dragged into it by force), but only authoritarian regimes — Russia, China, Cuba, Vietnam, and so on?

One would think that this elementary question would compel a truth-seeker at least to reflect. But is Solzhenitsyn seeking the truth — or only a justification for his political concept? If so, then he is seeking the impossible. Russian history does not confirm his outlook. This was proved, by those very same Slavophiles whom he so passionately defends yet so carelessly read. It was they, as we know, who called the alleged enlightened authoritarianism of the Russian Orthodox empire 'a governmental system rendering the subject a slave' and 'a police state'. It is true that in criticizing Russia's 'soul-destroying despotism', they too considered it the result of a 'dark whirlwind' from the West, only the villain of Russian history in their time, naturally, was not Lenin with his Communism, but Peter I with his police state, allegedly copied from European models. That was when Aksakov believed the 'dark whirlwind' had descended on the Russian land, while before Peter enlightened authoritarianism was in full bloom and 'both the physical and spiritual health of her people were still intact.' Thus who is right — Solzhenitsyn or his spiritual forefather? Is Lenin or Peter to blame for the 'dark whirlwind'? Who is really responsible for the destruction of Russia's enlightened authoritarianism?

If one is to believe Grigorii Kotoshkhin, who in the middle of the seventeenth century fled to Sweden and wrote a book about the horrors of pre-Petrine Russia, Aksakov and Solzhenitsyn are both wrong. How far back are we to go? Must we refer to the letters of Andrei Kurbskii, which unmask with explosive force the arbitrariness and ferocity of the first Russian counter-reform in the mid-sixteenth century? Or to the *Journal of Ivan Timofeev*? Or to the *History of Russia* by Prince Shcherbatov, who described the second half of the sixteenth century as a time when 'love for the fatherland died out and its place was taken by baseness, slavishness, and concern only for one's own property'?[26] Was this when Russia was 'morally elevated'? And if not then, when?

One thing that no Russian conservative utopian ever seems to have noticed is the autocratic nature of Russia's political system — that cursed 'anti-democratic' authoritarianism which doesn't allow the country to break out of its vicious circle of reform and counter-reform, piling one bloody dictatorship on top of another. To look for a validation of 'enlightened' authoritarianism in this terrible history is to look for a philosopher's stone.

The Religious Validation

By no means are all these arguments and deliberations on the theme of Russian history academic. Current political strategies follow directly from them. If the Soviet system is indeed the result of a 'dark whirlwind' from the West, then it is a natural and even necessary for Russia to isolate herself. For the positivist Danilevskii (who raised isolationism to the status of a natural law of history), such 'organic' validation of the imperial-isolationist strategy was quite sufficient. *Veche* too found it satisfactory, as we have seen. But for Solzhenitsyn's followers, both as people who profess Russian Orthodoxy and as politicians, an organic historical validation alone is not enough. They cannot allow themselves the luxury of accepting a positivist as a teacher. They also need an explanation from the metaphysical standpoint of Russian Orthodoxy. How else are they to attract support for the isolationist strategy from the growing numbers of Russian Orthodox intelligentsia? In short, a religious sanction for their isolationist strategy is imperative to them. Can it be justified from the perspective of Christianity, which — whatever one may say — is in its essence universal and for which — alas — there is, in principle, neither Hellene nor Jew? For this reason, we should not be surprised that the political collection *From Under the Rubble* should include passionate metaphysical tracts by Solzhenitsyn's young friends, aimed at a theoretical justification, in the twentieth century, of the authoritarian-isolationist strategy, in much the same way as Danilevskii had done one hundred years earlier.

In his brilliantly executed essay 'The national renaissance and the nation as a personality', Vadim Borisov tells the dramatic story of the collapse of the myth of 'humanistic consciousness' for which 'the freedom of individuals and the unity of the world as a whole are the alpha and omega.'[27] This myth, in Borisov's opinion, 'lacks an adequate *rational* basis',[28] inasmuch as *'personality* in its original sense is a religious and even specifically Christian concept.'[29] In general, 'the individual is . . . a fragment of nature, self-contained and absolute . . . Personality, as opposed to the individual, is not part of some whole, it contains the whole within itself.'[30] Not containing within himself the necessary 'whole,' the individual cannot claim the status of a personality. Luckily, on the other hand, something does exist which contains this 'whole' — namely, the 'nation as a personality',[31] the 'nation as a whole',[32] without which the individual cannot have either autonomous significance or autonomous value.

This, says Borisov, is confirmed, in particular, 'by the events of the Pentecost where the Holy Spirit descended on the Apostles and they were endowed with the gift of speaking in *different tongues*.'[33] Borisov does not assert that humankind — which is still in bondage to secular 'humanism' — is already aware of all this. No, this 'is merely a theoretical fixture of Christian consciousness.' However, he is full of optimism inasmuch as *'every* people must strive to realize its full personality,' and he is firmly convinced that, 'the nation is one of the levels in the hierarchy of the Christian cosmos, a part of God's irrevocable purpose.'[34]

At the risk of profaning the metaphysical pathos of Borisov's tract, let us simply state its point as follows: humankind is quantified, so to speak, not by single individuals, as 'humanistic consciousness' had naively assumed up to now, but by nations.

F. Korsakov's essay 'Russian destinies,' in which discussion of 'the nation as a personality' is brought down from the metaphysical heights of the cosmos to the Russian Orthodox earth, is close in theme to Borisov's article. In a passionate, symbolic stream of speech, full of emotion — indeed, almost a poem — he explains the incompatibility of the 'God of Abraham, Isaac, and Jacob' with 'the God of the philosophers and scholars', since 'behind the moralistic nonsense of the intellectuals', 'behind that modern humanistic phraseology', there is still the same 'devil with horns and hooves', the same 'form of the Antichrist'. The intellectual, in order to gain access to the Truth, must first of all renounce the need to understand — the freedom to think independently — which is, according to Korsakov, the same as pride, the first mortal sin. In other words, he must cease being an intellectual. Without this renunciation he can never believe that, 'the Orthodox Church is the only true church and that all the other Christians, as well as non-believers . . . are living in a state of untruth, enticed and deluded by the devil.'[35] Further on we learn that the riddle of the uniqueness of the Russian nation is beyond understanding, and that Russia differs fundamentally from 'the whole of the rest of the world, which exists within an entirely different, more open, framework'.[36] 'All the obvious advantages of that allegedly free and open system are constantly nullifying themselves . . . whereas here [in Russia] everything remains with us.'[37] In short, the Truth which is being sought 'merges' with the image of Russia.[38]

Given my hopeless ignorance in questions of the hierarchy of the cosmos, I would not dare dispute either the interpretation of the Pentecost which Borisov offers us, or Korsakov's measure of the power of diabolical delusion, under which 97 per cent of all mankind finds itself. I am interested only in the political function of the scholastic works briefly outlined here. In my view, this function is obvious: it is to provide religious validation for the authoritarian-isolationist strategy and to demonstrate the organic incompatibility of the intelligentsia with the credo of the Russian Idea. Let the West crumble ('the allegedly free and open systems nullify themselves'); let the intelligentsia with its humanistic phraseology perish ('the devil with his horns and hooves is ever behind it'). The Truth will remain because it is with us, because it is inside us, because it is Russia.

The 'Smatterers'

I am not a theologian, but an historian. I cannot judge whether the religious validation of the isolationist strategy is more convincing to young Russians than the historical one we have considered. I can only

state that a group of talented young people have devoted themselves
to attempting this task at the risk of their freedom — and perhaps
their lives. The passion and the polemical fervour with which they do
so indicates that within the complex and, to my knowledge, as yet
unexplained phenomenon of the Russian Orthodox renaissance, a
fierce struggle is underway. It is a struggle for the *political orientation*
of this cultural phenomenon by which Russia's future will, perhaps in
considerable degree, be formed. In a more general way, it can be said
that a struggle is taking place for the political orientation of the next
generation of the Russian intelligentsia. Will it be liberal-ecumenical
or authoritarian-isolationist, Westernizing or Tatar-messianic? In other
words, will Russia play a responsible part in the world political
process or will it be a threat to that process, maturing in isolation
until the Day of Judgement, that is the Year 2000? Once again, the
outcome would appear to depend on the answer to the basic question
which has always divided the Russian intelligentsia: Is Russia a
'European' country, or should it seek 'its own special path'? More
specifically, *pace* Solzhenitsyn, whose answer has already been
accepted by many: Was the catastrophe of October 1917 the result of
Russian history or of a 'dark whirlwind' from the West?

In 1970 the journal *Vestnik russkogo khristiyanskogo dvizhenia*
[*Herald of the Russian Christian Movement*] published a series of
essays by Soviet authors writing under pseudonyms and representing
the liberal-ecumenical wing of the 'Russian Orthodox Renaissance'. In
an essay by N. N. we read:

> Bolshevism . . . is not a Varangian invasion, and the Revolution was not
> made only by Jews. For this reason the Communist regime is not an
> external force but an organic product of Russian life — a concentration
> of all the filth of the Russian soul, the whole sinful outgrowth of
> Russian history, which cannot be mechanically cut off and thrown
> away.[39]

V. Gorskii formulated this viewpoint even more clearly:

> Overcoming the national-messianic consciousness is Russia's most
> urgent task. Russia will not be able to rid herself of despotism until she
> abandons the idea of national grandeur. Therefore, it is not 'national
> rebirth' but the struggle for freedom and spiritual values which must
> become the central creative idea of our future.[40]

There can be no doubt that Gorskii here had touched on the
contemporary Russian Right's sore point. The response that this

provoked in the nationalistic samizdat press is scarcely credible. For a brief historical instant, all the factions of the dissident Right — isolationist and messianic, 'good' and 'bad' nationalists — united in a fit of indignation, forgot their disagreements and strove to wipe the author of this blasphemous 'anti-Russian' appeal for a 'struggle for freedom' off the face of the earth. The enraged throng included a former leading member of the VSKhSON (Leonid Borodin), both Osipov and his 'Antonovist' opponents from *Veche*, Gennadii Shimanov (who will be discussed later) and, alas, Solzhenitsyn. For anyone still in need of further proof that all these figures developed their ideologies from the same intellectual source, then it was to be found here in this united front.[41]

But what had really happened? What is so terrible about an appeal for the abandonment of national messianism, and for a struggle for freedom and spiritual values? Is the Russian nation really being oppressed by some other nation, rather than its own leaders? They, after all, are also Russians, who even Solzhenitsyn assumes 'are not alien to their origins — to their fathers, grandfathers, and great-grandfathers, to the expanses of their homeland'.[42] It should be obvious that the obstacle to the true rebirth of Russia lies within the Russian nation and not between Russia and other peoples. Moreover, is it not obvious that this messianism (in the form of Marxism) is one of the cornerstones of that Ideology — that 'Lie' — which Solzhenitsyn has devoted his life to oppose? Nevertheless, the entire Russian Right, including Solzhenitsyn, took Gorskii's essay as a slap in the face.

But unlike others, Solzhenitsyn in his article 'The smatterers' did not grieve, weep, or prophesy. Solzhenitsyn struck, putting all his prestige and world renown into the blow. Solzhenitsyn lashed out not at the 'leaders' (with whom he was prepared to enter into a dialogue), but at his own admirers. He attacked his former dissident allies, the samizdat thinkers, the intellectuals who were torturously seeking a way out for Russia (some of whom had earlier risked supporting him). He was merciless. He did not take account of the fact that, as Yulia Vishnevskaia wrote, 'when "The Smatterers" was written, Solzhenitsyn knew only too well that his prestige in "smatterer" circles was immense and that any criticism of his views would be interpreted as almost a collaboration with the KGB.'[43]

When the VSKhSON programme was discussed, I noted the political intolerance of its authors, who were prepared to accept only those 'close in spirit' to themselves. But that was when the Russian Right was in its infancy. Only now — in the bloom of its young adulthood — had it become so overwhelmingly obvious that the Russian nationalist frame of mind is *organically* incapable of accepting differences of political opinion. If these people ever come to power in Russia, there would be no 'flowering of thought', as Solzhenitsyn promises. No opposition would be tolerated, let alone any 'anti-Russian' one. Something else had also become obvious: if, from the Right's point of view, a 'dark whirlwind' from the West was at the root of all the calamities in Russia's past, then the European, anti-isolationist, anti-messianic orientation of the Soviet intelligentsia would be the logical culprit of all future disasters as well. This is why the Russian Right was so unfailingly united in their attacks on the intelligentsia in the early 1970s.

In introducing the contemptuous term smatterers into his article, Solzhenitsyn virtually denied the existence of a contemporary Russian intelligentsia, refusing to permit it either human dignity or a moral world outlook, and thereby isolating it from the process of the country's 'spiritual rebirth'. I do not wish to dwell on the injustice of this verdict, or on the complete absence of logic it demonstrates (comparing the pre-revolutionary Russian intelligentsia with the modern one, Solzhenitsyn is repelled by the former's 'self-sacrifice', and by the latter's lack of it.). I wish to call the reader's attention to a different and, from my point of view, much more ominous circumstance. Reading 'The smatterers' attentively, one cannot help being struck by opinions such as 'lack of education is not the greatest loss one can suffer in life',[44] and recommendations for the creation of a new 'sacrificial elite' — a new nucleus of the nation, 'brought up not so much in libraries as on spiritual suffering'.[45] Furthermore, it would seem that 'educational qualifications and the number of scholarly works published are utterly irrelevant', for we will go to the people alongside 'semi-literate preachers of religion'.[46] Is there not in all this something very reminiscent of Chalmaev — something which leads one to the conclusion that Solzhenitsyn's 'smatterers' is only another name for Chalmaev's 'educated shopkeepers'? Let us recall that, according to Chalmaev, all the national feats of heroism in Russian history were performed by 'preachers of religion' in alliance with the 'leaders' of Russia — and, furthermore, performed *against* the 'educated shopkeepers'.

Of course, Chalmaev and Solzhenitsyn, the National Bolsheviks and Dunlop's *vozrozhdentsy*, are all opposed to each other in almost everything concerning Russia's present. Yet, we have seen how miraculously they transformed themselves into allies in all things concerning her past — and, what's more important, her future. Are not Chalmaev's 'anchorites', who saved Russia from the abyss of sin, and Solzhenitsyn's 'semi-literate preachers of religion' twins, and Chalmaev's 'tsars' a model for Solzhenitsyn's 'leaders'? We have already spoken of the similarity between the educated shopkeepers and the smatterers. Thus both Solzhenitsyn and Chalmaev have pinpointed three chief components that determine the structure of Russian society, and they have proved to be identical for both the National Bolsheviks and the *vozrozhdentsy*.

Summary of *From Under the Rubble*

(1)   The concept of a world crisis, 'reminiscent of the transition from the Middle Ages to modern times' — a crisis arising from the total secularization of culture in the Renaissance and inevitably leading either to the correction of this mistake, that is, the creation of a new religious civilization, or to the ruin of humankind.

(2)   The concept of democracy as an historical distortion, which arose from the great mistake of the Renaissance and led mankind into the dead end of irreligion and the Gulag.

(3)   The concept of 'two freedoms' — internal and external — which leads to 'moral freedom' as 'the moral goal of the nation' being counterposed to intellectual and political freedom.

(4)   The concept of 'enlightened authoritarianism' as an alternative to both totalitarianism and democracy.

(5)   The concept that the contemporary world is made up of three principal components (common to both *From Under the Rubble* and *Veche*): a threatening 'totalitarian' China, a decaying democratic West, and a Russia trying to resurrect herself with an 'enlightened authoritarian' system. There is, in addition, the related concept that Soviet society is also made up of three principal components (common to both *From Under the Rubble* and *Molodaia gvardia*): namely, the dangerous 'smatterers', the 'leaders' and 'the semi-literate preachers of religion'.

(6)   The concept of 'the nation as personality' being 'God's irrevocable plan for the world', which justifies imperial isolationism.

(7)   The concept of the intelligentsia as a harmful secular growth on the body of society, which effectively simulates a national elite and thereby hinders the formation of a real one.

(8)   The concept of a new 'sacrificial elite, brought up not so much in libraries as on spiritual suffering', summoned to enter into a

dialogue with the 'leaders' and, on the basis of the need for a 'national rebirth', to assure Russia's progress toward a salutary 'enlightened authoritarianism'.

Notes

1   I certainly cannot be satisfied with such naive explanations as, for example, John Bowling offers when he says that, '[Solzhenitsyn's] soul is Russian and not Western' and therefore '[he] cannot be understood in Western terms' (*Commentary*, September 1974, p. 14). This is the explanation which in the nineteenth century Chaadaev heard from Yazykov, and Herzen from Bulgarin. Russian reactionaries have always justified their devotion to authoritarianism by their mysterious 'Russian soul' which is not to be understood in Western terms.

2   Solzhenitsyn, *Pis'mo vozhdiam Sovetskogo Soiuza*, Paris: YMCA Press, 1974, p. 49 [English translation by Hilarie Sternberg, New York: Harper and Row, 1976, p. 57.]; Konstantin Aksakov in *Teoria gosudarstva u slavianofilov*, St. Petersburg: 1898, p. 41.

3   *Vestnik RKhD*, No. 112–13, p. 226.

4   No matter how one interprets this startling coincidence, for me it once again tends to confirm — experimentally — my central hypotheses: (a) the political system which became established in Russia as a result of her first counter-reform (or 'revolution from above'), that of Ivan the Terrible in the mid-sixteenth century, developed not progressively but in a spiral way; (b) in each new cycle of the historical spiral, similar ideological currents have to start their development all over again from the beginning, thus recapitulating all the stages through which their predecessors passed in the preceding historical cycle.

5   Solzhenitsyn, *Letter*, p. 5.

6   Ibid., pp. 17, 21.

7   Ibid., p. 45.

8   Ibid.

9   Jeanne Kirkpatrick, *Dictatorship and Double Standards*, Simon and Shuster, N.Y., 1982.

10   Solzhenitsyn, 'Na vozvrate dykhania i soznania' ['On the Return of Breathing and Consciousness'] in *Iz-pod glyb*, Paris, YMCA Press: 1974, pp. 7–28.

11   Let me cite just one example — that of myself. As the reader already knows, I, in Solzhenitsyn's opinion, harbour a 'hatred for all things Russian'. In other words, I am accused of the same thing which the author of the 'Critical Notes' on *Veche* accused Solzhenitsyn of. Moreover, I was also 'a communist journalist in Moscow for seventeen years known to no one' inasmuch as I was 'published only in *Young Communist* and lesser [fora]'. It is true that the open and easily verifiable lie about *Young Communist* and lesser [fora] he himself deleted from subsequent reprints, so we won't bother to discuss that. But what about my alleged seventeen years of journalism however? Where did he get this figure from? My

book jacket biography says nothing of the kind. It is obvious that Solzhenitsyn made this up. But why not say ten or twenty years? One has to assume that he thought an unexpected, non-round number would sound more authentic and give the impression he could back it up with evidence. This old tried-and-true bluff was highly effective under the Stalinist terroristic system, where a plausible sounding denunciation could cost someone his or her life. So much for Solzhenitsyn's call on us to 'Live Not by Lies'. For an analogous case see Ilya Zilberberg 'Neobkhodimyi Razgovor s Solzhenitsynm' (*A Needed Dialogue with Solzhenitsyn*), Great Britain, 1976.

12 *Iz-pod glyb*, p. 20.
13 Ibid., p. 21. Compare: 'Look at the West. The peoples . . . have been carried away by vain strivings, . . . and have started to believe in the possibility of a perfect government, have made republics, and have built constitutions, . . . and have become poor in their souls, and on the point of collapsing . . . any minute.' This was Aksakov in 1856 (*Teoria . . .* , p. 31).
14 *Iz-pod glyb*, p. 25.
15 Ibid., p. 22. Emphasis added.
16 Ibid., p. 25.
17 Ibid.
18 Ibid., p. 27.
19 Solzhenitsyn, *Pis'mo* . . . , p. 11.
20 Ibid., p. 17. Capital letters in the original.
21 *Vestnik RKhD*, No. 118, p. 170.
22 Ibid.
23 Solzhenitsyn, *Pis'mo* . . . , p. 45.
24 *Voprosy literatury*, 1969, No. 5, p. 91.
25 *Vestnik RKhD*, No. 117, p. 139.
26 M. M. Shcherbatov, *Istoria rossiyskaia s drevneishikh vremen*, St. Petersburg: 1903, v. 5, p. 832.
27 *Iz-pod glyb*, p. 201.
28 Ibid., p. 203.
29 Ibid., p. 208.
30 Ibid., p. 210.
31 Ibid., p. 206.
32 Ibid., p. 207.
33 Ibid., p. 209.
34 Ibid., p. 211.
35 Ibid., p. 165.
36 Ibid., p. 171.
37 Ibid.
38 Ibid., p. 176.
39 *Vestnik RKhD*, No. 97, p. 6.
40 Ibid., p. 61.
41 See L. Borodin's article in *Grani* No. 96; V. Osipov's reply in 'Letter to the Editorial Board of the *Vestnik RKhD*', *Vestnik RKhD*, No. 106, p. 295; the letters of I. Ibragimov and K. Radugin in the same issue of *Vestnik*, p. 309—19; G. Shimanov's article in *Arkhiv samizdata*, No. 1132. This was, as it were, simultaneously a witches' Sabbath, a lament

by the waters of Babylon, and a storm of prophesies. To give the reader some idea of the thinking of the authors of these 'refutations', I will cite only one extract: 'In the 13th—15th centuries, Russia, by shedding its blood, stopped the Tatar-Mongols. The civilized world was thus saved from conquerors who were obviously inspired by dark forces. . . . In the 17th century, the Russian people . . . destroyed the Pretender, which made the wars of the epoch of the "time of troubles" . . . a prefiguration of the struggle with the Antichrist. . . . The pathos of the struggle with the Antichrist inspired the Russian people in the 1812 war as well . . . Within the memory of the generations now living the sacrificial fate of Russia was again fulfilled. There are many indications that the Fascist invasion was not only a military but also a mystical intervention, comparable to the incursion by the heirs of Genghis Khan in the 20th century [read, the Chinese] who are declaring their claim to the territories conquered in the Middle Ages by their ancestors. . . . Orthodox Rus' still exists . . . [and] will fulfil its religious destiny to the end' (*Vestnik RKhD*, No. 106, pp. 311—12, 314).

42   Solzhenitsyn, *Pis'mo* . . . , p. 7.
43   *SSSR. Demokraticheskie al'ternativy*, Achberg: 1976, p. 187.
44   *Iz-pod glyb*, p. 259.
45   Ibid., p. 251.
46   Ibid., p. 255.

14
Diabolerie One

I trust that I have already provided the reader with enough evidence to judge that all the doctrines of the Russian New Right, even the most liberal of them, are distrustful of the intelligentsia. They suspect it of being dangerously inclined toward 'secularity' and 'Europeanism'. Even assuming they would allow the differences of opinion in the area of culture that their proposals for Russia's future include, they none the less have no desire to permit political heterodoxy. They all ignore the crucial question of a political opposition.

Is it not fair to say then that Chalmaev's invective against satiety and education, Antonov's call for a new cosmopolitan campaign, the 'patriotic masses' call for pogroms, the Osipov/Solzhenitsyn 'Siberian gambit' (advocating the ex-urbanization and deindustrialization of society) and *The Nation Speaks* manifesto's proposals for the 'ideological reorientation of the dictatorship', are despite their apparent differences, really all pursuing the same goal? That goal is to construct an economic and cultural model for Russia in which there would be no place for intelligentsia sympathetic toward the West — a model which would require their total removal from participation in the country's decision-making process and replacement by an alternative elite composed of a certain 'truly Russian' combination of 'leaders' and 'semi-literate preachers of religion'. In this scenario, Russian Orthodoxy, as a national ideology, would once again constitute the most reliable barrier against 'heretical' European currents, as it did in Muscovite times. In this way the nationalists are trying to safeguard Russia, once and for all, from any new 'dark whirlwinds' springing from the West's 'satanocratic' tendencies. For as long as these tendencies possess such a powerful social ally within Russian society, any attempts to hermetically isolate the country, to immunize it against Western infection, would prove fruitless.

If our assumptions about the Russian New Right are correct, we discover, in the consciousness of contemporary Soviet subscribers to the Russian Idea, the following logical progression:

(1) From the moment of its secularization, the West proved an easy prey for Satan.
(2) In the centuries that have passed since the Renaissance, it has steadfastly fallen under the power of Satanocracy.
(3) The existence of Orthodox Russia, which has fortunately avoided the 'mighty Renaissance embrace' of the West, constitutes the principal barrier to the total secularization and, thereby, satanocratization of the world.
(4) The West regularly unleashes 'dark whirlwinds' on Russia, intended to undermine the source of her internal strength — which is her loyalty to Orthodoxy.
(5) It does this through secular 'demons', who call themselves the intelligentsia.

Thus, though the general outlines of the problem are clear, the technical aspects of Western satanocratic manipulation, its mechanism, so to speak, remained unexplored and obscure — that is, until the appearance of Solzhenitsyn's *Lenin in Zurich*. Here, for the first time, a massive attempt was made relentlessly to expose the satanic nature of Lenin and the Bolshevik 'dark whirlwind' that took hold of Russia with the help of the 'demons' of the Russian intelligentsia poisoned by Europeanism. It is for this reason that *Lenin in Zurich*, in an historical sense, represents the quintessence of the contemporary Russian Idea. In this respect it was its most significant work, until the publication of the second edition of *August 1914* (which I shall discuss in the next chapter).

   In principle, I seek to avoid using Solzhenitsyn's literary works to judge his political views. However, what he has been writing since he left the Soviet Union seems to me closer to a series of political pamphlets than *belles-lettres*. In any case, that is the viewpoint from which I shall examine *Lenin in Zurich* here.

Lenin in Zurich

Lenin is portrayed in this book as half Russian (or more precisely, one-quarter Russian by blood), and furthermore as despising Russia.[1] That his goal, according to Solzhenitsyn, consisted in 'completely dismembering Russia'[2] is also readily clear. But less obvious, at first glance, is why Solzhenitsyn makes him encounter a person who is not only his equal — in force of character, in his non-Russianness, and in his hatred of Russia — but who even, by Lenin's own admission, is superior to him in all these respects. A born fighter, Lenin dod not know fear of anything or anyone. 'With this man alone he felt unsure of himself. He did not know whether he would be able to stand up to [him] as an enemy.'[3] 'Lenin knew the key to every Social Democrat in the world, knew the shelf to put him on,' and it was only this one who 'would not open, would not be put anywhere and stood across [his] path.'[4]

This person was a monstrous 'amalgam of theorist, operator, and politician'[5] — the only one in the world who was stronger than Lenin in all respects — in his amazing far-sightedness, unparalleled political intuition and ability to see what no one else did. If he wished, he could deprive Lenin of everything he lived for — his position of political leadership. He had already done this once, at the time of the first Russian revolution in 1905. Then, 'never straying for a moment, [he] had filled the road ahead and robbed Lenin of the will to go forward, of all initiative.'[6] 'In that Revolution, Lenin had been bruised [by this man] as if he had stood too close to an elephant . . . He sat at meetings of the Soviet, listening to the Hero of the Day, with his head in his hands.'[7] He even had 'nothing to say from the platform of the Soviet', since 'everything was going . . . so well' under the leadership of that other that 'there was no room left for the Bolshevik leader.'[8]

This man was a 'behemoth with genius'.[9] He possessed some kind of unbelievable 'seismographic sense of movement in the depths [of society]',[10] and 'ruthless inhuman intelligence'.[11] He 'had knocked around Europe for twenty-five years like the Wandering Jew'[12] and at the same time was always able to 'prophesy earlier, and farther into the future than anyone else'.[13] This man even now, in 1916 (when the action of Solzhenitsyn's book takes place), sees things more clearly and knows more than Lenin. He could once again take political leadership away from Lenin and thereby ruin him for good. When Lenin is totally crushed and disillusioned, when he no longer believes in anything any more and is planning to go off to America, suddenly this man comes to him and quietly says, 'I am setting the date of the Russian Revolution for the ninth of January next year!'[14] (and he is out by only one month.)

This person is the real 'author . . . the father of the first Revolution'.[15] He is the real inventor of the Soviet regime who has every right to say, in Solzhenitsyn, 'my Soviets'.[16] This 'Wandering Jew', this 'Behemoth', not only does not intend to distance Lenin, this time he himself comes to him, to his weak, beaten and powerless rival, to propose an alliance.

Why? What for? That is the most interesting and important question for us to decide here. Is it not because, in the first revolution, in 1905, he made a mistake in backing a *Jew*, Trotsky, as the potential leader of a *Russian* revolution? Is it not because he suffered defeat and Russia survived 1905? She must not survive the next revolution. That is why Lenin, the Russian (even if he's just one-quarter Russian), is now needed. That is why, in his memorandum to the German government, he 'had specifically mentioned Lenin . . . as his main support. With Lenin at his right hand, as Trotsky had been in the other revolution, success was assured.'[17]

Certainly this person is a German agent. Naturally, he is getting millions from the Germans. Of course, he only wants to hire Lenin to carry out his scheme (as an indigenous Russian 'demon') to destroy Russia. This much is understandable and even obvious. But does this automatically explain his inhuman intellect, his seismographic sense of movement in the depths, his ability to predict things earlier and farther into the future than anyone else (a capacity which completely overshadowed even Lenin's 'demonic' genius)? Is he serving the German General Staff or are they serving him? After all, the plan is his and not the Germans', and he is playing his own game, not theirs. It's quite clear that the Germans are no more to him than Lenin is — just tools. He is simply using them to achieve his own satanic objective, as he once used Trotsky and as he now intends to use Lenin. No, he is no 'demon'; he is a tempter of demons ('He always tried to operate behind the scenes, not to get in front of cameras, not to feed biographers'[18]). He is the Mephistopheles of demonry: the instigator, the grey eminence, the true master of history in whose hands both the Bolsheviks and the Germans are merely puppets on a string to be manipulated as he chooses. At least, this is how Solzhenitsyn depicts him. Yet here one involuntarily begins to doubt whether this is a human he is describing.

Yes, this figure has a name — he actually existed — Izrail' Lazarevich Parvus (whose real last name was Gel'fond). He was a Russian Jew who wandered around Europe with the sole purpose in mind of mobilizing its resources in order to unleash a 'black whirlwind' upon Russia. Whether by war or revolution, with German money or socialist ideas — what's the difference? An enormous, inhuman goal inspires this inhumanly intelligent creature. And if any doubts still remain that this character is himself Satan (the Jew Antichrist, emerged from the bowels of Russia, as foretold by Konstantin Leont'ev), then Solzhenitsyn destroys these in one remarkable scene.

The Coming of the Antichrist

It takes place in the oppressed and downtrodden Lenin's shabby little room, when the German Jew Sklarz brings him Parvus's proposal, the one which is to determine the course of Russian history for decades to come. It is twilight outside. There's no kerosene in the lamp, but for some reason it continues to burn without giving any light. It's dark in the room, but Lenin is somehow managing to read. Sklarz has tossed his luxurious hat on the poor table and left his leather trunk in the middle of the room. Lenin reads Parvus's letter and at this point unbelievable things begin to occur. 'His [Lenin's] eyes happened to fall on Sklarz's case. It was heavy, so tightly packed. How did he lug it around? . . . Why did he need it?'[19] Then: 'The hat behind the lamp shifted and revealed its satin lining. No, it was lying quietly, just as Sklarz had left it.'[20] Suddenly a strange thought occurred to Lenin: 'What did Sklarz want with that case? It looked as big as a boar.'[21] Then without warning, of its own accord, 'the handle of the big case flopped to one side . . . Snap!'[22] At this point the reader already begins to smell the unmistakable whiff of sulphur, especially since 'there was no kerosene in the lamp, but it had been burning for an hour. . . .'[23] (Is this not a tiny tongue of hell's fire?)

> Snap! The suitcase had finally burst open . . . and freeing his elbows, straightening his back, he unfolded, rose to his full height and girth, in his dark blue three-piece suit, with his diamond cuff-links and, stretching his cramped legs, came one step, two steps closer. There he stood, life-sized, in the flesh . . . the elongated dome of his head, the flashy bulldog features, the little imperial — looking with pale watchful eyes. Amicably, as ever.[24]

Satan had appeared. Izraill Lazarevich Parvus — risen from the darkness — was standing before Lenin personally and speaking, although he wasn't there. And Lenin answered him. 'Although speech was still difficult . . . Even without words they understood each other perfectly.'[25] This mysterious (though traditional) appearance out of nothing and this speech 'without words', and the fact that Parvus 'breathed in his [Lenin's] face with a marshy breath' makes the skin crawl, doesn't it? But the main thing is what Satan said to Lenin; how diabolically flattering and disarmingly compelling the demonic logic of his speech was. The reader feels how 'Parvus's behemoth blood spurted from the latter into Lenin's feverish hands, poured into his veins, swirled threateningly in his bloodstream.'[26] And then everything vanished. 'No table, no Sklarz. Just a massive Swiss iron bed, with the two of them upon it, great men both, floating above a world pregnant with revolution, a world which looked up to them expectantly . . . and the bed sped again around its dark orbit.'[27] Satan had 'forced, pumped . . . his behemoth blood' into Lenin.[28]

Summary

And now, after crossing ourselves, let's sum things up. Naturally, we are not so much interested in Parvus's real role in the Russian Revolution as in his imaginary one in Solzhenitsyn's book. And this role is clearly unambiguous: to raise up a defeated 'demon' who will visit a satanic orgy of destruction upon Russia.

The image of 'satanocracy', as the reader will no doubt recall, haunted the Russian New Right from its very beginning, even VSKhSON. In the Antonovist 'Letter of the Three', published in *Veche*, it had already provided a pretext for alliance with the regime. But all that was pale, fleshless, and written with a bloodless political pen. In Solzhenitsyn, with his talent for the anthropomorphization of dead symbols, this image comes to life before us — powerful, convincing, frightening. This, apparently, is how satanocracy looks in the flesh. This is evidently how the Antichrist bought the Russian intelligentsia (in the person of Lenin) with German money. This is how the 'dark whirlwind' was born. How can the intelligentsia be trusted after this? Do they not indeed deserve political annihilation? How can they not be excluded from deciding the fate of the country? Must not the devil be expelled from the sick body of Holy Rus'?

Earlier we saw how Solzhenitsyn's thought unintentionally became intertwined with that of Chalmaev. Here we see how it intertwines with that of Antonov and how the 'dark whirlwind' of struggle against the 'lumpen' drives it irrevocably into the arms of Black Hundreds Nationalism.

Notes

1   'And why was he born in that uncouth country? Just because a quarter of his blood was Russian, fate had hitched him to a ramshackle Russian rattletrap. A quarter of his blood, but nothing in his character, his will, his inclinations made him kin to that slovenly, slapdash, eternally drunken country' (A. Solzhenitsyn, *Lenin v Tsiurikhe*, Paris: YMCA

Press, 1975, p. 87) [English edition: *Lenin in Zurich*, trans. by H. T. Willetts (New York: Bantam Books, 1976), p. 95. The bracketed page references in subsequent footnotes refer to this edition.]

2   Ibid., p. 30 [30].
3   Ibid., p. 99 [108].
4   Ibid., p. 99 [109].
5   Ibid., p. 114 [126].
6   Ibid., p. 102 [112].
7   Ibid., p. 105 [115—16].
8   Ibid. [116].
9   Ibid., p. 15 [12].
10 Ibid., p. 112 [124].
11 Ibid., p. 111 [122].
12 Ibid., p. 100 [109].
13 Ibid., p. 101 [111].
14 Ibid., p. 111 [122].
15 Ibid., p. 115 [127].
16 Ibid., p. 129 [143].
17 Ibid., p. 121 [134].
18 Ibid., p. 106 [116].
19 Ibid., p. 100 [109].
20 Ibid., p. 106 [117].
21 Ibid., p. 102 [112].
22 Ibid., p. 107 [118].
23 Ibid., p. 106 [119].
24 Ibid., p. 107 [118].
25 Ibid., p. 108 [119].
26 Ibid., p. 99 [108].
27 Ibid., p. 110 [121].
28 Ibid., p. 131 [145: slightly modified].

15

August 1914: Solzhenitsyn versus Solzhenitsyn

One thing that strikes anyone who attempts to take in Solzhenitsyn's political evolution at a glance are his dramatic and repeated renunciations of his own earlier views. Moreover, in every case the process of renunciation has been complicated by the fact that all his prior convictions had seemed to him at the time to be the only views possible (*'the truth is one'*, he stressed in 1982).[1] One might suppose that to a dogmatic mind believing in the singularity of truth, not having experienced the crucible of a sceptical liberal education and thus unaccustomed to self-criticism, the renunciation of each succeeding absolute truth would, in its own way, represent the end of the world. Yet, Solzhenitsyn has managed to survive all these ideological metamorphoses. For each of them, however, he has had to pay a price.

Three recantations

In his youth, at the end of the 1930s, when for the first time he thought of writing a giant epic about the Russian revolution, his truth amounted to a rather trivial, for Russia at the time, anti-tsarism. From this, apparently, came the plan of opening his epic (which is now called *The Red Wheel*) with the fearsome annihilation of the Russian forces that occurred in East Prussia in August 1914. From the point of view of his truth at the time, this approach was perfectly adequate. It exposed the hopeless corruption of the Orthodox monarchy and its ineluctable doom in precise terms. This, one must assume, is where he, at that time, saw the higher justification for the revolution — its inevitability.

In the Gulag, the revolution lost its charm for Solzhenitsyn. He renounced his previous anti-tsarism and became, as did we all then, an anti-Stalinist and a fighter against political idolatry and 'soul-destroying despotism'. We owe *One Day in the Life of Ivan Denisovich* and *Cancer Ward* to this, the first of his recantations. It produced in him an explosion of artistic inspiration. However, toward the end of the 1960s, while he was writing his *Gulag Archipelago*, came his second recantation. Solzhenitsyn became an anti-Leninist (thereby winning the hearts of his Western anti-Communist fellow-travellers) and a Russian nationalist (to which these fellow-travellers did not attach at the time any particular significance).

Just as the dissidents had considered him one of their own in the 1960s, so the extremist anti-Communists began to consider him one of *their* own in the following decade. From the point of view of his fellow-travellers, many of whom called themselves neo-liberals, his political evolution should have reached its completion at this point. In fact, where is there to go further to the right than neo-liberal anti-Communism? Further is fascism.

The neo-liberals face the same disappointment which befell Soviet dissidents before them. In the historical epic which Solzhenitsyn is writing today, the ideological key to which is his new two-volume edition of *August 1914*, he recants a third time. According to his current version of the truth, Leninism itself turns out to be 'almost an episode' and 'in any event, a consequence', of liberalism. The new Solzhenitsyn sees the source of Russia's misfortune not in Leninism, but in liberalism. Thus the source of the approaching worldwide disaster for him now lies not so much in Communism *per se* as in his recently acquired neo-liberal fellow-travellers (who are allegedly clearing the way for it).

If the reader still needs more proof of the ideological degeneration of 'good' nationalism, all he need do is examine the new edition of *August 1914* and the articles, interviews and letters accompanying it. Reading this, however, might prove to be somewhat of a trial in and of itself. Solzhenitsyn's series of ideological recantations have punished him with the worst thing that can happen to a writer — artistic sterility and the loss of balance and sense of proportion, something which a writer cannot do without.

A new truth

'For six years I read neither their collections of essays, nor pamphlets, nor magazines, even though many of the articles were attacking me specifically. I was working at a distance, and was obliged not to meet with any of them, anywhere, or to get to know them or talk with them. Occupied by my *uzly**, I dozed through all their attacks and polemics during these years. The vast mass of printed matter had already shown that their hackles were raised. I had already been spattered with the black oil from two dozen [muckraking critics'] brushes . . . they choked on their own venom.'[2] This is how Solzhenitsyn complained in his letter 'Our pluralists' [*Nashi pliuralisty*], addressed this time not to the leaders of the Soviet Union, but to the Russian people, and directed not against a 'black whirlwind' from the West, but against their own contemporary intellectual elite.

Solzhenitsyn now imagines himself a heroic knight, alone in his quest to save Russia. He sees himself opening the eyes of a city and a world which had been languishing for so many decades in ignorance. Even his academic fellow-travellers and the neo-liberal anti-Communists have so far not yet gone beyond Solzhenitsyn's earlier conviction, that a band of Bolshevik conspirators destroyed Russia, and the October Revolution is the root of her misfortunes. Having become wiser from the experience of fighting with the Russian Westernizers in the emigre community, who 'choked on their own venom', Solzhenitsyn has now moved on.

Today his truth consists in the following: 'Properly speaking, there was [only] one revolution in Russia. Not the one in 1905 and not the October one. It was the February Revolution that was the decisive one which *changed the course of our history* as well as that of the whole earth. The October Revolution is almost an episode and, in any event, a consequence of the February one.'[3] As he explains in *August 1914*, 'In the foreseeable time, Russia could not have moved or even survived if her monarchical image and foundations had been demolished.'[4]

In other words there cannot be a Russia without an Orthodox monarchy is Solzhenitsyn's current truth. In fact, a Russia which is not autocratic and not Orthodox is not recognized as Russia at all. It is painful for him to observe his liberal critics' attempts to immortalize the overthrow of tsarism, and he sees it as another of their efforts once more to unleash a 'February catastrophe' upon his country: 'If suddenly tomorrow the party bureaucracy were to fall', he warns,

---

* [Translator's note: *uzly*, the plural of *uzel*, roughly meaning a 'cluster' or 'knot' of activity centred around a particular event. Solzhenitsyn's narration in *Red Wheel* moves from one such 'cluster' of actions focused around a particular point of time to the next, quite discrete, 'cluster'.]

'these *cultural forces* would also come to the surface — and we'd hear their constant wailing not about the people's needs, not about land, and not about [our] extinction, . . . but about rights, rights, rights . . . and what's left of us they would see smashed apart in yet another February, in yet another disintegration [of the nation].[5] Ten years of struggle in the emigre world with liberals and opponents of Communism has convinced him that the root of Russia's troubles is not at all in Communism but rather in the ruinous 'wailing about [human] rights.'

The Leont'ev connection

The reader may perhaps recall that earlier I spoke of a paper I delivered at the 7th Congress of American Slavists in 1975, called 'The Paradox of Solzhenitsyn: Halfway to Konstantin Leont'ev'. At the time, I had in mind the danger which Solzhenitsyn's political evolution faced from the moment he began to serve as spokesman for the reborn Russian Idea. He had begun by distinguishing himself in the 1960s by his struggle against political idolatry, like Konstantin Aksakov a hundred years before. Now his search for a 'truly Russian' alternative to the Soviet regime threatened to slip into an apology for Orthodox monarchy that would be no different from Konstantin Leont'ev's. For this metamorphosis to occur, all that would be needed was a crisis — the catalyst for ideological degeneration. I could not have known in 1975 just what that fateful catalyst would be. I knew only that he was then already half-way into this transformation. Now we know what happened: it was a decade of struggle within the emigre community that acted as the catalyst. Solzhenitsyn was actually transformed into a latter-day Konstantin Leont'ev. The metamorphosis was complete.

> God forbid that the majority of Russians reach the point that, step by step, already many Frenchmen have, i.e., [to become] accustomed to serving and loving any kind of France. What good to us is a Russia that is non-autocratic and non-Orthodox? What use is such a Russia? Such a Russia could be served only out of need and dumb fear.[6]

It was Konstantin Leont'ev who said that, and for just that reason he proposed 'freezing Russia, so that she won't decay.'[7] He wouldn't have forgiven her a liberal, westernizing revolution. For him that would have been the beginning of the end of Russia. Yet isn't this just what we are now hearing from Solzhenitsyn?

Even if Russia freely voted for a republic instead of an Orthodox monarchy (as she, in fact, did do in the elections to the Constituent Assembly in 1917), Leont'ev would have refused to accept her choice. He had no need for a Russia that was not both autocratic and Orthodox. It wasn't Russia he loved, but the autocracy in Russia. Solzhenitsyn in the 1980s, like Leont'ev in the 1880s, has no need of a non-autocratic, non-Orthodox Russia either. In *August 1914* he himself found the words which epitomize that branch of Russian thought to which he now belongs: 'the intolerant extreme right, which doesn't wish to see any development of society, any movement in thought, nor, moreover, any compromises, but only the prayerful worship of the tsar and the country's stony immobility — one more century, one more century, one more century.'[8]

Solzhenitsyn ignored

One way or another, today's Solzhenitsyn does not doubt, any more than did Leont'ev before him, that his critics are enemies of the Russian people. Otherwise, why should they remain silent about his epic, which he offers as the main means of averting a new catastrophe for Russia? He has dedicated his life to this epic. He has renounced the world for its sake and, like the mythical Atlas, has taken the whole weight of the universe upon his shoulders. Meanwhile, the critics take no notice. They squabble with him as if with some rank-and-file politician, judging him by his speeches and interviews, but behaving as though his gigantic literary masterpiece, which unravels all historical riddles and answers all questions, simply did not exist.

> Well there they are, my ten volumes. And there's a dozen historical chapters — attack them! Smash them! Such an expanse [of ideas] for you! Here is a complete *program* to be disseminated — Shipov's [program] (at present still deeper than anything which has been offered by our pluralists). Is the print too tiny? Don't their eyes pick it up? No! They squabble with me like with some party propagandist. They fall all over one single paragraph of some interview.[9]

As a human being one cannot but feel sorry for Solzhenitsyn. A man spends years in self-imposed confinement writing volume upon volume of a gigantic epic masterpiece not just of literature, but of philosophy and history too, and a group of his fellow-countrymen — 'smatterers' (among whom, by the way, number some of the best Russian editors and literary critics) — ignore the product of his labour — a work which includes within it a new *War and Peace*, a new *Devils* and a new *Fathers and Sons*. They can spatter him with 'two dozen [muckraking] oil-laden brushes' if they like, but what really hurts is that they ignore his profound *programme* for Russia's rebirth as though it didn't exist.

Later we will examine more closely the Shipov—Solzhenitsyn programme for 'combining autocracy and self-rule'. More important however, is that, for the first time in all these years Solzhenitsyn has finally referred to the source of his inspiration. For now, we ask only one question: why are Solzhenitsyn's stubborn countrymen so insensitive to the greatest literary masterpiece of our era? Why do they so doggedly refuse not only to acknowledge his spiritual leadership, but even to recognize his epic as a work of art? Is there indeed not a mystery in all this — especially since we're talking about the same people who just a few years ago were his most devoted and ardent readers and admirers? These are the same people who cried over his 'Matriona's Household', who felt Ivan Denisovich's grief as their own and who swore revenge when reading his *Gulag Archipelago*.

Solzhenitsyn's explanation we already know: it is a conspiracy against Russia. 'Various levels of development, various ages, various degrees of independent thought, but all of them,' he accuses, 'singing one deafening tune: against Russia! As if they had made an agreement.'[10] But this is hardly an explanation. What reason would all these sons of Russia have to conspire against their homeland? Why should they renounce the new works of the respected and admired author of *The First Circle* and *Cancer Ward*? They might not have agreed with his view in the 1960s either, but that didn't stop them from acclaiming him as the brightest new star in the Russian literary firmament and a new hope for a literary revival. So why do they avoid discussing his new books, and criticize, or even mention them?

Had Solzhenitsyn asked himself these questions, and had he not been too proud ever to meet or talk to anyone about it, he might have discovered the answers to the mystery years ago. But the truth might have been too terrible to accept.

The critics

To one American neo-liberal critic, very well-disposed toward Solzhenitsyn and valuing him for his anti-Communism, there is no mystery here at all. He read *August 1914* (in its first edition), and compared it not only with *One Day in the Life of Ivan Denisovich* but also with *War and Peace*. His conclusion is devastating:

> *War and Peace*, one of the greatest of all novels, is alive in every detail, and *August 1914* is, to put it plainly, dead from beginning to end. Neither the fictional nor the historical personages are truly realized, and though the combat scenes are scrupulously rendered, they remain staged set pieces with no power to arouse the emotions or to draw the reader in. As for the narrative line, it is driven by the grim energy of the author's will and not by the inner compulsion through which the living organism of a genuine work of novelistic art always unfolds itself. In short, judging by *August 1914*, Solzhenitsyn's epic of the Revolution fails utterly in its claim to stand beside *War and Peace*. Beyond this, it bespeaks the collapse of the hope that Solzhenitsyn would rescue and revive the great stifled tradition of the 19th-century Russian novel.[11]

Such is the merciless verdict of a well-wishing American critic who is in no sense an 'enemy of the people' nor one who in any way 'hates all things Russian'. On the contrary, he is filled with the sincerest sympathy for the Russian people, suffering under Communist oppression. So, even to his political allies, Solzhenitsyn's epic is no literary masterpiece. Indeed, to those who read the new edition of *August 1914*, whatever parallels it contains to *War and Peace, Fathers and Sons* or even *The Devils* seemed utterly out of place. They were books created by great masters of literature. Alas, all that emerges from under Solzhenitsyn's pen these days is merely a raw, helplessly constructed and, at times, densely confused mass of print, devoid of any artistic sense. Everything is so poorly focused that some chapters could have been left out, or others added, without damaging the work as a whole. Unfortunately, it is also excruciatingly boring to read.

A well-wishing emigre critic, in a magazine controlled by the Russian New Right, could not manage to say anything more complementary about the new edition of *August 1914* than the following:

> we see . . . columns, a ceiling overhead, pieces of superstructure, pullies, all the things that one can see where a palace or a warehouse is being built. Who knows what it will be: maybe an as yet unheard-of temple or maybe a disorderly agglomeration of various types of structures . . . The impression is that one has read through something of a series of separate works: at first, the opening of a large novel . . . secondly, a fictionalized chronicle of military operations in East Prussia . . . and then three stories — the tale of the terrorist Dmitrii Bogrov, a hagiographic portrait of Petr Stolypin and a satirical pamphlet about

Nicholas II. (Plus a satirical novellette about Lenin.) Thus, the fleeting comparisons to *War and Peace* in the first critical reviews seem very shallow . . . The true precursor to the genre of *Red Wheel* . . . is documentary chronicles . . . The question of whether it's reasonable to consider documentary chronicles as artistic works remains, however, debatable.[12]

Yet it was the old edition, which is incomparably more vibrant than the new, that provoked an American critic, not feeling the emigre's compulsion to speak in Aesopian language and to perform the ritual homage to a living classic, to describe it as 'dead from beginning to end'.

Collective guilt

Admittedly, it is easy for an American critic to pronounce such judgements, and not only because he is not party to emigre censorship. He also didn't cry over 'Matriona's household' or swear to take revenge while reading *Gulag Archipelago*. He even fails to see artistic merit in *Cancer Ward*.

As in *August 1914* — and as in *Cancer Ward*, another long and thickly populated novel set in a hospital for patients suffering from cancer — Solzhenitsyn doggedly does all the things a novelist is supposed to do. He constructs plots, he catalogues details of scene and character, he transcribes conversations, he sets up dramatic conflicts, he moves toward resolutions. Yet all to no avail. Edmund Wilson once said of F. Scott Fitzgerald that despite everything that was wrong with his novels, they never failed to live. The opposite can be said of Solzhenitsyn's novels: despite everything that is right about them, they always fail to live.[13]

None of the Russian 'smatterer' intellectuals could ever force themselves to say such a thing about *Cancer Ward*. For them, it would be like killing a piece of their own soul. They would defend 'their Solzhenitsyn', in whom are concentrated all their 1960s' hopes that great Russian literature, the nation's conscience, lives on. They would recoil from our friendly American critic's statement that Solzhenitsyn 'was moved by ordinary, completely conventional literary ambitions'.[14] Even in *August 1914* they seek to find the vanishing traces of his once inspired pen, if only in just a few battle scenes, individual characters or snatches of dialogue.

It simply pains them as human beings to witness such talent being squandered, and the man blessed with it so tragically reduced to a fanatical dogmatist who still considers himself a thundering Zeus. They are embarrassed by his fatal metamorphosis and their own unrealized hopes. It is as if they must share the blame for what has happened to him: how could they have failed to save such a writer! That is why their arguments with Solzhenitsyn do not refer to his epic and, in particular, the second edition of *August 1914*, which contains the quintessence of his present-day truth. In contrast to well-wishing American critics, such an undertaking for them would be too traumatic.

I do not intend to breach this unwritten convention. In the preceding chapter I analysed *Lenin in Zurich* as a political pamphlet. Here I shall analyse *August 1914* from the point of view of what I call 'the sociology of literature'. Stated simply, I intend to compare and contrast Solzhenitsyn the Russian New Right party propagandist with Solzhenitsyn the novelist, as I did in Moscow at the beginning of the 1970s with the leading lights of Socialist Realism.[15] Experience showed then that the staunchest adherents of Soviet party canons suddenly became the most merciless critics of these same canons when faced with such an approach. Let's look at what the new edition of *August 1914* has to tell us about Solzhenitsyn's party's canons.

Who is to blame?

The main question posed in *August 1914* is, Who was responsible for the destruction of the Russian army in the woods and swamps of East Prussia in the space of one fatal week? To whom does Russia owe her most tragic military disaster — one which set the tone for the rest of the war as well as its outcome, and ultimately led to the political catastrophe of 1917? In other words, whoever was to blame for the August slaughter is, in Solzhenitsyn's eyes, also to blame for Russia's fate in the twentieth century.

Who were these villains then, who were responsible for the defeats of August 1914 and hence for the February Revolution — the only one, as we now know from Solzhenitsyn, that changed the course of Russian history? For Solzhenitsyn the propagandist, the answer is unambiguous: they were liberals, terrorists, Bolsheviks and Jews — in a word, 'demons' inspired by the decadent, disintegrating West. According to the imperative of the Russian Idea, there can be no other answer. Otherwise, the decadence of the Orthodox monarchy and its lamentable incapacity to cope with the empire's historical decline would have to be blamed, as the earlier anti-tsarist Solzhenitsyn of the 1930s believed. To acknowledge this, would mean that the guilty party is precisely the ideal to which today's Russian New Right is calling its country 'homeward' — Russia's pre-Communist political tradition — and not any Russian or foreign-born 'demons'. To Solzhenitsyn as propagandist, such a recognition would be tantamount to political suicide. He knows his party obligations and does all he can to carry them out in his book, where, he believes, history is the judge.

From the very beginning of the book the West appears in the role of the accused. The French ambassador Paleologus writes to the tsar, 'I beg Your Majesty to order your forces to begin the attack immediately. Otherwise the French army runs the risk of being crushed.'[16] A few chapters later, we read a letter from the French Minister of Foreign Affairs to his ambassador,[17] followed by the author's ironical commentary that, 'Instead of allowing for 29 days of preparation after mobilization, the attack was launched after only 15 days of preparation, while the rear was still unprepared — such was the nervous rush to save Paris that gripped everyone.'[18] After a few more chapters the theme of 'saving France'[19] appears again as one of the reasons for the difficulties experienced by the Russian army in Prussia. Thus, the West, as New Right party canon dictates, assumes its rightful place in the dock.

Of course, after a few more chapters, the Bolsheviks join them there, in the person of Lenin, who 'acted as if some powerful force [dictated his actions]'[20] (we already know what kind of satanic force this was), and who — significantly — was driven by this at the very moment when the traitorous slogan of transforming the imperialist war into a civil one was conceived.[21] Even if the monologue attributed to him by Solzhenitsyn is of doubtful literary merit, it is nevertheless revealing:

A-a, got you now you rapacious carrion-crow from the coat of arms! You won't pull yourself out of the clutches that grasp you this time! You chose this war yourself! Let them chew you up — all the way to Kiev! to Kharkov! to Riga! Let them beat your great power spirit so you drop dead! You're only fit to squeeze others, nothing more! Amputate Russia all around. Poland, Finland — cut them off! The Baltic region — cut if off! The Ukraine — cut it off! The Caucasus — cut it off! Drop dead![22]

In this remarkable tirade there's only one small thing that's unclear: why, in point of fact, does the separation of Poland or Finland, or the

Baltic region, or even the Ukraine and the Caucasus qualify here as an amputation of *Russia* rather than of her *empire*? If, as is obvious from the text, it's the empire that's being amputated, then why should Solzhenitsyn object? What is it he is actually fighting for today, Russia or her empire? 'Why can't we live together with Poland as two free and equal nations? Why must we force everyone into serfdom to us? What makes us better than them?'[23] It was not Lenin who said this, but rather Herzen. Is he also guilty in Solzhenitsyn's opinion, of having intended to amputate Russia? Sometimes Solzhenitsyn rather gives himself away.

Anyway, the Bolsheviks also assume their rightful place in dock among those accused of guilt for the August debacle — even if there is nothing, apart from a tasteless monologue, to hold them responsible for. The nihilist intelligentsia — the smatterers — are represented in the army by ensign Sasha Lenartovich, who, in fact, makes no contribution to the August disaster other than thinking about the senselessness of the war and attempting to surrender himself to the Germans after the Russian army has been defeated. Both his 'smatterer' aunts are given much wider coverage. Yet their contribution to the defeat consists merely in trying to convince their student niece that the tsarist monarchy is a disgrace to Russia. This, of course, could provoke indignation among party 'patriots', but it doesn't have any direct relevance to military operations.[24]

As for terrorists, they are represented in the court of history by an impressive parade of 'Anarchists, Social Revolutionaries and Maximalists'.[25] However, they too appear only in the recollections of Lenartovich's aunts and not on the field of battle in East Prussia. The story of Stolypin's murderer, Mordechai Bogrov, which occupies over two hundred pages, is also presented as evidence against terrorists. To Solzhenitsyn it was important that Bogrov's 'great-grandfather on his father's side and his grandfather on his mother's side were wine concessionaires',[26] while Stolypin was 'the son of an adjutant general and the great-grandson of a senator'.[27] However, this story deserves special discussion and we'll return to it in the next chapter. The point that needs to be made here, however, is that since these things happened three years prior to August 1914, they couldn't have had a direct effect on the events in question.

Finally, of course, the theme of the West's guilt arises, in the concluding scene of the novel where Colonel Vorotyntsev, the author's alter ego, delivers an impassioned speech before the Russian High Command 'with the same directness as a dying man saying his last words'.[28] Just as Solzhenitsyn, in his *Gulag Archipelago*, spoke with the leaders of the Soviet empire on behalf of those who perished innocently, so Vorotyntsev makes a similar appeal to the leaders of the Russian empire. Even in this state of mind Vorotyntsev clearly realized that it wasn't the desire to save France that caused the destruction of the Russian army, but rather the mind-boggling incompetence of its very own leaders, their complete, total and hopeless inability to lead an army, conduct a war or guide Russia. 'We don't know how to lead any unit larger than a regiment — there's a conclusion for you.'[29]

That is how Solzhenitsyn the novelist, in the heat of indignation, having momentarily forgotten his obligations as a New Right party propagandist, characterizes the people who the Orthodox monarchy entrusted with the fate of the army, the front, the war and Russia itself. Postovskii is described as 'a wan, indecisive, but assiduous major general who had never in his life been to war';[30] 'this paperweight never understood anything nor could he ever.'[31] Kondratovich is a 'notorious coward'.[32] Blagoveshchenskii — a 'Sack of shit. Dripping-wet shit, too.'[33] Kliuev — 'a dough trough, not a general!'[34], who 'has never been to a war in his whole life.'[35] Artamonov is 'nothing but a braggart and a liar'; 'an errand-boy disguised as a general . . . But how did he get to be a General-of-the-Infantry? How did 64,000 Russian troops end up under his negligent supervision?'[36]

If the generals are all 'fools or cowards',[37] then higher up, it gets worse. Zhilinskii, a front commander, is a 'living corpse' and 'a gravedigger'.[38] Yanushkevich, head of the general staff, is a 'velvet milksop'.[39] 'It is obvious from each of his effeminate movements,' says Solzhenitsyn, 'that this is a mock-general, yet how could he possibly occupy the post of head of the High Command? And nothing can be done to prevent him from destroying even the whole of Russia's entire army.'[40] Danilov, the main strategist of the Russian army, is 'a ruminant';[41] 'his head was empty! . . . and his ideas feeble!'[42] Finally, the Supreme Commander himself is described as 'his Most August Fairy . . . of course he had the height, the look, the voice . . . but in his head — not a thing.'[43]

None of these people were liberals or Jews, or terrorists. None were, in a word, 'demons'. They were not given their positions of authority by Lenartovich's aunts, by Lenin or even by Parvus. The principal 'fairies', 'ruminants' and 'milksops' were appointed personally by the Orthodox monarch himself.[44] They, in turn, chose people like themselves to command the fronts, the armies and the corps in their charge. As for the 'living corpse' and 'gravedigger', 'he was close to the court of Maria Feodorovna',[45] the dowager empress and Stolypin's only supporter at court.

How did it happen that they all — from the corps commanders

right up to the High Command — represent, in Solzhenitsyn's portrayal at any rate, a total freak show, a collection of monsters — to use the author's phrase, a 'sack of shit'? Who destroyed the Russian army in the woods and swamps of East Prussia in August of 1914 — and with it Russia herself? Was it the 'demons' with their 'endless wailing about rights'? Shouldn't they be the ones to bear the blame, according to Solzhenitsyn the propagandist and the imperative of the Russian Idea? Or was it the monsters, created and placed at the helm by that very same Orthodox monarchy which Solzhenitsyn and his cohorts behind the Russian Idea now present as the political ideal for Russia's future?

Solzhenitsyn the novelist answers this question unequivocally: tsarism is to blame. It's this answer by Solzhenitsyn the novelist that turns the book *August 1914* into a personal August 1914 for Solzhenitsyn the party propagandist.

Novelist or propagandist?

Incompetent military and political leadership is by no means the monopoly of Orthodox monarchy. Such things can happen under any kind of political system, including under Solzhenitsyn's hated 'parliamentarism'. However, it is hard to imagine a democratic government that would not be removed from office immediately, if its policies led to a military debacle and the loss of a major war. Under 'parliamentarism' there exist legal procedures which make such a change of government minimally damaging to the country in a crisis situation. In other words, a military disaster does not at all necessarily become a catastrophe for the nation. The fatal flaw of medieval Orthodox monarchy is that there is no painless way of correcting major mistakes in state policy. That's why it makes a national catastrophe inevitable.

Solzhenitsyn the novelist demonstrates this graphically in the final scene of his novel in which the monarchist monsters achieve total and complete victory over Vorotyntsev, a character who was nourishing the faint utopian hope (Solzhenitsyn's) that the Orthodox monarchy could still be saved at the last minute — from itself. This proved to be impossible.

Solzhenitsyn the novelist knows all too well, just as Konstantin Aksakov did, that the Orthodox monarchy represented a social institution under which 'universal corruption or relaxation of moral principles reached enormous proportions'. He knows that this corruption 'became no longer a private sin but a public one', and '[therein lies] the immorality of the whole social structure.' Solzhenitsyn the novelist furiously denounces this immorality as follows: 'The higher the headquarters . . . the sharper and more immediately one expects to find narcissists, careerists and fossils there . . . Not singularly, but whole mobs of them, who think of the army as a comfortable, carpeted and shiningly polished staircase, on the steps of which stars and medals are handed out.'[46] This 'carpeted staircase of promotions', constructed under the Orthodox monarchy, is such that 'it isn't the independent ones who move up so much as the obedient, not the smart, but the meticulous and dependable, and whoever manages to please his superiors more.'[47] Promotion, here, is governed 'by seniority of incompetence and court influence'.[48]

However, for Solzhenitsyn the novelist, the most deadly condemnation of the Orthodox monarchy is that 'the key tone for it all was set by His Majesty.'[49] Therefore, even if by some miracle (or, more precisely, in the event of an extraordinary national crisis) a genuine statesman, like Petr Stolypin, rises to the helm of the Orthodox monarchy, he remains unappreciated, unprotected and, ultimately, is betrayed. He is then remembered in history as a 'hangman' by the Left and a 'traitor' by the Right:[50] 'Russia will inter her best head of government in a hundred or two hundred years amidst derision, hate, and abandonment by left-, semi-left-, and right-wingers alike. From emigre terrorists all the way to the pious tsar.'[51]

For Solzhenitsyn the novelist, the Orthodox monarchy 'is a slough. Tar water. It doesn't even go around in circles',[52] no matter what its loyal servants do to save it. Vorotyntsev 'threw himself into the operation because he thought the army's fate and victory would be decided in the ranks on the field. But when *they felt the way they did* at the top, that was already beyond the limits of tactics and strategy.'[53] Thus, Solzhenitsyn the propagandist's truth in the realm of politics, which he judges to be so conclusive and irrefutable, is insistently, line by line and word by word, dislodged from its position by Solzhenitsyn the novelist.

Solzhenitsyn's entire criticism of 'our pluralists' is based on the assertion that 'the truth is one' (and therefore pluralism is a lie and an unnecessary one). Yet clearly in *August 1914* there are at least two truths: one possessed by Solzhenitsyn the novelist and another by Solzhenitsyn the party propagandist. Which of these two Solzhenitsyns, each mercilessly contradicting the other, should we believe?

A final appeal

At the very end of *August 1914*, one of these Solzhenitsyns unexpectedly blurts out: 'Suddenly I have a distressing feeling about all of us — we're in the wrong place . . . Lost. We're doing the wrong thing.'[54] This is just what 'our pluralists' have been saying to Solzhenitsyn and his comrades of the Russian Idea: You're lost. You're doing the wrong thing. You're calling the country in the wrong direction. Russia's Orthodox monarchy has already once pushed her over the brink. So why should you expect salvation from this monarchy in the awesome age of nuclear weapons? Might not another Nicholas II, not to mention another Paul and Peter, annihilate Russia once and for all so that not even a memory of her remained?

To conclude my picture of the conflict between the two Solzhenitsyns, I can quote nothing more apt than Solzhenitsyn's appeal.

> I have written all this in one last hope and I appeal [to you] . . . gentlemen, comrades, wake up! Russia is not just a geographical expanse, a picturesque backdrop for your 'self-expression.' If you continue to expound yourselves in the Russian language, then [at least try to] bring in addition something good, sympathetic, just a bit of love and an attempt at understanding to the people who have created that language.[55]

But no. They just continue to go on and on about monarchy and Orthodoxy. Don't they know that 'to apply one's own values in evaluating someone else's judgement is ignorance and violence'?[56] Yet all they do is to continually apply their own values, repeating after Leont'ev, 'What good to us is a Russia that isn't autocratic and isn't Orthodox? What use is such a Russia to us?'

Notes

1   *Vestnik RKhD*, No. 139, 1983, p. 134.
2   Ibid., p. 133.
3   Ibid., No. 138, p. 162.
4   A. I. Solzhenitsyn, *Collected Works*, Paris: 1983, v. 12, pp. 188—9.
5   *Vestnik RKhD*, No. 139, 1983, p. 154.
6   K. N. Leont'ev, *Works*, St. Petersburg: 1913, v. 7, pp. 206—7. Of course, Solzhenitsyn's metamorphosis took place purely in ideological terms. As

a politician and thinker, the distance from Solzhenitsyn to Leont'ev is like from here to the stars. Therefore, in the political sense, he very likely will always remain a sectarian of the 'immobile Aksakov cast', one of those whom Leont'ev so despised. It was not Solzhenitsyn who marked the start of F-Nationalism in modern times. That remained to be done by another more realistic dissident politician, as the reader will discover.

7   Ibid., p. 124.
8   Solzhenitsyn, op. cit., p. 305.
9   *Vestnik RKhD*, No. 139, p. 156.
10 Ibid., p. 135.
11 Norman Podhoretz, 'The Terrible Question of Alexander Solzhenitsyn', *Commentary*, Feb. 1985, p. 20.
12 Lev Losev, 'Velikolepnoe budushchee Rossii' ['Russia's Marvellous Future'], *Kontinent*, No. 42, 1985, pp. 292–3.
13 Podhoretz, op. cit., p. 21.
14 Ibid., p. 23.
15 I would have probably long since lost count of all the discussions I have ventured in the Soviet literary press on the theme of 'the sociology of literature', had not one of my Soviet opponents, in an enraged article remarkably reminiscent of Solzhenitsyn's jeremiads, presented a long bibliography of my transgressions. Here it is: 'A. Yanov, "The Young Hero Movement, Sociological Notes on the Fiction of the 60s" ["Dvizhenle molodogo geroia. Sotsiologicheskie zametki o khudozhestvennoi proze 60-kh godov"], *Novyi mir*, 1972, No. 7; A. Yanov, "The Working Theme. Sociological Notes on Literary Criticism" ["Rabochaia tema. Sotsiologiches-kie zametki o literaturnoi kritike"], *Literatura i sovremennost'*, No. 11, Moscow: 1972; A Yanov, "The Production Play and the Literary Hero of the 1970s" ["Proizvodstvennaia p'esa i literaturnyi geroi 1970-kh"], *Voprosy literatury*, 1972, No. 8; A. Yanov, "Cinema and the Scientific-Technical Revolution. Sociological Notes" ["Kino i nauchno-tekhnicheskaia revoliutsia. Sotsiologicheskie zametki"], *Iskusstvo kino*, 1972, No. 11; A. Yanov, "Blue Aeolis and Grey Reality" ["Goluboi Eolis i seraia deistvitel'nost". Sotsiologicheskie zametki"], *Detskaia literatura*, 1973, No. 2; A. Yanov, "Emotions and Arguments, Critical Notes on One Reader Discussion" ["Emotsii i argumenty. Kriticheskie zametki ob odnoi chitatel'skoi diskussii"], *Molodoi kommunist*, 1973, No. 3. Criticisms of A. Yanov's articles were made by G. Brovman (*Iskusstvo kino*, 1972, No. 11); V. Kantorovich (*Iskusstvo kino*, 1973, No. 4); F. Chapchakhov (*Literaturnaia gazeta*, 16 Aug. 1972) and others. How-ever, I think the time has come to look more thoroughly and, so to speak, systematically, into what A. Yanov so insistently dwells on' (Valentin Khmara, 'Make No Graven Images' [Ne sotvori sebe kumira'], *Literaturnoe obozrenie*, June, 1973).
16 A. I. Solzhenitsyn, op. cit., v. 11, p. 21.
17 Ibid., p. 53.
18 Ibid., p. 89.
19 Ibid., p. 108.
20 Ibid., p. 208.
21 Ibid., p. 231.
22 Ibid., p. 230.

23   Quoted from A. Yanov, 'Alternative' ['Alternativa'], *Molodoi kommunist*,
     1974, No. 2, p. 71.
24   Solzhenitsyn, op. cit., v. 12, pp. 66—113.
25   Ibid., p. 87.
26   Ibid., p. 114.
27   Ibid., p. 167.
28   Ibid., p. 525.
29   Ibid., p. 528.
30   Ibid., v. 11, p. 98.
31   Ibid., p. 297.
32   Ibid., p. 160 [p. 153 of English translation of first edition].
33   Ibid. [153].
34   Ibid., p. 336.
35   Ibid., p. 289.
36   Ibid., pp. 161, 246.
37   Ibid., p. 363.
38   Ibid., v. 12, p. 519.
39   Ibid., p. 511.
40   Ibid., pp. 529—30.
41   Ibid., p. 529.
42   Ibid., p. 520.
43   Ibid., p. 511.
44   Ibid., p. 497.
45   Ibid., v. 11, p. 92.
46   Ibid., p. 116.
47   Ibid., p. 120.
48   Ibid.
49   Ibid., v. 12, p. 306.
50   Ibid., p. 305.
51   Ibid., pp. 305—6.
52   Ibid., p. 512.
53   Ibid., p. 513.
54   Ibid., p. 514.
55   *Vestnik RKhD*, No. 139, p. 154.
56   Ibid., p. 134.

16
Diabolerie Two

So far we have observed the prophets of the Russian Idea over the course of four generations — three under Orthodox monarchy and one under Soviet rule. This should be enough to enable us to recognize some standard patterns of behaviour and techniques of argumentation. How do they react, for example, when a contradiction between their doctrine and reality forces them to the wall (as happened to Solzhenitsyn over *August 1914*)? We have already seen one of these patterns: it consists in the removal of a political dispute to the realm of metaphysics, to a struggle between absolute Good and absolute Evil, Russia vs. the Devil. That was what the VSKhSON ideologists and *Veche* readers did by resurrecting the idea of 'satanocracy'. It is also what Vladimir Maksimov and Boris Paramonov are doing by replacing contemporary politics with metaphysics and Slavophile political doctrine with 'cultural philosophy'.

Another typical pattern, we observed, is to blame non-Russians for Russia's misfortunes. Thus, for second generation Slavophiles, the role of the devil/serpent was fulfilled by parliamentary Europe:

> There was a time when the Russian upper classes, seduced by the temptation of Western civilization . . . rushed to renounce their nationality . . . Not having the opportunity to be *reborn* as Westerners, they hurried to *disguise themselves* as them instead. The lie of alien nationality swaggered about openly in a powdered wig . . . Another time came . . . Russian people . . . the upper classes of society *were* born again . . . [with] the fullest spiritual servility toward Europe.[1]

That was Ivan Aksakov. The third generation of Slavophiles firmly shifted the guilt for all of Russia's maladies onto the Jews.

Finally, the third, and most remarkable, pattern of argument resorted to by adherents of the Russian Idea in an extreme situation is to combine the Jews and the Devil into one rhetorical figure representing all the world's Evil. Yu. M. Odinzgoev did this, and so did Solzhenitsyn in his first descent into diabolerie, where Izrail' Parvus proved conveniently to be both a Jew and Satan.

The Jewish calling

Solzhenitsyn's ideological about-face in *August 1914* left him with the following insoluble problem that the liberals who, according to the Russian Idea's dictum, were supposed to be responsible for the collapse of the Orthodox monarchy, were not, in fact, guilty according to Solzhenitsyn the novelist. Instead of coming up with a potent confirmation of the party line, he had created confusion. The first edition of *August 1914* was relentless in leaving no loopholes in its denunciation of the Orthodox monarchy. How could he reconcile this contradiction?

In line with the second traditional pattern of behaviour of preachers of the Russian Idea, and with little regard for the damage he might do to the artistic integrity of his novel, Solzhenitsyn introduced the Jewish theme into his new edition. At the centre of the novel are two characters who have no relation to the history of the August catastrophe — Petr Stolypin, who transparently symbolizes Russia, and the Jew, Mordechai Bogrov, who kills this symbol of Russia and is thus true to the certain[1] 'three-thousand-year-old calling'[2] of his cunning race. In the artistic sense this story line ruins *August 1914*, while intending to save it in the partisan political sense. Yet there was apparently no other way to show that, despite its decay, so amply demonstrated by Solzhenitsyn himself, the Orthodox monarchy did not die on its own but was toppled by 'demons'.

Solzhenitsyn leaves his readers not the slightest doubt that Stolypin symbolized the happy future of Orthodox monarchy in Russia — and its sole hope of resisting the 'demons'. 'True to his name, he really was a *pillar* ['stolp' in Russian means 'pillar'] of the state. He became a centre of Russian life as none of the tsars had done. (And really, his qualities were tsar-like). There was once again a *Peter* over Russia.'[3] Under the guidance of this new Peter, 'Russia was recovering irreversibly.'[4] Once again there can be no doubt that when Mordechai Bogrov shot Stolypin, he was shooting at the very 'heart of the state'.[5] He killed 'not only the prime minister, but an entire state program', thus altering the 'course of history of a people 170 million strong'.[6]

At the same time, Solzhenitsyn's reader is not allowed to forget that the course of this history was altered by a Jew. 'Permit me to remind you', Bogrov says, 'that to this day we live under the domination of Black Hundreds leaders. The Jews will never forget the Krushevans, Dubrovins, and Purishkeviches. And where is Gertsenshtein? And Yollos? Where are thousands of mutilated Jews [men, women and children with their stomachs ripped open and their noses and ears cut off]?'[7] Even a disciplined emigre critic, who does not permit himself to go beyond the bounds of Aesopian language, was compelled to note that, 'From the very beginning, the name Bogrov is surrounded in the book by almost exclusively Jewish names . . . There are almost no non-Jewish names to be found around Bogrov's [in the book] although in the [historical] documents they are more than half . . . For Solzhenitsyn it is not so important that Bogrov was a sleaze as it is that he was a Jew.'[8] 'I have fought for the good and happiness of the Jewish people', Bogrov says on the day of his hanging. Solzhenitsyn underscores this: 'That was his sole piece of testimony which didn't change.'[9] 'Here Bogrov was not scheming or inventing a story. He remained true to his people to the end.'[10]

An evil design

Thus, on the second of September of the year 1911, in the Kiev city theatre, the Jew Mordechai Bogrov, heeding the 'three thousand-year-old calling' of his cunning race, murdered the Russian Orthodox monarchy: 'with these bullets an entire dynasty was killed.'[11] 'The course of history of a people 170-million strong' was severed that day forcibly and irreversibly — and in this Solzhenitsyn manages to establish the 'demon's' guilt. In this way, the central contradiction of *August 1914* was cleared aside by the second pattern of behaviour of the Russian Idea's proponents . . . or was it?

In fact, haven't we already heard from Solzhenitsyn that, a certain 'decisive revolution . . . altered the course of our history and of the entire earth as well' — not the bullets of Mordechai Bogrov? There, one recalls, he was talking about February 1917 rather than September 1911. The 'decisive' character of the February Revolution was that the liberals with their 'constant wailing for rights' 'smashed apart' the Orthodox monarchy and toppled a 300-year-old dynasty. How was it then that Bogrov, hanged a few years earlier, managed to murder this very same dynasty with one shot? What was it that actually 'altered the course of our people and the entire earth' — a Jewish terrorist or the liberal revolution?

As we see, Solzhenitsyn is again faced with a dramatic dilemma. In the process of removing one contradiction, there has arisen a new and deeper one. Can it be that those 230 pages that ruin the structure of the novel are all for nothing? How can this new problem be resolved? How can we equate the liberal revolution with the single act of a Jewish terrorist? This problem is so vast that a Diabolerie II has to be programmed into its solution. Only by attributing superhuman significance to a single terrorist act, only by raising it to the status of absolute Evil, whose sinister designs we are not able to fathom — just as we cannot know God's plans — is the author able to span the chronological gap and combine September 1911 and February 1917 into one. Both the despicable Bogrov and the hateful liberals eventually turn out to be tools of the same all-encompassing Evil that has raised its sword against Russia. Like Parvus, Bogrov has to combine in his character traits of both a Jew and the devil. But whereas the demonic essence of Izrail' Parvus was presented to us as a behemoth, Mordechai Bogrov's appears to the reader in a more traditional form of the biblical serpent.

The demon Jew

The demonizing of Bogrov happens gradually. It is introduced carefully, at first by completely unnoticed strokes. Bogrov manages to 'slip through noiselessly and invisibly between the revolution and the police'.[12] A few pages later, someone talking with him suddenly sees him 'with his two front teeth protruding, they pushed forward when his upper lip rose in conversation.'[13] A little further on, he crawls along a pole that is 'perfectly smooth and without notches or knots. It will have to be crawled up . . . without holding on to anything',[14] 'his whole body rubbing and creeping along in an unreal manner'.[15] Pages later, the resemblance grows: Bogrov 'with his elongated squeezed head, constantly a bit tilted to one side, and lips perpetually ajar'.[16] Neither fangs nor venom are yet mentioned, only his 'narrow head a bit tilted to the side',[17] only how he 'casts a spell, like the song of a rare bird, stretching out his neck and seeming kind even to his enemies at such moments'.[18] But here, for the first time, the metaphor becomes very clear: 'he wanted only to deposit between them an enervating drop of venom.'[19]

Now the reader has no doubt: a serpent is before him. Bogrov climbed up that pole 'twisting himself around and around',[20] with his 'bewitching gaze and flattish head a bit to the side'.[21] The author even feels sorry for him — 'how tired all the muscles of his coils must have been!'[22] But all this time 'those few drops necessary for the fatal moment must have been accumulating, oozing — into his brain? his craw? his tooth?'[23] Finally, this is how Stolypin saw Bogrov when the 'fatal moment' arrived: 'he walked like he was coiling and uncoiling. Thin and tall, in black tails . . . a long-faced young Jew.'[24] Then he struck, and 'slithering along his black back, ran away.'[25] The image of the young Jew blended with that of the serpent. Only was it really the biblical one?

The allegorical snake

Undoubtedly, Solzhenitsyn resorted to this new Diabolerie out of desperation — because of the impossibility of reconciling by any earthly artistic means the contradiction between reality, which repudiates the Russian Idea, and the party line. But in order to do so, doesn't he himself — all too often and all too precariously — have to 'creep in an unreal manner'? Isn't the fine line 'without notches or knots' that separates anti-liberalism from the Black Hundreds and the Black Hundreds, in turn, from Nazism itself all too smooth?

'The allegorical snake', says Walter Lacqueur, 'which played a great role in the Russian anti-semitic literature was imported into Germany in the twenties.'[26] In the next decade, already under the Nazis, Grigorii Bostunich — 'the missing link between the Black Hundreds and the Nazis'[27] — searched out in some archives an ancient map of Europe being encoiled by a snake. According to his commentary, this snake symbolized exactly the same thing that it symbolizes in Solzhenitsyn (only with the well-read Bostunich it was on a global scale): a history of successful attempts by the Jews to 'break' states that have stood in the way of their drive for world domination. Among these were Athens in 429 BC, Augustus's Rome, Carl V's Spain, Louis XIV's France, and, of course, Russia in 1917. It was for this very 'discovery' that Bostunich was made an honorary professor in the SS. The parallel drawn by Solzhenitsyn between Bogrov as serpent and the traditional symbolism of the Black Hundreds and Nazism did not escape the attention of emigre literary critics: 'in the very image of the Serpent who strikes down a Slavic knight while he is making the sign of the cross, an anti-semite could without difficulty see a parallel with his favourite book *The Protocols of the Elders of Zion*.'[28] However, one hardly needs to be an anti-semite to see this transparent parallel in the new edition of *August 1914*. What is it that keeps 'accumulating' in Solzhenitsyn's 'brain? or craw? or tooth?' that makes him incapable of resisting the demonic temptation to identify the Jew with Satan?

Stolypin vs. Solzhenitsyn

The saddest part of the story, however, is that not even Satan manages to save *August 1914*. As Solzhenitsyn the novelist painstakingly shows, Bogrov's bullets wounded a political corpse. By September 1911, Stolypin had long been finished as a key public figure.

As with the military disaster of August 1914, the West, the liberals, the Jews and Satan were none of them to blame for the political catastrophe that befell Stolypin — that is, of course, unless one considers Grigorii Rasputin to be a liberal or a Westernizer. Solzhenitsyn notes that he once 'offered to the governor of Nizhnii Novgorod province the post of minister of internal affairs' — that is, Stolypin's job, while he still held it. Six months before Stolypin was shot, 'sensitive court noses recognized that his Majesty had irreversibly cooled and even become hostile toward Stolypin. And in *upper circles* an atmosphere of being finished had started to form around Stolypin';[29] 'somewhere behind the scenes and without it being declared, his Majesty had already repudiated the chairman of his cabinet.'[30]

Already by spring of 1911, in the State Council where Kurlov, who was rumoured to succeed Stolypin as minister of internal affairs (Stolypin's second post), had many supporters, 'it was openly said that [Stolypin] was living out his last weeks, if not days, and he would be moved over into some kind of useless honorary position.'[31] Moreover, 'the chairman had obviously become so insignificant . . . that it was almost a humiliation for Kurlov to break with the general tone and take serious cognizance of his former chief.'[32] 'Kurlov looked astonished and indeed was, at how the chairman of the cabinet had utterly lost his importance. On the journey to Chernigov, he [Stolypin] had even had to ask Kurlov for a place in his railway carriage.

What, you mean your Excellency doesn't have a place on the tsar's train?

I was not invited.

The ultimate sign of humiliation and ungraciousness! Yes, in a few short days he was to lose his post.[33]

Was it really the case then that Bogrov pierced the very 'heart of the state'? Is it true that he murdered 'not only the prime minister, but a whole state program'? Is it true that his shot 'altered the course of history of a people 170-million strong'? No, it is not, and Stolypin knew this better than his latter-day apologist. Solzhenitsyn asserts,

'Russia was recovering — irreversibly.' Stolypin corrects him: 'They can go on a few more years yet on the reserves I have built up, like a camel living off the fat he has saved up, but after that it will all fall apart.'[34] And, in contrast to Solzhenitsyn, Stolypin doesn't blame either the liberals, the terrorists or the West for the impending collapse.

The two Peters

Solzhenitsyn writes as though Stolypin were the first Russian reformist leader whose bold programme to restructure the state fell through. Before Stolypin, however, there was Alexander II, whose plans were overturned by the counter-reform of another Orthodox monarch, Alexander III. Before him there was Alexander I, whose reformist attempts were succeeded at first by political stagnation and later by the soul-destroying despotism of yet another Orthodox monarch, Nicholas I. Also after Stolypin there were reformist leaders who arrived on the Russian political scene: Kerenskii, Bukharin and, most recently, Khrushchev. Their attempts at reform, however, resulted in the same way as earlier efforts made by the emperors and their prime ministers. They were all followed by either counter-reform or political stagnation. Russia's political history, as we have already noted, is in effect a tragic series of failed and reversed reforms.

But let us return to Stolypin. For the Left he has gone down in history as a tsarist satrap who put down the revolution and dispersed the Duma. The Right remembers him as a 'traitor' and 'revolutionary'. Neither his contemporaries nor his successors properly understood him. Had Solzhenitsyn tried to recreate Stolypin's true role in history, that would have been a noble endeavour. Solzhenitsyn, however, has written an apology, a biography of the holy saint Peter. This hagiolatry does a disservice to the memory of Stolypin. 'Just as it is impossible for a believer to accomplish anything serious at all saying and thinking that he is doing it by his own power rather than by the grace of God,' says Solzhenitsyn's Stolypin, 'so a monarchist cannot pursue great deeds for the motherland outside the bounds of devotion to the monarchy.'[35] Thus Solzhenitsyn transforms Stolypin into a trivial restorer of the Orthodox monarchy, whereas in reality he was one of its leading destroyers — which it understood quite well and therefore devoured him. By comparing Stolypin with Peter I, one of the main pillars of 'soul-destroying despotism' (who was responsible for the dual slavery of the Russian peasantry — to the landlords and to the commune), Solzhenitsyn insults the memory of Stolypin, whose efforts were directed at wiping this slavery out. The two belong not only to different, but to mortally opposed, Russian political traditions, Peter was the father of one of the most terrible counter-reforms in Russia's history, which brought the country, even in the opinion of his closest collaborators, 'to the edge of final extinction'. Stolypin, on the other hand, despite his suppression of revolution and dispersal of the Duma, was a reformer.

It is hard to put in a few words what sets these two Peters apart, when their mortal opposition to each other began so long ago — before there were emperors, or prime ministers, or, moreover, secretaries of the Central Committee. It started with a fifteenth-century Stolypin, the Grand Prince of Moscow, Ivan III, who undertook the first Russian reform, and with his grandson, Ivan IV, who a few decades later responded to his grandfather's challenge with a crushing counter-reform. In short, whereas the reformers have always tried to destroy Russia's medieval political system, the counter-reformers have sought to perpetuate it. In Europe, the main means of dismantling a medieval political system has always been the creation of a strong middle class. The only way to prevent this from happening has been to prevent the emergence of that middle class (we said this earlier and will discuss it further in the conclusion).

As European history shows, the creation of a strong middle class depends, in the first instance, on the differentiation of the peasantry, and it is this that had to be forcibly stopped. Serfdom, the peasant commune, and the collectivization of agriculture were all different means of artificially keeping the peasantry in its medieval state, in other words, the institutionalization of Russian counter-reform. It is the tradition of Orthodox monarchy, according to which, Solzhenitsyn says, 'consciously or unconsciously, the whole ruling class trembled and greedily clung to its lands — gentry lands, grand ducal lands, crown lands: at the first sign of any kind of movement for [peasant] land ownership — [they shout] oh, what if it should be our turn next!'[36]

Over the course of centuries the Orthodox monarchy has resolutely held out against the middle class and peasant differentiation. The political ideal of its builders has been a powerful military empire, for which a strong middle class would have been an obstacle, a potential rival to the ruling military and bureaucratic elites. This empire was created for the purpose of war, not to encourage a flourishing society. Their goal and chief claim to fame was not the well-being of their subjects, but imperial expansion and domination over other nations.

Therefore, for centuries the empire cemented over all cracks that could potentially lead to peasant differentiation. In this sense, Joseph Stalin, with his kolkhoz slavery, was a worthy successor to Ivan IV and Peter I, under whom Russia's peasants owed their slavery to the landlords and the commune. In this sense Nikita Khrushchev, with his peasant reforms, was continuing the work of Alexander II and Petr Stolypin to dismantle serfdom and the commune, and hence — consciously or unconsciously — the medieval empire.

Russia's tragedy

It has been Russia's great tragedy that, whereas her reformers have always suffered defeat, her counter-reformers, whether in the context of Orthodox monarchy or its Soviet incarnation, have always been triumphant. The most fundamental question in Russian history is, I believe, why Russia has proved to be the only country in Europe where — without exception — all attempts at reform aimed at clearing the way for peasant differentiation have failed. Following the dicta of the Russian Idea, Solzhenitsyn doesn't even notice this problem. Nevertheless, in describing the defeat of one of Russia's reformers, he inadvertently casts some light on the mechanics of the constant failure of Russian reform.

In dozens of pages of tiny print he informs the reader of the details of Stolypin's 'state programme', his reformist plans. Nowhere, however, does the author or his hero give us as much as a single word about *how* these plans were to be implemented: via which political coalitions, with the help of which institutions, what manoeuvres would be necessary, and what kind of political base would be needed. Very quickly, the reader starts to doubt whether Stolypin had any kind of overall political strategy at all, or any political base. Solzhenitsyn then convinces us that indeed *he had neither*.

Here again, contrary to his intentions, the author points up the fatal weakness of all Russia's reformist leaders. They had 'state programmes' all right, yet none of them had developed a realistic and serious *political strategy* for the realization of their programmes. Unlike, for example, Bismarck or Cavour, none of them knew *how* to implement their ideas. But even given this general weakness of Russian reformers, Stolypin was outstanding in his desperate political helplessness. Repeatedly, Solzhenitsyn tells the reader that with Stolypin 'a radically new period in Russian history could have begun and was beginning.'[37] 'The 3rd of June was the start of the great reconstruction of Russia.'[38]

However, from the facts he introduces, the reader is persuaded that the opposite is true: Stolypin was utterly dependent on the whims of a worthless tsar, to whom his 'state programme' meant nothing and who at any moment could 'easily step back and betray his minister'.[39] At the same time, the tsar, according to Solzhenitsyn, was a puppet of 'the upper military and court aristocracy,' people about whom Stolypin thought: 'there are so many dozens — or hundreds? — of these self-seeking careerists that make up the ruling strata in Russia.'[40] The 'ruling strata', naturally, resented him in much the same way. To them, Stolypin was a 'schemer who had bewitched and beguiled his Majesty and so succeeded in hanging on to his post for too long — but by all accounts it was time for him to clear off!'[41]

Betrayal

Already by the autumn of 1908, that is, three years before he was assassinated, Solzhenitsyn's Stolypin was not unlike general Jaruzelski in today's Poland. He had disbanded the Duma (as Jaruzelski did with Solidarity), earning the hatred of Russian liberals and the West (also like Jaruzelski). In the eyes of the right-wing dinosaurs of his time, Stolypin was a 'traitor' and 'schemer' though he had saved them from the 1905 revolution. (Similarly, Jaruzelski is seen as a schemer by Poland's party dinosaurs, whom he rescued from Solidarity in 1981.) But as soon as he had managed this, 'Stolypin's politics became intolerable and impossible to them all . . . them *all* . . . the court camarilla, who under a constitutional structure would have nothing left to do but disappear; the retired bureaucrats, all of them failed rulers, who thronged the right wing of the State Council (it was overflowing with retired idlers who had come to a standstill, as the blood stops in a senile organism); and — those die-hards among the nobility who imagined they could dominate Russia for centuries to come without yielding an inch.'[42]

Politically, the difference between Jaruzelski and Stolypin is that the former is kept afloat by Moscow while the latter was not held up by anyone. That's why, even as early as autumn 1908, Stolypin was already politically dead. This produced in him eventually 'an almost total sensation — of utter defeat, and not just in the matter of his reform law, but in his whole five years of rule, in all his life's plans'.[43]

Once again we see that same freak show, that same menagerie of monsters of the Orthodox monarchy which led the Russian army to its devastation in August 1914 — only it was the generals who dominated

Russia's military policy, while it was the 'court camarilla', the 'retired idlers' and the 'die-hards' who dominated the Orthodox monarchy's state policy. It was they who crushed Stolypin, just as 53 years later it was their successors who annihilated Khrushchev. They steered Russia on to the reefs of counter-reform, just as her military monsters (Solzhenitsyn's 'sacks of shit') led her into the debacle of August 1914.

In vain, it would seem, has Solzhenitsyn profaned his muse by heeding the deceptive one-hundred-year-old calling of the Russian Idea. In vain, has he forced hundreds of pages devoted to the perfidious liberals and satanic Jews into the new edition of *August 1914*. In vain, has he defiled his work with yet another sortie into diabolerie, resurrecting the biblical (or Nazi?) image of the serpent. Just as the Orthodox monarchy betrayed its heroes Vorotyntsev and Stolypin, so has the Russian Idea betrayed Solzhenitsyn. The new edition of *August 1914* was destined to become Solzhenitsyn's own personal and artistic August 1914.

Shipov's programme

Solzhenitsyn, in his words, borrowed his 'state programme' for Russia's future from Dmitrii Shipov. It was by ignoring this programme that his opponents so offended him. ('Is the print too tiny? Don't their eyes pick it up?' he asked bitterly about the 'smatterers'.) I can't speak for the others, but my eyes pick up only Aksakov's old programme for a 'State of the Land' (a *Zemskoe gosudarstvo* — which the reader will recall was a hopeless anachronism even in the 1860s). Later, in 1881, Ivan Aksakov once again dragged it out of the Slavophile attic in a desperate attempt to convince Alexander III to assemble a *Zemskii Sobor**, 'capable of putting all the constitutions in the world to shame'.[44] Aksakov did not conceal his concern that, 'this is a *last gamble*: should it not pay off, but fail totally, there will be no more salvation.'[45] However, this 'last gamble' did fail in the 1880s, just as a similar one failed two decades ago. It met with a final failure in 1904, when the Russian Idea, you may recall, veered off in another direction, leaving those Slavophiles of the 'immobile Aksakov cast' (as Leont'ev characterized them), or 'the *zemstvo* Mensheviks', (as Solzhenitsyn calls them), by the

---

* [Translator's note: The Muscovite 'Assembly of the Land', a medieval Russian assembly called together by the tsar in the manner of a medieval parliament.]

wayside. In Solzhenitsyn's words, they represented a 'minuscule minority',[46] 'a minority frail'[47] even among those involved in the early twentieth-century *zemstvo* movement itself.

It was this sectarian band of Slavophile conservationists that Dmitrii Shipov headed. Three times over the course of half a century their programme was rejected by the Orthodox monarchy, and now Solzhenitsyn offers it to us as the means for saving Russia in the nuclear age. To anyone familiar with the historical drama of the Russian Idea, there is certainly nothing new in the Shipov—Solzhenitsyn programme. Its kernel is contained in the assertion that the state is not society's potential adversary (which is the basis of traditional Western political thought and of the founders of the American constitution), but rather its potential ally: 'The Russians from time immemorial have not thought about struggle against authority, but about co-operation with it in order to establish a life patterned after God.'[48] The programme, of course, resurrects the Slavophile myth, that 'The tsars of ancient Rus' believed similarly, not separating themselves from their people . . . Previous sovereigns sought not to impose their will, but to express the collective [*sobornaia*] conscience of the people — and it is not yet too late to recreate the spirit of that order.'[49] Moreover, Solzhenitsyn says, 'such an order is higher than a constitutional one, since it assumes not struggle between the sovereign and society, not a fight between parties, but the harmonious search for good.'[50] Therefore the '*Zemskii Sobor* ought to be recreated in a new form, to establish a state/land order',[51] in other words, a combination of autocracy and local self-government. 'Without mutual trust [between the state and society],' says Solzhenitsyn, 'success in organizing the state cannot be expected . . . Yes, that was what the programme of Shipov and his minority was about!'[52]

It doesn't matter that such a 'state/land order' never existed in Russia (or anywhere else for that matter). It doesn't matter that neither Aksakov, nor Shipov, nor Solzhenitsyn have *ever* been able to cite a *single* example to support this Slavophile myth. It doesn't even matter that this ideological programme combining autocracy with local autonomy, and explicitly recognized as doing so by all the Slavophiles of the time, has, for the overwhelming majority of third-generation Slavophiles, mingled with the most savage chauvinism, racism and naked imperial ambitions. Finally, it doesn't matter that the very slogan, 'the combination of autocracy and local self-government is our historical path', served as one of the cornerstones of the imperial utopia of degenerate Slavophilism at the turn of the century. What matters, however, to Solzhenitsyn is that he has a programme and 'smatterers' have nothing to match it. Yet, in view of its banality, it's hardly fair to reproach them for refusing to take it seriously.

But even supposing it is a worthwhile programme, the old question still remains: why didn't Alexander II, or Alexander III, or Nicholas II accept it? Why was it snuffed out by the very same Orthodox monarchy which Solzhenitsyn, after his most recent political recantation, now eulogizes? What grounds have we to expect that, say, an Alexander IV or a Nicholas III would not turn out to be the fascist *Führer* of a *Neues Russland* rather than the majestic Russian sovereign of old taken from Slavophile mythology?

Alas, just as *August 1914* proved to be Solzhenitsyn's artistic Waterloo, so Shipov's programme proves to be his ideological one.

Notes

1   Ivan S. Aksakov, *Sochineniia*, Moscow: 1886, v. II, p. 256.
2   A. I. Solzhenitsyn, op. cit., v. 12, p. 146.
3   Ibid., p. 223.
4   Ibid., p. 226.
5   Ibid., p. 223.
6   Ibid.
7   Ibid., p. 132. In brackets is the part of Bogrov's speech that was omitted by Solzhenitsyn.
8   L. Losev, op. cit., pp. 314—15.
9   Solzhenitsyn, op. cit., v. 12, p. 320.
10   Ibid., p. 287.
11   Ibid., p. 250.
12   Ibid., p. 124.
13   Ibid., p. 131.
14   Ibid., p. 138.
15   Ibid., p. 141.
16   Ibid., p. 142.
17   Ibid., p. 143.
18   Ibid., p. 144.
19   Ibid.
20   Ibid., p. 157.
21   Ibid., p. 158.
22   Ibid., p. 163.
23   Ibid., p. 146.
24   Ibid., p. 248.
25   Ibid., p. 249.
26   Walter Laqueur, op. cit., p. 123.
27   Ibid., p. 101.
28   L. Losev, op. cit., p. 315.
29   Solzhenitsyn, op. cit., v. 12, p. 239.

30   Ibid., p. 232.
31   Ibid., p. 262.
32   Ibid., p. 265.
33   Ibid., pp. 266—7.
34   Ibid., p. 243.
35   Ibid., p. 188.
36   Ibid., p. 192.
37   Ibid., p. 210.
38   Ibid., p. 205.
39   Ibid., p. 189.
40   Ibid., p. 213.
41   Ibid., p. 227.
42   Ibid., p. 217.
43   Ibid., p. 239.
44   P. A. Zaionchkovskii, *Krizis samoderzhavia na rubezhe 1870—1880 godov* [*The Crisis of Autocracy On the Eve of 1870—1880*], Moscow, 1964, p. 452.
45   L. G. Zakharova, *Zemskaia kontrreforma 1890 godov* [*The Land Counter-reform of the 1890s*], Moscow, 1968, p. 462.
46   Solzhenitsyn, op. cit., v. 13, p. 81.
47   Ibid., p. 83.
48   Ibid., p. 84.
49   Ibid.
50   Ibid.
51   Ibid., pp. 84—5.
52   Ibid., p. 86.

17
When the Sleeper Awakened

Long before the second edition of *August 1914*, *Veche*'s reader mail
and *The Nation Speaks* manifesto demonstrated clearly that a gulf
had opened up between the national-liberal intellectuals of the Russian
Idea and the 'Orthodox patriotic' masses. There are grounds to suppose
that some leaders of L-Nationalism and in particular Solzhenitsyn,
were troubled by this growing rift and tried to reduce it, moving in a
direction to meet the wishes of the masses. Long before the publication
of the *Gulag Archipelago*, one of Solzhenitsyn's readers wrote to him
with the following criticism: 'In your copious camp digressions one
finds no mention that a Natan Frenkel' was the head of the Gulag, a
Berman the head of the Belomor canal construction project,* a Kogan
the head of the Kotlas-Vorkuta road construction project and so on'.[1]
Subsequently, Solzhenitsyn obligingly introduced all these names
(even photographs) into the text of the *Gulag Archipelago*. The author
of 'Critical Notes' on *Veche* complained of the absence of Grigorii
Rasputin from *August 1914*.[2] Rasputin appears in the pages of the
second edition. A reader protested in 1971, 'I don't know who you are
— a Russian or a Jew? . . . Perhaps you are a Russian pressured by
your environment, a Jewish wife . . . In that case I request one thing
— think for a moment about your own people. Understand that there
is no returning to a bourgeois Jewish republic, that soviets are the
Russian form of rule by the people which will yet find strength.'[3]
Solzhenitsyn later paid homage toward soviets as a governmental
institution in his 'Letter to the Leaders of the Soviet Union', and the
desperate cry 'think for a moment about your own people' was also
heeded in the letter. Likewise, he condemned the 'bourgeois Jewish
republic' of February 1917 in 'Our Pluralists'. As far as Solzhenitsyn's

* [Translator's note: The Belomor canal (The White Sea canal in the extreme
arctic north of Russia) was constructed by prisoners.]

credentials as an Aryan are concerned, these were to be so eloquently demonstrated by his sorties into diabolerie that even the most sceptical 'patriot' could no longer have any racial reservations about him.

Despite all this, however, neither Solzhenitsyn, nor his comrades of liberal Nationalism, nor certainly his Western fellow-travellers, have proved capable of bridging the divide between themselves and the 'Orthodox patriotic' reader. They cannot, after all, follow the advice of the Christian nationalist Archdeacon Varsonofii and 'seek out means of practical rapprochement' with the Communist state. Still less can they accept a 'reorientation' of the Communist dictatorship that would put an end to 'disorderly hybridization' and thus 'fulfil its duty before the nation and the race'. Their Orthodoxy, in contrast to Antonov's, precludes any unification with Leninism. Like Osipov before them, they too refuse to campaign for 'percentage quotas' for Jews or to denounce Einstein as a pseudo-scientist (as the theoretical physicist Tiapkin did). They have no desire to rehabilitate Stalin — even on the ground that 'he loved to discuss things with the patriarch'. In short, they cannot overcome their revulsion for 'soul-destroying communism', just as in his time Ivan Aksakov could not share Sergei Sharapov's enthusiasm for 'soul-destroying despotism'.

The old Slavophile drama is repeating itself once more, only this time in a twentieth-century setting. Like the Slavophiles of the last century, these people were the first to speak about an 'Orthodox renaissance'. Also like the Slavophiles, they expended a great deal of effort in awakening the 'Orthodox patriotic' patriarchal simpleton of their utopian dream. Now — exactly like the Slavophiles before them — they find they have awoken a monster, quite unlike anything they expected and to whom they cannot even speak in the same language. The 'Orthodox patriotic' reader they awakened demanded not only that they be reconciled with the detestable 'soul-destroying communism' in the name of saving Russia, but also proof of their own Aryan credentials.

The transition

Thus, *The Nation Speaks* and the 'Critical Notes of a Russian Man' showed that national-liberalism is doomed to become the philosophy of an isolated sectarian group of preservers of antiquated Slavophile museum pieces — latter-day Shipovs — whose worn-out programmes interested no one at the beginning of the twentieth century and interest no one today (least of all their own readers, who have already gone way ahead of them). To please these readers, they could still create epic allegorical images of the Jew/Satan/Destroyer of Russia or publish a journal like *Kontinent*, where they could permit themselves to flirt ever so slightly with fascism, declaring it a 'movement of the era [and] sign of the times'.[4] But to state that, 'only the socialist system stands in the way of [the Jews'] world domination,'[5] or to publish a journal entitled 'Death to the Zionist Invaders!', that is beyond them. It turns out that there are limits to how far contemporary liberal Nationalism will go, just as there were for classical Slavophilism.

To make the jump across the gulf that separates them from the theoretical physicist Tiapkin a kind of intellectual revolution is needed. All their old idols and ideals have to be scrapped, and a totally new vision of history adopted instead. In other words, what is required is a transition from L-Nationalism to F-Nationalism. That is why in the 1970s the Russian New Right desperately needed a Sergei Sharapov of its own, a man who would emerge from the 'Orthodox patriotic masses' (sharing their basic beliefs) and who could channel their dark hatred toward non-Russians into an intellectual alternative to national-liberalism. An 'instrumental leader', as sociologists say, was required, someone capable of reconciling the intellectual vision of the Russian Idea with the expectations of its grass roots, of ending the breach between the two and decisively casting aside the liberal illusions of the old Slavophiles of an 'immobile Aksakov cast'.

The next chapter is devoted to the first attempt, by Gennadi Shimanov, to re-create an ideology of F-Nationalism, to the first candidate for the role of a Sergei Sharapov (a rebel and heretic within the Russian Idea) for the Russian New Right. For now I will only try to show what mind-bending complexity Shimanov's task presented him with.

Russia vs. Judaea

We find among Solzhenitsyn the novelist's causes for the collapse of the Orthodox monarchy — the 'court camarilla', the 'retired idlers' in the state council, the 'die-hard portion of the nobility', the symbolic behemoth Parvus and serpent Bogrov, and even the 'certain thousand-year-old calling' of the cunning Jewish race. Solzhenitsyn's thinking on the subject is thus dominated by a mixture of sociological and demonic factors. The 'Orthodox patriotic' reader, however, had grown sick of symbolism and metaphysical allegory, and sociology was as good as useless to him. Such a person is, above all eminently practical: he needs the names and secret rendezvous addresses of the conspirators; he needs what Solzhenitsyn provided in the *Gulag Archipelago* — photos of those responsible for bringing down the Orthodox monarchy — the Jew villains.

> But you don't have one word about the true reasons for the defeat and collapse [of the monarchy]. There is no trace of the vile activities of the band of Jew capitalists to whom almost the entire press and a large part of industry in Russia belonged. There is no Rasputin, who was placed in power and used to divide and demoralize the country by the Vinaver and Aron Samuilovich Simanovich clique, no treachery, no Mit'ka Rubinshtein and the other international Zionist bankers who strove to crush Russia come what may, no [mention of how the] Russian and German peoples were set upon one another [so that] the Rothschilds in London, Paris and Vienna and the Russian [Jewish] Poliakovs and Ginzbergs could make their gold from these nations' blood.[6]

Thus, in the vision of the world held by the awakened 'Orthodox patriotic' consciousness, Jews not only brought down the Russian Orthodox monarchy, but also unleashed World War I. Essentially, the reader demands of Solzhenitsyn, if he is going to be his spiritual guide, the very thing which Solzhenitsyn demands of the Soviet leadership — to 'live not by lies'. In so far as the reader, like Solzhenitsyn, is convinced that 'the truth is one', and that this truth is known to him, he simply cannot understand why a person who has awakened this realization in him would play the hypocrite. Why doesn't his mighty voice let his thunder across the whole face of creation, as it did across Russia, leaving no doubt in any honest soul that the Jews are the source of all the world's evil? Is he really a follower of Orthodoxy? 'Perhaps he is a proselyte . . . proselytes are usually more cruel than native Judeans.'[7] Maybe he is just afraid?

> They assure me you are a brave person. It's easy to be brave when you are printed in Zionist organs, when at the slightest jamming of you every [Radio] Free Europe starts to cry out. You know very well that special zionist councils are involved in the control of these stations. Just try to speak out against the zionists! Do you have enough courage for that? You have patrons in our country as well . . . With this letter I am subjecting myself to greater danger than you. Not one radio station will ever broadcast it.[8]

Yes, it was Solzhenitsyn who had himself instilled this reader with the Russian Idea; he who had given him this source of insight. But after this reader had matured, among the many other things that he saw for the first time, was the spectacle of his teacher not daring to take the last decisive step to the 'truth'. Thus he began to doubt his teacher — to lose faith in his human qualities and even his Orthodoxy. Eventually, he became disillusioned with him altogether and denounced him: 'Your Orthodoxy is also a false pose. A vainglorious knowledge of folk adages, customs, and holidays, not faith, draws your blasphemous pen across the paper. You even call Christ a Jew, though even I, a person . . . unschooled in theology, understand that God has no use for nationality.'[9]

Like Solzhenitsyn, the author of this letter writes the word God with a capital G. He too stands on the firm soil of Orthodoxy and feels not the slightest personal enmity toward Solzhenitsyn ('God forbid, I do not wish you ill'),[10] yet everything in Solzhenitsyn seems suspect to him. For example, a Jewish engineer Il'ya Isaakovich Arkhangorodskii appears in *August 1914*, who, it turns out, also dreams about 'the creation of Russia'. What could this mean to the reader Solzhenitsyn has awakened? Just one thing: 'a pack of lies'.[11]

> Where did Il'ya Isaakovich get ideas about the creation of Russia from if the Judaean religion . . . teaches him that non-Jews are worse than dogs, that a Jew is duty-bound to deceive non-Jews . . . that he belongs to the chosen people, whose destiny it is to subjugate all other peoples and force them to work for their benefit . . . And he had to pay his 'shekel', a tax in gold, (as is paid throughout the world today) to provide the means for an organization which fights to assert the world supremacy of the Jews.[12]

Moreover, the Jews 'have always hated the Russians and always thought only about themselves, both things which they are trained to do from childhood.'[13]

Such differences of opinion about *August 1914*, however, might come under the heading of literary criticism. The real conflict between the 'patriotic reader' and Solzhenitsyn, the anti-Communist and advocate of Orthodox monarchy, is political.

The 'patriotic' thesis

The 'patriotic' reader is by no means enthralled by Communism. One might sooner say he has a utilitarian attitude towards it: it is simply the lesser evil. 'To shatter [the Communist regime] would be easy! But then what? If the Bolsheviks were toppled, Zionists and only Zionists would come to power. They have the money and the agents plus brilliant organization — we have nothing except the Bolshevik party which still protects us, albeit not very well.'[14] On the other hand, the reader knows from *August 1914* that under an Orthodox monarchy the Russians would prove defenceless against the Zionists — just as their fathers and grandfathers proved defenceless against the Jewish band of Rubinsteins, Vinavers and Simanoviches. Under the monarchy Jews not only took control of industry and the Russian press, but also plunged the empire into World War I — and so forced it to commit political suicide.

Thus, which of the following would be better as a form of political organization for Russia's future: an impotent Orthodox monarchy which would allow itself to be controlled by the Jews; or a Jewish bourgeois republic, under which Russia would literally become enslaved to the Zionists ('This was exactly the issue — whether or not Russia was to be made a colony of Israel'[15]); or a Soviet regime, where the Bolshevik party would offer some protection against all these horrors? When the question is posed like this, the logic of the patriotic reader makes perfect sense. According to this logic, Solzhenitsyn's choice is the wrong one.

Like all national-liberals, Solzhenitsyn has made a crude mistake in his advocacy of an 'Orthodox renaissance'. He had assumed, like the eighteenth-century French philosophers of the Enlightenment, that his sermon was falling onto a *tabula rasa*, a virgin soil ready to accept any seed. In fact, he was appealing to people who had been raised within the system of Soviet political education and who had deeply internalized the elementary truths of vulgarized Marxism. It was precisely in connection with the ideas of an Orthodox renaissance that these people, for the first time in their lives, felt the need independently to apply their 'political education' to analysing the country's future. They reached similar conclusions to those of Antonov a decade earlier.

'Patriotic' truths were layered on top of the elementary principles of Soviet political education to form an ominously explosive mixture in which 'ownership of the means of production' became bound up with the idea of 'Christian nationalism' and the *Protocols of the Elders of Zion*. Thus, according to one correspondent: 'The Soviet regime, which replaced the autocracy, has done the main thing — deprived the Zionists in our country of the right to private ownership of the instruments and means of production. Perhaps that phrase has set some people's teeth on edge, but were it not for this, the year 2000 would long ago have come for the children of Israel and all the problems of the Russian people would be lying at the bottom of ovens in Zionist crematoria.'[16] 'Everything that in our system of political education is called capitalism, imperialism, exploitation, and oppression', another reader asserts, 'all refers to rich Jews.'[17]

The reductionists

It was a tragic episode in the history of the Russian Idea of the last century, when, in the 1880s, the Slavophiles finally succeeded in awakening the 'patriotic' consciousness of the masses. The dualism of 'world evil' that had served as the ideological foundation for liberal nationalism unexpectedly crumbled. Before, as we recall, Slavophilism had fought on two fronts: against native 'soul-destroying despotism' and against Western 'parliamentarism'. But as soon as the Russian Idea left the framework of intellectual struggle and was transformed, to use Marx's phrase, into a material force, the dualistic structure of 'world evil' proved inoperable; the equilibrium between its two 'devils' was disturbed. Hatred of the evil of 'parliamentarism' was translated into attempts to recruit the other evil in the struggle against it, so that parliamentarism now represented the only real threat to the existence of the world. In effect, what was taking place was a kind of 'reduction of world evil' in the Russian Idea's progression from an ideology confined to intellectual circles to one of mass appeal. Evil became concentrated and personified in the Jews. The movement had become fascism.

We have witnessed the same thing happen to the contemporary Russian Idea. The intellectuals of national liberalism, who have continued to insist on the duality of world evil, are behind the times. To them, 'soul-destroying Communism' is still a 'devil'. So, like the Slavophiles before them, they are rejected by the 'patriotic masses', in whose consciousness the 'reduction of world evil' has already taken place.

The end of the second Christian millennium represents a date of epic significance for these masses; it is the time when the Jews will try to storm the last bastion of national independence on earth — Russia. They do not wish to become slaves of the Jews. 'It cannot be ruled out that tomorrow Russian blood will once again be shed in sacrifice to Jehovah . . . Do you want to be a slave, Solzhenitsyn? I don't! I'd rather die with a gun in my hands.'[18]

Such was the rift between the national-liberal teachers and the 'Orthodox patriotic' readers they had awakened. Gennadii Shimanov was to throw a bridge across that divide.

Notes

1   *Novyi zhurnal*, No. 118, 1975, p. 205.
2   Ibid., p. 220.
3   Ibid., p. 218.
4   *Kontinent*, No. 20, 1979, p. 257.
5   *Novyi zhurnal*, No. 118, 1975, p. 226.
6   Ibid., p. 206.
7   Ibid., p. 207.
8   Ibid., p. 207.
9   Ibid., p. 207.
10   Ibid., p. 216.
11   Ibid., p. 207.
12   Ibid.
13   Ibid., p. 215.
14   Ibid., p. 223.
15   Ibid., p. 210.
16   Ibid., p. 227.
17   Ibid., p. 209.
18   Ibid., p. 218, 216.

18
The Politics of Russian Fascism

During my time in Moscow, I did not know Gennadii Shimanov personally. I only heard about him and his cohorts — the 'Shimanovites' (or 'Ultras', as they were called by my acquaintances from the Russian Club[1] and the editorial board of *Veche*) — and read some of his works. Shimanov appears to be one of a number of contemporary Russian intellectuals who have left behind all dreams of worldly success and deliberately descended to a level of meagre material existence in order to find freedom at the 'bottom' — freedom to think, to write and to preach. He is an elevator operator. In this role — 'in the cellar, where it is damp, beside the garbage chute'[2] — he is almost invulnerable to attack from the regime. This has afforded him the opportunity to sit and ponder and write dozens of articles, which have been collected together in two samizdat books.[3]

But Shimanov not only writes about politics: he is also (as we have noted) the leader of the 'Ultras'. Before 1974 — that is, prior to the exile of Solzhenitsyn, the split in *Veche* and the arrest of Osipov — Shimanov's 'Ultras', though active in the Russian Club, remained somewhat in the background — a sort of a shadow cabinet. At that time the views of the 'Ultras' were too extreme for either the VSKhSON wing of the Dissident Right or the supporters of *Veche*, who (together with such eminent representatives of the Establishment 'Rusists' as P. Palievskii, V. Kozhinov, and A. Lanshchikov) dominated the Russian Club in the early 1970s. Among the highbrow liberal nationalists, the 'Ultras' even seemed to provoke a certain disgust.

I was therefore particularly surprised to find a programmatic article by Shimanov entitled 'Moscow: The Third Rome' in *Moskovskii sbornik* [*Moscow Anthology*] — a samizdat journal which, after the demise of *Veche*, attempted to replace it as an organ of the Dissident Right. The editor of *Moskovskii sbornik* was L. Borodin, one of the members of VSKhSON who had been arrested and served a term in prison. He wrote a brief introduction to 'Moscow: The Third Rome', stating that in his opinion 'Shimanov's point of view on some questions of the nation and of religion is today *extremely popular* among the nationalistically inclined Russian intelligentsia.'[4]

One has to suppose either that the views of the former member of VSKhSON had undergone a significant evolution in the decade since the collapse of his organization, or that Shimanov's views in the mid-1970s had become a force that could no longer be ignored (or maybe both are true). Whatever the explanation, there is no doubt that VSKhSON would not even have allowed a person holding Shimanov's views through its doors — and he certainly would not have been tolerated in *From Under the Rubble*. Moreover, his programmatic statements were not permitted in *Veche*. On 29 April 1973, Osipov wrote a rather stiff 'open letter' to him in which, while disassociating himself from the line of the 'revolutionist' (read VSKhSON) underground, he no less decisively repudiated the views of Shimanov.[5] Thus, none of the factions of L-Nationalism recognized Shimanov and his 'Ultras' as belonging to them. For Shimanov to have advanced into the foreground of the dissident Right, and for Borodin to testify in flattering tones to the wide popularity of his views 'among the nationalistically inclined intelligentsia,' meant that all these factions must have suffered a defeat — or had found their positions severely weakened. The wind must have changed in the nationalistic dissident movement. Perhaps the hour had arrived for the public appearance of F-Nationalism.[6]

Sources of the Coming Catastrophe

Shimanov's very existence as a political writer is an expression of the intellectual crisis through which Russia was passing in the 1970s. It is revealing to look at the way he himself describes this crisis:

> The obvious collapse of the Communist utopia, which cannot be covered up indefinitely, and from which we must somehow emerge with dignity; the worthlessness of Western ways, which cannot attract any sympathy; the advancing industrial-ecological crisis, which compels us to search frantically for a path to a different civilization; the military danger from China . . . and the internal processes of bourgeoisification and spiritual and moral degradation, which must be resisted not with words . . . all of this . . . must push the Soviet regime, first to partial and half-hearted reforms, and then to decisive ones, in the face of the catastrophe threatening the state.[7]

If we try to formulate more rigorously the reasons for this advancing 'catastrophe', we find the following three sources:

(1) The regime, by nature mobile, whose dynamism is based on movement toward a clear and exalted goal, has lost its goal and consequently become immobilized. Movement was first reduced to marching on the spot, then 'putrefaction'. The nation is disoriented and degraded, and hence dying in a spiritual sense. This is shown by the catastrophic drop in social and labour discipline, which undermines the vital forces of the nation.[8]

(2) The colossal sacrifices made by the people on the road to the supposed goal have lost their meaning. The Revolution, the Civil War, the Gulag, the deaths of millions, famine and collectivization, World War II, self-sacrifice — everything which could be justified by the movement toward Communism — has proved to be meaningless. 'God is dead.' (This terrible conclusion, which the Soviet people instinctively reject and fear as much as their own death, is the basis of Shimanov's fearless doctrine).

(3) In this situation of general confusion and putrefaction, the country finds itself in its worst crisis of its history — between two fires, China and the West, equally dangerous and equally merciless. At present, the nation has nothing with which to counter this mortal threat.

'Everybody despises the Russians'

Thus, according to Shimanov's logic, the time has come 'to save the Russian nation'.[9] It is time for all Russians, regardless of their station in life, to unite in a spiritual and intellectual effort to return their nation to power and glory. Shimanov bitterly resents, what to him is a fact, that 'everybody despises the Russians.'[10] Indeed, his suffering is so great that it amounts to a national inferiority complex. To save Russia means, for Shimanov, not only to return his country to greatness and prosperity, but to transform her into the centre of humankind's spiritual history — to make her the leader of the world; to show that all the other peoples are inferior, and therefore not worthy of that responsibility; to show that Russia holds the key not only to her own destiny, but because she provides the solution to the crisis through which the world is now passing — to the fate of the whole human race.

To achieve salvation, Russia must rid herself of the three sources of the advancing catastrophe. Only by doing so, will her lost sense of purpose be returned, will meaning be restored to all the sacrifices the people have made, and will she be capable of withstanding China and the West. But how is this to be done? The paradox of Shimanov's answer to the challenge of history deserves special discussion.

The Concept of History

Shimanov's historical doctrine proceeds from the premise that Christianity as a universal tool for saving the world 'has failed' — that emerging into the world from the catacombs, it has been seduced by the glitter of material culture and has exchanged its world mission for a mess of pottage and worldly power. Having been seduced, Catholicism gave birth to 'the ulcer of Protestantism', which in turn bore the 'bourgeois era', which has overwhelmed mankind with the 'cult of profit and cold cash'. Finally, the bourgeois era begot the great and sinful mutiny of socialism. Hence, 'corrupted' (European) Christianity is the thesis, socialism the antithesis, and the world can be saved only by a synthesis. (The immortal Hegel as interpreted by the popular textbooks of dialectical materialism still triumphs!) But where is this synthesis to be found? It turns out that there is one people which has been preserved by God and has escaped the corruption of Catholicism and the bourgeois ulcer. They were preserved in a terrible, but in the final analysis blessed, way — by sending the Tatars upon them to cut them off from the 'mighty Renaissance embrace' of Europe. Thus, alone among the nations, Russia is the only one to possess the 'true faith', and by a miracle to have preserved it from the bourgeois flood.

Here is seen the basic methodological principle of Shimanov's historical doctrine: when God wishes to preserve and purify his chosen people, he sends upon it a plague, a national disaster. Shimanov, having been fortunate enough to have discovered the *modus operandi* of Providence, goes on to apply it to the history of Russia. He acknowledges that the Petrine reforms, the October Revolution and the Gulag were great calamities for the people, but urges us to see a Great Mystery and Divine Providence behind all the blood and squalor, behind their apparent meaninglessness. No, he says. The innumerable sacrifices of the Russian people have not been in vain: they are justified; they are steps on the road to a great goal and the price of the people's historical destiny. So, hold your heads high, Russians!

The collapse of the Communist utopia, Shimanov says, has cleared the way for a renewal of Russian Orthodox Christianity. Once the ancient Russian faith is united with the internal, immanent-religious nature of Communism, there will emerge — in place of the false idol — God. The people may have been led along a thorny path to reach him, but it was God who led them. This is the dawn of the new millennium.

> I say that after the experience of a thousand years which has driven humankind into an intolerable impasse, is it not clear that only a genuine, reborn Christianity can offer the way out? — that we need a different, new civilization, not pagan-bourgeois, but ascetic and spiritual?[11]

Where will this new gospel come from, if not from the single source of the true faith which the Lord has preserved and purified by the ordeals of the Tatar yoke, the October Revolution, the Great War, the Gulag and the KGB?

In today's Russia, it seems dangerous to underestimate the political potential of Shimanov's interpretation of history, in which even the Gulag (sacreligious as this may sound) is justified. For is not one of the causes of the fatal isolation of the Soviet dissident movement — a movement which has courageously fought to expose the pointlessness of the sacrifices exacted on three generations of the nation — that the people themselves are not interested in these revelations? Is it an accident that these exposés come up against the obstacle of socio-psychological stereotypes, perhaps planted in the depths of the nation's consciousness for the purpose of national self-preservation? This instinctive striving of the mass consciousness to make black white, to assign meaning to the meaningless, to turn the shame of the nation into its glory, becomes a powerful instrument for Shimanov. What Versailles was to Hitler, so the Gulag was to Shimanov.

The Political Concept

The most original aspect of Shimanov's work is his interpretation of the Soviet system. Shimanov was the first of the 'Rightists' to understand that the purely negative, accusatory function of the dissident movement had outlived its usefulness — that from there on only a positive concept could work. Rather than accusing the regime, such a conception would use its immanent-religious nature to achieve positive national goals. This is the basis of Shimanov's understanding that the Soviet system is the only political organization which, on the one hand, is capable of withstanding the temptations of 'rotten Western democracy' and, on the other, can mobilize the people for new historical feats:

> Today the Soviet system can no longer seriously strive toward the spectre of Communism — but at the same time it cannot yet abandon the grandeur of its tasks, for otherwise it would have to answer for fruitless sacrifices which are truly innumerable. But in what then can the Soviet system find its justification? Only in the consciousness that it was unconsciously in the past, as it is now quite consciously, God's instrument for constructing a new Christian world. It has no other justification, and this is . . . a genuine and great justification. By adopting it, our state will discover in itself a truly inexhaustible source of Truth, spiritual energy and strength, which has never before existed in history . . . The old pagan world has now finally outlived its era . . . In order not to perish with it we must build a new civilization — but is Western society, whose foundations have been destroyed, really capable of this? Only the Soviet system, having adopted Russian Orthodoxy . . . is capable of beginning THE GREAT TRANSFORMATION OF THE WORLD.[12]

To achieve this, it is not economic reforms or civil rights which are needed. It is not the Soviet system which must adapt itself to the people, but the people who must adapt themselves to the system, understand it and take it to their hearts as their own native source of authority 'which is from God'. For only by accepting and dissolving it into themselves, can it be made truly a people's regime.

Here is the blueprint for the bridge that will span the gulf which in the 1970s separated the intelligentsia of Russian Idea from its grass-roots supporters. In all the metamorphoses of modern-day L-National-ism we have considered so far, from VSKhSON's revolutionary theocracy in the 1960s to Solzhenitsyn's apologia for Orthodox monarchy in the 1980s, Communism has consistently figured as a phenomenon alien to Russia and inimical to her historical tradition. Shimanov is the first in the post-Stalinist era to have legitimized Communism by fitting it into the Russian political tradition,[13] as one of a series of tribulations — sent by God to save and preserve Russia.

As before, Communism, of course, remains an evil, but an evil that is not just incomparably less than those which threaten the nation from without, but is Russia's own indigenous evil, which can always be reconciled. This evil cannot simply be expunged from Russian life, as the national-liberal sectarians believed, rather it must be transcended through a co-operative effort by the whole nation at the spiritual and intellectual levels.

Shimanov thus provides the theory for the idea *Veche*'s 'Orthodox patriotic' readers were trying to express more instinctively: namely, the reduction of world evil to a single focus. He has managed to construct an ideological justification for the Orthodox masses' intuitive drive to make peace with the regime in the face of the impending nation-wide threat. He pacifies and comforts these masses whom Solzhenitsyn had aroused and then cast out into the wilderness, declaring them to be living by lies. He absolves the Orthodox believers of the sin of collaborating with an atheistic regime. To counter the teachers of national-liberalism, who cannot abandon their sectarian anti-Communism, he declares, 'To protest against our regime means to go against God.'[14] He persuades 'patriots' that only by collaborating can they make the regime truly national. Shimanov not only writes God with a capital letter, but also Soviet Authority. He understands perfectly that to construct a bridge to the 'patriotic' reader, he must banish the sectarian illusions and utopianism of his predecessors.

The VSKhSON, we recall, was dedicated to the idea of a 'revolution of national liberation' and the armed 'overthrow of the Communist oligarchy'. *Veche* proposed, not a revolution, but the creation of a second, Orthodox, Russia in Siberia that would be separated geographically from Communism. Solzhenitsyn attempted to realize *Veche*'s plan by appealing to the 'Russian souls' of the Soviet leaders to renounce their 'alien', 'Western' ideology. (Later, at the end of the 1970s, he realized it was impossible to change the leaders' minds with words, and began to appeal to the 'Russian souls' of the Soviet military instead — thus, in a sense, he came back to the ideas of VSKhSON[15]).

Despite the differences within these approaches, they all originated from the same assumption: that a true Russian renaissance could only begin without the Communists. Nonsense, replies Shimanov in concert with the 'patriotic' masses, Russia is already undergoing a renaissance. Moreover, Communism, far from hindering the process, is aiding it, first and foremost by preserving Russia from the ravages of bourgeoisification and so forming a protective shield around it which makes the renaissance possible. Soviet Authority, says Shimanov, has, since 1917 already 'accomplished an enormous turnaround and continues to change perceptibly before the eyes of those *who know how to look*.'[16] Moreover, Communism, through its immanent religiousness, keeps that flicker of faith alive among the masses, without which any renaissance would be impossible. Because of this, the Russian people strive not to liquidate Communism, but to take possession of it. It is also for this reason that the second-hand utopianism with which national liberals seek to distract the people from their true purpose — that of transfiguring the system in order to transform the world — are extraneous.

For the national liberals, the West — though hopeless and 'rotten' — is their sole ally, who, however weakly, still defends them from the Communists. In other words, the national liberals need the West the same way that 'patriotic' readers need Communism. For Shimanov, the West is a plague, the source of 'pagan-bourgeois' infection which must be wiped out if humanity is to survive. Of course, to Shimanov, like Solzhenitsyn, the hateful 'smatterers' are Jewish or Judaizing intellectuals — 'civilized savages', as he calls them. He hates them for the same reasons the Young Guards did — because they 'feed on the refuse of Western civilization.' Not surprisingly, Andrei Sakharov's programme is 'Kike-Freemason' to Shimanov. Nor does he have any sympathy for the national liberals, who, in his opinion, dress up like patriots while echoing the 'Kike-Freemasons'. He ridicules them mercilessly.

'From a reading of his [Solzhenitsyn's] *Letter to the Soviet Leaders*,' says Shimanov, 'it may appear that Solzhenitsyn has already outgrown democracy and passed over from it to autocracy (that is, Russian style monarchy),' but, he adds wryly, 'this is true only if one reads inattentively. He has actually taken this step just with one foot, while the other remains . . . where it was.'[17] Shimanov's critique of Solzhenitsyn 'from the Right' is very important for us, because it leads straight to the core of his political concept. To Solzhenitsyn's call on the leaders to abandon the state ideology, Shimanov says 'nonsense', because 'for an ideocratic state to abandon its ideology means simply to commit suicide . . . The Marxist ideology . . . is the foundation of our state . . . [And] it is necessary to see to it, not that Marxism is mechanically discarded, but that it is transformed by life itself and . . . transcended.'[18]

'Comical and miserable democratic void'

Thus in the ideology for Russia's future charted by Shimanov, he not only plans to use the religious elements in Marxism, which is to become an organic 'union of Nil Sorskii with Lenin' (a mixture of Russian Orthodoxy with Leninism), but also he believes that this future state must *remain ideocratic* — that is, having a single, monopolistic ideology that excludes any differences in thinking.[19] Shimanov, like his pre-revolutionary counterpart Sergei Sharapov, believes in dissidence only so long as he is not in power. This is why he viciously attacks Solzhenitsyn's early speculation as to the 'free flowering' of ideas in a future Russia. He will not tolerate any such freedom; it is not needed by anyone in Russia apart from the small band of Judaizing cosmopolitans: 'It is time to abandon the ridiculous prejudice that a lukewarm atmosphere of "freedom of thought" and "freedom of creativity" is the best one for the maturation of truth and great art.'[20]

Note the paradox of Shimanov's doctrine. Here is a dissident, a free-thinker, who openly preaches the totalitarian suppression of hetero-doxy and hates the very principle of dissidence. When we try to analyse the basis of this paradox, however, we see that it is only the logical consequence of Shimanov's concept of the state. 'In Russia,' says Shimanov, 'there has been too much suffering and God will not permit it to be resolved in the comical and miserable democratic void. There must be no Western democracy for us.'[21] Earlier, Leont'ev had put the case more precisely when he declared that, 'The Russian nation has expressly not been created for freedom.'[22]

But why must there be no democracy? By answering this question we can explain all of Shimanov, even his justification of political informing which he shamefacedly tries to support with a long quotation from Dostoevskii;[23] and even his appeals to 'create an ambience of allegiance' to the state 'as the only one possible for Orthodox Russian patriots.'[24]

Shimanov asks, 'Can we really, with valid authority, label as democratic, regimes *which have emancipated themselves from solving moral problems* in favour of purely fiscal and police functions?'[25] To Shimanov, a state can only exist in the full sense if it assumes responsibility for the moral tasks of society, if it defines the nation's goals and leads the nation towards them. This is because the state must be a 'tool for the transformation of the world', for a new crusade. It must therefore have total control over its subjects, in a way that democracy cannot.

How do the Western democrats relate to the regime? Why, whoever wants to, approaches it . . . and begins to shake its breast . . . arguing his rights . . . until the poor regime no longer knows whom it is supposed to serve and to whom it should be subject . . . is demoralized . . . and in effect abandons power . . . instead of *firmly defining what must be and what must not.*[26]

In other words, a state which is not absolute, not autocratic, and does not possess 'a highly developed nervous system in the form of a Party which embraces the entire organism of society almost down to its smallest cell',[27] is not a state at all, according to Shimanov. Democracy is bad because it is not totalitarian in principle, and thus cannot 'exercise such a degree of control.' Conversely, the Soviet system is good because it contains the potential for totalitarianism and thus is able to provide such control.[28] This is the price, Shimanov says, the people must pay for their chosen status: they must be aware that it is their fate, their cross and their secret that they shall be the slave of a totalitarian state.

Not even the most fanatical foreign Russophobe has ever ventured to pronounce so definitive a death sentence upon Russia. Only a person who kneels reverently before the church altar out of love for the Russian people can permit himself to proclaim so openly that his people — the only vessel of the 'true faith' in the world, destined to be the moral teacher of mankind — are in fact slaves. Moreover, what Shimanov's people have to teach mankind is the fine art of slavery.

Thus we have Shimanov's F-nationalist utopia, based on profound distrust of the individual, who — though supposedly created in God's own image — is deprived of the most elementary right of free choice and condemned to be merely a tool in the hands of an all-powerful and all-benevolent state. The state takes the place of God in this totalitarian paradise — and legitimately so because it is the sole embodiment of the pagan image of the nation, which, in the minds of Shimanov and his 'Ultras', has replaced God. For, according to Shimanov, 'Russia is an object of faith.'[29]

Russia: Nation or Empire?

We turn now to the main paradox of Shimanov's concept. On the one hand, he asserts that nations must not 'have communion with foreigners when there is no need', and 'national organisms must be self-contained and impenetrable to each other,'[30] while on the other hand, he attacks Solzhenitsyn's early proposal (which would seem to follow logically from this premise) that the Soviet peoples should be permitted to secede from the USSR. How are we to reconcile isolationism with imperialism? Unlike Danilevskii, Shimanov calls on the help of Providence, for which, of course, there are no paradoxes:

The Soviet Union is not a mechanical conglomeration of nations of different kinds . . . but a MYSTICAL ORGANISM, composed of nations mutually complementing each other and making up, under the leadership of the Russian people, a LITTLE MANKIND — a spiritual trigger for the explosion of the great mankind.[31]

In other words, the USSR is merely the chosen people's laboratory for conducting experiments into the future 'Orthodoxization' of the world. In this sense the Russian people are an exception. Translating Shimanov's mystical revelations into the language of practical politics, it means that the Russian people are the only ones allowed to have an *empire* — one that is closed, 'impenetrable', isolated from other nations — until such time as these nations are willing to speak with it in its own language — that is, in the language of the Third Reich — sorry, 'Third Rome' (to quote Shimanov). Briefly, that is how Shimanov tries to turn his utopian scheme into a realistic programme for an imperial-isolationist Russia.

Strategy and Politics

In analysing Shimanov's works, one senses a kind of strange dualism — as though you have before you not one, but two writers, who change places with each other minute by minute. The mystical language of miracles alternates with cold officialese; fiery prophecies of the 'Third Rome' give way to the style of a commonplace clerk; pious anathemas against Western democracy are interspersed with vulgar propagandistic invective. This literary 'split personality' of Shimanov's calls for careful interpretation and analysis. Here is an example of one style:

Russia has literally suffered through a NEW THEOCRACY . . . for it is quite obvious that we need a patriarchal structure of society different from the present one . . . and a new . . . mystical attitude toward the land . . . [This] task is not within the capacity . . . of Western democracy . . . but then who can do it? I think . . . that the best instrument may prove to be that force which from its very beginning has made war on God — the system that wrestles with God, which decided . . . to turn the whole world around to suit itself — that is what might serve the glory of God better than anything else. I have in mind, of course, the Soviet system, with its essentially autocratic structure, its maximalist aims, and which is so contradictory in its nature and its ideology that it is able, thanks to this circumstance, under the influence of the truth of life to change itself from a minus to a plus, and only win from such a metamorphosis.[32]

This Shimanov addresses to the Russian intelligentsia of the era of 'Russian Orthodox renaissance' — an intelligentsia deeply disillusioned with socialism, which is sceptical about the miraculous potential of the 'transformation' he promises. Here Shimanov is a sincere defender of the Soviet system; he speaks in a lofty pulpit style; he prophesies; his language is full of pathos and fire.

Then, in a nearby passage of the same book, another Shimanov speaks, discussing the 'Draft of the Basic Law of the USSR on Public Education' and trying to convince the 'leaders' that a clique of Soviet 'priests' (i.e., Marxist anti-religious propagandists) have written the draft in such a way that

> the objective contents of this . . . draft will do enormous harm to the Soviet state and will damage in the eyes of the progressive world the authority of Communist morality. [For this reason the draft should be rejected], so as not to compromise our Soviet system by an accusation of violence . . . done to freedom of conscience — and whose? . . . not the exploiters, not the landlords and capitalists, but plain Soviet working people . . . Is it not a sign of [Marxism's] weakness that we should abolish the well-known Leninist position on the freedom both of religious and of anti-religious propaganda? . . . Here, I think, it would be appropriate to recall those hard times when our society, faced by a heavily-armed, advancing German Fascist enemy . . . abandoned the self-torment that was weakening it, and conquered the foe by the moral and political unity of all our Soviet people. This moral and political unity . . . proved to be superior to all ideological divisions and was of such undoubted value, tested by life itself, that it would be criminal, from the point of view of state policy, for us to give it up. The moral and political unity of the entire Soviet people is something that we must strengthen, not dissipate, by incitement to conflict within our society, because, at the acute turning points of history, our state will more than once have to encounter dangers no less than that of the past Great Patriotic War. In the face of the very real and growing Chinese chauvinist threat . . . we must strengthen all the healthy forces of society so that, at the moment of crisis, they can come to the aid of the state.[33]

This other voice is that of Shimanov the Party propagandist, who seems to have borrowed phrases such as 'well-known Leninist position', 'the moral code of Communism' and 'the moral and political unity of our entire Soviet people' from an editorial in *Pravda*. This Shimanov, using the bureaucratic and pragmatic language characteristic of the 'leaders', cautiously tries to sell them his own tactical concept of a 'transformation'. He tries to convince the Soviet state of the loyalty of the 'patriotic masses', and of the fact that they, and not the Marxist ideological clique are the 'healthy forces' ready to come to the state's aid. The price of this loyalty, however, is that the state return to the 'well-known Leninist position', remember the Stalinist 'moral and political unity', and agree to 'peaceful coexistence' with the devout Orthodox masses.[34]

What is of interest here, above all, is the fact that in the 1970s the Russian Idea was *acquiring its own politics*. Not only did it no longer call for the overthrow of the Soviet regime (as VSKhSON had done), but it no longer confined itself to global strategies or historical parallels (in contrast to *Veche* and *From Under the Rubble*); it was starting to speak to the Soviet state *in its own language*. It was beginning to demonstrate the concrete advantages the system can derive from allying itself with the Russian Right — against the clique of Marxist 'priests'. In essence, it was already accusing its opponents of *anti-Sovietism*.

It accuses them of undermining the influence of the USSR 'in the eyes of progressive world opinion', of 'inciting internal conflicts' within Russia itself. It puts before the 'leaders' a practical proposition: weigh up how much you stand to gain or lose before relying on the Marxist ideological clique. It attempts to compete with this clique on the basis of practical politics by showing that the 'leaders' have more to gain by relying on the Russian Right than on its competitors. It addresses the leaders' deeply hidden subconscious fears and asks them with an air of innocence: which is more important to you — tattered Marxist dogma or real power? If power, then reliance — at the moment of crisis — on the 'patriotic masses' is far safer than an alliance with an impotent ideological clique. Unlike other factions of the New Right, Shimanov conducts his own PR and does business: he advertises his own wares to the consumer and runs down his competitors'.

To the Russian Orthodox intelligentsia he sells the *strategy* of transformation. For this, high pathos and impassioned preaching are needed. To the leaders, he sells the politics of transformation and the guarantee of their rule. This requires business-like prose and vulgar advertising jargon. In both cases, he speaks in a language that is easily understood by the consumer.

To their former allies Shimanovites were 'Ultras'. Yet, in fact, they are not militant at all: they are practical politicians offering the leaders more flexible and effective tactics, a deeper social base, and a broader field of operations for political manoeuvre in case of crisis. In fact, Shimanov is suggesting nothing more than a Russian variant of the 'historic compromise'. If this is possible for the Italian Communist

Party — and it can remain chaste in spite of it — then why shouldn't it be possible for the Soviet Communist Party?

The Ideology of Russian Fascism

In Shimanov, the Russian New Right has, for the first time, found not only an ideologist who can address the awakened 'Orthodox patriotic masses' in their own language, but also someone who is a potential political leader, capable of transforming a sectarian anti-Communist doctrine into a real mass political movement. Isn't this just what the 'patriotic' readers of *Veche* and Solzhenitsyn were clamouring for? But whereas they could offer only resettlement in Siberia or an Orthodox monarchy in mothballs, Shimanov offers the 'patriots' the possibility of a real struggle: gradually and legally to transfigure the Soviet state, to remobilize it and transform it into a vital and powerful weapon for repelling the 'Zionist imperialist' global assault scheduled for the year 2000.

Compared with Shimanov, Osipov and Solzhenitsyn really are generals without armies. Shimanov can speak to 'the leaders' on behalf of a political constituency. He is not posturing before the 'patriotic' masses or lecturing them. He is an ordinary man, an elevator operator and a patriot, a true man of the people. He does not bother to appeal to the leaders' 'Russian souls.' He appeals directly to their interests, instead.

In the eyes of the 'patriotic' reader, both Solzhenitsyn and Osipov were compromised by their support from the 'Zionist' West. They were interviewed by Zionist journalists, published by Zionist publishers, and discussed on Zionist radio stations. Shimanov is clean in this respect, and has had no such dealings with the hated West. He represents a sector of Soviet public opinion whose strength 'the leaders' can easily verify by the most elementary sociological survey (the KGB has a number of highly experienced sociologists at its disposal).

Of course, *Veche* was the first to discover this source of political capital, but it was Shimanov who discovered how to make use of it. He was the first to lay claim to the role of intermediary between 'the leaders' and the 'Orthodox patriotic masses'. In the present climate of reform, and with the arrival of Gorbachev and a new generation of Soviet leaders, the phenomenon of Gennadii Shimanov might seem insignificant. However, looking back over the past 500 years of Russian history, and looking forward to the year 2000 from the perspective of

Shimanov and his 'patriotic' masses, we get a rather different impression. For, in reality, Shimanov — and at present he alone — promises to heal the empire's most vulnerable and sorest point: its rapidly growing inferiority complex.

In fact, in the eyes of the world, the Russian empire is ceasing to be a realistic alternative to its principal age-old rival, the West. It is skidding again — as it did at the end of the seventeenth and the nineteenth centuries. Its ideology is increasingly being seen as a scandalized utopia. Even the Communist Parties of Italy, in the West, China, in the East, Hungary in the Warsaw Pact itself, have been jettisoning everything Russian from their Communist practice and doctrine. They are turning to the concept of a mixed economy, with a state and private sector, borrowed from the West, or to pluralistic — liberal Marxist — ideology. Of course, Russia too could choose to succumb to the reformist impulse, right behind the Hungarians, the Chinese and the Italians. But then she would cease being a leader. She would be reduced to the status of follower, of imitator, and thus no longer unique. She would be trading her spiritual birthright for the mess of pottage offered by Western material prosperity. For adherents of the Russian Idea and for the Orthodox patriotic masses, such a course would signify a national humiliation of awesome proportions — comparable to Russia's ideological and political capitulation to the 'Americanization of the spirit', in the language of Young Guardism, or to 'the Jewish drive for world dominion', according to the readers of *Veche*.

Is there any chance for Russia to regain her spiritual birthright? Is there a realistic alternative to the Soviet system's humiliating demobilization and surrender to the West? If so, then Shimanov's alternative is the only one on offer. His 'new Russian ascetic and spiritual civilization', has no use for 'markets' or material prosperity and thus doesn't need to mimic the Chinese or the Hungarians. This is why Shimanov is important, but his significance has been largely overlooked by Western sovietology. (I shall return to this subject in my concluding chapter.)

At first glance, Shimanov's historical and political concept appears to contain little that is original. He borrowed theocracy from the VSKhSON programme, imperial isolationism from *Veche*, and the 'combination of Nil Sorskii with Lenin' from Antonov. From Solzhenitsyn he lifted hatred of the 'smatterers' and a devastating critique of democracy, while directly from the Orthodox patriotic masses he took their rabid anti-semitism. However, the principal novelty of his concept is that he has unrelentingly discarded all the utopian and sectarian elements of national liberalism. He drained VSKhSON's theocracy of its adventuristic conspiratorial flavour, separated out the 'Siberian gambit' from *Veche*'s isolationism, and the retrospective utopia from Solzhenitsyn, and severed *From Under the Rubble* of its mystical anti-Communism. Most importantly, he contributed something to the Russian Idea which its political constituency had been passionately seeking — the affirmation of an 'atmosphere of allegiance' to the Soviet state as the 'only possible one for Orthodox Russian patriots.'

That is how the politics of Russian nationalism looked after its shell of bombastic rhetoric had broken and had fallen away. Instead of Orthodox monarchy's double-headed eagle, hatched by the Russian Idea at the turn of the century, this time there emerged a hideous twisted reptile — Russian fascism.

Summary of the 'Ultras'

(1)   The concept of the Russians as a chosen people, saved by God only thanks to the exceedingly cruel trials he has imposed upon them over the course of their history. These very tests can be viewed as testimony to Russia's select status.

(2)   The concept of the religious nature of Communism, within which the very scope of its activity in opposition to God is transformed into evidence of its having been chosen as his vehicle.

(3)   The concept of the Soviet state as an unconscious tool of the Lord, destined to save Russia and, in the final analysis (through 'Orthodoxization'), the world too. Recognition of the principle that the Soviet system is potentially 'Russian in spirit', thus bringing Shimanov closer to Young Guardism and creating an objective basis for the ideological merger of the establishment and the dissident branches of the Right.

(4)   The concept of a 'state catastrophe' threatening Russia if the Soviet leaders and 'patriotic' masses do not manage to find a common language and begin to work together.

(5)   The development of political devices for uniting 'Russian Orthodoxy with Leninism' and exploiting and re-interpreting the slogans of Soviet propaganda.

(6)   The replacement of muted anti-semitism (VSKhSON and *Veche*) or symbolic anti-semitism (Solzhenitsyn) by overt anti-semitism linked to the exposure of 'Kike-Freemasonry' (identified with the

liberal dissident movement) as an agent for the forces of global chaos.

(7) The attempt to introduce the image of the 'year 2000' — the appointed time for the final confrontation between Russia and the West — into political dialogue with the Soviet regime.

(8) The concept of Russian fascism as an alternative strategy for Russia as it stands on the threshold of that year 2000.

Notes

1 Officially the 'Russian Club' was called 'The Society for the Preservation of the Monuments of Antiquity' and was an entirely legal affair. In reality, however, this was a 'party' institution where Russian Idea dissidents regularly gathered with their establishment comrades in order to exchange views and develop strategies. Passions came to a boil in the Russian Club in the 1960s resulting in the formation of the Russophile factions.

2 G. M. Shimanov, *Ideal'noe gosudarstvo* [*The Ideal State*] (Keston College Archives), p. 2.

3 *Pis'ma a Rossii* and *Protiv techeniia*.

4 *Moskovskii sbornik*, No. 1 (Keston College Archives), p. 68. Emphasis added.

5 '[Our] line is "further right" than that of the "revolutionary underground", but "further left" than that timid position of universal admissability on which you stand . . . I think that *super-obedience*, just like rebellion, will not bring Russia anything good' (*Vol'noe slovo*, No. 17 — 18, p. 19).

6 The works of Konstantin Leont'ev suffered approximately the same fate a century before. His first work, later famous, *Vizantizm i slavianstvo* [Byzantinism and the Slavic World], was rejected by all the organs of the nationalist press and published in an obscure journal — *Chtenia v Imperatorskom obshchestve istorii i drevnostei rossiiskikh* [Proceedings of the Imperial Society of Russian History and Antiquities] — in 1875, where it remained unnoticed until 1885, when the first volume of his collection *Vostok, Rossia i slavianstvo* [The East, Russia, and the Slavic World] appeared, causing a sensation. This seems to indicate that an ideology's timeliness is not a simple matter of who lived or wrote after whom. In the nineteenth century such antagonists as Ivan Aksakov, Danilevskii, Leont'ev, and Sharapov were also contemporaries. A whole brew of nationalist conceptions can boil at the same time in the cauldron of right-wing ideas. What matters is the sequence with which — because of changes in historical circumstances — certain doctrines which had until recently shone on the ideological scene, fade into the background, while others, which had previously been in shadow, move into the light.

7 Shimanov, *Kak ponimat' nashu istoriu* [How to Understand Our History], p. 5.

8   'The Russian nation is increasingly vanishing in a spiritual and physical sense. . . . The soul of the Russian person is degenerating too: in the current spiritual and intellectual emptiness, as if deprived of air, it is fading and wilting. Morality is drying up . . . The most complete disorientation in life . . . the decay of the family, spiritual disorganization, drunkenness, perversion, feeling trapped' (*Protiv techeniia,* [Against the mainstream] p. 62).

9   Ibid.

10   Ibid., p. 18.

11   Shimanov, *Kak ponimat' nashy istoriu,* p. 5.

12   Ibid., p. 6. Capitalized in the original.

13   Here Shimanov, of course, is also taking his cue from Berdiaev. However, unlike VSKhSON, he is not using *The New Middle Ages* as his guide, but *Istoki i smysl' russkogo kommunizma* [The Sources and Sense of Russian Communism], YMCA Press, Paris: 1955. This book was unanimously condemned by nationalists of every shade for its heretical assertion that communism has Russian roots.

14   Shimanov, *Protiv techeniia,* p. 23.

15   *Vestnik RKhD,* No. 127, 1979, p. 295.

16   Shimanov, *Protiv techeniia,* p. 90.

17   Shimanov, *Kak ponimat' nashy istoriu,* p. 8.

18   Ibid., p. 9.

19   If we assume for a moment that in a situation of serious crisis, brought on, say, by the collapse of Gorbachev's reforms, power in Russia came into the hands of the military, they would clearly have an easier time coming to terms with Shimanov than with Solzhenitsyn.

20   Shimanov, *Kak ponimat' nashy istoriu,* p. 8.

21   Shimanov, *Protiv techeniia,* p. 24.

22   *Russkoe obozrenie* No. 1, 1895, p. 264.

23   Shimanov, *Protiv techeniia,* pp. 97—8.

24   Ibid., p. 101.

25   Shimanov, *Ideal'noe gosudarstvo,* p. 6. Emphasis added.

26   *Moskovskii sbornik,* p. 26. Emphasis added.

27   Shimanov, *Ideal'noe gosudarstvo,* p. 14.

28   Here again it is difficult not to notice how extraordinarily convenient Shimanov's doctrines are for ideologically justifying the regeneration of the mechanism of totalitarian rule — in other words, for a new counter-reform.

29   Shimanov, *Protiv techeniia,* p. 20.

30   Shimanov, *Ideal'noe gosudarstvo,* p. 6.

31   Ibid., p. 16.

32   Shimanov, *Protiv techeniia,* p. 89.

33   Ibid., pp. 76—83.

34   In a private Moscow conversation in 1976, Shimanov also spoke of 'peaceful coexistence' as a source for improving the Soviet economy, putting an end to the universal embezzlement of socialist property, and drunkenness, as well as increasing the productivity of labour.

III

Conclusion

19
Fascism takes to the Streets

In the last century, history was pulled by oxen. It took two generations for the Russian Idea to be transformed from a protest against despotism into an apology for it. Only by its third generation did it prove ready to embrace fascism. Of course, even by the 1870s, an astute observer could have foretold, with some degree of certainty, that an ideological doctrine that preached a spiritual return to the middle ages, would, very likely, toward the end of the century, also return there politically: to *The Protocols of the Elders of Zion*; and, that, by the start of the next century, it would take to the streets in an effort to reverse the wheel of history by brute force. Before such an observer's eyes a kind of historical experiment would have been unfolding, and the confirmation of his hypothesis would have promised an outstanding academic result.

No such observers, however, existed in the 1870s. The very concept of historical experiment as a strategy for political research was only to be born a century later in the West.[1] As for native liberal critics of the Russian Idea, they — for all their diatribes against its 'teeth-gnashing obscurantism' — did not take it seriously as a political alternative (recall V. Solov'ev's tirade about its 'reckless bantering'). All we can say now, looking at the metamorphosis of the Russian Idea in retrospect, is that it came on to the streets in 1905, as a result of what I call a 'regime' crisis within the Russian political system. But for it to be capable of adopting Hitler's swastika as its official emblem, and total war against the 'kike-Freemasons' as its official ideology, the 'systemic' crisis of 1917 was needed.[2]

We have already several times remarked on the repetition of this metamorphosis begun in the second half of this century. The main difference is that this time it has happened astonishingly quickly. In Petersburg Russia it took eighty years for the Russian Idea to come as far as it has today over the course of just one Soviet generation: from a dedicated struggle against 'soul-destroying Communism' in the mid-1960s to being prepared, in the early 1980s, to take to the streets wearing the swastika.

This is how an anonymous samizdat author described this phenomenon in August 1983:

> Lately, on the streets, squares and parks of many Soviet cities, particularly at night, you will increasingly meet groups of young people whose clothes, speech and behaviour are uncannily reminiscent of the sadly familiar patterns of Germany in the 1920s, [including] semi-home-made swastika charm bracelets. Last year Moscow already witnessed an attempt to stage a fascist demonstration by Pushkin's monument, on the 20th April — Adolf Hitler's birthday. This year, several days before that date, the principals and party secretaries of secondary schools met for special briefings on what to do in the event of the public appearance 'of pro-fascist elements within a number of groups of youths ignorant of their social obligations' . . . And indeed, on the 20th April, public appearances by fascist youths were recorded in a string of cities. These appearances varied in form: in different cities and districts, the fascists marched in formation in the streets and courtyards, chanting 'Heil Hitler!' and 'Sieg Heil!'; in others, clothed in their uniforms with [swastika] armbands, they moved into coffee bars and discos to declaim their slogans; in still others, there were demonstrations at night. In many cases the fascists started brawls, sometimes they beat up war veterans wearing their service ribbons. They used not just fists, but also knuckle dusters. Those who were involved, were mainly students, young workers, and older pupils from academic and technical secondary schools.[3]

This might have seemed like exaggeration or rumour had not Evgenii Evtushenko for the first time given publicity to the phenomenon of Russian fascism in the September 1985 issue of *Novyi mir*. He describes in verse much the same thing as our samizdat author has described in prose, concluding with the sad question:

> How could it have happened that these, as we say, units,
> were born in a country of twenty million and more — shadows?
> What allowed them, or rather, helped them to appear,
> what allowed them to reach out for the swastika within her [Russia]?[4]

Russian fascism abroad

An emigre observer, describing the emergence in New York of 'Russian

Call' [*Russkii Klich*], a fascist publishing house which publishes Russian translations of 'rare books, which have been physically destroyed both in the USSR and the West',[5] asked himself the same question as Evtushenko. Already since 1982 — the same year that the first fascist demonstration took place in Moscow — 'Russian Call' has published 87 titles, including Hitler's *Mein Kampf*, the speeches of Alfred Rosenberg, *The Protocols of the Elders of Zion*, the manifesto of the 'Union of the Russian People' and V. Mikhailov's brochure 'New Judea', which I quoted from earlier. The publisher, a certain Nikolai Tetenov, explains that, 'the value of these books is that they expose the TRUE enemies of our people and aid the formation of spiritual and national self-awareness.'[6] He asks those 'who love our much-suffering people' to despatch to Russia 'via tourists, sailors and even by regular mail', books which 'give a CLEAR impression of what happened to Russia and of what morass of decadence and decay the Western world is floundering.'[7]

The same publisher also produces a magazine entitled *Russian Self-Awareness* [*Russkoe Samosoznanie*], which preaches the following maxims: 'The Semites have spoiled our motherland, and only anti-semitism will save her. Revulsion toward kikes is implanted in us by the Lord God himself. Anti-semitism is a sacred emotion. He who stifles it in himself is not only sinning, but also ruining both himself and his country.'[8] Just like the Moscow fascists, Tetenov leaves not the slightest doubt with whom his sympathies lay in the confrontation between fascism and the West: 'As for Hitler, it was he who brought Germany out of hunger and collapse, who liquidated unemployment, provided his people with a high standard of living and who showed the predator Jews the door.' According to Tetenov, 'The West with its human rights has already, with the help of drugs, sexual perversion, advertising and pop music, transformed its people into a weak-willed mass of consumers, in the historical perspective good only as fertilizer.'[9]

Unanswered questions

How can one explain the emergence of overt Russian fascism (as opposed to Shimanov's theorizing or even the samizdat 'patriotic' reader mail) simultaneously in both Moscow and the emigre community (where, as in Moscow, it was unheard of since the 1930s)? Evtushenko, of course, has no answer to this question. It is a credit to him just to have posed it. An American journalist David Shipler, who lived in Moscow between 1975 and 1979, understood very well the power of the degenerate Russian Idea (which he calls Russianism) and vividly relates a discussion he had with an elderly Soviet writer. 'We are ruled now by sated wolves', he was told, 'but among those people [nationalists] there are hungry wolves.'[10]

Shipler's explanation of the phenomenon is, however, too abstract. 'The potential force of Russianism, whose best-known apostle is Solzhenitsyn', says Shipler, 'lies in its coincidence with the most powerful impulses of both the political hierarchy and the people. As it shares Soviet communism's devotion to political unanimity, it also taps the deepest Russian wellsprings of obedience to authority and such a visceral aversion to diversity that some liberal dissidents find the Russianists even more frightening than the Communists in power.'[11] Like the majority of American intellectuals who have encountered Russian nationalism, Shipler falls back on the fundamental stereotypes of political culture. But these stereotypes are age-old and static. They cannot explain the dynamic of the Russian Idea: why it vanished from circulation after the 1920s and then was reborn in the second half of the 1960s; why Shimanov, with whom the author discussed many things, so despises Solzhenitsyn, who is represented in Shipler's book as an 'apostle of Russianism'. Moreover, these stereotypes cannot explain why the Russian Idea took to the streets and why its disciples await the year 2000 with such tragic intensity.

The explanation of our samizdat author is, of course, much less abstract. He observes that, 'today among party, state, and Komsomol activists all possible sorts of "reflections", "appeals", and "memoirs" printed up on mimeograph machines are being circulated which are unofficial in form, but openly apologetic and simultaneously menacing in content. It is becoming exceedingly fashionable to praise the firmness of the leaders of the Third Reich — Hitler, and Himmler and Bormann even more . . . Books about the Third Reich are becoming favourites, especially among young functionaries.' The author talks as well about a general 'fascisization of apparatus functionaries', and concludes that, 'the fascist, radical right movement among various layers of Soviet youth that is arising and gathering strength, though containing elements of spontaneous protest, plays into the hands of certain groups in the political leadership of the USSR and [even] if they may not be directly inspiring it, they covertly support it, counting on the possible use of this movement to achieve particular strategic goals.'[12] But if the fascist movement was *not* inspired by 'certain political circles' then what *did* inspire it? Why was the 'fascisization of young functionaries' taking place at this particular time? Why fascism, of all things?

These questions have remained unanswered, not least because the leading American sovietologists simply ignore them, or at best treat them as exotic eccentricities — lunatic-fringe phenomena. Conventional sovietological thought has no place for Russian fascism. For conservatives, who anyway have difficulty distinguishing between Nazi and Soviet 'totalitarianism', all this fuss about fascism in Moscow is completely trivial. What difference does it make? they would ask. Liberals, on the other hand, tend to ignore the uncomfortable fact because it compromises their general view, according to which Moscow 'functionaries', especially the younger ones, are supposed to become increasingly liberal, not turn fascist. One way or another, neither of these groups of experts wishes to see Russian fascism as a problem that requires serious explanation. Some of them, we have seen, confuse the Russian Idea with patriotism, while others mix it up with chauvinism, everybody is satisfied. However, the issue cannot be made to disappear like this, and still needs to be explained.

An historical parallel

It is here that the theoretical analysis of the degeneration of the pre-revolutionary Russian Idea might be of some practical help. In fact, it is hardly possible to suggest any plausible explanation of the sudden emergence of fascist mobs on the Moscow streets in the early 1980s unless we remember that they were there once before. In 1905, it was precisely the powerful appeal of the degenerate Russian Idea, its logic and argumentation that inspired the 'patriotic masses' to take to Moscow streets under fascist slogans. What it signalled then was the arrival of the 'regime' crisis in the Petersburg empire — as well as the approach of its 'systemic' crisis.

Let us recall briefly the circumstances under which the fascist mobs took to Moscow streets in 1905. The unsuccessful Russo-Japanese war had provoked a 'regime' crisis which resulted in an immediate sharp polarization between the two Russias. The 'patriotic masses' led by the fighters against 'Kike-Freemason schemes' readily adapted a fascist coloration while at the same time a moderate coalition at the top of the Russian establishment had been formed initiating Stolypin's reforms. These represented a desperate attempt to save the system by means of *changing the regime* and so avert the approaching 'systemic' crisis which both fascist demonstrations from the right and revolutionary terrorism from the left foreshadowed. Reformist Russia stayed face to face with its extremist (revolutionary—reactionary) antagonist. By 1908 the reformers won the first round of this confrontation.

Now what have we seen in Moscow in the early 1980s? The collapse of a long drawn out regime of political stagnation; the emergence on the streets of fascist mobs; and the formation of a moderate coalition at the top of the Soviet establishment initiating Gorbachev's reforms. These seem to represent a desperate attempt to save the system by means of *changing the regime* and so avert the approaching 'systemic' crisis. Once again reformist Russia stayed face to face with her extremist antagonist. By 1986 the reformers won the first round of this confrontation.

Obviously, the 1905—08 'regime' crisis, just as the one of the early 1980s, cannot simply be reduced to fascist demonstration and Stolypin's reforms. There were other significant developments: the tsarist manifesto, and the creation of the Duma, liberal parties and soviets. The specific details of every historical confrontation are indeed unique. However, I am speaking of the *patterns* of political change in Russia, not of the peculiarities of a particular crisis.

The implications of the suggested historical parallel are as follows: by the early 1980s Brezhnev's political stagnation reached the proportions of a 'regime' crisis comparable with that produced by Russia's defeat in the 1904—05 war with Japan; in the situation of imperial decline and approaching 'systemic' crisis it couldn't help but provoke both fascist demonstrations and the formation of Gorbachev's reformist coalition; whereas in the 'regime' crisis of 1905 moderate Russia was opposed by left- and right-wing extremist alternatives, in the Soviet Union of the 1980s the only political force having an ideological platform and capable of capitalizing on the collapse of reform is right-wing extremism; the success or failure of the Russian Idea by the year 2000 depends totally on the success or failure of Gorbachev's reforms.

A Soviet fascist programme

On 10 January 1977, long before the appearance of the Russian Idea on the streets, a tactical programme for the fascist 'transformation' of Russia by the year 2000 was proposed, in its most developed form so far, by Nikolai Emel'ianov to the CPSU Central Committee. According to Emel'ianov:

It is perfectly obvious that the struggle against the highly diversified and highly organized network of Zionism and Freemasonry . . . can be successfully conducted only on a level of still higher organization, which [it] is only in the power of our country and all countries of the socialist system in concert with many developing countries [to achieve]. Concrete measures along these lines could be as follows:

A. On the International Level:

The formation of a broad WORLDWIDE ANTI-ZIONIST AND ANTI-FREEMASON FRONT, after the model of the anti-fascist fronts of the 1930s and '40s, because the menace of Zionist world hegemony, scheduled for the year 2000, threatens all goys of the earth, independently of race, religion or party affiliation (a projected charter for this front was presented a year ago to the International Department of the CPSU Central Committee).

Taking into account the fact that this will be a front against 80 per cent of all the world's capital, then the ULTIMATE VICTORY OF THE FRONT WILL BE THE FINAL VICTORY OVER THE ENTIRE SYSTEM OF CAPITALISM ON A WORLD SCALE.

Time does not wait: while the Zionist-Freemason train continues its journey on schedule toward the year 2000, it can be stopped only by a WORLDWIDE FRONT; only this can derail it from the track of world history. If not, inevitable genocide awaits ALL GOYS.

B. On the Intra-Union Level:

The formation of specialized scientific institutes (provisionally, the Institute for the Study of Zionism and Freemasonry of the CPSU Central Committee), whose [criteria for] electing cadres would exclude from employment individuals who might be potential carriers of the ideas of Zionism and Freemasonry [read: Jews]. If West German capitalist government can bar from a broad range of activities individuals who belong to democratic organizations [read: Communists], then why must the country which was the first DICTATORSHIP of the proletariat in the world deny itself analogous measures against individuals who could be carriers of anti-socialist ideas? Isn't that why we're a *dictatorship* . . . If this stipulation were not observed, the creation of an institute would be pointless (an expanded proposal for this was presented to the Presidium of the 25th CPSU Congress) . . .

The introduction of a section on 'scientific Antizionism and anti-Freemasonry' into the social science courses of all secondary schools . . . and into educational programme on television.

The publication of standard textbooks on this subject for institutions of higher education. . . .

The inclusion of this subject into the mandatory programme of all levels of the system of political education [as well as] into the mandatory programme of political preparation for all personnel of the USSR Armed Forces — from common soldier to marshal.

The inclusion in the all union republics' criminal legislative code articles which stipulate severe punishments for belonging to Zionist and Freemason organizations . . . concealment of belonging to Zionism or Freemasonry ought to be viewed as the infiltration of a hostile agent into our socialist society, with all the ensuing criminal consequences.

The declaration in legislative form (as an edict of the Supreme Soviet of the USSR) that Zionism and Freemasonry are outside the law.

[Waging] a relentless struggle against all forms of ORGANIZED Freemason-Zionist activity like the 'Sakharov Committee', 'The Committee for Monitoring the Implementation of the Helsinki Accords on Human Rights', 'The Solzhenitsyn Fund to Assist Political Prisoners in the USSR', 'The Soviet Branch of Amnesty International', various kinds of 'international seminars on the issues of Jewish culture' and other self-appointed organs, and [instituting] severe criminal punishment for all their participants.[13]

As we see, for Emel'ianov the time for contemplation (or, as Skobelev once put it 'civilian theories') is over. The hour has come to roll up one's sleeves and prepare for the year 2000. Emel'ianov does not busy himself with ideological tracts, like Osipov, or with metaphysical sorties into the realm of demonology, like Solzhenitsyn, but presents a concrete point-by-point plan of action, written in the standard bureaucratic parlance in which a mid-level pro-fascist Soviet functionary of the regime of political stagnation is accustomed to express himself. Significantly, he makes no mention of the 'Orthodox-ization of Russia and the world', nor is he interested in Shimanov's subtle division of 'Orthodox patriotic transformation' into a *strategic* part (convincing the Russian New Right of the necessity of an alliance with the regime) and a *tactical* part (convincing the regime of the need to ally with the Russian New Right). Emel'ianov focuses *exclusively on tactics*. Any appeal to Orthodoxy is irrelevant to his purpose. Even so, there is a noticeable link between Emel'ianov's document and the ferocious diatribe contained in the 'Letter of the Three', against the 'organized forces of broad Zionism and satanism', which conduct a 'secret struggle against our state from within and without'. In fact, Emel'ianov's programme represents no more than a detailed expansion of *The Nation Speaks* Russian Orthodox manifesto's proposal for an 'ideological reorientation of the dictatorship'.

Solzhenitsyn did not manage to formulate a precise ideological response to *Veche*'s 'patriotic' readers, or to the 'Critical Notes of a Russian Man'. Shimanov did succeed in doing so, but offered no concrete programme of preparation for the year 2000. This void in the Russian New Right's arsenal could only be filled by a person such as Emel'ianov, who himself had for many years been a 'pro-fascist functionary'.

From this it is clear that the 'pro-fascist functionary' Emel'ianov, the Young Guardist Chalmaev, the Nobel laureate Solzhenitsyn and the elevator operator Shimanov all had common enemies, whether they called them educated shopkeepers, kike-Freemasons or smatterers (the one difference being that Emel'ianov included Solzhenitsyn's supporters among that damned). Thus, Emel'ianov's fascist programme was firmly built into the Orthodox patriotic temple of the Russian New Right.[14]

The role and function of the Russian Idea

The Russian Idea, an ideology of imperial nationalism, arises in situations where the autocratic system has reached a peak and is starting to slip into decline (as Figure 1 of the Appendix illustrates). That is what happened in the nineteenth century, and is being repeated in the twentieth. To put it another way, the emergence of the Russian Idea is associated with the progressive exhaustion of the empire's resources: political, social and economic, but — most importantly — ideological, or spiritual as the Russian Idea's followers say. Its emergence signals the empire's inability to mobilize the masses, or retain their support, and also signals the alienation of the intelligentsia. In the last century, these resources were used up more slowly. This, it seems, accounts for the slowness of the Russian Idea's metamorphosis into a shadow ideology of counter-reform capable, in a situation of 'systemic' crisis, of restoring to the empire its mobilizational character and the support of both the 'patriotic' masses and extremist elements among the intelligentsia.

Once it has arisen, however, the Russian Idea develops according to its own internal logic, gradually changing from an instrument of struggle against internal and external evil into one of mobilization against an 'outward foe', so assisting the rebirth of a garrison-state mentality among the 'patriotic masses'. The nucleus of this evolution is contained in it from the start — in the quest for a third, specially Russian, path between democracy and 'soul-destroying despotism' (as we saw from the examples of the early Slavophiles in the nineteenth century and VSKhSON in the twentieth). At the next stage, faced with a choice between 'human rights' and 'saving the nation', the Russian Idea will always choose the latter. (We have the examples of Ivan Aksakov in the nineteenth century and Osipov in our own time.) From here, the path lies open toward defining liberalism as an evil of the contemporary world. (Konstantin Leont'ev in the last century and

Solzhenitsyn today). Then follows the imperial dream of having done with the devil once and for all by means of the 'Orthodoxization' of the world (Sharapov at the turn of the century and Shimanov in the 1970s.) Finally, a gigantic image of Satan planning to take over the world is drawn out, which only Russia (with her monopoly on political righteousness) is capable of withstanding. Thus the Russian Idea approaches its natural completion (Odinzgoev at the start of the 1920s and Emel'ianov at the end of the 1970s). When the 'Nation speaks', it is invariably about fascism.

Reform and Russian history

Judging from their reactions, it is clear that Brezhnevist strategists from Old Square* did not understand the meaning of the Russian Idea's rebirth. They, like American sovietologists, did not see it as a sign of the system's decline and slide into a state of 'systemic' crisis. To them, as to the Russian Idea's Western fellow-travellers, it was only another variety of dissidence, opposing the regime. They were not interested in analysing its signals, only in stopping them. Accordingly, the problem was given to the political police to deal with. They managed to track down and arrest the members of VSKhSON, exile Osipov internally and expel Solzhenitsyn, as well as stifle Chalmaev. What they obviously could not do was to change the Brezhnevist strategy which lay at the root of the problem.

This strategy was laden with political stagnation, social decay and cultural paralysis. It could succeed only so long as the country's resources were still growing, albeit slowly, and the regime's only problem remained how to distribute these resources between, on the one hand, the population with its growing demand for 'satiety' and, on the other, military-industrial complex with its growing demand for 'might'. It failed, however, as soon as the system's resources began to dwindle and the regime was forced to choose whether the interests of the people or the military should come first. It was only in trying to resolve this problem, at the end of the 1970s, by which time the economic and social decline had reached scandalous proprtions, that Soviet politicians, along with Western sovietologists, realized that a

---

*[Translator's note: *Staraia ploshchad'* = 'Old Square', where the Central Committee building is located.]

change of regime was necessary, a 'revolutionary change', as Gorbachev now calls it.

Once again, as at the turn of the century, Russia is at a crossroads. By destroying the backbone of Stalinist command economy and maximizing the interests of 'satiety', and correspondingly minimizing those of 'might', the system could pass over into a regime of reform. Judging by Gorbachev's speeches, this is just what he intends for Russia. Reformist speeches, however, have been heard countless times before — and not merely speeches. Yet there has never been a Russian reform, over the course of the last 500 years, which has proved to be irreversible. Even the most successful reforms, as we know, either ended in political stagnation, like Brezhnev's, or were reversed by a fierce counter-reform, like Stalin's. What evidence is there to suggest that Gorbachev might succeed where all his predecessors have, without exception, failed?

Let's face the fateful question: What if Gorbachev's reforms indeed meet the same fate as Stolypin's? How will the system then manage to justify its denial of the interests of 'satiety' other than by instituting a 'spiritual and ascetic' dictatorship in the name of the ultimate confrontation with worldwide 'kike-Freemasonry', which is supposedly preparing to storm Russia by the year 2000? The weight of historical evidence suggests that, in the event of the collapse of reform, the system would be forced to turn to the Russian Idea simply to survive — because it would have nowhere else to go by the end of the twentieth century. It would have to accept the strategy of Shimanov and the tactics of Emel'ianov.

Whom to believe?

To most Western experts on Russia, such a proposition is, of course, quite incredible. 'Who are all these "Orthodox patriotic" writers and readers?' they will ask. Even taken together, what do the 'Critical Notes', Solzhenitsyn's diabolerie, Shimanov's strategy and Emel'ianov's tactics really amount to? Who will follow them in risking everything to try to 'Orthodoxize' the empire and the world? Are they not just a bunch of eccentric fanatics who have very little power and influence, anyway? What chance do they really have of changing the course of history, when all the most reliable sources (Western experts' Soviet contacts from important circles close to the Kremlin) offer assurances that things are by no means as bad as they seem?

There is no doubt that Western experts work with the most modern and sophisticated analytical tools available. They have at their disposal statistics, numerous interviews with Soviet emigres, as well as exact methods of research and means of collecting quotations from the speeches of Soviet leaders as backup. Shimanov and those like him have nothing to counter this with except their own personal observations, feelings and presentiments. But, unlike the accurate and rational experts, the earth is shaking underneath their feet. In the very air of the motherland they sense the approach of a threat which brings with it such a fundamental crisis to the empire that even the wildest fantasies could become reality. Shimanov and his colleagues are living in anticipation of their own 1917 which they expect to come before the year 2000. Whom to believe — the Western experts or the preachers of the Russian Idea?

Certainly, no one will follow Shimanov or Emel'ianov if, at the end of this century, the empire does not undergo a 'systemic' crisis. But suppose it does? Even the most liberal sovietologists can't deny categorically that this is a possibility in the 1900s.[15] Indeed, as far as conservatives are concerned, some of them even preach that the Soviet system be pushed into this fateful crisis, not suspecting that they are actually working for Shimanov and his strategy for a fascist transformation of Russia.[16]

One of the most striking observations about the history of the twentieth century is contained in a book by English historian Norman Cohn; 'There exists a subterranean world, where pathological fantasies disguised as ideas are churned out by crooks and half-educated fanatics for the benefit of the ignorant and superstitious. There are times when that underworld emerges from the depths and suddenly fascinates, captures, and dominates multitudes of usually sane and responsible people . . . And it occasionally happens that this subterranean world becomes a political power and changes the course of history.'[17]

Cohn presents us here with his conclusions about one historical experiment — that of Germany in the 1920s. An analogous experiment took place in the 1970s in Iran, supporting Cohn's observation. In contrast to the preaching of Gennadii Shimanov, this observation cannot be dismissed as mere fantasy. Yet, this is precisely what we are doing. Why?

Notes

1   See David Singer, 'Historical Experiment as a Research Strategy in World Politics', *Political Inquiry*, 1 February 1974.

2   The difference between a 'regime' and 'systemic' crisis is discussed in my concluding chapter.
3   *Strana i mir*, 1984, No. 1−2, p. 51.
4   *Novyi mir*, 1985, No. 9, p. 32.
5   *Zerkalo,* [The Mirror], 1985, No. 3, p. 2.
6   Ibid.
7   Ibid., p. 7.
8   Ibid., p. 8.
9   Ibid., p. 10.
10 David K. Shipler, *Russia: Broken Promises, Solemn Idols*, Penguin Books, 1983, p. 328.
11 Ibid., p. 327.
12 *Strana i mir*, 1984, No. 1−2, p. 54.
13 *Russkoe samosoznanie* [Russian self-awareness], 1984, No. 4, pp. 11−12. Capitalized in the original.
14 It is of no consequence that, personally, N. Emel'ianov is, as one might expect, a maniac and in 1981 was imprisoned for murdering his wife. Fanatics, as is well known, can be ideological leaders, but rarely are well-balanced people.
15 Let us recall: 'If conservative or reactionaries gain the upper hand in the 1980s, or if bungled reforms come to naught . . . pressing problems will go unrectified. The likelihood would then be high that the 1990s would bring a crisis of legitimacy and far more searching dilemmas for the regime, with its core structures and values open to question and under attack as never before.' (Timothy J. Colton, *The Dilemma of Reform in the Soviet Union*, Council on Foreign Relations, 1984, pp. 78−9).
16 See, for example, Richard Pipes, *Survival is Not Enough*, Simon and Shuster, 1984.
17 Norman R. C. Cohn, *Warrant for Genocide,* Harper and Row, NY: 1966, pp. 17−18.

20

Is the West Ready for the 'Year 2000'?

In any science that concerns dynamic objects an historical approach is the standard investigative strategy. We cannot imagine a geologist studying the dynamics of the formation of the earth's core, a psychiatrist analysing a patient's illness, or even a market analyst, who would voluntarily deny themselves the opportunity of examining — in its entirety — the past of the object they are studying. Sovietology, though proud of its status as a social science, seems to be the only exception to this universal rule. Moreover, as Richard Pipes complains, it 'aggressively flaunts its ignorance of Russian history.'[1] It does not strive to determine the fundamental paradigms of change in the object it studies. It knows nothing about them and — something that genuinely makes it unique in the world of science — it doesn't want to know. It is as though sovietology has drawn around itself an imaginary chalk circle which includes only those events that occurred in Russia after 1917.[2] Sovietologists, believing in the magical power of generational change within the Soviet establishment, have — ironically — failed to notice that a change of generations within sovietology itself has not produced any kind of magical transformation in the Western public's perception of Russia, or even changed their own conceptions.

It is true that a younger, revisionist, generation of sovietologists rebelled against their teachers in the 1960s. They cast down the old idols. Yet the main taboos and stereotypes remained, and accordingly the rebels stayed within the limits of that imaginary chalk circle. Here we encounter the first paradox of America's Soviet debate: the rebellion in sovietology provoked by Krushchev's reforms met the same fate as those reforms themselves — it petered out into intellectual stagnation.

Those sovietologists who do dare to cross over the imaginary boundary line, such as Richard Pipes or George Kennan, are very rare.

Yet even they do not move forward with their models, but rather backward, attempting mechanically to transpose the traditional historiographic paradigms, popular in the last century, on to contemporary political reality.[3] Thus, they too end up inside an imaginary chalk circle, only a different kind — one that was drawn a century ago by pre-Soviet Russian historiography. This is the second paradox of the modern Western debate over Russia.

The third paradox, and perhaps the most amusing, is that Clio, the muse of history, has seen fit to punish both opposing camps for their neglect of her. She has not allowed them to escape the limitations of the past. As a result, today both sides diligently repeat the misconceptions and errors of those who were most involved in the debate over Russia's destiny at the turn of the century.

In fact, aren't the Western conservatives repeating the arguments of the old Russian extremists (first and foremost the Bolsheviks) in their zeal to deepen the empire's 'regime' crisis by every means possible, so as to bring it to the white heat of a 'systemic' crisis — and, thus, once and for all, to rid the world of the curse of Communism? On the other hand, aren't liberal sovietologists, in denying the possibility of a 'systemic' crisis, fraught with historical calamity, simply reiterating the arguments of the old Russian liberals? They complacently believed in the viability of the tsarist system, refusing to support Stolypin's reforms which were, in essence, the last desperate attempt to halt the empire's slide toward 'systemic' crisis. Western liberals today are just as certain as their Russian predecessors were that, even if they don't lift a finger to support Gorbachev's reforms, the Soviet system will still somehow, on its own, overcome its 'regime' crisis.

The result of this flight from history is plain to see: just as 1917 caught the West unawares, so the Russian Idea's Year 2000 is beyond the scope of any Western strategies (or 'game plans', as it is becoming fashionable to call them) related to the superpower rivalry at the end of this century. The Russian New Right has been preparing for this historical calamity — clearly and loudly — for the past two decades (just as the Bolsheviks prepared for 1917.) Yet the West still doesn't heed the signals, any more than it did at the turn of the century.

A Replay of the Past

Let us consider tsarist Russia at the fateful moment when she just seemed to be overcoming a 'regime' crisis, and Stolypin was desperately trying to hold her back from the brink of the abyss. What would the best strategy for the West have been then? To deliberately push tsarism over the edge? To involve it in global geopolitical games which it hadn't the strength to survive? To let things continue in the direction they were headed? Or to support Stolypin, tsarist 'apparatchik' that he was, in his attempt to save Petersburg Russia from a fatal 'systemic' crisis, whose outcome, as we now know, was the emergence in the world of a Communist Russia?

At first glance, this last alternative seems as unthinkable as would be a suggestion by someone today to support Gorbachev's reforms. True, Stolypin's Russia wasn't perceived then as a direct threat to the West the way Gorbachev's Russia is now. Still, it was the monstrous tsarist empire. The most abhorrent human rights violations were habitual there, including savage Jewish pogroms. Its political system was antiquated and oppressive, its military posture threatening. No one doubted at the time that Petersburg Russia was a medieval state, the Sick Man of Europe. Besides, who was this Stolypin if not a tsarist satrap through and through? The former governor of Saratov province and then minister of internal affairs — hardly an inspiring record. If one listened to Russian radicals of the time, Stolypin would emerge as a more sinister figure yet: the butcher of the revolution, the instigator of the court martials, the violator of the constitution.

This was an accurate picture. What it lacked was the context — a correlation with the alternatives. These were either a fascist dictatorship under someone like Purishkevich or a Communist one under someone like Lenin. Cruel as he was, Stolypin did abolish the medieval institution of the peasant commune and thus opened the gates for the development of the middle class. He also agreed to collaborate with a constitutional body, albeit a truncated one, and so gave the middle class a means of articulating its interests. In brief, for all his sins, Stolypin opened for the country a window on to political modernization, which in the Russian context means reform. His rivals at both ends of the political spectrum, be it Purishkevich or Lenin, would have (indeed, Lenin did) shut this window off for decades to come, which means counter-reform.

This was the situation in the empire at the time Stolypin was trying to pull it from the brink of the abyss, very much as Gorbachev is trying to do today. Thus, the ultimate criterion for the evaluation of any Western 'game plan' is, in my view, whether the Bolsheviks in Stolypin's time (or, the Russian New Right in Gorbachev's,) would perceive this plan to be in their interests, that is, conducive to Russia's transformation into a Communist, or fascist, state.

The Game Plans

The first, and perhaps most popular, of these was introduced into America's Soviet debate in 1984 by Richard Pipes's *Survival is Not Enough*. It is a most elaborate plan to accelerate Russia's decline, to push her over the brink: to deliver her to the Bolsheviks (in Stolypin's time) or the Russian New Right (in Gorbachev's). For Lenin, it would be one more manifestation of the imperialist nature of the West; for Shimanov, a confirmation that the West is indeed part of a worldwide 'kike-Freemason' conspiracy against Russia. For the Jews it would most probably mean a new holocaust. Even so, there can be little doubt that Richard Pipes's plan for a crusade against the 'evil empire' would be held in highest esteem by both the Bolsheviks at the dawn of the century and the Russian New Right at its twilight. It is intended to ensure that reform fails and thereby to accelerate Russia's slide toward the abyss.

Another strategy for dealing with a Russia in the throes of a 'regime' crisis was introduced into the debate in 1986 by Zbigniew Brzezinski in his book *Game Plan*. Unlike Pipes, Brzezinski was not writing a tract on the evils of the Russian empire compared to the merits of Western democracy. His book is intended as a practical guide for action in a nuclear geopolitical contest. What he is concerned with is Russia's global design to displace the United States as the world's principal power and primary stabilizing influence. This must not be allowed to happen. America must prevail. It can do this by achieving military preponderance, by building a two-tier strategic defence (Star Wars) and by weakening the adversary in any way it can. For example, the religion of 55 million Muslims, the nationalism of 50 million Ukrainians and 10 million Balts, not to mention 40 million Poles, are all potential targets for US exploitation of political unrest within the Russian empire. None of this, however, takes into account what happens to Russia as a result of a military contest projected into infinity.

The Bolsheviks would have liked such a game plan. For the Russian New Right it is a godsend. It actually looks as if Brzezinski has incorporated in his game plan the grandiose Young Guardist vision of the inevitability of an ultimate confrontation between Russia and the devil. It would confirm that Russia's conflict with the West is irreconcilable. It would strengthen the hand of the military-industrial complex, the most reliable ally of the New Right within the Soviet establishment. Finally, by trying to exploit the unrest of national minorities it would trigger the isolation of the empire from the world. The only way Russia would be able to resist such pressure would be the traditional one — to transform herself into a fortress. Thus a new garrison-state in Russia would be ensured, whether Communist (as after Stolypin) or fascist (as after Gorbachev).

Within American sovietology, there are also more moderate game plans. According to one of these, introduced in 1986 by Seweryn Bialer in *The Soviet Paradox*, Russia's reformist leadership is in a Catch 22 situation: an irreconcilable contradiction between, on the one hand, the urgent need for radical reform at home and, on the other, the fear of losing Russian dominance within the empire and in the superpower contest. Unlike Pipes and Brzezinski, however, Bialer understands that a policy of relentless confrontation may backfire. It would rally the Soviet people around the 'regime,' giving it the legitimacy it has been unable to win through its performance. But exactly which Soviet regime is Bialer talking about? We heard the Young Guardist Chalmaev and the dissident Stalinist Antonov passionately condemning the flabby and rotten Brezhnev regime of stagnation. Instead, they dreamed of a regime of dictatorship capable of combating the 'Americanization of the spirit', exterminating the 'civilized savages' and declaring war on the world-wide 'Freemason — Kike' conspiracy. To them, Khrushchev's reform regime that had actively fought for a permanent accommodation with the West seemed even worse than Brezhnev's torpor. Thus, to the preachers of the Russian Idea, it makes all the difference in the world which of these regimes the Russian people would rally behind if the confrontation with the West were projected into infinity as Pipes's and Brzezinski's game plans suggest. They would love such a game plan: a permanent confrontation would exclude a repetition of Khrushchev's reformist regime and make a new garrison-state bent on grand expansion and the 'Orthodoxization of the world' almost inevitable for Russia.

But would Russia's regime of dictatorship be alleviated if America took as a guide, instead of Pipes — Brzezinski, Bialer's game plan of 'managed rivalry'? Indeed, what is 'managed rivalry' if not a slightly civilized version of Brzezinski's game plan, that is, the same relentless and irreconcilable superpower contest, only with some rules to the game which both contestants are supposed to obey but which a Russian dictatorship might ignore anyway? Unfortunately, the author leaves us in the dark as to whether this strategy would help or hinder the Russian New Right's plan to topple the regime of reform and introduce a regime of dictatorship by the year 2000. Would Gorbachev's regime manage to survive this managed rivalry? Since the chances of this are slim, the Russian New Right would probably have little trouble in accepting Bialer's game plan — as long as it doesn't interfere with their own.

A fourth major American game plan was presented in 1983 in *The Nuclear Delusion* by George Kennan. At first glance it is altogether different from the Pipes — Brzezinski plan as well as from Bialer's. It passionately protests the nuclear arms race. It repudiates any superpower military rivalry projected into infinity, 'accelerated' or otherwise. It is not beyond comparing the major Soviet policies with those of the Petersburg empire or even Muscovite tsardom. It escapes the traps of the 'evil empire' and permanent geopolitical confrontation. Yet its political conclusions are rather uninspiring. They may be described as non-involvement — both in Soviet domestic affairs and in the arms race. They can actually be reduced to a common-sense formula: live and let live. But would this save Gorbachev's reform from the fate its predecessors met? Would it help to arrest a new brutal counter-reform? Unfortunately, Kennan's game plan does not address these questions.

As one of that rare and precious breed of sovietologist *and* historian, Kennan undoubtedly knows that Russia is no stranger to counter-reform: that its political past is permeated with historical calamities. Lenin's 'revolution from below' which followed from the 'systemic' crisis precipitated by the failure of Stolypin's reforms, was no less catastrophic for Russia than the 'revolutions from above' of Ivan the Terrible, Peter I, or Joseph Stalin. Each was unfailingly accompanied by mass terror and all the other horrors of garrison-state despotism, costing the nation millions of innocent lives. These historical disasters also deformed Russia's political culture, blocking her exit from the Middle Ages. They were the cause of the terrible fact that — alone among European nations — Russia has never managed to free itself of its empire, or separate church from state, or base its institutions on the principle of the separation of powers (the basis of every modern state).

Kennan, who knows a lot about Russian history, unlike the average sovietologist, might have found it rewarding to ask some searching questions. For example, can Russia, imprisoned for centuries in a vicious circle of bold reformist attempts and fierce counter-reforms, free herself without outside help? Doesn't her entire past look rather as a list of desperate efforts to struggle free from an historical trap, while each of them merely pulls the snare tighter? Isn't Russian history, from this standpoint, just a medical record of the Sick Man of Europe?

For centuries the rest of the world remained aloof of Russia's predicament. This is what Kennan's book, in full accordance with time-honoured tradition, recommends once more. Yet, as its very title — *The Nuclear Delusion* — suggests, we are living in a rather different age today. What if a new counter-reform should befall Russia in this nuclear era? Might it not, this time, spell disaster for the rest of the world too? Preventing such a scenario would seem to be the central problem of world politics till the end of this century. Unfortunately Kennan's game plan, though more deserving of sympathy than the others discussed here, does not address this problem.

There is, of course, no sovietological game plan that addresses the strategy of the Russian New Right for the year 2000. In Pipes, Brzezinski, Bialer, and Kennan, we have, as far as I know, presented all the colours of the Western sovietological rainbow as far as grand strategies for the rest of this century are concerned. Such is the price sovietology pays for its flight from history.

The terms in which we argue

The fact that the Russian New Right is not discussed in America's Soviet debate is only part of the problem. What is worse, is that we don't even have the terms in which to discuss it. The necessary instruments of analysis are lacking in our discourse. We know how indiscriminately Seweryn Bialer uses the term 'Soviet regime', but he is by no means exceptional. This alone denies us the possibility of probing beneath the surface of the Soviet political process to grasp its inherently antagonistic nature. We haven't yet grasped the fact on which the preachers of the Russian Idea build all their hopes: that the Russian autocracy is in reality a kind of a 'meta-regime' where every new element (new regime) is the antithesis of its predecessor — its negation, not its continuation, as sovietology presumes. Antonov, as we know, condemned the de-Stalinization of the system under Khrushchev. Others welcomed its de-Khrushchevization under Brezhnev. If they are now worried about its de-Brezhnevization under Gorbachev, it is because their preference was for re-Stalinization. Thus the notion of 'regime-change' in the Soviet Russian political system is central to all their calculations. Indeed, it seems to be a key notion for any analysis of the Soviet political process. Yet, sovietology doesn't even suspect its existence.

For us, the single term 'Soviet regime' is good enough to describe

War Communism (a garrison-state), NEP (liberalization of the 1920s), Stalin's dictatorship, Khrushchev's reform, Brezhnev's decay, and Gorbachev's desperate attempt at transition to new reform. Even the methodology of the Russian New Right is much more sophisticated than this. While we could calculate perfectly the number and throw-weight of Soviet missiles, and figure out who were the 'hawks' and the 'doves' in the Politburo, we were unable to predict either the phenomenon of de-Stalinization after Stalin, de-Khrushchevization after Khrushchev, or de-Brezhnevization after Brezhnev. We are not only unable to exploit the USSR's innate antagonisms, we cannot even discern their existence. For years we treated the regime of de-Stalinization as Stalinism without Stalin. We repeated the mistake by treating the regime of de-Khrushchevization as Khrushchevism without Khrushchev and we are still treating a regime of de-Brezhnevization as Brezhnevism without Brezhnev. Just like the generals of the old adage who are always preparing to fight the last war, so sovietologists are always ready to deal with the last Soviet regime. In our analysis of the Soviet system, we are always one regime behind. As another example of how far we are behind in our methodological ammunition, compared with the Russian New Right, let's take the notion of 'Soviet ideology', a term we use just as indiscriminately as 'Soviet regime'. For the ideologist of the Russian Idea, there is no such thing as a 'Soviet ideology', as the reader must have noticed many times throughout this book. The Young Guards' rebellion against the ideology of 'satiety' and 'education' is a prime example. Antonov and Emel'ianov, respective representatives of the *vozrozhdentsy* and 'National Bolshevism,' to use Dunlop's language, were calling for a radical ideological transformation *within* the confines of 'Soviet ideology'. *The Nation Speaks* made the 'ideological re-orientation' of the Soviet state a linchpin of its game plan. Shimanov's entire strategy is centred around the call for a metamorphosis in 'Soviet ideology'. In the final analysis, this is all that the Russian New Right in the 1980s is about (if we exclude the increasingly insignificant anti-Communist sectarians of an 'immobile Aksakov cast').

How does all this square with our own notion of a supposedly uniform and immutable 'Soviet ideology'? In fact, I devoted a section in one of my previous books to this last question.[4] The main point is that, just as we are dealing with a 'meta-regime' in the analysis of the Soviet political process, so in analysing the Soviet ideological process, we must deal with a notion of 'meta-ideology', — one that contains mutually exclusive denominations (or sub-ideologies) which are antithetical to each other.

There should hardly be anything surprising in this interpretation. After all, we know just as well as Shimanov does, that Soviet ideology is a secular religion, only he thought this notion through while we did not. For him it is a living truth, an instrument of analysis and for us merely a dead stereotype. For if we were to think it through, the complexity of the issue would be as obvious to us as it is to him. Aren't all major religions in fact meta-ideologies? Catholicism, Protestantism and Greek Orthodoxy are all denominations of Christianity: they share some fundamental beliefs, for example, in Jesus as the son of God, or the Holy Trinity. But that did not hinder them from becoming sworn enemies during the Middle Ages (as happened in Islam too). Why should Soviet secular religion be any different? Table 1 of the Appendix shows the crucial difference between its major denominations: the dictatorial (which I call National Communism), with its ascetic, paternalistic and isolationist values and a mystical belief in the revolutionary transformation of the world; and post-dictatorial (which I call Soviet Protestantism) with its belief in butter over guns, in the imperative of economic reform, in consumer satisfaction ('satiety') and peaceful coexistence.

Somehow we overlooked this great religious schism in Moscow in the 1950s. We didn't appreciate the role of Khrushchev as a Soviet Luther who introduced and legitimized the new denomination of Soviet Protestantism into the Soviet meta-ideology. The proponents of the Russian New Right understand it, however. They are preaching what, in the Soviet ideological context, is a religious counter-reformation — just as they preach counter-reform in the political context. What I call the 'denomination change' is just as important to them as 'regime change'. They fully understand the importance of Soviet secular religion (even if it calls itself Marxism—Leninism) as the most powerful resource of pre-modern system ruled by a secular church (even if it calls itself Communist party) at the end of the twentieth century. Unlike them, we sovietologists go on repeating the old stereotypes without even suspecting what 'denomination change' or a 'regime change' really mean — just as we don't distinguish between 'systemic' metamorphoses in the Russian empire and its ordinary 'regime' crises.

Perhaps here is the answer to the question asked at the end of the last chapter: Why is today's Western intelligentsia as insensitive to the signals of an approaching 'systemic' crisis in Russia as they were to similar omens at the beginning of the century? Now, however, we are able to formulate this question more explicitly: Why is it that not a single major American game plan for the end of the millennium takes into account the possibility of a new systemic metamorphosis in Russia similar to the one in 1917?

Admittedly, its previous metamorphoses, those of the 1560s and 1690s which ushered in the empire's Muscovite and Petersburg periods, are too remote for the public to recall or for the experts, in their 'flight from history', to take into account. But 1917 cannot yet have been so completely forgotten. The majestic spectacle of the 200-year-old Petersburg autocracy collapsing in a matter of weeks and being transformed into an almost unrecognizable Soviet empire, reminiscent more of its Muscovite grandmother than its immediate predecessor, could not, it would seem, have vanished from the minds of experts so soon. Yet somehow it did.

Unlike sovietology, the Russian New Right has never subscribed to the Soviet secular church's central dogma, which denies the USSR's political relation to Russia's imperial past. In fact, the opposite is true: the entire game plan of the Russian New Right is based on the assumption that what happened to the Petersburg empire might just as easily happen to its Soviet reincarnation. In other words, the Soviet period, along with the Muscovite and the Petersburg eras, are all, for the Russian New Right, merely transitory phases of one and the same 'meta-regime', not separate, let alone unique, political systems. Which of these two interpretations is correct?

The intellectual poverty of the Soviet secular church is legendary. In all truth one would sooner have expected sophisticated and secular Western experts, not the religious preachers of the Russian Idea, to have seen through its dogmas. Still, sovietology preferred to stick with Soviet orthodoxy rather than side with the heresy of that orthodoxy's opponents. But again, how do we know that the ideologists of the Russian Idea are right and Western experts (and the Soviet secular church) are wrong? To help answer this, let us just look briefly at the history of Russia's political crises over the last half-millennium to see what this can tell us about the nature and potential of these crises. Do the centuries-old patterns still hold?

Imperial Crises: An Attempt at a Typology

The principal difference between crises in Russian history seems to be that some of them (which I have called 'regime' crises) left the system's leadership the choice of regime change while others ('systemic' crises) did not. For example, it was the 'regime' crisis of 1905 that brought Stolypin to the helm (just as the 'regime' crisis of the early 1980s did so for Gorbachev), whereas it was the 'systemic' crisis of 1917 that led to the metamorphosis of the Petersburg empire into the Soviet one. One could cite other examples.

No matter how sharp or painful Russia's many 'regime' crises may have been, and irrespective of how the circumstances under which they occurred may have varied, in every case the leadership retained the option of a 'regime change'. On some occasions, this led to the establishment of a reformist regime, as happened in the early 1550s and the 1680s during the Muscovite period, in the Petersburg empire in the 1760s, 1801 and 1855, and in the Soviet empire in 1921 and 1953. It is happening again in the mid-1980s. In these cases the Russian leadership, faced with a crisis which didn't reach 'systemic' proportions and which it could control, chose the path of reform, thus opening the system up for political modernization. As Russian history shows, however, this wasn't the only path the leadership could have followed. In the 'regime' crises of 1796, 1825 and 1929, it opted for the alternative — counter-reform — closing the system to political modernization and establishing 'soul-destroying despotism'. Finally, in a number of other 'regime' crises (again covering the Muscovite, Petersburg and Soviet periods) such as those of 1503, 1613, 1812 and 1964, the leadership chose 'stabilization', which resulted in what I call regimes of political stagnation, where the system stands still, gradually rotting at the root.

Though we talk about the leadership 'choosing', it should be stressed that even in 'regime' crises the leadership's freedom of choice is somewhat limited by certain general rules of political change, as can be seen from Figure 2. For example, only a reform regime may follow a regime of counter-reform, whereas a regime of political stagnation may be succeeded by either reform or counter-reform. Furthermore there have so far not been more than two reformist attempts in any one of Russia's historical cycles. The collapse of the second of these has always, up to now, been accompanied by a regime of dictatorship. Finally, a failed reform may be succeeded by either a regime of political stagnation (as in 1730) or a counter-reform (as in October 1917), but not by a new reform (similarly, no dictatorship in Russian history has ever been followed by another dictatorship).

The other type of Russian political crisis — the 'systemic' crisis — deprives the system's leadership of control over the regime change, leaving the system with no option but counter-reform. In such cases, it isn't the fate of the regime that is at stake, but rather that of the system itself. The only way to avoid the collapse of the system in a 'systemic' crisis has, throughout Russian history, been by the establishment of a garrison-state based on a fortress mentality.

'Systemic' crises have been rare in Russia. When they have occurred, they have been the result either of powerful reforms that threatened to become irreversible (like the reforms of the 1550s or February 1917) or of the extreme spiritual and political exhaustion of the system which threatened its collapse (as in the 1690s and October 1917). Each of the resulting metamorphoses was a genuine and great revolution. However, they performed a function directly opposite to that of the great Western revolutions: they did not destroy, but rather renewed and strove to perpetuate, the system's pre-modern character. They required not only mass terror and a great purge of the old elites, but also radical changes in the mentality of the new elites. They not only brought about sweeping political and institutional changes, making Russia almost unrecognizable compared to its former self, they also made ideological revolutions. Each of them marked a catastrophe for the Russian middle class, and a return of the system to its initial mediaeval parameters — only on a higher level of complexity.

It is evident from Figure 2 that as far as political crises in the Russian autocracy are concerned, the centuries-old patterns still hold in the Soviet empire. Lenin's garrison-state was followed, according to the pattern, by a 'regime' crisis which in turn led to the establishment of a reformist regime (NEP). The failure of NEP created another 'regime' crisis which, again according to the pattern, led to the establishment of a counter-reformist regime and so began a new historical cycle. The end of dictatorship created one more 'regime' crisis which ended, appropriately, not with another dictatorship but in a new regime of reform. Where should the new 'regime' crisis created by the failure of this first reform in a new cycle lead? According to the pattern, into a regime of political stagnation. And so it did. This regime of political stagnation ultimately created a new 'regime' crisis. We witnessed it in the early 1980s. It could have led to a new regime of reform. To the dismay of the Russian New Right (but still true to our pattern), it did. What now?

In all previous 'regime' crises — without exception — and there have been quite a number of them (as we have seen), the Soviet empire followed the age-old patterns obediently. In this respect, Western sovietology's presumption seems to be wrong while that of the Russian New Right has been validated. Russia's historical record simply doesn't suggest any reasonable grounds to expect her to deviate from the general pattern — unless its current cycle is broken by an irreversible reform.

Our overview, however, yields another, much more ambivalent

conclusion. Apparently, Russia will not be able to escape a crisis in the 1990s irrespective of whether Gorbachev's reforms achieve a breakthrough and he succeeds in bringing Russia into the European family of nations. The crucial question is whether the approaching crisis will remain within the limits of a 'regime' crisis or go further and bring about a new metamorphosis, whether the reformist leadership will lose control of the situation and so make the Russian New Right's game plan for the year 2000 a credible alternative.

The answer depends on whether Russia's middle class is strong and articulate enough to be able to meet this crisis, to withstand a new extremist fit within the system. In 1917, as we know, Russia's middle class — even with free enterprise, political parties, a strong voice in the Duma (state assembly) and the initial success of Stolypin's reforms — proved unable to resist the Bolshevik counter-reform. Would it be able to stand up to a fascist counter-reform around the year 2000 — without political parties and without a Duma? Looking at it like this, it does seem that the Russian New Right's optimism is by no means ill-founded. A 'systemic' crisis in Russia at the end of this century is indeed a strong possibility. It might become a reality — unless the New Right's game plan is confronted with an equally powerful and realistic reformist strategy designed to strengthen Russia's middle class and prepare it for the coming 'regime' crisis. Yet to achieve this, the current reformist effort — unlike all its predecessors down through the centuries — must succeed in breaking the vicious circle of autocracy and become irreversible.

But what are the chances of this happening? What has taken place in Russia or in the world at large that sets the end of this millennium apart from all Russia's earlier experiences of reform? Given that Russia's political past is a history of failed and reversed reforms, why should the outcome be any different this time? Where is the elaborate strategy needed to confront the Russian New Right's game plan to come from — after all, it was not in evidence either in the 1960s, the 1920s, 1917, 1905, or indeed in any prior instance of Russian reform?

An Unprecedented Phenomenon

It would seem that such a strategy cannot be developed within the Russian leadership, perennially steeped in quasi-mediaeval ideology. Just as Stolypin was sincerely convinced of the unsurpassed advantages of Orthodox monarchy, so Khrushchev believed in the absolute superiority of what he called socialism. Today, Gorbachev still believes in this. There is virtually no chance that any of these leaders, for all their refined political instinct, energy and dynamism, could in the past — or can today — make the elevation of the middle class the primary focus of their political programmes. The very political culture in which they have been brought up, essentially religious, secretive, rooted in the traditions of censorship and self-censorship, deprived them of clarity or political vision. Add to this that Byzantine tangle of mutual fears and hatreds which is the Russian establishment and you will see that it is no accident that no viable reformist strategy has ever been developed within the Russian leadership.

The implications of this are somewhat grave, especially in this nuclear age. For it means that a suitable strategy could only be developed outside of the system. Such things rarely happen. True, modern history includes examples of emigres returning home in triumph to impose on their native land strategies developed outside of it. This happened in England in the 1660s and in France in 1815. More recently, it happened to Lenin in 1917 and Khomeini in 1979. But these were all examples of successful *counter-reformist* strategies. To the best of my knowledge there has been only a single case of an outsider, an emigre, who offered support in developing a strategy of *reform* to a government he couldn't help but dislike and distrust. This was Alexander Herzen, who, with his friends, tried to influence the course of Russian history from London in the early 1860s through his famous paper *The Bell*. Amazingly, though an exile, Herzen did for a short while achieve the prominence of a 'second Russian government'. His enormous influence was ruined, however, when Poland unexpectedly rose in rebellion in 1863. Herzen sided with the Poles, against the overwhelming majority of Russians who, to his surprise, appeared no less imperial-minded in a crisis situation than the imperial government itself.

Nevertheless, Herzen's short reign as a 'second Russian government' set an important precedent. It showed that only those who combine in themselves a superior knowledge about Russia with Western intellectual culture are capable of accomplishing that which has eluded Russia's reformist leaders for centuries: a strategy for Russian reform, however debatable. Might it not also be true that the permanent absence, outside the system, of a powerful intellectual group capable of developing such a strategy is one of the principal causes of the perpetual failure of all Russian reforms?

If so, this is a possibility that the Russian New Right certainly did not build into its game plan for the year 2000. Convinced that the West is Russia's eternal enemy (or, as Brzezinski would put it, permanent geopolitical adversary) — not to mention its being in the service of the Antichrist and ripe for Orthodoxization — the Russian New Right underestimates the compassion, the generosity, the powerful instinct for self-preservation the West possesses and, above all, its overwhelming intellectual power. In so doing, it has overlooked two important phenomena which indeed set the current situation apart from all Russia's prior experiences of reform.

The first of these is, of course, the very age we live in — the nuclear age. This alone would make the West think twice before following Pipes's or Brzezinski's advice and entering into the kind of relentless confrontation with the USSR needed by the Russian New Right to bring its game plan to fruition.

The second phenomenon overlooked by the New Right may be still more important. I refer to the unprecedented concentration of knowledge about Russia accumulated in the West over the last century, and having found expression in the equally unprecedented phenomenon of sovietology. So great is this knowledge, as many professionals in the field are aware, it surpasses in many instances what Soviet politicians, economists and sociologists themselves know about the performance of their own system. Thus, a superior knowledge of Russia (combined with relative immunity to mediaeval ideological aberrations), which led to Herzen's success a century ago, is being repeated now on a much grander scale. Indeed, some things do appear to have changed at the end of the twentieth century. These changes may even be decisive, if only we learn how to use them.

The Necessity of Reform

Of course, the parallel between *The Bell* and sovietology shouldn't be taken too literally. It is strictly functional. Although Herzen was called a Westernizer by his enemies and was as free from mediaeval ideological aberrations as any Russian could be, he still was a Russian emigre, a passionate political writer, a philosopher — one whose heart ached for Russia. In total contrast, sovietology comprises a motley group of academics trained to observe and analyse their subject rather than weep for it, let alone build strategies for reform. It is only the fact that we live in the age of the intercontinental ballistic missile that may compel sovietology to perform the same function as Herzen once did. For if a new disaster strikes Russia in the nuclear age, sovietologists may not only find themselves without a job, they may even end up unwilling actors in the tragic finale of Russia's political drama. Perhaps this sobering thought will lead Western experts down the same path that Herzen's aching Russian heart once led him. Perhaps its traditional academic detachment will be discarded for the sake of survival.

For Herzen, to support the cause of reform within a hated tsarist empire was no small matter either. He had to violate some unwritten but strict emigre rules, as anyone who is familiar with the standard reactions of Russian emigres to the present Russian reforms will understand. These people hate everything Soviet with a passion, reform included, just as Herzen hated everything tsarist. Before he and his friends at *The Bell* were able to offer, in place of the traditional emigre curses, their support to a reformist regime they radically had to reform themselves. There are also other parallels between the reformist situation of the mid-1980s and that of the early 1860s.

By the mid-1980s most sovietologists were agreed that what Russia needs is a thoroughgoing change, radical reform, and at the very least an end to the Brezhnevist era of stagnation, social decay and cultural paralysis. The Russian leadership also agrees with this enthusiastically. In this sense, the mid-1980s are repeating the early 1860s, when for the first time in imperial history the judgement of the imperial leadership coincided with that of reformist outsiders. Moreover, the imperial leadership of the mid-1980s does not explain what it means by 'radical reform'; nor did the leadership of the 1860s. The reason, one may surmise, is that, despite its confident reformist language, the leadership — now as then — simply does not know what it really means by 'reform'. That is bad enough. What is worse is that Gorbachev, like Alexander II (and, for that matter, Khrushchev) is quite confident that he does know. In reality, he reacts to the situation at hand. His policies are shaped more by the usual antagonistic response to the policies of the preceding regime than by any clearly devised reformist game plan. His policies are as lacking in strategy as those of the reformist emperor of the 1860s. But this should come as no surprise to anyone who has studied political change in Russia or watched its previous reformist attempts.

More importantly, the reformist outsiders of today — the sovietologists — also cannot agree on what they mean by radical reform in the Soviet context. Deep ideological schisms, party rivalries and the intellectual inertia of the Brezhnevist decades all conspire to deprive sovietology of its ability to confront the Russian challenge directly, in this new and much more sophisticated phase. Indeed, it would seem that sovietology is as much in need of radical reform as its unfortunate subject (just like Herzen and his friends in London in the 1860s). It cannot any longer allow itself to trail behind the Russian New Right in intellectual sophistication as it did through the Brezhnevist decades.

So far, as we saw from our brief survey of American game plans, the reformist outsiders of the 1980s are not doing very well. In fact, they are falling behind even the imperial leadership, which has already shown considerable flexibility, if only in repudiating the policies of the past regime. Like Khrushchev in his early days, the imperial leadership of the mid-1980s has shown ingenuity and dynamism in two major areas open to immediate improvement — agriculture and foreign policy. In a Moscow trying to shake the dust of Brezhnevist torpor off its feet, a cultural thaw is also gaining momentum. In contrast, sovietology is running on the spot. Its own de-Brezhnevization hasn't even begun yet. Some of the supposedly enlightened outsiders still behave like unwitting allies of the Russian New Right. Others are slow in confronting them with an alternative game plan. The very idea of using a Herzen-like phenomenon in a Herzen-like fashion is foreign to them. The cause of championing the Russian middle class, of putting their intellectual weight behind an attempt to make Russian reform irreversible this time, is as far from them as ever. Yet, despite all this, there undoubtedly exists the potential for a new and much more influential Herzen.

Another way in which the current situation resembles the early 1860s is that Poland is still an imperial province and still the powder-keg of Europe. In a few years' time it may once again explode as it did in 1863. It was this explosion that destroyed Herzen's credibility and ultimately Russian reform. It is known that Herzen, believing the Polish uprising to be premature, used his considerable influence with the Poles in an attempt to persuade them to postpone it. Of course, he failed. Poland was as unpredictable then as it is today.

The 1860s Russian reform failed, and in due time was reversed by a counter-reform. Once more, the Russian imperial leadership proved that it didn't know how to go about the business of reform. As soon as the influence of reformist outsiders vanished, the reform was doomed, making counter-reform, in the final analysis, inevitable.

Whether, today, a group of reform-minded outsiders will be able to do for Gorbachev's reform what Herzen attempted to do for Alexander II's, remains to be seen. All I can offer, by way of conclusion, are two examples (or elements) of a possible alternative Western game plan to counter the Russian Idea. They are intended to show that it is perhaps possible for sovietology to fulfil such a function.

The 'Eternal Tree of Life'

'Theory, my friend, is grey, but the eternal tree of life is green,' Mephistopheles explained to Faust. Suppose for a moment that we had never heard of any grey theories such as 'Soviet ideology' or 'the Soviet regime', that our minds were fresh and open to observations on the Russian tree of life. How would the problem of trade between the USSR and the West appear to us then? Would it be reduced to the single recurrent question, 'To trade or not to trade?', which we have been hearing from the experts for years? If this question makes any sense at all, then it is only from the point of view of those 'grey' theories. As soon as we start to look at things from the position of the Soviet middle class or Russia's political modernization, different questions arise.

Is it possible to use trade with the Soviet Union to strengthen the reformist groups within the Soviet establishment — and accordingly to weaken the counter-reformist ones? To put it another way, is it possible to use trade as leverage for deepening the innate antagonisms between Soviet elites and to encourage the elevation of the middle class? If this is possible, then how?

On the Soviet side, I see three principal actors, not a faceless monolithic 'Soviet regime', involved in the issue of trade with the West. The first is the gigantic foreign trade bureaucracy (an important component of the Central Economic Bureaucracy; group 9 in Figure 3). This was created by Stalin as an impermeable screen between Western corporations and their natural partners in the Soviet Union, the middle managerial class. This class itself represents the second of our principal political actors concerned with this issue on the Soviet side (group 4 in the same Figure). The third actor, whose voice may be decisive in the conflict between the first two, is the national leadership, which includes, in my view, the Politburo, the Central Committee Secretariat and the office of Secretary General. The national leadership occupies the central position in our Figure (group 6) and represents an independent, though also the most powerful, set of interests in the Soviet establishment. Naturally, these interests are not at all identical either with those of group 9, or with those of group 4. In the second half of the 1970s sovietologists observed the fluctuation of the national leadership between group 4, who demanded direct access to trade with Western corporations (following the example of the Hungarian middle managerial class) and group 9, who desperately opposed any attack on their prerogatives.[5] The struggle ended in a compromise, after the collapse of Russia's detente with the West at the end of the 1970s. The Soviet middle class did not receive 'Hungarian rights' in full measure, but it did make a breach in the foreign trade bureaucracy's monopoly, giving Soviet corporations the right to trade directly with their East European partners.

What is going on in the area of foreign trade in the Soviet Union is reminiscent, at least in one respect, of what happened in mediaeval Europe at the dawn of modern history. The reformist elements of the middle class have risen up against a bureaucratic hierarchy which was cutting them off from direct contact with the source of their inspiration — in much the same way as Protestantism rose against a Catholic hierarchy that was allegedly cutting believers off from direct interaction with God. This analogy may look superficial, but in fact, it boldly reflects the mediaeval character of the Soviet political system. Is the situation of the Soviet middle class in the mediaeval USSR hopeless? The Reformation's success in England, Germany and parts of Eastern Europe would suggest that it is not. This success is also evidence that, in each instance, the Reformation depended on the position of the national leadership: it succeeded where the national leadership agreed to dismantle the monopoly of the Catholic hierarchy. In no instance did the Reformation lead to the undermining of the national leadership's position, only to its reorientation. This is analogous to the way foreign trade reform did not undermine the position of the national leadership in Hungary when its 'Protestant' group 4 won out over 'Catholic' group 9. The middle managerial class simply took the place of the former bureaucratic hierarchy — entering on to the world scene and acquiring new skills and experience, new responsibility and new international connections. In so doing, it significantly strengthened its political position within the Hungarian establishment.

The prospect of repeating this experiment in the Soviet Union depends, therefore, on the position of the national leadership. We assume that its position is not rigidly fixed and that it is free to side with the 'Protestants', should it consider this course of action to be advantageous to its own group interests. Evidently, the maximization of Soviet—American trade is posited as one of the leadership's fundamental goals. In this respect, the position of the American national leadership, on whom such trade links depend, becomes decisive in the struggle between two elites within the Soviet establishment.

Therefore the traditional argument over whether to trade or not to trade with the USSR makes no sense. The real question is, 'Who should we trade with in the Soviet Union?' Should it be the 'Catholic hierarchy', which would strengthen the forces of counter-reform, or with the 'Protestant' middle class, which would reinforce the position of reform? The American national leadership could, for example, offer to maximize trade (and credits) on the condition that business be conducted directly between Soviet and American corporations without bureaucratic intermediaries. This kind of an offer would in no way resemble a political ultimatum — in fact, it wouldn't have anything to do with politics. It would be motivated exclusively by the pragmatic business objective of easing the trade process, and would correspond to the interests of both Soviet and American corporations. At the same time, it would be strengthening the Russian middle class and preparing it for the coming 'regime' crisis.

This is just one example of a possible American strategy oriented toward supporting the Soviet middle class. I mention it here only because over the course of many years in Moscow I had the opportunity to study the problems of the Soviet middle class professionally, trying, as best as I could, under the constraints of a censored press, to articulate its group interests. Western experts don't have to contend with censorship. They have described, analysed, catalogued and produced detailed statistics on each and every nuance of Soviet society. Has all this effort been expended so that this fabulous wealth of information should gather dust on library shelves, or so that sovietological conservatives and liberals go on picking holes in each other's arguments? Couldn't Western experts have at their disposal dozens of viable strategies, like the one just described, if only liberals and conservatives would work together on the *practical* problem of moving the Soviet system in the direction of political modernization? In fact, it is only through joint practical work that sovietology can become an effective counter to the Russian Idea — by helping to school the Russian middle class and the West for the 'Year 2000'.

Leont'ev's Dilemma

Another possible Western game, this time perhaps a little more complex, concerns what I call Leont'ev's dilemma.

In the 1880s Konstantin Leont'ev, the most incisive of the Russian conservatives of the past century, insistently advised the dictator Alexander III not to be swayed by pan-Slavic sentiments, but to leave

Eastern Europe in peace. Leont'ev's dilemma can be summed up as follows: we haven't been able to integrate Poland into our imperial, 'Byzantine' culture over the course of nearly a century; what would happen to us if we had to handle another half-dozen Polands? To Leont'ev, such a course could even lead to the destruction of Byzantine culture. In fact, he thought that the empire was doomed from the moment it conquered the Western Slavs. The middle class he so despised ('bourgeois Philistines') was traditionally much stronger and more articulate in Eastern Europe and would set about its destructive work, dragging behind it its Russian partner in a direction 'congenial to Western interests'.

A few decades later another dictator, Josef Stalin, who had no Leont'ev to advise him, was unable to resist the expansionist impulse of Russian dictatorship. He accomplished what the pan-Slavists had wanted Alexander III to do, or, from Leont'ev's standpoint, committed the crudest of errors, one fatal to the empire. As a result, Eastern Europe became the mediaeval empire's westernmost frontier. If Leont'ev was right — and he alone in the 1880s predicted a socialist revolution in Russia — then the problem for Stalin and his successors was whether the civilized world would take advantage of the situation to bring about what Leont'ev feared, the political modernization of the empire. Indeed, can the West transform the powerful potential of the Eastern European middle class into leverage for the elevation of its Soviet counterpart?

For understandable reasons, the peoples who have fallen into Russia's imperial orbit have so far shown little interest in Leont'ev's dilemma. They wish to break away from the empire's embrace, not to concern themselves with its modernization. The Germans in East Berlin in 1953 and the Hungarians in 1956 tried to do this 'Polish-style' — by frontal assault, a national uprising. This ended, of course, the same way as Polish attempts in the previous century, in bloodshed and failure. The mediaeval empire does not succumb to frontal attack. The Czechs, naively relying on socialist fraternity, tried to escape, in 1968, via the roundabout route of national democratization. Soviet tanks quickly crushed their hopes. Polish 'Solidarity' in 1980 thought it could succeed where the Czechs had failed. Poland is now under military dictatorship. As in tsarist times, the empire cannot be duped. So vanished the last hope that any single province might be able to break free of the empire's clutches — without modernization of the imperial centre.

This tragic history has a corollary, however. Just as Leont'ev predicted, 'half a dozen Polands' are indeed constantly working away at the empire's destruction. So far, over the course of a few decades, they haven't been able to find a fulcrum with which to overturn their mediaeval stepmother. But in 1968 it was as though one small province, having learned from its own bitter experience, had inadvertently hit upon Leont'ev's dilemma. Hungary began its process of liberalization not with an uprising, not with a revolutionary attempt at national democracy, but rather with the elevation of its own 'bourgeois Philistines'. Naturally, to achieve this, it first of all had to breach the empire's economic model which, as always, had been set up to block the upward movement of the middle class. Without any noise or fanfare, Hungary succeeded where both the Czechs and the Poles suffered defeat and failure. In less than two decades Hungary has been transformed into a prospering and — as far as possible within the framework of a mediaeval empire — liberal state, based on the strengthening of its middle class. Radical economic reform accomplished what neither revolt nor attempts at national democratization could. Consequently, Hungary has become the first province in the empire where, by law, two or more candidates are required to stand in each election, where there is an essentially open border with a capitalist state, where censorship has been reduced to a minimum and every citizen has the legal right to travel abroad, and where there are neither emigration problems, nor food crises, nor queues for consumer goods.

Hungary has demonstrated that liberalization is possible within the mediaeval empire, and has offered herself as a model for the rest of the empire to follow. No more than that can be expected of her. In the final analysis, she is a tiny country, with her own problems, frightened of her own success, and not daring to dream about seriously influencing the empire. In no way, can Budapest pretend to the role of a second, reformist, centre of the empire, competing for influence with Moscow. Warsaw, on the other hand, is a different matter. Poland has always been the key country of Eastern Europe. If Poland were to follow Hungary, and, in addition to this, were to enter into a kind of alliance with Hungary, utilizing Hungary's experience to strengthen her own middle class, a second, reformist, centre of the empire could become a reality. It could act as a magnet to the whole western flank of the empire and as a signal for the rebirth of the whole Eastern European middle class, including the middle class of the imperial centre. In other words, Poland could make Leont'ev's nightmare come true.

For this to happen, the peoples on the empire's Western fringes must first and foremost understand the main lesson of their struggle for liberation: that the path to national liberalization, and ultimately to the independence of Warsaw, Prague, Bucharest and Sofia, lies through the liberalization of Moscow, through successful — and irreversible — Soviet reform. If the Poles do manage to achieve liberalization, it's because the Hungarians have already shown them how it can be done within the mediaeval system. But the recognition of this fact by the peoples of Eastern Europe is, by itself, not enough to transform Leont'ev's nightmare into reality. It is naive to expect Poland's military government to be capable of a Hungarian-style initiative. They have neither the authority, nor the resources, nor even the necessary backing of the people, to break with command economy. The West, however, could offer Poland what its current government lacks.

Here, too, as in the case of trade with Russia discussed earlier, the situation demands a well thought-out Western strategy. A 'mini-Marshall Plan' for Poland predicated on the condition that she go the 'Hungarian' way would be analogous to the suggestion to maximize Soviet—American trade on condition that corporations deal directly with each other. Also, as before, it could by no means be called a political ultimatum. It would involve only the natural desire of creditors to receive what is due to them and help the borrower to avoid bankruptcy. It would be based solely on the desire to support radical reform within the Soviet system, shared — if we are to believe their own declarations — by both the national leadership in Moscow and Richard Pipes in Cambridge (judging from his last book).[6]

Sovietological liberals are also well disposed toward reform. In any event, they would certainly wish to avoid the unprecedented crisis predicted by Timothy Colton if reform should fail.[7] What is there to prevent both liberal and conservative sovietologists — Pipes and Colton in this instance — from sinking their ideological differences in favour of a concrete and practical opportunity to avert a major catastrophe — the 'Year 2000'?

The Mediaeval System's Resources

Of course, to Pipes and Colton, (as well as to American politicians) the 'Year 2000' can hardly be more than an abstraction. They wouldn't take seriously *Veche*'s reader mail or Solzhenitsyn's diabolerie. They probably never heard of Shimanov's strategy and Emel'ianov's tactics. After all, there can be no shortage of elevator operators in America who in their leisure time prophesize the imminence of Armageddon.

Having been reared under a modern system of values, experts naturally have difficulties to perceive the role ideology plays in a pre-modern state. The very idea of the USSR as a mediaeval state is completely alien to them. They will probably ask me the same questions about this book as the critics asked about *The Russian New Right*: How many supporters of the Russian Idea are there in the Soviet Union? How many of them are influential in the court circles in Moscow? I don't know, I'll tell them. Nobody knows. Then they'll turn away, shrugging their shoulders in bewilderment, totally convinced that Shimanov is just a lunatic and the plans of the Russian Idea for its 'Year 2000' are idle delusions.

These same questions, however, could have been asked about the Bolsheviks at the beginning of the twentieth century. Then, as now, such statistical reasoning is irrelevant to the matter at hand. How many supporters did the Bolsheviks have, say, a decade before their shattering victory in 1917? Very few — far fewer than the Russian New Right has today. Moreover, the Bolsheviks had no one in influential court circles. Yet they won. Why?

Statistics cannot answer this question. In 1908, the prediction of a Bolshevik victory would have been unthinkable using statistical methods. However, from the point of view of the hypothesis that lies at the core of this book, the Bolsheviks' victory is easily explained: they were the single group in Russia at the time possessing a genuine alternative ideology capable of saving the empire from collapse at the moment of its 'systemic' crisis. The fact that such an alternative ideology emerged within the mediaeval empire as it stood on the threshold of a 'systemic' crisis is at least as important as any statistical calculations. In a pre-modern system, the role of ideology differs significantly from its role in a modern secularized state — if only because the nature of such a system is essentially religious, however scientifically it chooses to explain itself to the world. To speak about a religious system solely in terms of statistical arguments is, at the very least, naive.

We have seen how Russian autocracy moves out of its crises by means of 'regime changes', accompanied by their religious-cultural equivalents, 'denomination changes' It was exactly this kind of 'denomination change' that the Bolsheviks were preparing for the empire at the beginning of the twentieth century to enable it to survive its 'systemic' crisis. It is also this kind of 'denomination change' that today's Russian Idea is preparing for the empire as the current millennium draws to a close. This is where its real danger lies, not in the number of its adherents in the Soviet Union or patrons in the Kremlin.

I understand how much more attractive Pipes's recommendation simply to pressure the empire until it begins to burst at the seams, or Brzezinski's call for unrelenting geopolitical confrontation, sound to conventional politicians. They don't want to have to bother with anything tricky like 'regime changes' or 'denomination changes'. The traditional approaches are simple and familiar. In essence, Pipes and Brzezinski are calling on American policy to put the same pressure on the Soviet empire as World War I put on the tsarist empire. The simpler a recommendation, the more seductive it is. Aren't the empire's resources limited? Won't its rulers face a choice between guns and butter as a result of Western pressure? Driven to the wall, they will at some point be forced to decide whether to build new rockets and completely deprive the population of meat, thus running the risk of provoking riots and undermining their own legitimacy. At some point, Pipes calculates, they will have to choose meat, unless they want to commit political suicide. Thus the problem will be solved. If we can't win a nuclear war, what remains is to win the nuclear peace. It is so natural. The main thing is to win.

There is only one thing wrong with this reasoning: the pressure of World War I did not give rise to reform in tsarist Russia, but to a garrison-state and Communism — i.e., to that very 'regime change' and 'denomination change' that Pipes is now fighting. Pipes's recommendation doesn't take into account that ideology is also a resource for a mediaeval system, and, indeed, its most powerful resource.

Suppose that, under a post-dictatorial ideology, the empire's rulers, in order to provide the population with meat, are required to produce 250 million tons of grain a year or make massive grain purchases from the United States. Under the alternative dictatorial ideology with its 'spiritual and ascetic values' which the Russian Idea would offer in the event of a 'systemic' crisis, the empire would not need to produce even 100 million tons of grain, or buy from abroad, because this ideology doesn't require the populace to be fed meat at all, because it is in principle vegetarian. In 1953, forty years after the Bolshevik counter-reform, the production of meat in Russia had not even attained the level it was at in 1913. The imperative of national survival successfully replaced meat — for a quarter of a century. Dictatorial ideology turned asceticism into a patriotic virtue and consumption into a national sin. No spontaneous riots were recorded. The dictatorial regime's legitimacy was not subjected to doubt until after the death of the dictator.

In other words, the rulers of the mediaeval empire will never end up faced with the fatal choice between rockets and meat postulated by Pipes. Their real choice at the point of a 'systemic' crisis will be something completely different: between a post-dictatorial denomination, which forced them to triple meat production after the dictator's death, and its opposite, a vegetarian ideology of dictatorship, which would allow them to concentrate all the system's resources on rocket production. Thus nuclear peace is as unwinnable as nuclear war, and the logic of Pipes and Brzezinski collapses.

Orthodox marxism has been exhausted as an ideological resource for the system, just as the ideology of tsarism was exhausted at the beginning of the twentieth century. Alternative ideological resources are needed to enable the empire to survive a 'systemic' crisis. The Russian Idea is offering these resources for the 'Year 2000' just as the Bolsheviks offered theirs in 1917. That's where Bolshevism's true strength lay, and that's where the Russian Idea's true strength lies today. If sovietology fails to comprehend the function of ideology in a pre-modern system and follows the logic of Pipes or Brzezinski, the 'Year 2000' will catch the West napping, just as it was caught by the events of 1917. Must we forever be condemned to understand such things only in hindsight? This time hindsight might be too late — for all of us.

Notes

1   Martin F. Herz, ed. *Decline of the West?*, Ethics and Public Policy Center, Georgetown University, 1978, p. 62.
2   The ultimate irony of this fundamental sovietological postulate is that it looks rather like a carbon copy of a corresponding Soviet dogma, according to which the October Revolution has produced an unprecedented political body that, except for geography and a common heritage in the fine arts, has nothing to do with its sombre imperial past.
3   I included several chapters about this unfortunate phenomenon in my book *The Origins of Autocracy*, an outline of which the reader will find in my essay 'Flight from Theory', *Slavic Review*, Fall 1983.
4   Alexander Yanov, *The Drama of the Soviet 1960s: A Lost Reform*, 'Notes on Terminology: Soviet Protestantism', pp. 127—30.
5   See Yanov, *Detente after Brezhnev*, pp. 37—8.
6   *Survival Is Not Enough.*
7   Timothy J. Colton, *The Dilemma of Reform in the Soviet Union*, Council on Foreign Relations, 1984, pp. 78—9.

Afterword

The book was already set up when the word from Moscow came: Andrei D. Sakharov is free from his internal exile. Did it last for seven years? To thousands of Russians it seemed to last for ages. Sakharov's re-emergence in Moscow has been a miracle for them. Apart from being the highest authority on things Russian, Sakharov is the conscience of the nation. For lack of comparison it is rather hard to explain to outsiders. For this we have to strain our imagination a bit. What would contemporary Americans feel if, say, Thomas Jefferson re-emerged among them, alive and well? Wouldn't they await with trepidation his judgement on whatever they do or say or write? So was I awaiting with trepidation Sakharov's judgement on the central issue of this book — should the West ally with Solzhenitsyn and his followers and thus ruin Gorbachev's reforms, or should it ally with reformers and support their desperate endeavour?

The usual fate of Russian Jeffersons being what it is, Sakharov fully experienced the misery of exile, isolation and torture. It would seem rather natural for him to become as embittered and contemptuous of the state which did this as Solzhenitsyn became. It would seem logical if he agreed with Pipes that unless this brutal police state is pushed to the wall nothing good could ever be expected from it. It would seem reasonable for him to call on the West not to trust Gorbachev or, at least declare along with A. M. Rosenthal, the former executive editor of *The New York Times*, 'Mr Gorbachev is certainly a smoother chap than most of his predecessors but he has not touched the police nature of the Soviet state and has not even hinted at it. How could he? He is part of it and rules through it . . . Myself, I will wait until Mr Gorbachev arrests and tries the men who sent . . . Dr Sakharov into exile.' In other words, it would seem logical for Andrei Sakharov to condemn everything this book stands for. Would he?

The central premise of the book is that there are two Russias — in perennial and mortal opposition to each other. And because of this what seems natural, logical and reasonable to the extremist Russia of Solzhenitsyn must be unnatural, illogical and unreasonable for the other Russia.

According to the extremist Russia and its Western fellow travellers, Gorbachev's reforms must be cancelled — by pressure, by disbelief, by Star Wars. According to the other Russia, it is vitally important for the West to see to it that the reforms succeed — if only to prevent the transformation of the USSR into a fascist nuclear monster. Which of these irreconcilably opposite stands would the Russian Jefferson take?

If the premise of this book is correct, then, however embittered, Sakharov back in Moscow would say something like this:

> It is in the interests of the West that these reforms should succeed so that the Soviet Union can be a more stable partner. The West must not try to corner the Soviet Union. A cornered nation is always dangerous.

And this is what Sakharov, in fact, said on 14 February, 1987. What he couldn't have said publicly — a pre-modern state with a human face is still pre-modern — is perhaps this: It is time to start the de-Brezhnevization of world politics. It is imperative to return to the Khrushchev-Kennedy political agenda of 1963 brutally interrupted by the fatal shots in Dallas and the Brezhnevist coup in Moscow. For all his polish and courage, Gorbachev is a pre-modern politician. He needs guidance, not resistance. He needs someone in Washington who would be able to do for him what Kennedy had done for Khrushchev — to clear the way for the idea of a world safe for diversity. If it comes to that, it is not Gorbachev who should ask the West to support his bold effort to prevent a garrison state in Moscow, it is the West who should guide him into this — for all of us to survive in the nuclear age.

Appendix

Table 1   Soviet Meta-Ideology

Dictatorial Era	*Post-Dictatorial Era*
Sub-Ideology of National Communism	**Sub-Ideology of Soviet Protestantism**
Major Beliefs:	**Major Beliefs:**
1 Socialism as a new era in the history of mankind	Socialism as a new era in the history of mankind
2 State ownership of the means of production — sole means of ending exploitation of man by man	State ownership of the means of production — sole means of ending exploitation of man by man
3 Paternalism (Father of the Fatherland)	Collective leadership
4 Inevitability of World War III	World War III is not inevitable
5 Imperative of national survival	Imperative of economic reform
6 Guns instead of butter	Butter instead of guns
7 Asceticism	Consumer satisfaction
8 Isolationism and fortress mentality	Detente with the West
9 Total control over culture	Cultural thaw
10 The permanent sharpening of the class struggle	No class struggle in socialism
11 Revolutionary transformation of the World	Peaceful coexistence

Table 2 Russia's Reformist Attempts and Their Outcomes

Attempt of the 1550s — reversed by a *counter-reform*
Attempt of the 1610s — faded into political stagnation
Attempt of the 1680s — reversed by a *counter-reform*
Attempt of the 1720s — faded into political stagnation
Attempt of the 1760s — faded into political stagnation
Attempt of 1801   — faded into political stagnation
Attempt of the 1820s — reversed by a *counter-reform*
Attempt of the 1860s — faded into political stagnation
Attempt of 1879—80   — reversed by a *counter-reform*
Attempt of 1905   — faded into political stagnation
Attempt of 1917   — reversed by a *counter-reform*
Attempt of the 1920s — reversed by a *counter-reform*
Attempt of the 1960s — faded into political stagnation
Attempt of 1985   —   ?

Russia's Counter-reformist Dictatorships

1560—1584
1689—1725
1796—1801
1825—1855
1881—1894
1918—1921
1929—1953

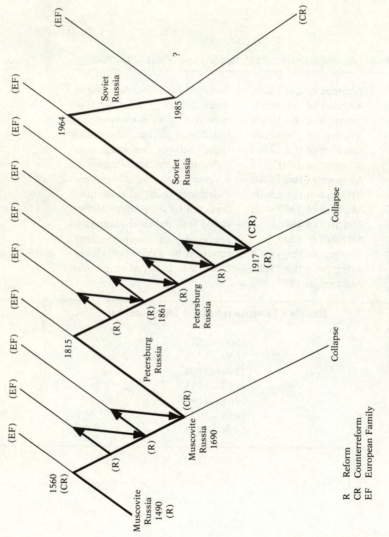

Figure 1 Five Centuries of Russian History in One Chart

R   Reform
CR   Counterreform
EF   European Family

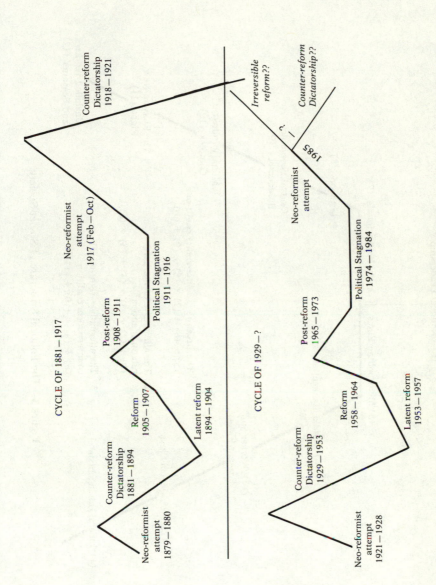

Figure 2 Structure of Russia's Historical Cycles

CYCLE OF 1881—1917

Neo-reformist attempt 1879—1880

Counter-reform Dictatorship 1881—1894

Latent reform 1894—1904

Reform 1905—1907

Post-reform 1908—1911

Political Stagnation 1911—1916

Neo-reformist attempt 1917 (Feb—Oct)

Counter-reform Dictatorship 1918—1921

CYCLE OF 1929—?

Neo-reformist attempt 1921—1928

Counter-reform Dictatorship 1929—1953

Latent reform 1953—1957

Reform 1958—1964

Post-reform 1965—1973

Political Stagnation 1974—1984

Neo-reformist attempt

1985

— ?

Irreversible reform??

Counter-reform Dictatorship??

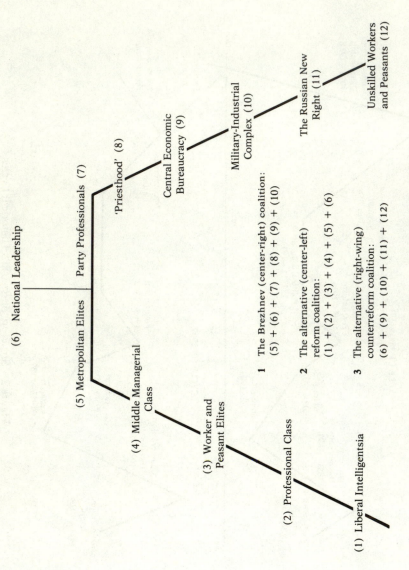

Figure 3 The Political Structure of Soviet Society

(6) National Leadership

Party Professionals (7)

'Priesthood' (8)

Central Economic Bureaucracy (9)

Military-Industrial Complex (10)

The Russian New Right (11)

Unskilled Workers and Peasants (12)

(5) Metropolitan Elites

(4) Middle Managerial Class

(3) Worker and Peasant Elites

(2) Professional Class

(1) Liberal Intelligentsia

1 The Brezhnev (center-right) coalition: (5) + (6) + (7) + (8) + (9) + (10)

2 The alternative (center-left) reform coalition: (1) + (2) + (3) + (4) + (5) + (6)

3 The alternative (right-wing) counterreform coalition: (6) + (9) + (10) + (11) + (12)

Index